WORLDLY SAINTS

The Puritans
As They
Really Were

Leland Ryken

ZondervanPublishingHouse
Grand Rapids, Michigan

A Division of HarperCollinsPublishers

For Al and Florence Graham

WORLDLY SAINTS
Copyright © 1986
by Leland Ryken

First paperback edition 1990

Requests for information should be addressed to:
Zondervan Publishing House
Grand Rapids, Michigan 49506

Library of Congress Cataloging-in-Publication Data

Ryken, Leland.
    Worldly saints.

        Includes index.
    Bibliography: p.
    Includes index.
        1. Puritans. 2. Reformed Church. I. Title.
    BX9323.R93   1986   285'.9   86-19869
    ISBN 0-310-32551-1

Edited by Judith E. Markham
Designed by Louise Bauer and James R. Buick

Printed in the United States of America

90 91 92 93 94 / DH / 5 4 3 2 1

Contents

The Puritans were worldly saints. As this painting of the first Thanksgiving in America shows, the Puritans had a zest for earthly life accepted as God's gift. Brownscombe, *First Thanksgiving;* courtesy of the Pilgrim Society

Why We Need the Puritans

J. I. PACKER

I

Horse racing is said to be the sport of kings. The sport of slinging mud has, however, a wider following. Pillorying the Puritans, in particular, has long been a popular pastime on both sides of the Atlantic, and most people's image of Puritanism still has on it much disfiguring dirt that needs to be scraped off.

"Puritan" as a name was, in fact, mud from the start. Coined in the early 1560s, it was always a satirical smear word implying peevishness, censoriousness, conceit, and a measure of hypocrisy, over and above its basic implication of religiously motivated discontent with what was seen as Elizabeth's Laodicean and compromising Church of England. Later the word gained the further, political connotation of being against the Stuart monarchy and for some sort of republicanism; its primary reference, however, was still to what was seen as an odd, furious, and ugly form of Protestant religion. In England, anti-Puritan feeling was let loose at the time of the Restoration and has flowed freely ever since. In North America it built up slowly after the days of Jonathan Edwards to reach its zenith a hundred years ago in post-Puritan New England.

For the past half-century, however, scholars have been meticulously wiping away the mud. And as Michelangelo's frescoes in the Sistine

Chapel have unfamiliar colors today now that restorers have removed the dark varnish, so the conventional image of the Puritans has been radically revamped, at least for those in the know. (Knowledge, alas, travels slowly in some quarters.) Taught by Perry Miller, William Haller, Marshall Knappen, Percy Scholes, Edmund Morgan, and a host of more recent researchers, informed folk now acknowledge that the typical Puritans were not wild men, fierce and freaky, religious fanatics and social extremists, but sober, conscientious, and cultured citizens, persons of principle, determined and disciplined, excelling in the domestic virtues, and with no obvious shortcomings save a tendency to run to words when saying anything important, whether to God or to man. At last the record has been put straight.

But even so, the suggestion that we *need* the Puritans — we late twentieth-century Westerners, with all our sophistication and mastery of technique in both secular and sacred fields — may prompt some lifting of eyebrows. The belief that the Puritans, even if they were in fact responsible citizens, were comic and pathetic in equal degree, being naïve and superstitious, primitive and gullible, superserious, overscrupulous, majoring in minors, and unable or unwilling to relax, dies hard. What could these zealots give us that we need? it is asked.

The answer, in one word, is maturity. Maturity is a compound of wisdom, goodwill, resilience, and creativity. The Puritans exemplified maturity; we don't. A much-traveled leader, a native American (be it said), has declared that he finds North American Protestantism — man-centered, manipulative, success-oriented, self-indulgent, and sentimental as it blatantly is — to be three thousand miles wide and half an inch deep. We are spiritual dwarfs. The Puritans, by contrast, as a body were giants. They were great souls serving a great God. In them, clear-headed passion and warm-hearted compassion combined. Visionary and practical, idealistic and realistic too, goal-oriented and methodical, they were great believers, great hopers, great doers, and great sufferers.

But their sufferings, on both sides of the ocean (in old England from the authorities and in New England from the elements), seasoned and ripened them till they gained a stature that was nothing short of heroic. Ease and luxury, such as our affluence brings us today, do not make for maturity; hardship and struggle do, and the Puritans' battles against the Evangelical and climatic wildernesses in which God set them produced a virility of character, undaunted and unsinkable, rising above discouragement and fears, for which the true precedents and models are men like Moses, and Nehemiah, and Peter after Pentecost, and the apostle Paul.

Spiritual warfare made the Puritans what they were. They accepted conflict as their calling, seeing themselves as their Lord's soldier-pilgrims, just as in Bunyan's allegory, and not expecting to be able to advance a single step without opposition of one sort or another. Wrote John Geree, in his tract *The Character of an Old English Puritane or Nonconformist* (1646): "His whole life he accounted a warfare, wherein Christ was his captain, his arms, praiers and tears. The Crosse his Banner and his word [motto] *Vincit qui patitur* [he who suffers conquers]."[1]

The Puritans lost, more or less, every public battle that they fought. Those who stayed in England did not change the Church of England as they hoped to do, nor did they revive more than a minority of its adherents, and eventually they were driven out of Anglicanism by calculated pressure on their consciences. Those who crossed the Atlantic failed to establish New Jerusalem in New England; for the first fifty years their little colonies barely survived, hanging on by the skin of their teeth. But the moral and spiritual victories that the Puritans won by keeping sweet, peaceful, patient, obedient, and hopeful under sustained and seemingly intolerable pressures and frustrations give them a place of high honor in the believers' hall of fame, where Hebrews 11 is the first gallery. It was out of this constant furnace-experience that their maturity was wrought and their wisdom concerning discipleship was refined. George Whitefield, the evangelist, wrote of them as follows:

> Ministers never write or preach so well as when under the cross; the Spirit of Christ and of glory then rests upon them. It was this, no doubt, that made the Puritans . . . such burning and shining lights. When cast out by the black Bartholomew-act [the 1662 Act of Uniformity] and driven from their respective charges to preach in barns and fields, in the highways and hedges, they in an especial manner wrote and preached as men having authority. Though dead, by their writings they yet speak; a peculiar unction attends them to this very hour. . . .[2]

Those words come from a preface to a reprint of Bunyan's works that appeared in 1767; but the unction continues, the authority is still felt, and the ripe wisdom remains breath-taking, as all modern Puritan-readers soon discover for themselves. Through the legacy of this literature the Puritans can help us today toward the maturity that they knew and that we need.

II

In what ways can they do this? Let me suggest some specifics. First, there are lessons for us in *the integration of their daily lives*. As their Christianity was all-embracing, so their living was all of a piece.

Nowadays we would call their lifestyle wholistic: all awareness, activity, and enjoyment, all "use of the creatures" and development of personal powers and creativity, were integrated in the single purpose of honoring God by appreciating all His gifts and making everything "holiness to the Lord." There was for them no disjunction between sacred and secular; all creation, so far as they were concerned, was sacred, and all activities, of whatever kind, must be sanctified, that is, done to the glory of God. So, in their heavenly minded ardor the Puritans became men and women of order, matter-of-fact and down-to-earth, prayerful, purposeful, practical. Seeing life whole, they integrated contemplation with action, worship with work, labor with rest, love of God with love of neighbor and of self, personal with social identity, and the wide spectrum of relational responsibilities with each other, in a thoroughly conscientious and thought-out way.

In this thoroughness they were extreme, that is to say, far more thorough than we are, but in their blending of the whole wide range of Christian duties set forth in Scripture they were extremely balanced. They lived by "method" (we would say, by a rule of life), planning and proportioning their time with care, not so much to keep bad things out as to make sure that they got all good and important things in — necessary wisdom, then as now, for busy people! We today, who tend to live unplanned lives at random in a series of noncommunicating compartments and who hence feel swamped and distracted most of the time, could learn much from the Puritans at this point.

Second, there are lessons for us in *the quality of their spiritual experience*. In the Puritans' communion with God, as Jesus Christ was central, so Holy Scripture was supreme. By Scripture, as God's Word of instruction about divine-human relationships, they sought to live, and here too they were conscientiously methodical. Knowing themselves to be creatures of thought, affection, and will, and knowing that God's way to the human heart (the will) is via the human head (the mind), the Puritans practiced meditation, discursive and systematic, on the whole range of biblical truth as they saw it applying to themselves. Puritan meditation on Scripture was modeled on the Puritan sermon; in meditation the Puritan would seek to search and challenge his heart, to stir his affections to hate sin and love righteousness, and to encourage himself with God's promises, just as Puritan preachers would do from the pulpit. This rational, resolute, passionate piety was conscientious without becoming obsessive, law-oriented without lapsing into legalism, and expressive of Christian liberty without any shameful lurches into license. The Puritans knew that Scripture is the unalterable rule of holiness, and they never allowed themselves to forget it.

Knowing also the dishonesty and deceitfulness of fallen human hearts, they cultivated humility and self-suspicion as abiding attitudes, examining themselves regularly for spiritual blind spots and lurking inward evils. They may not be called morbid or introspective on this account, however; on the contrary, they found the discipline of self-examination by Scripture (not the same thing as introspection, let us note), followed by the discipline of confessing and forsaking sin and renewing one's gratitude to Christ for his pardoning mercy, to be a source of great inner peace and joy. We today, who know to our cost that we have unclear minds, uncontrolled affections, and unstable wills when it comes to serving God, and who again and again find ourselves being imposed on by irrational, emotional romanticism disguised as superspirituality, could profit much from the Puritans' example at this point too.

Third, there are lessons for us in *their passion for effective action*. Though the Puritans, like the rest of the human race, had their dreams of what could and should be, they were decidedly not the kind of people that we would call "dreamy"! They had no time for the idleness of the lazy or passive person who leaves it to others to change the world. They were men of action in the pure Reformed mold — crusading activists without a jot of self-reliance; workers for God who depended utterly on God to work in and through them and who always gave God the praise for anything they did that in retrospect seemed to them to have been right; gifted men who prayed earnestly that God would enable them to use their powers, not for self-display, but for His praise. None of them wanted to be revolutionaries in church or state, though some of them reluctantly became such; all of them, however, longed to be effective change agents for God wherever change was called for. So Cromwell and his army made long, strong prayers before each battle, and preachers made long, strong prayers privately before ever venturing into the pulpit, and laymen made long, strong prayers before tackling any matter of importance (marriage, business deals, major purchases, or whatever).

Today, however, Christians in the West are found to be on the whole passionless, passive, and one fears, prayerless. Cultivating an ethos that encloses personal piety in a pietistic cocoon, they leave public affairs to go their own way and neither expect nor, for the most part, seek influence beyond their own Christian circle. Where the Puritans prayed and labored for a holy England and New England — sensing that where privilege is neglected and unfaithfulness reigns, national judgment threatens — modern Christians gladly settle for conventional social respectability and, having done so, look no further. Surely it is obvious that at this point also the Puritans have a great deal to teach us.

Fourth, there are lessons for us in *their program for family stability*. It is hardly too much to say that the Puritans created the Christian family in the English-speaking world. The Puritan ethic of marriage was first to look not for a partner whom you *do* love passionately at this moment but rather for one whom you *can* love steadily as your best friend for life, then to proceed with God's help to do just that. The Puritan ethic of nurture was to train up children in the way they should go, to care for their bodies and souls together, and to educate them for sober, godly, socially useful adult living. The Puritan ethic of home life was based on maintaining order, courtesy, and family worship.

Goodwill, patience, consistency, and an encouraging attitude were seen as the essential domestic virtues. In an age of routine discomforts, rudimentary medicine without pain-killers, frequent bereavements (most families lost at least as many children as they reared), an average life expectancy of just under thirty years, and economic hardship for almost all save merchant princes and landed gentry, family life was a school for character in every sense. The fortitude with which Puritans resisted the all-too-familiar temptation to relieve pressure from the world by brutality at home, and labored to honor God in their families despite all, merits supreme praise. At home the Puritans showed themselves mature, accepting hardships and disappointments realistically as from God and refusing to be daunted or soured by any of them. Also, it was at home in the first instance that the Puritan layman practiced evangelism and ministry. "His family he endeavoured to make a Church," wrote Geree, ". . . labouring that those that were born in it, might be born again to God."[3] In an era in which family life has become brittle even among Christians, with chicken-hearted spouses taking the easy course of separation rather than work at their relationship, and narcissistic parents spoiling their children materially while neglecting them spiritually, there is once more much to be learned from the Puritans' very different ways.

Fifth, there are lessons to be learned from *their sense of human worth*. Through believing in a great God (the God of Scripture, undiminished and undomesticated), they gained a vivid awareness of the greatness of moral issues, of eternity, and of the human soul. Hamlet's "What a piece of work is man!" is a very Puritan sentiment; the wonder of human individuality was something that they felt keenly. Though, under the influence of their medieval heritage, which told them that error has no rights, they did not in every case manage to respect those who differed publicly from them, their appreciation of man's dignity as the creature made to be God's friend was strong, and so in particular was their sense of the beauty and nobility of human holiness. Nowadays, in the collectivized urban anthill where most of us live, the sense of each individual's eternal significance is much eroded, and the Puritan spirit is at this point a corrective from which we can profit greatly.

Sixth, there are lessons to be learned from the Puritans' *ideal of church renewal*. To be sure, "renewal" was not a word that they used, they spoke only of "reformation" and "reform," which words suggest to our twentieth-century minds a concern that is limited to the externals of the church's orthodoxy, order, worship forms, and disciplinary code. But when the Puritans preached, published, and prayed for "reformation," they had in mind, not indeed less than this, but far more.

On the title page of the original edition of Richard Baxter's *The Reformed Pastor*, the word "Reformed" was printed in much larger type than any other; and one does not have to read far before discovering that, for Baxter, a "Reformed" pastor was not one who campaigned for Calvinism but one whose ministry as preacher, teacher, catechist, and role model for his people showed him to be, as we would say, "revived" or "renewed." The essence of this kind of "reformation" was enrichment of understanding of God's truth, arousal of affections Godward, increase of ardor in one's devotions, and more love, joy, and firmness of Christian purpose in one's calling and personal life. In line with this, the ideal for the church was that through "reformed" clergy each congregation in its entirety should be "reformed" — brought, that is, by God's grace into a state of what we would call revival without disorder, so as to be truly and thoroughly converted, theologically orthodox and sound, spiritually alert and expectant, in character terms wise and mature, ethically enterprising and obedient, and humbly but joyously sure of their salvation. This was the goal at which Puritan pastoral ministry aimed throughout, both in English parishes and in the "gathered" churches of congregational type that multiplied in the mid-seventeenth century.

The Puritans' concern for spiritual awakening in communities is to some extent hidden from us by their institutionalism. We are apt to think of revival ardor as always putting a strain on established order, whereas the Puritans envisaged "reform" at the congregational level coming in disciplined style through faithful preaching, catechizing, and spiritual service on the pastor's part. Clericalism, with its damming up of lay initiative, was doubtless a Puritan limitation, which boomeranged when lay zeal finally boiled over in Cromwell's army, in Quakerism and in the vast sectarian underworld of Commonwealth times. The other side of the coin, however, was the nobility of the pastor's profile that the Puritans evolved — gospel preacher and Bible teacher, shepherd and physician of souls, catechist and counselor, trainer and disciplinarian, all in one. From the Puritans' ideals and goals for church life, which were unquestionably and abidingly right, and from their standards for clergy, which were challengingly and searchingly high, there is yet again a great deal that modern Christians can and should take to heart.

These are just a few of the most obvious ways in which the Puritans can help us in these days.

III

In conclusion I would commend Professor Ryken's chapters, which these remarks introduce, as a fine presentation of the Puritan outlook. Having read widely in recent Puritan scholarship, he knows his way around. He knows, as do most modern students, that Puritanism as a distinctive attitude began with William Tyndale, Luther's contemporary, a generation before the word "Puritan" was coined, and went on to the end of the seventeenth century, several decades after "Puritan" had fallen out of general use. He knows that into the making of Puritanism went Tyndale's reforming biblicism, the piety of the heart that broke surface in John Bradford, the passion for pastoral competence that John Hooper, Edward Dering, and Richard Greenham, among others, exemplified, the view of Scripture as the "regulative principle" of worship and ministerial order that fired Thomas Cartwright, the comprehensive ethical interest that reached its apogee in Richard Baxter's monumental *Christian Directory*, and the concern to popularize and make practical, without losing depth, that was so evident in William Perkins and so powerfully influenced his successors.

Dr. Ryken also knows that in addition to being a movement for church reform, pastoral renewal, and spiritual revival, Puritanism was a world view, a total Christian philosophy, in intellectual terms a Protestantized and updated medievalism, and in terms of spirituality a kind of monasticism outside the cloister and away from monkish vows. His presentation of the Puritan view and style of life is perceptive and accurate. It should win new respect for the Puritans and should create a new interest in exploring the great mass of theological and devotional literature that they left us, so as to discover the profundities of their biblical and spiritual insight. If it has this effect, I for one, who owe more to Puritan writing than to any other theology I have ever read, shall be overjoyed.

Preface

This book is a survey of Puritan ideals. It explores Puritan attitudes on a broad range of topics that generally fall within the category of practical Christian living.

My purpose in writing this book has been threefold: (1) to correct an almost universal misunderstanding of what the Puritans really stood for, (2) to bring together into a convenient synthesis the best that the Puritans thought and said on selected topics, and (3) to recover the Christian wisdom of the Puritans for today. Evangelical Protestants are strangers to what is best in their own tradition; my hope is that this book will make a small contribution to remedying that situation.

I have taken most of my data from Puritan written sources. This is what my own scholarly training equips me to do, and it fits best with my purpose of focusing on Puritan ideals that remain relevant today.

I have looked at Puritanism with a "wide-angle lens" to provide as much scope as possible. I have ranged over both English and American Puritanism in both the sixteenth and seventeenth centuries. In achieving such scope, I have had to slight the nuances of historical development, the contexts of specific Puritan quotations, and the exception to the general rule. To compensate for those lacks, I have been able to capture some of the varied richness of the Puritan movement. I know of no other movement that produced so many good secondary spokesmen in addition to the major ones. I hope also to have left my readers assured that the views I attribute to the Puritan movement were representative of a majority of Puritans, not the atypical convictions of an individual Puritan.

Why are there so many quotations in the book? Because books that claim to tell us what the Puritans were like without documenting the claims cannot be trusted. As much as possible, I have tried to let the Puritans speak for themselves and to allow my readers to draw their own conclusions. The resulting book incorporates a wealth of choice Puritan quotations and of apt comments by leading historians of the Puritan movement.

Perhaps I should add that when I refer to Puritanism as a "movement," I use the term loosely. The structural or institutional organization of Puritan religion was sometimes very hazy. By the Puritan "movement," therefore, I mean Puritan religion, a spirit or attitude that bound Puritans together.

For the sake of readability, I would encourage my readers to ignore the footnotes on a first reading of the book. To make the Puritan quotations accessible to modern readers, I have modernized both spelling and punctuation.

In ascribing various views to the Puritans, I do not intend always to imply that they were exclusive to the Puritans. The Puritans often participated in the general trends of their age. My concern at every point has been to keep the record straight on what the Puritans believed, partly in an effort to correct modern misconceptions about them. Too often it is assumed that the Puritans did not share the most enlightened views of their cultures; I have tried to show that they usually did and were often responsible for them.

Although I have not had the space to "build bridges" between Puritan views and our own situation, the assumption underlying this book is that on many crucial issues the Puritans remain a guide for Christians today. My purpose in writing is partly to allow the Puritans to be a lens through which we can see what it means to live Christianly in the world. My sympathy with Puritan viewpoints will be obvious. Even Puritan faults, to which I have devoted a chapter, have a positive instructional value by showing us what to avoid.

Acknowledgments

This book became a reality only with the help of people to whom I here gratefully record my indebtedness: to Harold Myra, for unwittingly setting in motion a chain of occurrences that eventuated in the book; to Bob and JoAnn Harvey, for continuing to expect the book during my years of research and diversion; to Dan Bowell of the Wheaton College Library, for processing my unconscionable number of interlibrary loan requests; to Wheaton College, for a summer writing grant; to my wife Mary, for proofreading the manuscript; to Walter Elwell of the Wheaton College Graduate School, as well as colleagues in the archives of the Billy Graham Center and the special collections of the Wheaton College Library, for assistance in the illustrations for the book; to Mark Noll of the Wheaton College History Department, for his unfailingly helpful critiques of the chapters as I wrote them; and to James I. Packer of Regent College, for scrutinizing the entire manuscript and writing the foreword.

We must picture these Puritans as the very opposite of those who bear that name today.[6]

Very few of the so-called "Puritans" were "Puritanical" in the nineteenth-century sense of that word, obsessed by sex and opposed to fun: "Puritanism" of this sort was largely a post-Restoration creation.[7]

When you think about Puritanism you must begin by getting rid of the slang term "puritanism" as applied to Victorian religious hypocrisy. This does not apply to seventeenth-century Puritanism.[8]

In the introduction that follows, I have attempted under a variety of formats to suggest the main outlines of the Puritan "mind" or "temperament" or "spirit." The purpose of this overview is to provide a landscape that the remaining chapters will fill in with details. The opening chapter states my "thesis"; the rest of the book is documentation.

"Everybody Knows That the Puritans Were ..."

No group of people has been more unjustly maligned in the twentieth century than the Puritans. As a result, we approach the Puritans with an enormous baggage of culturally ingrained prejudice. As an entry into the subject, therefore, I propose that we take a brief look at the usual charges against the Puritans, noting the truth or falseness of those charges.

The Puritans were against sex. Ridiculous. An influential Puritan said that sexual intercourse was "one of the most proper and essential acts of marriage" and something in which a couple should engage "with good will and delight, willingly, readily, and cheerfully."[9] Another began his list of the duties between husband and wife with "the right and lawful use of their bodies or of the marriage bed, which indeed is an essential duty of marriage."[10]

The Puritans never laughed and were opposed to fun. Only partly true. The Puritans were serious people, but they also said such things as this: "God would have our joys to be far more than our sorrows";[11] "there is a kind of smiling and joyful laughter . . . which may stand . . . with the best man's piety";[12] Christians "may be merry at their work, and merry at their meat";[13] "joy is the habitation of the righteous."[14] Thomas Gataker wrote that it is the purpose of Satan to persuade us that "in the kingdom of God there is nothing but sighing and groaning and fasting and prayer," whereas the truth is that "in his house there is marrying and giving in marriage, . . . feasting and rejoicing."[15] William Tyndale described the

Acknowledgments

This book became a reality only with the help of people to whom I here gratefully record my indebtedness: to Harold Myra, for unwittingly setting in motion a chain of occurrences that eventuated in the book; to Bob and JoAnn Harvey, for continuing to expect the book during my years of research and diversion; to Dan Bowell of the Wheaton College Library, for processing my unconscionable number of interlibrary loan requests; to Wheaton College, for a summer writing grant; to my wife Mary, for proofreading the manuscript; to Walter Elwell of the Wheaton College Graduate School, as well as colleagues in the archives of the Billy Graham Center and the special collections of the Wheaton College Library, for assistance in the illustrations for the book; to Mark Noll of the Wheaton College History Department, for his unfailingly helpful critiques of the chapters as I wrote them; and to James I. Packer of Regent College, for scrutinizing the entire manuscript and writing the foreword.

This reconstruction of life at Plymouth Plantation suggests several leading traits of the Puritans: an urge for new beginnings, courage when confronted with hardship, an elemental simplicity. Courtesy of Plimouth Plantation

Chapter 1

What Were the Original Puritans Like?

I serve a precise God. — RICHARD ROGERS

P uritanism is the haunting fear that someone, somewhere, may be happy." So said a modern debunker of the Puritans.[1]

But a contemporary of William Tyndale, often considered the first Puritan, gave exactly the opposite assessment. Thomas More, the great Catholic, found the Protestant religion of Tyndale overly indulgent. He described its adherents as people who "loved no lenten fast" but instead "eat fast and drink fast and lust fast in their lechery."[2] Their theology, according to More, erred in the direction of making the Christian life too easy: "I could for my part be very well content that sin and pain and all were as shortly gone as Tyndale telleth us: but I am loathe that he deceived us."[3]

Puritanism, we are told today, "damages the human soul, renders it hard and gloomy, deprives it of sunshine and happiness."[4] This charge would have come as quite a surprise to the Quaker George Fox, a contemporary of the Puritans who despised their "ribbons and lace and costly apparel," their "sporting and feasting."[5]

When authorities such as C. S. Lewis, Christopher Hill, and A. G. Dickens say such things as the following, it will pay us to keep an open mind to the possibility that we have been seriously misled regarding the Puritans:

We must picture these Puritans as the very opposite of those who bear that name today.[6]

Very few of the so-called "Puritans" were "Puritanical" in the nineteenth-century sense of that word, obsessed by sex and opposed to fun: "Puritanism" of this sort was largely a post-Restoration creation.[7]

When you think about Puritanism you must begin by getting rid of the slang term "puritanism" as applied to Victorian religious hypocrisy. This does not apply to seventeenth-century Puritanism.[8]

In the introduction that follows, I have attempted under a variety of formats to suggest the main outlines of the Puritan "mind" or "temperament" or "spirit." The purpose of this overview is to provide a landscape that the remaining chapters will fill in with details. The opening chapter states my "thesis"; the rest of the book is documentation.

"Everybody Knows That the Puritans Were ..."

No group of people has been more unjustly maligned in the twentieth century than the Puritans. As a result, we approach the Puritans with an enormous baggage of culturally ingrained prejudice. As an entry into the subject, therefore, I propose that we take a brief look at the usual charges against the Puritans, noting the truth or falseness of those charges.

The Puritans were against sex. Ridiculous. An influential Puritan said that sexual intercourse was "one of the most proper and essential acts of marriage" and something in which a couple should engage "with good will and delight, willingly, readily, and cheerfully."[9] Another began his list of the duties between husband and wife with "the right and lawful use of their bodies or of the marriage bed, which indeed is an essential duty of marriage."[10]

The Puritans never laughed and were opposed to fun. Only partly true. The Puritans were serious people, but they also said such things as this: "God would have our joys to be far more than our sorrows";[11] "there is a kind of smiling and joyful laughter ... which may stand ... with the best man's piety";[12] Christians "may be merry at their work, and merry at their meat";[13] "joy is the habitation of the righteous."[14] Thomas Gataker wrote that it is the purpose of Satan to persuade us that "in the kingdom of God there is nothing but sighing and groaning and fasting and prayer," whereas the truth is that "in his house there is marrying and giving in marriage, ... feasting and rejoicing."[15] William Tyndale described the

Christian gospel as "good, merry, glad and joyful tidings, that maketh a man's heart glad, and maketh him sing, and dance, and leap for joy."[16]

The Puritans wore drab, unfashionable clothes. Untrue. The Puritans dressed according to the fashions of their class and time. It is true that black carried connotations of dignity and formality (as it does today) and was standard for clothes worn on Sundays and special occasions. But daily dress was colorful. The American Puritan William Brewster wore a blue coat, a violet coat, and a green waistcoat.[17] Anthony Wood described how John Owen looked during his days as vice-chancellor at Oxford University: "hair powdered, cambric band with large costly band strings, velvet jacket, breeches set round at knees with ribbons pointed, and Spanish leather boots with cambric tops."[18] Russet or various shades of orange-brown were the most common color for clothes, but surviving inventories also show many items in red, blue, green, yellow, purple, and so forth.[19]

The Puritans were opposed to sports and recreation. Largely false. A book-length study has shown that the Puritans enjoyed such varied activities as hunting, fishing, a form of football, bowling, reading, music, swimming, skating, and archery.[20] A Puritan pastor said regarding recreations that Christians should "enjoy them as liberties, with thankfulness to God that allows us these liberties to refresh ourselves."[21] It is true that the Puritans banned all recreation on Sundays and all games of chance, gambling, bear baiting, horse racing, and bowling in or around taverns at all times. They did so, not because they were opposed to fun, but because they judged these activities to be inherently harmful or immoral.

The Puritans were money-grubbing workaholics who would do anything to get rich. Generally untrue. The Puritans were obsessed with the *dangers* of wealth. In fact, they would hardly get off the subject when discussing business. Lord Montagu told his son, "Travail not too much to be rich. . . . He that is greedy of gain troubleth his own soul."[22] "Remember that riches are no part of your felicity," wrote Richard Baxter; "riches are nothing but plentiful provision for tempting corruptible flesh."[23] "I had rather be a miserable saint than a prosperous sinner," wrote Thomas Adams.[24] On the positive side, the Puritans *did* believe that work was a moral virtue, that idleness was a vice, and that thrift or deliberate underconsumption for the sake of moderation and avoiding debt was a good thing.

The Puritans were hostile to the arts. Partly true, but not as true as most moderns think. The misunderstanding stems from the fact that the Puritans removed music and art from the churches. But this was an objection to Catholic worship and ceremony, not to music and art themselves.[25] The Puritans removed organs and paintings from churches but bought them for private use in their homes.[26] In a treatise stating the usual objections to musical instruments in church, John Cotton added that he did not "forbid the private use of any instrument of music."[27] Oliver Cromwell removed an organ from an Oxford chapel to his own residence at Hampton Court, where he employed a private organist. When one of his daughters was married, he engaged an orchestra of forty-eight to accompany the dancing.[28] While confined to prison, John Bunyan secretly made a flute out of a chair leg.[29]

The Puritans were overly emotional and denigrated reason. Nonsense. They aimed at a balance of head and heart. "Man is a rational creature, and apt to be moved in a reasoning way," wrote Richard Baxter.[30] "The believer is the most reasonable man in the world," wrote Samuel Rutherford; "he who doth all by faith, doth all by the light of sound reason."[31]

Puritanism was an old-fashioned movement that appealed only to people over seventy suffering from tired blood. Exactly wrong. Puritanism was a youthful, vigorous movement. C. S. Lewis calls the early Puritans "young, fierce, progressive intellectuals, very fashionable and up-to-date."[32] The Puritans "thought young," whatever their chronological age. The youthfulness of Elizabethan Puritans was a common taunt against them by their Anglican enemies; in 1583 Archbishop Whitgift said condescendingly to a group of Puritan ministers, "You are . . . but boys in comparison of us, who have studied divinity before you . . . were born."[33] An Anglican bishop was alarmed by the way in which the Puritans had "drawn divers young ministers" into their ranks,[34] while at St. Albans it was the "young men and young women" who made a practice of "gadding" to the neighboring parish where the Puritan William Dyke preached.[35] One anti-Puritan father arranged for his son to be educated by a Puritan "to sicken him of Puritanism," only to find that his son became a Puritan.[36]

The Puritans were repelled by the human body and the physical world. Not true, except for a few Puritans suffering from psychological aberrations. Increase Mather wrote in his diary, "Jesus Christ intends to bestow eternal glory on my body as well as my soul, and therefore he will not deny unto me so small a matter as bodily health."[37] William Ames declared, "Our bodies are to be offered to God, Rom. 12:1, and God is to be glorified in our bodies."[38] As for the physical world, the Puritans said such things as this: "grace is hid in nature . . . as sweet-water in rose leaves";[39] "God hath given us several senses that so we might enjoy the delights of them all";[40] "this world and the things thereof are all good, and were all made of God, for the benefit of his creature."[41]

The Puritans were intolerant toward people who disagreed with them. True by modern standards, but not by the standards of their day. *No* group in the sixteenth and seventeenth centuries was prepared to grant full religious and political toleration. There was one official church and government, and dissidents were punished for their dissent.

Compared with other religious groups in England, Puritan tolerance receives high marks. W. K. Jordan, whose books on the development of religious toleration in England are the standard sources on the subject, credits Puritanism for contributing to "liberty of dissent," "religious liberty," and "the right of freedom of conscience."[42] Cromwell was prepared to allow Anglicans and Catholics to hold their services in private homes (something that had largely been denied to Puritans), and he permitted the Jews to return to England and to have their own synagogue and cemetery in London.[43] Despite all their anti-Catholicism, Puritans did not generally deny that many Catholics had been true Christians.[44] And part of the time, at least, Puritans rose above party spirit, as in Samuel Fairclough's statement, "If a man lives holily, and walks humbly with God, I shall ever love him, notwithstanding his conformity [to the Church of England]; and if he be proud, contentious and profane, I will never think well of him for his non-conformity."[45]

The Puritans were overly strict. Often true. Samuel Ward's college diary consists of a cataloging of his failings, and his self-accusations include such offenses as these: going "to bed without prayer," falling asleep without his last thought being about God, "unwillingness to pray," not preparing adequately for Sunday on the preceding Saturday night, immoderate eating, "also my immoderate laughter in the hall at nine o'clock," impatience, and talking on Sunday of "other matters than are meet to be talked of on the Sabbath."[46]

When the English Puritan preacher Richard Rogers was lecturing at Wethersfield, Essex, someone told him, "Mr. Rogers, I like you and your company very well, but you are so precise." To which Rogers replied, "O Sir, I serve a precise God."[47] One of the names by which the Puritans were first called was "Precisionists." Of course, everyone is strict about the things he or she values most highly. Athletes are strict about training, musicians about practicing, business people about money. The Puritans were strict about their moral and spiritual activities.

The Puritans repressed normal human feelings in the name of religion. Not so: the Puritans were warmly human in their feelings. They spoke repeatedly about nurturing good "affections," that is, emotions. The American Puritan Samuel Willard wrote,

Stoicism . . . would hamstring nature, and cut off the affections from their natural activity, as if they had been given to . . . men for nothing else but to be suppressed . . . : whereas the Word of God and the rules of religion teach us, not to destroy, but to improve every faculty that is in us, and in particular our affections, to the glory of God who gave them to us.[48]

John Bunyan wrote of his imprisonment, "The parting with my wife and poor children hath often been to me in this place as the pulling of my flesh from my bones."[49]

The Puritans were legalistic moralists who judged people by their external behavior only. Largely untrue of the original Puritans. The word "moral" was a negative term for the Puritans because it suggested works without faith.[50] "That which is seen," wrote William Adams, "is nothing in comparison of that which is not."[51] "Civility is not purity," said Thomas Watson; "a man may be clothed with moral virtues — justice, prudence, temperance — and yet go to hell. If we must be pure in heart, then we must not rest in outward purity."[52] Samuel Willard wrote, "Nor indeed do I know of anything which doth more threaten the undermining of true Christianity . . . than the putting of moral virtues into legal dress."[53] In short, distrust of outward appearances was one of the Puritans' most salient traits.

The Puritans indulged in too much self-loathing. Partly true. Cotton Mather wrote this type of thing in his diary:

A Christian ought always to think humbly of himself, and be full of self-abasing and self-abhorring reflections. By loathing of himself continually, and being very sensible of what are his own loathesome circumstances, a Christian does what is very pleasing to Heaven.[54]

We should not, however, take such comments out of their context. The exaggerated descriptions of human worthlessness occur in passages where the writer is exploring human sinfulness before God's holiness. A study of the Puritans does not leave one with the impression that they suffered from poor self-images. If anything, they seem overly confident. Then, too, we can balance passages of self-loathing against statements such as these:

Never did God declare against self, or call a man to deny himself in that which hinders his own salvation and happiness. . . . There is a love which is due to a man's self, without which he cannot perform the duties of the law. . . . I owe charity to others, but it must begin at home.[55]

The Puritans were ignorant people who opposed education. Absolutely untrue. No Christian movement in history has been more zealous for education than the Puritans. The adjective "learned" was one of their most frequently used positive titles for a person. A modern scholar describes Puritanism as "a movement of the 'learned godly,' the religious intellectuals of the day, a movement that found its strongest support in university circles."[56] The founders of the Massachusetts Bay Colony established their first college (Harvard) only six years after landing. The colony itself, "with over 100 graduates of Oxford and Cambridge, was surely the best educated community the world has ever known, before or since."[57]

Exactly Who Were the Puritans?

Puritanism was part of the Protestant Reformation in England. No specific date or event marks its inception. It first assumed the form of an organized movement in the 1560s under the reign of Queen Elizabeth, but when we identify the traits of that movement we can see that its roots reach back into the first half of the century. Its intellectual and spiritual forebears include figures like the Bible translator William Tyndale, the popular preacher-evangelist Hugh Latimer, and Thomas Becon. And surely the roots of Puritanism include the Protestant exiles who fled to the Continent during the persecution under the Catholic Queen Mary (1553–1558).

Puritanism began as a specifically church movement. Queen Elizabeth established "the Elizabethan Settlement" (also know as "the Elizabethan Compromise") within the Church of England early during her reign. That compromise drew together Reformed or Calvinistic *doctrine*, the continuation of a liturgical and (in the eyes of the Puritans) Catholic *form of worship*, and an episcopal *church government*.

The Puritans were impatient with this halting of the Reformation. In their view, the English Church remained "but halfly reformed." They wished to "purify" the church of the remaining vestiges of Catholic ceremony, ritual, and hierarchy. This early quarrel with the state church quickly broadened to include other areas of personal and national life. Puritanism was thus partly a distinctly English phenomenon, consisting of discontent with the Church of England. But from the beginning it was also part of European Protestantism. Horton Davies says that "puritanism began as a liturgical reform, but it developed into a distinct attitude towards life."[58]

As the movement progressed, more and more Puritans were unable to "conform" sufficiently to the state church to remain as good members

John Bunyan's tomb in Bunhill Fields, London. Several famous Puritans, including John Owen, lie buried in this nonconformist cemetery. Puritanism was in important ways an outsider's movement in England, where it was destined to influence rather than dominate English society.

within it. Puritan pastors frequently found themselves ejected from their positions. For purposes of this book, I have generally tried to keep the Puritans distinct from "separatists" and "nonconformists," but as the seventeenth century wore on, Puritans were in fact increasingly, and against their will, nonconforming separatists.[59]

Just as Puritanism had no specific birth date, it had no precise termination. For purposes of this book, I have fixed its limit at the end of the seventeenth century.

Some Landmark Dates in the Puritan Movement

This book is not a history of Puritanism, but an outline of some key events in the movement will provide a useful historical skeleton.

1526	William Tyndale's English New Testament reaches England.
1536	Henry VIII and the English Parliament separate the Church of England from Rome.

1547	Edward VI becomes king. The Protestant Reformation in England advances dramatically.
1553	Mary, Roman Catholic, becomes queen. Three hundred English Protestants are martyred, and eight hundred flee to the Continent, where they imbibe the doctrinal tenets of the Continental Reformers.
1558	Queen Elizabeth I accedes to the throne and establishes the Elizabethan Compromise, which is insufficiently reformed to satisy those who would soon be known as Puritans.
1559	The Act of Uniformity authorizes the Anglican Prayer Book for public worship and lays down penalties for those who refuse to use it or who speak against it.
1567–1568	A vestments controversy of long standing reaches its height in the Church of England. The immediate question is whether preachers had to wear the prescribed clerical garments at church services, but this is only a symbol of the bigger issue of ceremony, ritual, and liturgy in the church. The controversy marks growing impatience among the Puritans over the situation of a "halfly reformed" church.
1569–1570	Thomas Cartwright, professor at Cambridge University, upsets the Anglican establishment (and loses his position) with his lectures on the first two chapters of Acts, in which he argues for a simplified Christianity and a Presbyterian form of church government.
1583	John Whitgift becomes Archbishop of Canterbury and enforces conformity to the ceremonies of the Anglican Church, leading to oppression of Puritan nonconformists.
1603	James I becomes king. Puritans initially have hopes that their situation will improve. In 1604 they meet with the new king at the Hampton Court Conference to present their requests. The king threatens to "harry them out of the land, or else do worse."
1618	The Book of Sports is first published (renewed in 1633), encouraging sports on Sunday afternoons in direct contradiction of Puritan Sabbatarianism. This is cited by the seventeenth-century British church historian Thomas Fuller as one of the leading causes of the English civil war.
1620	Puritan Separatists found the Pilgrim colony at Plymouth, Massachusetts.
1625	Charles I, unsympathetic to the Puritans, becomes king.

1628	William Laud becomes Bishop of London (and Archbishop of Canterbury in 1633) and undertakes stringent measures to stamp nonconformity out of the Anglican Church. Laudian oppression is a leading contributor to Puritan migrations to America.
1630	John Winthrop leads the first large body of Puritans to Massachusetts Bay.
1636	Harvard College is founded.
1640	Summoned into session by Charles I, the Long Parliament curtails the power of the king. Migration to New England largely stops.
1643–1646	The Westminster Assembly, a synod called by Parliament to act as a consulting council on matters of church polity and doctrine, prepares a *Directory of Worship*, the *Westminster Confession*, a *Larger Catechism*, and a *Shorter Catechism*.
1645–1646	Oliver Cromwell's parliamentary army defeats the king's army to end the civil war.
1646	The episcopalian form of church government is abolished in the Church of England.
1647	The army debates at Putney, England, over the question of how universally the vote will be extended.
1649	Charles I is executed, whereupon Oliver Cromwell assumes the leading role in English government until his death in 1658. As Lord Protector of England, Cromwell tries to implement Puritan ideals in church and state.
1660	As Charles II accedes to the throne, the monarchy is restored in England and episcopal polity is reestablished in the Church of England.
1662	By a new Act of Uniformity, exclusive use of the newly revised Anglican Book of Common Prayer is enforced, as more than two thousand Puritan pastors resign or are ejected. Non-Anglicans are prevented from taking degrees at Oxford and Cambridge universities, leading to the founding of many Dissenting academies.
1688	With William and Mary proclaimed king and queen of England, the "Glorious Revolution" restores the liberty of Puritans to preach and establish independent churches.

Some Leading Traits of Puritanism

Earlier I tried to clear the air of some common misconceptions about the Puritans. It is time now to look at some of the positive traits of the movement. If we had been contemporaries of the Puritans, what would have struck us as their distinguishing characteristics?

The Puritan movement must be understood first of all as *a religious movement*. The secular interpretation of Puritanism is the product of an irreligious age and overlooks that, even in its political and social and economic manifestations, Puritanism expressed a religious outlook. A modern historian writes, "When we have finished our efforts to modernize and secularise Puritanism, it remains an obstinately religious phenomenon."[60] In both its private and public manifestations, the Puritan movement was populated by God-obsessed people. John Bunyan's haunting question, "How can I be saved?" was ultimately the important question for every Puritan. An army general wrote to Cromwell, "My lord, let waiting upon Jehovah be the greatest and most considerable business you have every day; reckon it so, more than to eat, sleep, or counsel together."[61]

Puritanism was also characterized by *a strong moral consciousness*. For Puritans, the question of right and wrong was more important than any other. They saw life as a continuous struggle between good and evil. The world was claimed by God and counterclaimed by Satan. There was no neutral ground.[62] Richard Sibbes expressed this mindset in typical form:

> There are two grand sides in the world, to which all belong: there is God's side and those that are his, and there is another side that is Satan's, and those that are his; two kingdoms, two sides, two contrary dispositions, that pursue one another.[63]

Believers could, with God's help, achieve victory through such means as *watching*, *exact walking*, and *mortification*.

Puritanism was *a reform movement*. Its identity was determined by its attempts to change something that already existed. At the heart of Puritanism was the conviction that things needed to be changed and that "business as usual" was not an option. It is hard to overestimate the impact that such an outlook produces in a person's life. It also explains, incidentally, why the Puritans in their day adopted such an aggressive stance and why, as one reads the polemical literature of the age, the Puritans' opponents seem always to be on the defensive.

Of all the key terms used by the Puritans, the foremost were *reform*, *reformation*, or the adjective *reformed*. These terms were not the coinage of later historians but were the words on everyone's lips during the Puritan era itself. It was an age in which rulers were urged "to reform their countries," churchmen to effect "the reformation of religion," and fathers "to reform [their] families."[64] At a more personal level, the Puritan impulse was to "reform the life from ungodliness and unrighteous dealing."[65]

The Puritan movement was *a visionary movement* energized by nothing less than a vision of a re-formed society. Someone has aptly summarized the Puritan program thus: "The summons to a reformation was a call to action, first to transform the individual into an instrument fit to serve the divine will, and then to employ that instrument to transform all of society."[66]

Puritanism was also *a protest movement*, as was the Protestant movement in general. Again and again in the pages that follow, Puritan views will fall into place more clearly if we are aware that the Puritans are protesting against attitudes of Roman Catholicism and, less often, Anglicanism. On such subjects as work, sex, money, and worship, a good starting point for understanding the Puritans is to see what they were against. As Christopher Hill puts it, "There was an element of social protest in almost every Puritan attitude."[67]

One thing that makes Puritanism seem modern is the extent to which it was *an international movement*. For one thing, many of the original leaders of the movement spent months and even years on the Continent, especially during times of persecution. They absorbed the tenets and worship practices of "the best Reformed churches," the phrase they used to denote European Protestantism. Furthermore, after the migration to America became a feature of Puritanism, there was a continuous interaction among leaders of the movement on the two sides of the Atlantic. "Behind the Puritans," writes M. M. Knappen, "was the force of a rising international Protestantism."[68] The international nature of Puritanism explains why I have mingled English and American Puritans in this book and why I have used the footnotes to draw attention to parallels between Puritan thought and the views of Luther and Calvin.

English Puritanism (though not American Puritanism) was *a minority movement*. Although the English Puritans gained immense power within their society (especially in Parliament), they were never a numerical majority. Puritanism, therefore, evinced some of the same traits that characterize other minorities: a strong sense of internal loyalty to common principles, a feeling of vulnerability, a tendency toward bipolar thinking in which the world is divided into two camps: we and they. A. G. Dickens rightly regards Puritanism "as a force more suited to pervade than to dominate the English spirit,"[69] while Paul Seaver thinks that the Puritans "thrived on failure."[70]

In New England, where the Puritans more thoroughly dominated society and institutions, Puritanism was, in my view, a less attractive phenomenon — more prone to intolerance and heavy-handedness, to complacency, to legalism, to inner decay. In England, by comparison, the movement existed without stable institutional structures and was spared from the tendency of its adherents to place their allegiance in institutions rather than ideals.

The Puritans were not only a minority, but also *a persecuted minority.* In England they were subjected to harassment and persecution at virtually every stage of their history (excepting, of course, the mid-seventeenth century, when they became the ruling party in the government and church). Puritan leaders were in and out of prison as a way of life. Laypeople were hauled into court for holding religious meetings in their homes. Puritan young people who would not sign the Act of Uniformity could not get degrees from Oxford and Cambridge universities. Ministers who refused to wear Anglican vestments or support Anglican ceremony or read services from the Prayer Book were ejected from their positions. Consciousness of alienation gave the Puritans their major archetype, the pilgrim passing through an alien world to his or her true country.[71]

Despite the significant role played by Puritan preachers and professors, the success of the movement depended in the final analysis on its being *a lay movement.* As one scholar says, "The Puritan movement was notable for its vigorous lay participation."[72] It is true that the clergy and professors provided the intellectual theory for the movement. They were the ones who harnessed the laypeople's superior numbers into the power to challenge existing structures. There was, of course, plenty of paradox in the situation: in the very act of undermining traditional clerical hierarchy and privilege, Puritan preachers attracted huge followings of laypeople and ended up enjoying a position of power themselves. Their power, however, extended only as far as their ability to influence the thinking of the ordinary layperson.

Puritanism was *a movement in which the Bible was central to everything.* There is a sense in which the foremost issue of the Puritan movement (as of the Reformation in general) was the question of authority. The Puritans resolved the question of authority by making the Bible the final authority for belief and practice. John Owen, often regarded as the greatest of the Puritan theologians, said that "Protestants suppose the Scripture to be given forth by God to be . . . a perfect complete rule of . . . faith."[73] "Who, then, were these early Puritans?" asks Derek Wilson; "basically it was their attitude towards the authority of the Bible which marked them out as different from other English Protestants."[74]

The Puritan movement was *an educated movement.* Its goal was the reform of religious, national, and personal life, and its adherents quickly sensed that one of the most effective ways of influencing their society was through the schools. In both England and America, the Puritan movement was closely linked with the universities.[75] John Knowles wrote to Governor Leverett of Massachusetts that "if the college die, the churches . . . will not live long after it."[76] A modern authority speaks of "the pre-eminence and continuity of university leadership of the Puritan movement."[77] It is not surprising, therefore, that Puritanism was *a highly literate movement* that possessed a "vital rage for utterance."[78]

Puritanism was, finally, *a political and economic movement.* This may be clearer to us today than it was to the Puritans, since we can see the long-term effects of the movement. In a day when the church was under the control of the state, it was inevitable that the Puritans' attempt to change the church involved them at once with the government. In this sense we can agree with the designation of the Puritans as incurably political. As for economics, by stressing the values of work, thrift, and honest gain, the Puritans created a climate that accorded well with the rise of capitalism, regardless of whether they actually caused that rise. The Puritans had a great deal to say about the topics of work and money.

Some Key Puritan Doctrines

Like other Christian movements, Puritanism had some doctrinal distinctives that it emphasized within the more general framework of Christianity as a whole. Doctrinally the Puritans were Calvinistic, as were most separatists and most Anglicans until the time of Archbishop Laud. This means that such doctrines as the sovereignty of God, salvation by faith in Christ, God's election of people to salvation, the irresistibility of God's grace, and human depravity were axioms for the Puritans.

The doctrine of grace permeated Puritan thinking in many areas, from salvation to material prosperity. At the heart of Puritanism was the belief that God's grace is the source of all human benefit and that it cannot be earned by human merit. Samuel Willard's comments on the gift of salvation sound the keynote:

> There are no other conditions required . . . but acceptance of this gift,
> and acknowledgement of the kindness of the bestower. Faith is the
> hand that receiveth it. . . . And what is our obedience, but our
> thankfulness to God for so unspeakable a gift?[79]

For the Puritans, *personal regeneration* or conversion was, in the words of Cromwell, "the root of the matter."[80] Conversion was so closely linked with sanctification or *holy living* that the Puritans used the word *salvation* to cover them both. Richard Sibbes linked redemption and sanctification when he commented that "the sense of the love of Christ in pardoning of sins will constrain one to a holy violence in the performing of all duties."[81] Thomas Becon said that the purpose of his writings was "to teach people to know themselves and their salvation in the blood of Christ through faith, and to walk worthy of the kindness of God."[82]

The concept of *covenant* provided a basis for virtually all the relationships that were important to the Puritans. Covenant denoted a relationship of mutual trust and obligation. It explained God's dealing with the individual person and was the philosophic basis for such Puritan institutions as family, church, and state. The foundation of everything was God's covenant of salvation extended to every believer, in return for which He demanded human obedience and faithfulness. In turn, people covenanted among themselves to form a church, a family, or a state, with God as the third party or guarantor of the contract. This emphasis on covenant made Puritanism a strongly relational religion.[83]

On the question of authority, the Puritans stood for *Scripture alone as the final authority for religious belief and practice.* Of course, the Bible requires interpretation, and once the Puritans began to interpret it they did so in terms of one or another Protestant tradition. In that sense, there was no final escape from human tradition. "Scripture alone" is itself a Protestant tradition. Still, there is an enormous watershed between the Puritan conviction that any belief or practice must be based on biblical warrant and rival theories that traditions beyond the Bible are a sufficient foundation for believing or practicing something.

The Puritans had a completely developed *doctrine of Creation.* They believed that God had created the physical and human world and therefore it was good in principle. They believed that the physical world pointed to God. They were in this specific sense the real "sacramentalists" of their day, much more so than those who multiplied visual ceremony within the walls of a church building. One Puritan said that a Christian can regard "his shop as well as his chapel as holy ground."[84] "The world is God's book," said Richard Baxter, "and every creature is a letter, or syllable, or word, or sentence . . . declaring the name and will of God."[85] Thomas Taylor wrote, "The voice of God in all the creatures and by them all speaketh unto us always and everywhere."[86] One consequence of the Puritan doctrine of Creation is that it led logically to a repudiation of the old sacred-secular dichotomy that had dominated thinking for so long.

Related to the doctrine of Creation was the strong Puritan emphasis on *Providence.* The Puritans were par excellence the people who saw God in everyday events. They wrote diaries in which they traced God's grace in their daily lives. They confidently expected to find God in "the milkhouse, the stable, the barn, and the like, where God [visits] the soul."[87] The Puritans also interpreted contemporary historical events within a framework of God's providence and biblical analogues.

The Puritan doctrine of *calling,* or vocation, was a specific application of God's providence to the personal life of every Christian. Puritans customarily divided God's call of the individual into a *general calling* and a *particular calling*. The general calling was the calling to be a redeemed and holy Christian in every area of life. The particular calling was God's direction of a person into a specific life's work or career.

The Puritan *view of the person* is an immense topic on which much has been written. In brief, the Puritans combined a thoroughgoing restatement of the doctrines of original sin and total human depravity on the one hand and a high view of the worth of the individual transformed by God's grace on the other. Puritanism postulated a threefold view of the person: perfect as created by God and therefore good in principle, sinful by virtue of Adam's original sin imputed to them and their own evil choices, and capable of redemption and glorification by God's renewing grace.

The great either-or in this scheme is the presence or absence of regeneration in the individual heart, accounting for the extremes of optimism and pessimism about people that we find in Puritan writings. Consciousness of sin runs strong in Puritan diaries, but so does consciousness of divine grace. Puritan attitudes toward social institutions combine a pessimistic awareness of their corruptibility with expectant visions of a re-formed society that today strike us as naïvely optimistic.

What the Puritans Liked and Disliked

Any movement can be identified by its likes and dislikes. For the Puritans, too, it is possible to discern what qualities and activities excited their strongest affirmations and what aversions awakened their disgust. Sensitivity to Puritan vocabulary and master images tells us a lot about the Puritan temperament.[88]

Some major positive terms in Puritan vocabulary were *reform* (or its variants *reformed* and *reformation*), *godly*, *well-ordered*, the adjective *learned*, *plain*, *profitable*, *simple*, *grave*, and *painful* ("painstaking, meticulous"). The Puritans wanted activities to be *lawful*, all the way from work to play and from worship to government. *Pure*, *purge*, *holy*, *true*, and *sound* (as opposed to unsound) were among their positive qualities.

The Puritans were less interested in the idea of self-fulfillment than *duty*, which they regarded both as a responsibility of the covenant and a condition of life within any social unit. As Samuel Willard wrote, "It is certain that from all the relations that men bear each to other, there are reciprocal duties incumbent on them."[89] The early Puritans were nicknamed *disciplinarians*. It is no surprise that they spoke repeatedly of a *good conscience* as a prerequisite to human happiness.

The Puritans were distrustful of flashy external appearances and placed their confidence in what Baxter called the "internal principle of life in a person."[90] Richard Greenham complained about sermons that were "glassy, bright and brittle . . . , so cold . . . that the simple preaching of Christ doth greatly decay."[91] To use a modern phrase, with the Puritans "what you see is what you get." "Truth loves the light," wrote Baxter, "and is most beautiful when most naked."[92] "Truth feareth nothing so much as concealment," said Richard Sibbes, "and desireth nothing so much as clearly to be laid open to the view of all: when it is most naked, it is most lovely and powerful."[93] Cromwell asked to be painted as he really looked, "warts and all."

The Puritans placed a high premium on religious *truth*. The intellectual content of a person's faith was not an indifferent matter for them. Thomas Hooker claimed that "all truth, though the least that God reveals, is it not better than all the world?"[94] John Owen urged Christians to "look on truth as a pearl, as that which is better than all the world, bought with any price."[95]

Corresponding to these positive values were some common Puritan aversions. *Tradition* was something that they treated with scorn; they equated it with *superstition* when speaking of Roman Catholic ceremonies in worship. *Tyranny* was another word that elicited strong negative feelings, especially in political and ecclesiastical contexts.

The idea of *cold* or *coldness*, and the synonyms *dull* and *dullness*, were major spiritual aversions for the Puritans. Richard Rogers recoiled from "the coldness and half service . . . which is in the world," while Cotton Mather warned, "Beware of . . . a strong head and a cold heart."[96] Samuel Ward recorded in his diary the self-accusation "how on the 15 and 16 of February thou was very dull in God's service."[97] As a counterpart to these rejections of coldness, *zeal* and *zealous* were recurrent positive value-terms in Puritan vocabulary.

Spiritual complacency and mediocrity were the greatest of all Puritan aversions. Richard Baxter wrote,

> As mere idleness and forgetting God will keep a soul as certainly from heaven as a profane, licentious, fleshly life, so also will the usual company of such idle, forgetful, negligent persons as surely keep our hearts from heaven, as the company of men more dissolute and profane.[98]

Samuel Willard lamented that in New England "forwardness and zeal for God is almost out of date" while "lukewarm-confession is much in credit."[99]

The Puritans were repelled by partying and carousing. Anything that had even the appearance of unrestraint raised their ire. A typical job description for a Puritan schoolmaster tells us a lot about Puritan aversions: he is not to be a gamester . . . or a frequenter of taverns or alehouses, or a drunkard or . . . given to wanton dalliances and unseemly behavior with women, or lavish in unnecessary expenses, in following vain gaudy fashions of apparel, or . . . wear long curled or ruffian-like hair, or . . . be a swearer or curser. . . .[100]

In 1677, Massachusetts empowered officers known as tithingmen to arrest "all Sabbath-breakers and disorderly tiplers, or such as keep licensed houses, or others that shall suffer any disorder in their houses on the Sabbath-day or evening after."[101] The English Puritans could scarcely restrain their disgust for Anglican preachers such as Robert Palmer, who had a bowling alley in his orchard and could be discovered there "daily and weekly," and that with "a great swarm of men."[102]

For an interesting glimpse into what the Puritans rejected, we might consider the following church and civil court proceedings:

1. Robert Sykes of Dorchester (Mass.) was brought to trial "for not attending the public worship of God, negligence in his calling, and not submitting to authority."[103]

2. William Scant of Braintree was brought before the Suffolk Court for "not ordering and disposing of his children as may be for their good education."[104]

3. When the First Church of Boston excommunicated James Mattock, one of his offenses was "that he denied conjugal fellowship [sexual intercourse] unto his wife for the space of two years."[105]

4. Temperance Sweete, belying her name, was admonished "for having received to house and given entertainment unto disorderly company and ministering unto them wine and strong waters, even unto drunkenness."[106]

The Puritans are known to us partly in their preferred activities. Reading the Bible, listening to sermons, and attending Bible studies and prayer meetings were conspicuous on the list of desirable activities. John Winthrop said that after his conversion he "had an unsatiable thirst after the Word of God and could not miss a good sermon, though many miles off, especially of such as did search deep into the conscience."[107] At one aristocratic Puritan wedding, Lady Russell dispensed with the usual music and dancing and replaced them with "a sermon and dinner" for the pleasure of the guests.[108]

An extension of this Puritan zest for worship was their prizing of

Christian *conference*, by which they meant conversation w
like mind in spiritual matters.[109] Richard Rogers recorde
"sweet conference I have had . . . with Newman and M
John Winthrop similarly recorded a "conference with a
or two," adding that "God so blessed it unto us, as we we..
quickened and refreshed by it."[111]

The Puritans valued hard work, were suspicious of much recreation, and made no attempt to conceal their scorn for lazy and idle people:

> It is a blessing upon every one that feareth the Lord, and walks in His ways, that he shall eat the labor of his hands. And he that without his own labor either of body or mind eats the labor of other men's hands only, and lives by their sweat, is but like unto lice, and such other vermin.[112]

To sum up, a great deal of what the Puritans liked and disliked is captured in the following resolve that John Winthrop recorded in his diary:

> I made a new covenant with the Lord, which was thus: Of my part, that I would reform these sins by His grace: pride, covetousness, love of this world, vanity of mind, unthankfulness, sloth, both in His service and in my calling, not preparing myself with reverence and uprightness to come to His Word. Of the Lord's part, that He would give me a new heart, joy in His Spirit, that He would dwell with me, that He would strengthen me against the world, the flesh and the devil, that He would forgive my sins and increase my faith.[113]

A Portrait of the "Typical Puritan"

The typical Puritan was married and had a family. The family was "well-ordered" and hierarchical in authority.[114] The husband/father was the accountable head of the family, especially in religious exercises, although the wife/mother had her spheres of authority. The education of the children and family worship (especially Bible reading and prayer) received high priority in this Puritan family.

Much of the family's religious life centered around the local church. It was under the church's auspices that doctrine was inculcated, corporate worship took place, and children were catechized. The church was not so much a building as a group of believers joined together under the pervasive influence of the pastor. A midweek home meeting would have been a standard part of church life whenever the political authorities would have allowed such meetings.

The weekly routine for the typical Puritan was a busy affair. Life was a serious matter, and there was no time for idleness. The average

ritan believed that hard work was a virtue and that God had called
every individual to perform worldly business in a Christian, moral
manner. He or she felt no guilt about everyday work nor about the money
that it might produce. The high point of the week was Sunday. Sports on
this day were absolutely prohibited. The family attended church twice
each Sunday and assembled after dinner and/or in the evening to repeat
the key points of the sermons.

If we had worked beside this typical Puritan or been a neighbor, he
or she would have impressed us as being religious but not odd. He or she
would not have been distinguished by outward appearance. As Samuel
Willard noted, "the children of God . . . outwardly . . . look like other
men, they eat, drink, labour, converse in earthly employments, as others
do; the communion which they have with God in all of these is a secret
thing."[115] The typical Puritan dressed as other members of the same
social class did. Conversation would have turned much of the time to
topics of Christian belief and experience.

Overall, the typical Puritan would have impressed us as hardworking, thrifty, serious, moderate, practical in outlook, doctrinaire in
religious and political matters, well-informed about the latest political and
ecclesiastical developments, argumentative, well-educated, and thoroughly familiar with the content of the Bible. To attain all this, Puritans
had to be self-disciplined. For anyone prone to laxity in these matters,
being around a Puritan would of course have made one uncomfortable,
and therein lies a partial explanation of why the Puritans have been so
strongly attacked by people not sharing their outlook and lifestyle.

Summary

To bring this introductory sketch of Puritanism into focus, I have
collected the most helpful brief definitions that I have encountered:

> At the risk of oversimplification, it could be said that Reformation
> Protestantism was a religion of literacy, domestic prayer, and the
> family bible in the family home, all buttressed by the public
> sermon.[116]

> To assess the true character of the Puritan movement inside and
> outside the Church we must free our minds from the popular use of
> the term. . . . We might reasonably claim that it flourished most as a
> social religion among townsmen, that it required a modicum of
> education, thoughtfulness and independent spirit, again that in time it
> helped to produce minds passionately addicted to certain limited yet
> important notions of civic and personal freedom.[117]

In its early stages Elizabethan Puritanism was a confederation of ministers and laity, semi-sectarian but still within the fold of the Church. It pressed . . . for reform of liturgy and ceremony, and for a cleaning up of administrative abuses and corruption, it was active locally in preaching and practising the new ethic of godliness.[118]

Seventeenth-century Puritanism was tight-lipped, severe, and pious, but it was simultaneously frank, strongly sexed, and somewhat romantic. . . . It was as much an offshoot of the Renaissance as a reaction against it.[119]

FURTHER READING

The best overviews of Puritanism that I have encountered are these:

M. M. Knappen, *Tudor Puritanism: A Chapter in the History of Idealism* (1939).

Perry Miller, *The New England Mind: The Seventeenth Century* (1939).

John Thomas McNeill, "English Puritanism," pp. 15–48 in *Modern Christian Movements* (1954).

Gerald R. Cragg, *Puritanism in the Period of the Great Persecution* (1957).

John Dykstra Eusden, *Puritans, Lawyers, and Politics in Early Seventeenth-Century England*, especially chap. 1 (1958).

Charles H. George and Katherine George, *The Protestant Mind of the English Reformation, 1570–1640* (1961).

Christopher Hill, *Society and Puritanism in Pre-Revolutionary England* (1964).

H. G. Alexander, *Religion in England, 1558–1662* (1968).

Everett Emerson, *Puritanism in America, 1620–1750* (1977).

For people who like a strongly historical approach based on a wealth of specific dates and figures, the following are standard sources:

William Haller, *The Rise of Puritanism* (1938).

A. G. Dickens, *The English Reformation* (1964).

Patrick Collinson, *The Elizabethan Puritan Movement* (1967).

In a different category is Percy Scholes's book *The Puritans and Music in England and New England* (1934). I regard it as one of the first books that an honest inquirer should read because it assaults the "deep structure" of modern prejudices and leaves one convinced that at least some of the anti-Puritan propaganda is a deliberate lie.

On the origin and developing meanings of the word *Puritan*, one can best consult Christopher Hill, *Society and Puritanism in Pre-Revolutionary England*, chap. 1 ("The Definition of a Puritan") and Basil Hall, "Puritanism: the Problem of Definition," pp. 283–96 in *Studies in Church History*, vol. 2, ed. G. J. Cuming (London: Thomas Nelson, 1965).

The Puritan work ethic declared the inherent dignity of all legitimate types of work.
From Bartolomeo Scappi's *Opera;* courtesy of the Folger Shakespeare Library [TX 711 S4 1605 Cage sig. R2r]

Chapter 2

Work

God hath made man a societal creature. We expect benefits from human society. It is but equal that human society should receive benefits from us.

— COTTON MATHER

Even people who know little about the Puritans bandy the phrase "Puritan work ethic" with confidence. When we explore what they mean by that phrase, it becomes apparent how little specific content the phrase holds for most people today. For many the phrase "Puritan ethic" is simply a catchall label for what they dislike about the Puritans.

Even when the phrase is restricted to the topic of work, it tends to be clouded with a host of misconceptions about what the Puritans really thought. The label "Puritan work ethic" is used today to cover a whole range of current ills: the workaholic syndrome, drudgery, competitiveness, worship of success, materialism, and the cult of the self-made person.

It has become such an axiom that the Puritans started all this that it comes as a shock to learn that what is called the Puritan work ethic is in many ways the opposite of what the Puritans of the sixteenth and seventeenth centuries actually believed about work. For the past three centuries Western civilization has been dominated by a secularized perversion of the original Puritan work ethic. I begin my survey of Puritan beliefs, therefore, with the topic that is ostensibly best known to moderns but actually very misunderstood.

The Background: The Division Between Sacred and Secular

To understand Puritan attitudes toward work, we must take a look at the background against which they were reacting. For centuries it had been customary to divide types of work into the two categories of "sacred" and "secular." Sacred work was work done by members of the religious profession. All other work bore the stigma of being secular.

This cleavage between sacred and secular work can be traced all the way back to the Jewish Talmud. One of the prayers, obviously written from the scribe's viewpoint, is as follows:

> I thank thee, O Lord, my God, that thou hast given me my lot with those who sit in the house of learning, and not with those who sit at the street-corners; for I am early to work and they are early to work; I am early to work on the words of the Torah, and they are early to work on things of no moment. I weary myself, and they weary themselves; I weary myself and profit thereby, and they weary themselves to no profit. I run, and they run; I run towards the life of the age to come, and they run towards the pit of destruction.[1]

The same division of work into categories of sacred and secular became a leading feature of medieval Roman Catholicism. The attitude was formulated already in the fourth century by Eusebius, who wrote,

> Two ways of life were given by the law of Christ to his church. The one is above nature, and beyond common human living. . . . Wholly and permanently separate from the common customary life of mankind, it devotes itself to the service of God alone. . . . Such then is the perfect form of the Christian life. And the other, more humble, more human, permits men to . . . have minds for farming, for trade, and the other more secular interests as well as for religion. . . . And a kind of secondary grade of piety is attributed to them.[2]

This sacred-secular dichotomy was exactly what the Puritans rejected as the starting point of their theory of work.

The Sanctity of All Legitimate Types of Work

It was Martin Luther, more than anyone else, who overthrew the notion that clergymen, monks, and nuns were engaged in holier work than the housewife and shopkeeper.[3] Calvin quickly added his weight to the argument.[4] The Puritans were unanimous in following the lead of Luther and Calvin.

Like the Reformers, the Puritans rejected the sacred-secular dichotomy. William Tyndale said that if we look externally "there is difference betwixt washing of dishes and preaching of the word of God; but as touching to please God, none at all."[5] William Perkins agreed: "The action of a shepherd in keeping sheep . . . is as good a work before God as is the action of a judge in giving sentence, or a magistrate in ruling, or a minister in preaching."[6] This Puritan rejection of the dichotomy between sacred and secular work had far-reaching implications.

For one thing, it renders every task of intrinsic value and integrates every vocation with a Christian's spiritual life. It makes every job consequential by making it the arena for glorifying and obeying God and for expressing one's love (through service) to one's neighbor. Thus Hugh Latimer saw in the example of Christ the true dignity of all work:

> This is a wonderful thing, that the Savior of the world, and the King above all kings, was not ashamed to labor; yea, and to use so simple an occupation. Here he did sanctify all manner of occupations.[7]

John Dod and Robert Cleaver wrote that "the great and reverend God despiseth no honest trade . . . be it never so mean, but crowneth it with his blessing."[8]

The Puritan conviction about the dignity of all work also has the important effect of sanctifying the common. John Cotton said this about the ability of Christian faith to sanctify common life and work:

> Faith . . . encourageth a man in his calling to the homeliest and difficultest. . . . Such homely employments a carnal heart knows not how to submit unto; but now faith having put us into a calling, if it require some homely employment, it encourageth us in it. . . . So faith is ready to embrace any homely service his calling leads him to, which a carnal heart would blush to be seen in.[9]

William Perkins declared that people can serve God "in any kind of calling, though it be but to sweep the house or keep sheep."[10] Nathaniel Mather said that God's grace will "spiritualize every action"; even the simplest actions, such as "a man's loving his wife or child," become "gracious acts," and "his eating and drinking [are] acts of obedience and hence are of great account in the eyes of God."[11]

For the Puritans, all of life was God's. Their goal was to integrate their daily work with their religious devotion to God. Richard Steele asserted that it was in the shop "where you may most confidently expect the presence and blessing of God."[12] The Puritans revolutionized attitudes toward daily work when they raised the possibility that "every step and stroke in your trade is sanctified."[13] John Milton, in his famous

Areopagitica, satirized the businessman who leaves his religion at home, "trading all day without his religion." Thomas Gataker saw no tension between the sacred and secular when he wrote,

> A man must not imagine . . . , when he is called to be a Christian, that he must presently cast off all worldly employments . . . and apply himself wholly . . . to prayer and contemplation, but he must retain the calling still as well as the other, following the one still with the other.[14]

The Puritan goal was to serve God, not simply *within* one's work in the world, but *through* that work. John Cotton hinted at this when he wrote,

> A true believing Christian . . . lives in his vocation by his faith. Not only my spiritual life but even my civil life in this world, and all the life I live, is by the faith of the Son of God: He exempts no life from the agency of his faith.[15]

And Cotton Mather said,

> A Christian should be able to give a good account, not only what is his occupation, but also what he is in his occupation. It is not enough that a Christian have an occupation; but he must mind his occupation as it becomes a Christian.[16]

With the Puritan emphasis on all of life as God's, it is not surprising that a late seventeenth-century pamphlet entitled *St. Paul the Tentmaker* could note that the Protestant movement had fostered a "delight in secular employments."[17]

The Puritan Concept of Calling

A second strong affirmation by the Puritans, in addition to declaring the sanctity of all types of work, was that God calls every person to his or her vocation. Every Christian, said the Puritans, has a calling. To follow it is to obey God. The important effect of this attitude is that it makes work a response to God.

To begin with, the Puritans' emphasis on such doctrines as Election and Providence made it easy for them to assert that every person has a calling in regard to work. The Puritan divine Richard Steele wrote,

> God doth call every man and woman . . . to serve him in some peculiar employment in this world, both for their own and the common good. . . . The Great Governor of the world hath appointed to every man his proper post and province.[18]

William Perkins, in his classic *Treatise of the Vocations or Callings of Men*, wrote,

> A vocation or calling is a certain kind of life, ordained and imposed on man by God, for the common good. . . . Every person of every degree, state, sex, or condition without exception must have some personal and particular calling to walk in.[19]

The doctrine of calling was even more prominent in American Puritanism. Cotton Mather asserted, "Every Christian ordinarily should have a calling. That is to say, there should be some special business . . . wherein a Christian should for the most part spend the most of his time; and this, that so he may glorify God."[20] John Cotton spoke in similar terms:

> Faith draws the heart of a Christian to live in some warrantable calling; as soon as ever a man begins to look toward God and the ways of his grace, he will not rest till he find out some warrantable calling and employment.[21]

One effect of the Puritan concept of calling is to make the worker a steward who serves God. God, in fact, is the one who assigns people to their tasks. In this view, work ceases to be impersonal. Moreover, its importance does not lie within itself; work is rather a means by which a person lives out his or her personal relationship to God. "Whatsoever our callings be," claimed one Puritan source, "we serve the Lord Jesus Christ in them."[22] Richard Steele viewed work as a stewardship when he wrote,

> He that hath lent you talents hath also said, "Occupy till I Come!" How is it that ye stand all day idle? . . . Your trade is your proper province.[23]

"God is the General," Perkins wrote, "appointing to every man his particular calling. . . . God himself is the author and beginning of callings."[24]

If God is the one who calls people to their work, then such work can be a form of service to God. John Cotton put it this way:

> A man therefore that serves Christ in serving of men . . . doth his work sincerely as in God's presence, and as one that hath an heavenly business in hand, and therefore comfortably as knowing God approves of his way and work.[25]

To work in one's calling, in the Puritan view, is to work in the sight of God. Cotton Mather exclaimed, "Oh, let every Christian walk with God when he works at his calling, act in his occupation with an eye to God, act as under the eye of God."[26]

Another practical result of the doctrine of Christian calling is that it leads to contentment in one's work. If a Christian's calling comes from God, there is inherent in that belief a strategy for accepting one's tasks. Cotton Mather wrote that

> a Christian should follow his occupation with contentment. . . . It is the singular favor of God unto a man that he can attend his occupation with contentment and satisfaction. . . . Is your business here clogged with any difficulties and inconveniences? Contentment under those difficulties is no little part of your homage to that God who hath placed you where you are.[27]

The sense of calling as a stewardship and as a reason for contentment come together beautifully in the poem that a young Puritan wrote on the occasion of his twenty-third birthday. Milton's famous seventh sonnet opens with self-rebuke at the poet's lack of achievement to date. But the consolation expressed in the aphorism with which the poem concludes is typically Puritan:

> All is, if I have grace to use it so,
> As ever in my great task-Master's eye.

The most plausible interpretation of the lines is this: "All that matters is that I have the grace to use my time as though I am always living in my great taskmaster's presence." Milton obviously viewed himself as responsible to God, and the epithet "my great task-Master" vividly captures the Puritan awareness of God as the one who calls people to tasks.

If everyone has a calling, how can people know what they have been called to do? The Puritans evolved a methodology for determining their calling; they did not mysticize the process. Richard Steele, in fact, claimed that God rarely calls people directly "in the latter days," and that anyone who claims to have had a revelation from God "must produce extraordinary gifts and qualifications, else it be but conceit and delusion."[28]

The Puritans preferred to trust such things as a person's "inward endowments and inclinations," "outward circumstances which may lead . . . to one course of life rather than another," the advice of "parents, guardians, and in some cases magistrates," and "nature, education, or gifts . . . acquired."[29] They also believed that if people were in the right calling, God would equip them to perform their work: "When God hath called me to a place, he hath given me some gifts for that place."[30]

The Puritans believed in loyalty to a calling. A vocation was to be neither entered into nor abandoned lightly. On the subject of choosing a vocation, Milton, who from childhood had a strong calling to be a poet, wrote that "the nature of each person should be especially observed and not bent in another direction, for God does not intend all people for one thing, but for each one his own work."[31] Richard Steele cautioned that it was "preposterous" to choose "a calling or condition of life without a careful pondering it in the balance of sound reason."[32] John Cotton stressed the idea of talents in choosing a vocation:

> Another thing to make a calling warrantable is when God gives a man gifts for it. . . . God leads him on to that calling, 1 Cor. 7:17. . . .
> When God hath called me to a place, he hath given me some gifts fit for that place, especially if the place be suitable and fitted to me and my best gifts; for God . . . would have his best gifts improved to the best advantage.[33]

The Puritan idea of the calling was equally resistant to the casual leaving of a vocation. While the Puritans did not generally believe that a person could never legitimately change occupations, they were clearly cautious about the practice. William Perkins spoke of "a perseverance in good duties" and warned against "ambition, envy, impatience," adding that "envy . . . when we see others placed in better callings and conditions than ourselves . . . is a common sin, and the cause of much dissension in the commonwealth."[34] Cotton Mather agreed:

> A Christian should follow his occupation with contentment. A Christian should not be too ready to fall out with his calling. . . . Many a man, merely from covetousness and from discontent throws up his business.[35]

To sum up, the Puritan idea of calling covered a cluster of related ideas: the providence of God in arranging human tasks, work as the response of a steward to God, contentment with one's tasks, and loyalty to one's vocation. These were admirably captured in John Cotton's exhortation to "serve God in thy calling, and do it with cheerfulness, and faithfulness, and an heavenly mind."[36]

The Motivation and Rewards of Work

Puritan beliefs about the motivation and goals of work need to be carefully distinguished from what has passed for three centuries as the "Puritan work ethic." From the time that Benjamin Franklin uttered his worldly wise proverbs about wealth as the goal of work to our own century when industrial giants have claimed that their success was proof that they were God's elect, our culture has viewed work primarily as the means to wealth and possessions. This secularized work ethic has been

An etching of a roper and a cordwainer. From Johann A.
Comenius, *Orbis Sensualium Pictus*; courtesy of the Folger Shakespeare
Library [Wing C5525 p. 166]

attributed to the Puritans and their forerunner Calvin, and it has become
accepted as an axiom that the Puritan ethic is based on wealth as the
ultimate reward of work and prosperity as a sign of godliness.

But is this what the Puritans really believed? The rewards of work,
according to Puritan theory, were spiritual and moral, that is, work
glorified God and benefited society. By viewing work as stewardship to
God, the Puritans opened the way for a whole new conception of the
rewards of work, as suggested in Richard Steele's comment, "You are
working for God, who will be sure to reward you to your heart's
content."[37] That those rewards are primarily spiritual and moral is
abundantly clear from Puritan comments.

William Perkins asserted that

> the main end of our lives . . . is to serve God in the serving of men in
> the works of our callings. . . . Some man will say perchance: What,
> must we not labor in our callings to maintain our families? I answer:
> this must be done: but this is not the scope and end of our lives. The
> true end of our lives is to do service to God in serving of man.[38]

John Preston said that we must labor "not for our own good, but for the
good of others."[39]

Richard Baxter shared this view of the spiritual and moral ends of
work. The purpose of work, he said, is "obeying God and doing good to
others." Furthermore, "the public welfare, or the good of the many, is to
be valued above our own. Every man therefore is bound to do all the
good he can to others, especially for the church and commonwealth." As
for the riches that might come from work, they "may enable us to relieve
our needy brethren and to promote good works for church and state."[40]

American Puritans espoused the same viewpoint. According to Cotton Mather, the reason a person should pursue a calling is "that so he may glorify God, by doing good for others and getting of good for himself."[41] And again,

> God hath made man a societal creature. We expect benefits from human society. It is but equal that human society should receive benefits from us. We are beneficial to human society by the works of that special occupation in which we are to be employed, according to the order of God.[42]

John Cotton stated that in our calling "we may not only aim at our own, but at the public good. . . . And therefore [faith] will not think it hath a comfortable calling unless it will not only serve his own turn but the turn of other men."[43]

What is noteworthy about such statements is the integration among God, society, and self that converges in the exercise of one's calling. Self-interest is not totally denied, but it is definitely minimized in the rewards of work.

In keeping with their view of the spiritual and moral ends of work, the Puritans drew the logical conclusion that these same goals should govern one's choice of a vocation. Richard Baxter urged:

> Choose that employment or calling in which you may be most serviceable to God. Choose not that in which you may be most rich or honorable in the world; but that in which you may do most good, and best escape sinning.[44]

Elsewhere Baxter wrote that in choosing a trade or calling, the first consideration should be "the service of God and the public good, and therefore that calling which must conduceth to the public good is to be preferred." Furthermore, "when two callings equally conduce to the public good, and one of them hath the advantage of riches and the other is more advantageous to your souls, the latter must be preferred."[45]

The counterpart of this emphasis on the spiritual and moral rewards of work is the frequent denunciation of people who use work to gratify selfish ambitions. Contrary to what many think, the idea of the self-made person did not appeal to the Puritans, if by "self-made" we mean people who claim to have been successful by their own efforts and who ostentatiously gratify their materialistic inclinations with the money they have made.

Baxter spoke slightingly of ambitious self-aggrandizement: "Take heed lest, under the pretense of diligence in your calling, you be drawn to earthly-mindedness, and excessive cares or covetous designs for rising in the world."[46] "Every man for himself, and God for us all," wrote Perkins, "is wicked, and is directly against the end of every calling."[47] He then added,

> They profane their lives and callings that employ them to get honors, pleasures, profits, worldly commodities, etc., for thus we live to another end than God hath appointed, and thus we serve ourselves, and consequently neither God nor men.[48]

The early Puritan Hugh Latimer said regarding wealth that "we may not do as many do, that greedily and covetously seek it day and night."[49]

Success Is God's Blessing, Not Something Earned

Did Puritanism and Calvinism more generally regard work as the means by which people earn their own success and wealth? It is commonly asserted that they did, but I look in vain for substantiation of the claim. Calvinism does not teach an ethic of self-reliance, as our modern work ethic does. It is instead an ethic of grace: whatever tangible rewards come from work, they are the gift of God's grace.

Calvin himself had denied that material success is always the result of work. It was Benjamin Franklin, and not the early Protestants, who had the confidence that "early to bed and early to rise make a man healthy, wealthy, and wise." In the Calvinistic view, not only does work not guarantee success; even if God blesses work with prosperity, it is his grace, and not human merit, that produces the blessing. In the words of Calvin, "Men in vain wear themselves out with toiling, and waste themselves by fasting to acquire riches, since these also are a benefit only by God."[50] And again, "Far be it from us to think we have any right to vain confidence. Therefore, whenever we meet with the word 'reward' or it crosses our minds, let us realize that it is the height of the divine goodness towards us."[51]

The same spirit permeates Puritan thinking about the relationship between human effort and divine blessing. Cotton Mather asserted, "In our occupations we spread our nets; but it is God who brings unto our nets all that comes into them."[52] Robert Crowley told an audience at London's Guildhall that neither covetousness nor hard work could make them rich, since God alone blesses people with success.[53] According to George Swinnock, the successful businessman can never say that his own efforts were responsible for his success; even though humans play their active part, "there is not the least wheel in the frame of nature which doth not depend upon God for its motion every moment."[54]

It is true that the Puritan lifestyle, a blend of diligence and thrift, tended to make people relatively prosperous, at least part of the time. The important thing, however, is how the Puritans looked upon their wealth. The Puritan attitude was that wealth was a social good, not a personal possession — a gift from God, not the result of human effort alone or a sign of divine approval. Richard L. Greaves's massive survey of the primary sources reveals that the Puritans "asserted that no direct correlation exists between wealth and godliness. . . . Not riches, but faith and suffering for the sake of the gospel are signs of election."[55]

The Puritans never conceived of work apart from a spiritual and moral context of service to God and man. Richard M. Nixon's much-quoted Labor Day message of 1971 probably summed up the popular conception of the "Puritan work ethic," but if so, it is an inaccurate picture:

> The "work ethic" holds that labor is good in itself; that a man or woman becomes a better person by virtue of the act of working. America's competitive spirit, the "work ethic" of this people, . . . the value of achievement, the morality of self-reliance — none of these is going out of style.

I trust that I have shown that the Puritans would not have been content with such a theory of work. Their ideals were obedience to God, service to humanity, and reliance on God's grace. In the Puritan ethic, the virtue of work depended almost wholly on the motives with which people performed it.[56]

Moderation in Work

A final inheritance that the Puritans bequeathed in their view of work was the need for a sense of moderation in work. They tried in theory to maintain a middle position between the extremes of idleness or laziness on the one hand and slavish addiction to work on the other. In practice, they may have often erred in the direction of overwork.

There is one point at which the modern interpretation of the Puritan work ethic is correct — that the Puritans scorned idleness and praised diligence. Baxter displayed his usual curtness on the subject of idleness: "It is swinish and sinful not to labor."[57] Robert Bolton called idleness "the very rust and canker of the soul."[58] "God doth allow none to live idly," wrote Arthur Dent in his influential book *The Plain Man's Path-way to Heaven*.[59] Elizabeth Joceline wrote in *The Mother's Legacy to Her Unborn Child*, "Be ashamed of idleness as thou art a man, but tremble at it as thou art a Christian."[60] It is obvious from such statements that the Puritan work ethic made work an individual responsibility as well as a social obligation.

The Puritans' critique of idleness was matched by their praise of diligence in work, not so much because it was inherently virtuous but because it was God's appointed means of providing for human needs. Baxter wrote, "God hath commanded you some way or other to labor for your daily bread."[61] Thomas Watson theorized that "religion does not seal warrants to idleness. . . . God sets all his children to work. . . . God will bless our diligence, not our laziness."[62]

Part of the Puritan revulsion against idleness and praise of work was their conviction that labor was a creation ordinance and therefore a necessity for human well-being. "Adam in his innocence had all things at his will," wrote William Perkins, "yet then God employed him in a calling."[63] According to John Robinson,

> God, who would have our first father, even in innocency, . . . to labour . . . , would have none of his sinful posterity lead their life in idleness. . . . Man is born to sore labour, in body or mind, as the spark to fly upward.[64]

And Baxter wrote, "Innocent Adam was put into the Garden of Eden to dress it. . . . And man in flesh must have work for his body as well as his soul."[65] By viewing work as a creation ordinance as well as a calling, the Puritans recognized the dignity of labor for its own sake as well as a response to God.

Even "spirituality" was no excuse for idleness in the view of the Puritans. Richard Steele spoke against "neglecting a man's necessary affairs upon pretense of religious worship."[66] Thomas Shepard had the following advice for a religious zealot who complained that religious thoughts distracted him while he was at work:

> As it is sin to nourish worldly thoughts when God set you a work in spiritual, heavenly employments, so it is, in some respects, as great a sin to suffer yourself to be distracted by spiritual thoughts when God sets you on work in civil . . . employments.[67]

But doesn't the Puritan ethic lead inevitably to the workaholic syndrome? Not according to the Puritans. They attempted to balance their diligence with definite curbs against overwork. Once again their ideal was moderation. "Take heed of too much business or intending it too much, or inordinately," warned John Preston.[68] Philip Stubbes cautioned that "every Christian man is bound in conscience before God" not to allow "his immoderate care" to surpass "the limits of true godliness," adding,

> So far from covetousness and from immoderate care would the Lord have us that we ought not this day to care for tomorrow, for (saith he) sufficient to the day is the travail of the same.[69]

The Scottish divine Robert Woodrow commented,

> The sin of our too great fondness for trade, to the neglecting of our more valuable interests, I humbly think will be written upon our judgment.[70]

On the subject of "moonlighting," Richard Steele claimed that a person ought not to "accumulate two or three callings merely to increase his riches."[71]

The goal of the Puritans was moderation between extremes. To work with zeal and yet not give one's soul to his or her work was what they strove for. John Preston expressed it thus:

> You might meddle with all things in the world and not be defiled by them, if you had pure affections, but when you have an inordinate lust after anything, then it defiles your spirit.[72]

The middle way between the idler and the workaholic was also the ideal of John Cotton:

> There is another combination of virtues strangely mixed in every lively holy Christian, and that is diligence in worldly business and yet deadness to the world; such a mystery as none can read but they that know it. . . . Though he labor most diligently in his calling, yet his heart is not set upon these things, he can tell what to do with his estate when he hath got it.[73]

Summary

For a summary of the Puritan doctrine of work, we do well to turn to John Milton's epic *Paradise Lost*. Milton embodied much of what the Puritans believed about work in his portrayal of Adam and Eve's life of perfection in the Garden of Eden. Milton repeatedly emphasized that work in Paradise was not only pleasant but also necessary. Someone who made a thorough comparison of Milton's paradisal vision with those of earlier writers found that to portray work as necessary was "the most strikingly original feature of Milton's treatment."[74] What set Milton apart from his medieval predecessors in this regard was his Puritanism.

There is no better summary of the original Puritan work ethic than these words of Adam to Eve in *Paradise Lost:*

> Man hath his daily work of body or mind
> Appointed, which declares his dignity,
> And the regard of Heaven on all his ways.[75]

We can glimpse here the Puritan belief about God as the one who calls people to tasks, about the dignity of work, about how the proper attitude toward the goals of work can transform every task into a sacred activity.

FURTHER READING

Several key Puritan texts have been excerpted in modern anthologies, and these texts are such a succinct and organized version of Puritan attitudes toward work that they are well worth consulting. They can be found in these places:

John Cotton, *Christian Calling*, pp. 319–27 in vol. 1, rev. ed., of *The Puritans*, ed., Perry Miller and Thomas H. Johnson (1963).

Cotton Mather, *A Christian at His Calling*, pp. 122–27, in Michael McGiffert, ed., *Puritanism and the American Experience* (1969).

William Perkins, *A Treatise of the Vocations or Callings of Men*, pp. 35–59, in Edmund S. Morgan, ed., *Puritan Political Ideas, 1558–1794* (1965), or pp. 446–76 in Ian Breward, ed., *The Work of William Perkins* (1970).

Secondary sources include these:

R. H. Tawney, *Religion and the Rise of Capitalism* (1926).

Richard B. Schlatter, *The Social Ideas of Religious Leaders, 1660–1688* (1940).

Robert S. Michaelsen, "Changes in the Puritan Concept of Calling or Vocation," *New England Quarterly* 26 (1953): 315–36.

H. M. Robertson, *Aspects of the Rise of Economic Individualism* (1959).

Charles H. George and Katherine George, *The Protestant Mind of the English Reformation, 1570–1640* (1961).

Christopher Hill, *Society and Puritanism in Pre-Revolutionary England* (1964).

M. J. Kitch, ed., *Capitalism and the Reformation* (1967).

The great and reverend God despiseth no honest trade.

— JOHN DOD AND ROBERT CLEAVER

The main end of our lives . . . is to serve God in the serving of men in the works of our callings. — WILLIAM PERKINS

Man hath his daily work of body or mind
Appointed, which declares his dignity,
And the regard of Heaven on all his ways.

— JOHN MILTON

"Speak for yourself, John," Priscilla Mullens told John Alden when he came to court her for his master, Captain Miles Standish. American poet Henry Wadsworth Longfellow later made this classic Puritan love story famous. Priscilla married John, and here is one artist's picture of the wedding procession. *Priscilla and John Alden,* by Charles Yardley Turner; courtesy of Colonel and Mrs. Emanuel A. Pelaez

Chapter 3

Marriage and Sex

All married persons must above all things love, respect and cherish grace in one another.

— THOMAS TAYLOR

The Puritans, as we all know, were sexually inhibited and repressive. Or were they?

When a New England wife complained, first to her pastor and then to the whole congregation, that her husband was neglecting their sex life, the church proceeded to excommunicate the man.[1]

A leading Puritan preacher, in giving an exposition of Proverbs 5:18–19 (which compares a wife to "the loving hind and pleasant roe"), claimed that the hind and roe were chosen because they are most enamoured of their mates "and even mad again in their heat and desire for them."[2]

When young Seaborn Cotton was a Harvard College student, he copied some passionate passages of Renaissance love poetry in his notebook. In his later years, after becoming minister at Hampton, New Hampshire, he saw no incongruity in using the same notebook for his notes of church meetings.[3]

To the embarrassment of the theory of the sexually repressed Puritans are statements from supposedly staid Puritan preachers. Cotton Mather called his second wife "a most lovely creature and such a gift of Heaven to me and mine that the sense thereof . . . dissolves me into tears of joy."[4] William Secker's book *A Wedding Ring* pictured husband and wife as two instruments making music and two streams in one current.[5] Most impressive of all is the following description by Thomas Hooker:

39

The man whose heart is endeared to the woman he loves . . . dreams of her in the night, hath her in his eye and apprehension when he awakes, museth on her as he sits at the table, walks with her when he travels. . . . She lies in his bosom, and his heart trusts in her, which forceth all to confess that the stream of his affection, like a mighty current, runs with full tide and strength.[6]

The modern stereotype stubbornly refuses to be reconciled with the statements of the Puritans themselves. Can it be that the modern image is wrong? One authority who thinks so describes the Puritan marriage ideal as "a perfect sharing" and calls it "Puritanism's greatest and most admirable cultural achievement."[7]

Sex in the Middle Ages

To understand Puritan attitudes toward marriage and sex, we must see them in their historical setting. When we do so, it is obvious that the Puritans were revolutionary in their day. With amazing quickness they uprooted a Catholic tradition that had persisted for at least ten centuries.

The dominant attitude of the Catholic church throughout the Middle Ages was that sexual love itself was evil and did not cease to be so if its object were one's spouse.[8] Tertullian and Ambrose preferred the extinction of the human race to its propagation through sin, that is, through sexual intercourse. For Augustine the sexual act was innocent in marriage but the passion that always accompanies it was sinful. Gregory the Great agreed, adding that whenever a husband and wife engage in sexual intercourse for pleasure rather than procreation, their pleasure befouls their sexual act.

Albertus and Aquinas objected to the sexual act because it subordinates the reason to the passions. Origen took Matthew 19:12 so literally that he had himself castrated before being ordained.[9] Tertullian claimed that "marriage and adultery . . . are not intrinsically different, but only in the degree of their illegitimacy."

These rejections of sex resulted in the Catholic glorification of virginity and celibacy. By the fifth century, clerics were prohibited from marrying. Athanasius declared that the appreciation of virginity, which had never before been regarded as meritorious, was the supreme revelation of Christ. Augustine frequently commended married couples who abstained from sex. Jerome said that the good of marriage is that it produces virgins, and he also asserted that while there have been married saints, these have always remained virgins.

Virtually all the church fathers have statements praising virginity as superior to marriage. Jovinian was excommunicated for daring to suggest that marriage was no worse in God's sight than virginity. A common interpretation of the parable of the sower was that the thirtyfold harvest represented marriage, the sixtyfold harvest widowhood, and the hundred-fold harvest virginity. This tradition culminated in the Council of Trent's denouncing people who denied that virginity was superior to the married state.

Along with the praise of virginity there was constant disparagement of marriage, which was at the same time a rejection of sex. According to Ambrose, "married people ought to blush at the state in which they are living." The church kept multiplying the days on which sex was prohibited for married people until half of the year or more was prohibited, with some writers going so far as to recommend abstinence on five of the seven days of the week. According to Jerome, God refrained from pronouncing a blessing on the second day of creation because the number two prefigured marriage, which Jerome associated with sin.

The medieval Catholic commentaries on early Genesis are a good index to the prevailing attitudes toward sex and marriage. Chrysostom said that Adam and Eve could not have had sexual relations before the Fall. Origen agreed, and he inclined toward the theory that if sin had not entered the world, the human race would have been propagated by some mysterious angelic manner rather than by sexual union. Bishop Gregory of Nyssa claimed that Adam and Eve had originally been created without sexual desire and that if the Fall had not occurred, the human race would have reproduced itself by some harmless mode of vegetation.

The Puritan Rejection of the Medieval Attitude

The Catholic attitudes of the Middle Ages provide the necessary background against which we must understand the Puritan view of sex and marriage. In general, the Puritans affirmed what the Catholics denied and denied what the Catholics had traditionally affirmed. Many of the Puritan pronouncements, in fact, occurred in head-to-head debates with Catholics.

After the Reformation broke out in the early sixteenth century, the Catholic Thomas More and the Puritan William Tyndale conducted a bitter printed debate about whether clergymen were free to marry. Tyndale argued not simply that ministers were free to marry, but that Paul had commanded them to marry, citing verses such as 1 Timothy 3:2 ("Now a bishop must be the husband of one wife"). Thomas More, with his Catholic views about penance and asceticism, regarded Tyndale's Puritan theology as indulgent to the point of license, charging Protestants with "sensual and licentious living."[10] More spoke of the Protestants as people who "eat fast and drink fast and lust fast in their lechery."[11]

Puritan preachers were outspoken in their repudiation of the Catholic viewpoint. Again and again they ascribed the Catholic prohibition of sex to the devil. William Gouge wrote that "it is accounted a doctrine of devils to forbid to marry. For it is a doctrine contrary to God's word."[12] "It was the devil that brought in a base esteem of that honorable condition" of marriage, wrote Richard Sibbes.[13] According to Thomas Gataker, "The marriage bed (saith the Apostle) is of itself free from filth. . . . But saith the Spirit of Satan speaking by these men or beasts rather: marriage is dishonourable."[14]

In his treatise on marriage the Catholic theologian Erasmus had praised as ideal a marriage in which husband and wife learned to live without sexual intercourse. By contrast, the New England Puritan John Cotton preached a marriage sermon in which he called marital abstinence "the dictates of a blind mind . . . and not of that Holy Spirit which saith, It is not good that man should be alone."[15]

Catholic church policy had for centuries insisted on celibacy as a condition for ordination; the Puritan William Gouge denounced "the impure and tyrannical restraint of the Church of Rome, whereby all that enter into any of their holy orders are kept from marriage."[16] Catholic doctrine had declared virginity superior to marriage; the Puritan reply was that marriage "is a state . . . far more excellent than the condition of single life."[17] Many Catholic commentators claimed that sexual intercourse had been a result of the Fall and did not occur in Paradise; the Puritan comeback was that marriage was ordained by God, "and that not in this sinful world, but in paradise, that most joyful garden of pleasure."[18]

It is not only in physics that every action produces an equal reaction. Centuries of Catholic doctrine had denigrated sex and marriage. The Puritans were equally vehement in reacting to that attitude, and they established a tradition that has persisted to the present day.

Puritan Affirmation of Marriage

Few ideas unleashed such wellsprings of feeling among the Puritans as their praise of the ideal of the companionate marriage. One of them wrote:

> There is no society more near, more entire, more needful, more kindly, more delightful, more comfortable, more constant, more continual, than the society of man and wife, the main root, source, and original of all other societies.[19]

Gataker wrote that marriage is "one of the greatest outward blessings that in this world man enjoyeth."[20] For Thomas Adams, "There is no such fountain on earth as marriage."[21]

The ideal of friendship, which in classical antiquity had been largely confined to male friends, now became transferred to the marriage relationship. In marriage, wrote one Puritan, "thou . . . unitest unto thyself a friend."[22] Richard Baxter wrote regarding the companionate marriage,

> It is a mercy to have a faithful friend that loveth you entirely, . . . to whom you may open your mind and communicate your affairs. . . . And it is a mercy to have so near a friend to be a helper to your soul and . . . to stir up in you the grace of God.[23]

The Catholic tradition had tended to view women as a temptation. The Puritans had another idea. A good wife, claimed Henry Smith, is "such a gift as we should account from God alone, accept it as if he should send us a present from heaven with this name on it, *The gift of God*."[24]

The Goodness of Sex in Marriage

Given the Catholic background against which they wrote and preached, the Puritans' praise of marriage was at the same time an implicit endorsement of marital sex as good. They elaborated that point specifically and often. This becomes clearer once we are clued into the now-outdated terms by which they customarily referred to sexual intercourse: "matrimonial duty," "cohabitation," "act of matrimony," and (especially) "due benevolence."

Everywhere we turn in Puritan writing on the subject we find sex affirmed as good in principle. Gouge referred to physical union as "one of the most proper and essential acts of marriage."[25] It was Milton's opinion that the text "they shall be one flesh" (Gen. 2:24) was included in the Bible

> to justify and make legitimate the rites of the marriage bed; which was not unneedful, if for all this warrant they were suspected of pollution by some sects of philosophy and religions of old, and latelier among the Papists.[26]

William Ames listed as one of the duties of marriage "mutual communication of bodies."[27]

So closely linked were the ideas of marriage and sex that the Puritans usually defined marriage partly in terms of sexual union. Perkins defined marriage as "the lawful conjunction of the two married persons; that is, of one man and one woman into one flesh."[28] Another well-known definition was this: Marriage

> is a coupling together of two persons into one flesh, according to the ordinance of God. . . . By yoking, joining, or coupling is meant, not only outward dwelling together of the married folks . . . but also an uniform agreement of mind and a common participation of body and goods.[29]

Married sex was not only legitimate in the Puritan view; it was meant to be exuberant. Gouge said that married couples should engage in sex "with good will and delight, willingly, readily, and cheerfully."[30] An anonymous Puritan claimed that when two are made one by marriage they

> may joyfully give due benevolence one to the other; as two musical instruments rightly fitted do make a most pleasant and sweet harmony in a well tuned consort.[31]

Alexander Niccholes theorized that in marriage "thou not only unitest unto thyself a friend and comfort for society, but also a companion for pleasure."[32]

In this acceptance of physical sex, the Puritans once again rejected the asceticism and implicit dualism between sacred and secular that had governed Christian thinking for so long. In the Puritan view, God had given the physical world, including sex, for human welfare. Robert Croftes wrote that

> he that useth these external felicities of the world, such as this of nuptial love, to the glory of God and to good ends, . . . is better to be reputed than he that . . . neglects so great a good, which God freely offers to our acceptance.[33]

In the Puritan view, God was no celestial Scrooge who deprived his creatures of good things:

> Wisest Solomon among his gravest Proverbs countenances a kind of ravishment . . . in the entertainment of wedded leisures; and in the Song of Songs . . . sings of a thousand raptures between those two lovely ones far on the hither side of carnal enjoyment. By these instances, and more which might be brought, we may imagine how indulgently God provided against man's loneliness.[34]

The Puritans rejected asceticism because of their firm grip on the doctrine of creation. In their view, it was God who had created people as sexual beings. Thus William Whately could claim that "the Author of nature hath appointed this union betwixt one man and one woman," while William Perkins was assured that marriage "was ordained by God in Paradise."[35] Robert Cleaver spoke of marriage as a "coupling together of two persons into one flesh . . . according unto the ordinance of God."[36]

Contrary to a popular misconception, the Puritans were not squeamish about physical or erotic contact between couples. Thomas Gataker said that "the Holy Ghost did allow some such private dalliance and behaviour to married persons between themselves as to others might seem dotage."[37] Many Puritan writers used Genesis 26:8, which describes Isaac's fondling of Rebekah, to argue that erotic love was legitimate.[38] One of them commented that in marriage "a play-fellow is come to make our age merry, as Isaac and Rebecca sported together," while Gouge cited the same passage to charge husbands who reject such contact as taking no more delight in their own wives than in any other women.[39] Perkins described one of the ways by which couples should show "due benevolence" to each other as "by an holy kind of rejoicing and solacing themselves with each other," in connection with which he mentioned kissing.[40]

The Nature of Sex

Although Puritan writers and preachers did not give an anatomy of what sex is, with a little analysis we can easily piece together their thinking. In the first place, sex is a God-implanted *natural or biological appetite*. Edward Taylor, New England poet and minister, spoke of "the use of the marriage bed" as "founded in man's nature."[41] William Perkins classified marriage as one of the things that are spiritually "indifferent," adding that "the kingdom of God stands no more in it than in meats and drinks," again exhibiting an assumption that sex is as natural as the appetite for food.[42]

If sex is thus a natural impulse, it is at the same time intended to be *more than a physical act*. It is part of a total union of two persons, including their minds, emotions, and souls as well as their bodies. For Robert Cleaver, sexual union in marriage implied "an uniform agreement of mind" as well as "common participation of body."[43] Milton argued regarding the marriage union that "by loneliness is not only meant the want of copulation," since "man is not less alone by turning in a body to him, unless there be within it a mind answerable."[44]

Thirdly, sex is *necessary in marriage*. Marriage is the God-ordained means of satisfying the sexual urge. Perkins called marriage "a sovereign means to avoid fornication."[45] William Whately told spouses that marriage "will keep their desires in order, and cause that they shall be well satisfied each in other, as in God's gifts."[46]

The need for sexual satisfaction as a human condition led the Puritans to say a great deal about sex as a marriage duty, with 1 Corinthians 7:1–5 serving as the central text. Henry Smith called verse 3 of that passage "a commandment to yield this duty [of sexual intercourse], . . . and not to do it is a breach of commandment."[47] According to Whately, neither husband nor wife can "without grievous sin deny" sexual intercourse to the other.[48] To deny sexual union, said Gouge, "is to deny a due debt, and to give Satan great advantage."[49]

The fear of physical separation between spouses was a major theme of Puritan writers on the subject of sex. Typical was Benjamin Wadsworth's advice that married couples not allow quarrels to "make you live separately, nor lodge separately neither: for if it once comes to this, Satan has got a great advantage against you."[50]

To regard sex as a marriage duty was not, however, to make it a joyless thing. William Whately encouraged marriage partners to love each other "with an ardent love" and admonished them that they must not "yield themselves with grudging and frowardness, but readily, and with all demonstrations of hearty affection."[51]

Fourthly, the Puritans taught that *sex is private*, not because it is bad, but because of its inherent nature as a total union between two people who commit themselves to each other permanently. The Puritans had an abhorrence of erotic displays in public, where the sexual urges of others might be inflamed.[52] But this negative attitude toward public dalliance did not extend to private love. Gouge claimed that "much greater liberty is granted to man and wife when they are alone than in company."[53]

Nowhere do we come closer to the revolutionary core of the Puritans' teaching on sex than in their insistence that *married sex is a form of chastity*. Catholic doctrine had equated chastity with virginity, a misconception that is still with us. William Gouge attacked the position of the Council of Trent with the statement:

> Here by the way note the dotage of our adversaries, who think there is no chastity but of single persons: whereupon in their speeches and writings they oppose a chastity and matrimony one to another, as two contraries.[54]

William Ames defined "virginal chastity" as "that which should be kept . . . until . . . marriage," and "conjugal chastity" as "that which should be kept in wedlock," adding that "a marriage lawfully contracted and observed goes with conjugal chastity."[55] The Protestant poet Edmund Spenser devoted a whole book of his poem *The Faerie Queene* to a portrayal of chastity, by which he meant abstinence before marriage and "active, honest, and devoted love" after marriage.[56]

As this portrait of a Puritan woman dressed in Sunday clothing suggests, the Puritans were far from indifferent to physical attractiveness. From Wenceslaus Hallar, *Ornatus Muliebris Anglicanus;* courtesy of the Folger Shakespeare Library [STC 13599.5 pl 20]

The Purpose of Marriage and Sex

The Puritans also had a fully developed theory of the purposes of marriage and sex. The larger context into which we must put their comments is the unified Protestant tradition that included both Anglicans and Puritans. While individual writers might modify the scheme, the general framework was a threefold purpose for marriage — procreation, a remedy against sexual sin, and mutual society.

The distinctive contribution of the Puritans within this framework was to shift the primary emphasis from procreation to companionship.

The order adopted in the Book of Common Prayer was (1) the procreation of children, (2) the restraint and remedy of sin, and (3) mutual society, help, and comfort. James Johnson has written a whole book to show that as Puritan thought developed, the first and third purposes of marriage became reversed from the list in the Prayer Book. Johnson provides numerous quotations from the Puritans, which I do not have space to reproduce, but his summary is worth pondering:

> It is the result of the Puritan emphasis on companionship in marriage that the first and last reasons change place. Another way of saying this is to note that the Puritans normally look to a verse from the second chapter of Genesis — "God said, It is not good that the man should be alone; I will make him an help meet for him" instead of the one normally cited from the first, "Be fruitful and multiply" — for their explanation of why marriage was instituted by God in the first place.[57]

In Catholic doctrine, the only thing that had salvaged sex in marriage was the procreation of children. The Puritans disagreed. Perkins stated that "some Schoolmen do err who hold that the secret coming together of man and wife cannot be without sin unless it be done for procreation of children."[58] This is similar to Milton's opinion that

> God in the first ordaining of marriage taught us to what end he did it, . . . to comfort and refresh him against the evil of solitary life, not mentioning the purpose of generation till afterwords.[59]

If the main purpose of married sex is the expression of mutual love and companionship, it is a perversion of sex to reduce it to a merely physical act. "How can two . . . become one flesh lawfully," asked Cleaver, "when as there wanteth the union and conjunction of the heart, the true and natural mother of all marriage duties?"[60] Perkins had something similar in mind when he wrote, "Nothing is more shameless than to love a wife as though she were a strumpet."[61] And Milton wrote,

> Although copulation be considered among the ends of marriage, yet the act thereof in a right esteem can no longer be matrimonial than it is an effect of conjugal love. When love . . . vanishes, . . . the fleshly act indeed may continue, but not holy, not pure, not beseeming the sacred bond of marriage, being at best but an animal excretion.[62]

Integrating the Spiritual and Physical Ends of Marriage

With all their emphasis on the human and physical purposes of marriage, the Puritans did not, of course, neglect the primacy of the spiritual purpose. The integration of spiritual and physical that is a hallmark of Puritanism did not forsake them here. Daniel Rogers called romantic love "a sweet compound of both religion and nature."[63] John Robinson believed that God had ordained marriage "for the benefit of man's natural and spiritual life."[64]

The Puritans never doubted that married love should be subordinate to the love of God, though they viewed the two as complementary rather than opposed. In John Winthrop's first letter to his wife Margaret after their marriage he called her "the chiefest of all comforts under the hope of salvation."[65] The complementary nature of human and divine love was beautifully captured by Milton's poetic definition of married love in *Paradise Lost:*

> love refines
> The thoughts, and heart enlarges, hath his seat
> In reason, and is judicious, is the scale
> By which to heavenly love thou mayest ascend.[66]

Thomas Gataker held out as an ideal God's turning his gift of marriage between husband and wife both "to his own glory and their mutual good."[67]

What the Puritans insisted on, here as elsewhere, was that an activity carry a purpose higher than itself. John Cotton warned against the error of aiming "at no higher end than marriage itself" and encouraged people to look upon spouses "not for their own ends, but to be better fitted for God's service and bring them nearer to God."[68] Thomas Taylor wrote,

> All married persons must above all things love, respect and cherish grace one in another: ground not thy love upon beauty, riches, portion, youth, or such failing foundation: but pitch it first in God and grace, and it will take hold.[69]

The Puritan view of the purposes of marriage, encompassing sexual union but going beyond it, is well capsulized in the following definition from the pen of Thomas Becon: matrimony is a

> high, holy and blessed order of life, ordained not of man, but of God,
> . . . wherein one man and one woman are coupled and knit together in
> one flesh and body in the fear and love of God, by the free, loving,
> hearty, and good consent of them both, to the intent that they two
> may dwell together as one flesh and body, of one will and mind, in all
> honesty, virtue and godliness, and spend their lives in equal partaking
> of all such things as God shall send them with thanksgiving.[70]

Romantic Love as the Context for Sex

Did the Puritans go beyond the ideal of godly and companionate marriage to romantic passion? It is usually said that they were too rational, practical, and domestically oriented to qualify for what today we would call romantic passion. I would suggest that if we listen to what the Puritans said about sexual love, we can catch the resonance of romance.

The American poet and minister Edward Taylor wrote to his beloved that his passion for her was "a golden ball of pure fire."[71] Reverend John Pike called his wife "the desire of mine eyes."[72] William Whately said that the mutual love of husband and wife should be "most fervent and abundant."[73]

The letters of John Winthrop to his wife are an especially well-known example of Puritan romanticism. Winthrop typically closed his letters to his wife with phrases such as these: "I kiss and love thee with the kindest affection"; "so I kiss thee and wish thee Farewell"; "I kiss my sweet wife and remain always thy faithful husband"; "many kisses of love I send thee"; "so with the sweetest kisses and pure embracings of my kindest affection I rest thine."[74]

The love of which these Puritans speak is an emotional rapture that sweeps the lover into its orb. Henry Smith told his parishioners that in marriage there must be "a joining of hearts and a knitting of affections together."[75] William Gouge urged wives "to be lovers of their husbands, as well as husbands to love their wives," adding, "Under love all other duties are comprised: for without it no duty can be well performed. . . . It is like fire, which is not only hot in itself, but also conveyeth heat into that which is near it."[76]

A few Puritan writers were even intent on preserving the mystery of romantic love. Thomas Gataker wrote:

> As faith, so love cannot be constrained. As there is no affection more forcible, so there is none freer from force and compulsion. . . . There are secret links of affection that no reason can be rendered of.[77]

Daniel Rogers sounded a similar note:

> Husbands and wives should be as two sweet friends, bred under one constellation, tempered by an influence from heaven whereof neither can give any reason, save mercy and providence first made them so, and then made their match; saying, see, God hath determined us out of this vast world each for other.[78]

It has been rightly said that "from magnifying the religious significance of marriage Puritan thought easily proceeded to magnify the emotional, romantic, and idealistic aspects of the marriage relation."[79]

There is another reason to credit the Puritans with fostering romantic love, and it comes from literary history. Throughout the Middle Ages, love poetry and love stories had celebrated adulterous romantic love. By the time we reach the end of the sixteenth century, the ideal of *wedded* romantic love had replaced the adulterous courtly love ideal of the Middle Ages as the customary subject for literature. C. S. Lewis has shown that "the conversion of courtly love into romantic monogamous love was . . . largely the work of English, and even of Puritan, poets."[80] Someone else claims that the Puritans "did what courtly lovers had never dared to do; by combining the romantic love relation and the marriage relation, they created the new social institution of *romantic marriage*."[81]

The Puritan ideal was wedded romantic love. Without such love, sex in marriage was doomed to be a disappointment. "As for love," wrote William Whately, "it is the life, the soul of marriage."[82] Benjamin Wadsworth claimed that people should not marry "unless they can have a real cordial love" to their spouse, "for God strictly commands mutual love in this relation."[83] According to John Wing, a husband's love to his wife "must be the most dear, intimate, precious and entire that heart can have toward a creature; none but the love of God . . . is above it, none but the love of ourselves is fellow to it, all the love of others is inferior to it."[84] A modern scholar has summarized the situation by saying that "love was the cement of the Puritan family and sex was viewed as one of the means of expressing that love."[85]

Marriage Is for Sinners

Despite all the idealization of marriage that I have delineated, the Puritans were under no illusions about marriage. They combined realism with their idealism. They knew that marriage did not escape the effects of the Fall.

A Boston Puritan noted that marriage is "very difficult because of your many infirmities"; knowing this, a couple must exercise "patience and meekness, forbearing, forgiving, and forgetting provocations."[86] "Look not for perfection in your relation," advised Thomas Thatcher; "God reserves that for another state where marriage is not needed."[87]

John Oxenbridge recommended that spouses could prepare for the rigors of marriage "by limiting the expectation" and by remembering that "you marry a child of Adam."[88]

Attitudes Toward Women

An authority on the history of attitudes toward romantic love has observed that "in any culture there is usually a close connection between the prevailing view of marriage and physical sexuality, and the attitude adopted towards women."[89] The Puritan glorification of sex and marriage had a correspondingly positive effect on views toward women. This elevation of the status of women has been variously attributed to the doctrines of creation and the priesthood of all believers, and to the role of the wife as consort in a companionate marriage.[90]

Whatever the reason, Puritans exalted women, especially in their role as Christian wives and mothers. Daniel Rogers called a wife "a true friend" and "next to the soul's peace with God . . . the greatest content under the sun."[91] Robert Cleaver wrote:

> Most true it is that women are as men are reasonable creatures, and have flexible wits, both to good and evil. . . . And although there be some evil and lewd women, yet that doth no more prove the malice of their nature than of men, and therefore the more ridiculous and foolish are they that have inveighed against the whole sex for a few evil.[92]

Some of the Puritan praise of women was quite obviously an implied refutation of medieval Catholic attacks on women. Volumes of patristic writing had viewed women as snares to men. The Puritan attitude was well expressed in this advice to newly wedded husbands: "Thy wife shall be a blessing, no snare; thy liberties shall be pure unto thee, and thou shalt visit thine habitation without sin."[93] John Cotton wrote that

> women are creatures without which there is no comfortable living for man. . . . They are a sort of blasphemers then who despise and decry them, and call them a necessary evil, for they are a necessary good.[94]

Cleaver similarly wrote:

> A wife is called by God himself an helper, and not an impediment or a necessary evil, as some unadvisedly do say. . . . These and such like sayings, tending to the dispraise of women, some maliciously and undiscreetly do vomit out, contrary to the mind of the Holy Ghost, who said that she was ordained as a helper, and not a hinderer.[95]

In a subsequent chapter on the topic of the Puritan family, I will have occasion to note a strong Puritan emphasis on the husband's headship and the wife's subordination. In the context of the present chapter, it is important to note that Puritan ideas on sex and marriage had the effect of mitigating hierarchy in the direction of marital equality. Lawrence Stone sums it up by saying that "Puritan desire to preserve male . . . authority was in practice undermined by Puritan zeal for holy matrimony."[96]

In Puritan discussions of hierarchy in the marriage relationship, the word "equality" keeps appearing. "Of all the orders which are unequals," wrote Samuel Willard, those of husband and wife "do come nearest to an equality, and in several respects they stand upon even ground. These do make a pair, which infers so far a parity."[97] No Puritan believed more fervently in the headship of the husband than John Milton, yet observe how he tries to hold to equality under the umbrella of hierarchy: "Man . . . receives her into a part of that empire which God proclaims to him, though not equally, yet largely, as his own image and glory."[98]

According to William Secker, God made Eve a "parallel line drawn equal" to Adam, not created from the head "to claim superiority, but out of the side to be content with equality."[99] For Rogers, "the subjection we treat of is not slavish, but equal and royal in a sort."[100] "Of all degrees wherein there is any difference betwixt person and person," said Gouge, "there is the least disparity betwixt man and wife." He explained:

> Though the man be as the head, yet is the woman as the heart, which
> is the most excellent part of the body next the head, far more excellent
> than any other member under the head, and almost equal to the head
> in many respects, and as necessary as the head.[101]

Such statements do not obliterate the headship of the husband. Rather, they show that the Puritan ideal of the companionate marriage tended to soften the claims of male dominance and to produce an enlightened version of marital hierarchy.

Summary

The Puritan doctrine of sex was a watershed in the cultural history of the West. The Puritans devalued celibacy, glorified companionate marriage, affirmed married sex as both necessary and pure, established the ideal of wedded romantic love, and exalted the role of the wife.

This complex of ideas and values received its most eloquent and beautiful expression in Milton's picture of the married life of Adam and Eve in his epic *Paradise Lost*. In portraying the perfect marriage in Book 4, Milton went out of his way to show that Adam and Eve enjoyed sexual union before the Fall. As Adam and Eve retire to their bower for the evening, we read,

> Straight side by side were laid, nor turned I ween
> Adam from his fair spouse, nor Eve the rites
> Mysterious of connubial love refused:
> Whatever hypocrites austerely talk
> Of purity and place and innocence,
> Defaming as impure what God declares
> Pure, and commands to some, leaves free to all.

> Our Maker bids increase, who bids abstain
> But our Destroyer, foe to God and man?[102]

Having dissociated himself from the Catholic tradition, Milton proceeds to give his famous apostrophe (address) to wedded love:

> Hail wedded love, mysterious law, true source
> Of human offspring, sole propriety
> In Paradise of all things common else.
> By thee adulterous lust was driven from men
> Among the bestial herds to range, by thee
> Founded in reason, loyal, just and pure,
> Relations dear, and all the charities
> Of father, son, and brother first were known.
> Far be it, that I should write thee sin or blame,
> Or think thee unbefitting holiest place,
> Perpetual fountain of domestic sweets,
> Whose bed is undefiled and chaste pronounced.[103]

All the usual Puritan themes are here: the biblical basis for affirming sex (as evidenced by several key biblical allusions in the passage), the differentiation between animal lust and human sexual love, the domestic context into which sexual fulfillment is put, and the romantic overtones of the passage. This, and not the modern stereotype, is what the Puritans really said about sex.

FURTHER READING

William Haller and Malleville Haller, "The Puritan Art of Love," *Huntington Library Quarterly* 5 (1941–42): 235–72.

Roland M. Frye, "The Teachings of Classical Puritanism on Conjugal Love," *Studies in the Renaissance* 2 (1955): 148–59.

Derrick Sherwin Bailey, *Sexual Relation in Christian Thought* (1959).

Charles H. George and Katherine George, *The Protestant Mind of the English Reformation, 1570–1640*, chap. 7 (1961).

Edmund S. Morgan, *The Puritan Family: Religious and Domestic Relations in Seventeenth-Century New England*, (1944, rev. ed. 1966).

Robert V. Schnucker, *Views of Selected Puritans, 1560–1630, on Marriage and Human Sexuality* (1969).

James Turner Johnson, *A Society Ordained by God: English Puritan Marriage Doctrine in the First Half of the Seventeenth Century* (1970).

John Halkett, *Milton and the Idea of Matrimony* (1970).

Joyce L. Irwin, *Womanhood in Radical Protestantism, 1525–1675* (1979).

Roberta Hamilton, *The Liberation of Women*, chap. 3 (1978).

As for love, it is the life, the soul of marriage.
— WILLIAM WHATELY

Though the man be as the head, yet is the woman as the heart. — WILLIAM GOUGE

The man whose heart is endeared to the woman he loves . . . forceth all to confess that the stream of his affection, like a mighty current, runs with full tide and strength.
— THOMAS HOOKER

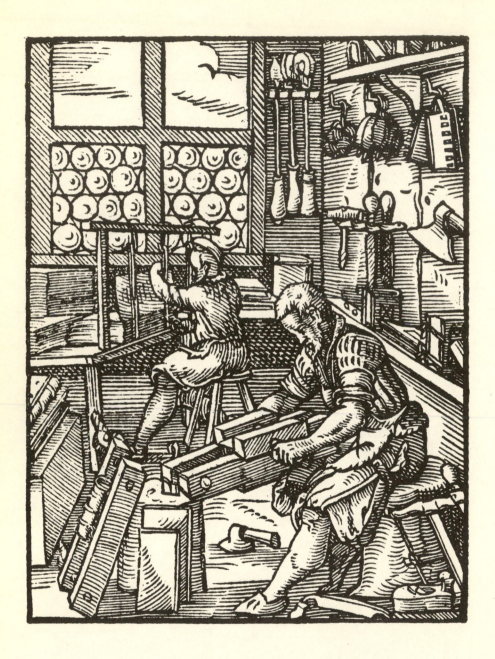

The Puritan work ethic, a blend of industry and thrift, sometimes produced wealth. The Christian use of money was an idea on which the Puritans lavished much attention.

Chapter 4

Money

God never gave a gift, but he sent occasion at one time or another to show it to God's glory. As if he sent riches, he sendeth poor men to be helped with it.

— HUGH LATIMER

One of the most influential and controversial books of our century was Max Weber's *Protestant Ethic and the Spirit of Capitalism* (1930). Beginning with the observation that the rise of middle-class trade occurred chiefly among Protestants, Weber set out to explore the connections between "the Protestant ethic" and "the spirit of modern capitalism." He found many connections: a belief that one can serve God in one's worldly calling, a tendency to live disciplined and even ascetic lives, a spirit of individualism, emphasis on working hard, and a good conscience about making money. Although Weber was highly selective in the data he chose to consider, his analysis uncovered much that is important about the Protestant movement.

The so-called Weber thesis produced some unfortunate results, however. Protestants have been pictured as elevating money-making to the highest goal in life, as viewing the amassing of wealth as a moral obligation, and as approving virtually every kind of business competition. A look at Puritan attitudes and practices toward money will show that the Weber thesis was a good idea that ended up seriously perverting the truth.[1]

Is Money Good or Bad?

When Martin Luther became a monk, he took a vow of poverty. This reflected a long-standing Catholic view that poverty is inherently

57

virtuous for a person. But the Reformers — including Luther himself — did not see it that way. The starting point in their thinking about money and possessions was that these things are good in principle.

The Puritans agreed with Calvin that "money in itself is good."[2] When Samuel Willard eulogized John Hull at his funeral, he saw no contradiction between the merchant's having been "a saint upon earth" who lived "above the world" and his having been industrious in his business, so that it could be said of him that "Providence had given him a prosperous portion of this world's goods."[3] According to Richard Baxter, "All love of the creature, the world, or riches is not sin. For the works of God are all good, as such."[4]

Samuel Willard theorized that "riches are consistent with godliness, and the more a man hath, the more advantage he hath to do good with it, if God give him an heart to it."[5] William Adams regarded economic endeavor as worthy of a Christian's affection; he wrote that the Christian "hath much business to do in and about the world, which he is vigorously to attend, and he hath . . . that in the world upon which he is to bestow affection."[6]

In affirming the goodness of money, the Puritans found it necessary to defend the legitimate aspects of money against its detractors. William Perkins did so in a sermon on Matthew 6:19–20, in which he listed what Christ did *not* forbid:

> Diligent labour in a main vocation, whereby [a person] provides things needful for himself, and those that depend on him. . . . The fruition and possession of goods and riches: for they are the good blessing of God being well used. . . . The gathering and laying up of treasure is not simply forbidden, for the word of God alloweth herefor in some respect. 2 Corinthians 12:14.[7]

The Puritans had no guilt about making money; to make money was a form of stewardship. One of the passages that the Weber thesis made mileage out of is the following statement by Richard Baxter:

> If God show you a way in which you may lawfully get more than in another way (without wrong to your soul, or to any other), if you refuse this, and choose the less gainful way, you cross one of the ends of your calling, and you refuse to be God's steward.[8]

In the broader context of Baxter's writing on economics, this call for efficiency and productiveness is simply an evidence of common sense and a strong sense of wishing to be a good steward of God's gifts.

Why were the Puritans so sure that money was a good thing? Chiefly because they believed that money and wealth were gifts from

God. "If we happen to have inherited much property," wrote Perkins, "we are to enjoy these in good conscience as blessings and gifts of God."[9] John Robinson commented, "The blessing of the Lord maketh rich. . . . And as riches are in themselves God's blessings, so are we to desire them, for the comfortable course of our natural and civil states."[10] If money and property are gifts from God, Richard Sibbes could affirm, "worldly things are good in themselves and given to sweeten our passage to Heaven."[11]

Because the Puritans viewed prosperity as a gift from God, they decisively dissociated it from the idea of human merit. If it is a gift, how can it be earned?[12] Not only does human effort not guarantee success; even if God blesses work with prosperity, it is God's grace and not human merit that produces the blessing. Cotton Mather asserted, "In our occupation we spread our nets; but it is God who brings unto our nets all that comes into them."[13] "If goods be gotten by industry, providence, and skill," wrote John Robinson, "it is God's blessing that both gives the faculty, and the use of it, and the success unto it."[14] The Puritan ethic is an ethic of grace, not of human merit.

The Puritans' defense of private property was an extension of their belief in the legitimacy of money.[15] William Ames wrote that private property is founded "not only on human but also on natural and divine right."[16] Elsewhere Ames wrote that there is justice "in the lawful keeping of the things we have."[17] When John Hull, one of the first merchant princes of Massachusetts, lost his ships to the Dutch, he took consolation in God's providence: "The loss of my estate will be nothing, if the Lord please to join my soul nearer to himself, and loose it more from creature comforts." But when his foreman stole his horses, Hull took the view that "I would have you know that they are, by God's good providence, mine."[18]

Puritan endorsement of money and property should not be construed as meaning that the Puritans elevated material goods above spiritual values. John Winthrop disparaged those who mistake "outward prosperity for true felicity."[19] Peter Bulkeley wrote that a Christian "may do many things for himself," yet only so long as "this is not in opposition, but in subordination, to God and his glory."[20]

Richard Rogers, in the privacy of his diary, summarized the perspective in which the Puritans affirmed wealth:

So it may be said of our outward prosperity that for as much as God giveth us such great encouragement, we can willingly delight with others in things which are good. But we must find that our hearty embracing of the doctrine of God and love of it and labouring after a good conscience to find joy in Christ's redeeming us is that which maketh our lives joyful, for this cannot by any malice of man nor devil be taken from us.[21]

What About Poverty?

If riches are a blessing from God, then poverty must be a curse and a sign of God's disfavor — right? Wrong, said the Puritans, who disagreed with a whole tissue of assumptions often attributed to them in the twentieth century.

In the first place, the Puritans disagreed that godliness is a guarantee of success. Thomas Watson went so far as to say that "true godliness is usually attended with persecution. . . . The saints have no charter of exemption from trials. . . . Their piety will not shield them from sufferings."[22]

If godliness is not a guarantee of success, then the converse is also true: success is not a sign of godliness. This is how the Puritans understood the matter. John Cotton stated that a Christian "equally bears good and evil successes as God shall dispense them to him."[23] Samuel Willard wrote, "As riches are not evidences of God's love, so neither is poverty of his anger or hatred."[24] Samuel Hieron said that just as many of God's "beloved servants do feel the smart of poverty, so even the most wicked . . . have a large portion in this life."[25]

With the causal link between success and godliness thus severed, the Puritans concluded several things about poverty. One was that poverty is not necessarily a bad or shameful thing. "Poverty in itself," wrote Ames, "hath no crime in it, or fault to be ashamed of: but is oftentimes sent from God to the godly, either as a correction, or trial or searching, or both."[26] Richard Baxter concluded:

> None are shut out of the church for want of money, nor is poverty any eyesore to Christ. An empty heart may bar them out, but an empty purse cannot. His kingdom of grace hath ever been more consistent with despised poverty than wealth and honour.[27]

In fact, the Puritans claimed that poverty may well be God's way of spiritually blessing or teaching a person. In dealing with biblical passages that promise God's blessing to believers, Samuel Bolton wrote:

> But shall we judge nothing to have the nature of blessing but the enjoyment of temporal and outward good things? May not losses be blessings as well as enjoyments?[28]

And Thomas Watson, in a list of "things that work for good to God's children," included poverty in the list, with this commentary:

Poverty works for good to God's children. It starves their lusts. It increases their graces. "Poor in the world, rich in faith" (James 2:5). Poverty tends to prayer. When God has clipped his children's wings by poverty, they fly swiftest to the throne of grace.[29]

In thus vindicating poverty, the Puritans were careful to distinguish themselves from Catholic teaching about poverty as meritorious in itself. William Ames made this clear when he denounced the monks' vows of poverty as "madness, a superstitious and wicked presumption, being that they sell this poverty for a work of perfection . . . which will much prevail for satisfaction and merit before God."[30] The Puritans used the phrase "evangelical poverty" to describe their ideal of learning spiritual lessons from such poverty as God might send them in their ordinary callings in the world.[31]

The Puritans did not *idealize* poverty as something to be sought. Contrary to Catholic monastic theory, the Puritans theorized that poverty is no sure way to avoid temptation. Richard Baxter commented:

Poverty also hath its temptations. . . . For even the poor may be undone by the love of that wealth and plenty which they never get: and they may perish for over-loving the world, that never yet prospered in the world.[32]

The Puritans also rejected the ethic of unconcern that is content to let the poor remain poor. In their view, poverty is not an unmitigated misfortune, but it is certainly not the goal that we should have for people. "The rich man by liberality must dispose and comfort the poor," said Thomas Lever in a sermon.[33] "God never gave a gift," preached Hugh Latimer, "but he sent occasion at one time or another to show it to God's glory. As if he sent riches, he sendeth poor men to be helped with it."[34] Latimer even went so far as to say that "the poor man hath title to the rich man's goods; so that the rich man ought to let the poor man have part of his riches to help and to comfort him withal."[35]

On the subject of poverty, then, the Puritans taught that it is sometimes the lot of the godly and that it can be a spiritual blessing. It is not, however, meritorious in itself, and poor people require the generosity of people who have the resources to help them.

The Dangers of Wealth

Instead of regarding success as a sign of God's approval or of their own virtue, the Puritans were much more likely to look upon prosperity as a temptation. A marginal note to Genesis 13:1 in the Geneva Bible speaks volumes: Abraham's "great riches gotten in Egypt hindered him not to follow his vocation," implying that his riches could easily have become a temptation to him. "Both poverty and riches," wrote John Robinson, "have their temptations. . . . And of the two states, . . . the temptations of riches are the more dangerous."[36] Thomas Lever claimed, "He that seeks to be rich . . . will fall into diverse temptations and snares of the devil."[37] Richard Rogers woke up a little after midnight and was convicted of the fact that the blessings of God "waxed too sweet to me, and . . . dangerous."[38]

Much to our surprise, the Puritans saw an *inverse* relationship between wealth and godliness. It did not *have* to turn out this way, but in their view it usually did. "Remember that riches do make it harder for a man to be saved," warned Richard Baxter.[39] Samuel Willard believed that "it is a rare thing to see men that have the greatest visible advantages . . . to be very zealous for God."[40] Richard Sibbes noted that "where the world hath got possession in the heart, it makes us false to God, and false to man, it makes us unfaithful in our callings, and false to religion itself."[41]

Edmund Morgan is thus right when he says that "the Puritans always felt more at ease when adversity made them tighten their belts."[42] "Seeking of abundance is a hazard to the salvation of the soul," said William Perkins, who elsewhere was even blunter: "Let us consider what moved Judas to betray his master: namely, the desire of wealth."[43] Richard Greenham claimed that "it is harder to believe in the abundance of worldly means, than it is in the want of them."[44]

In elaborating this theme of the dangers of wealth, the Puritans gave an anatomy of the reasons why money is dangerous. Foremost is the tendency of money to replace God as the object of ultimate devotion. Worldly goods "are veils set betwixt God and us, they stay our sight in them that it cannot pierce to God."[45] "How ready is [man] to terminate his happiness in externals," noted Thomas Watson.[46] John Robinson said the same: "If a man be rich, and full, he is in danger to deny God, and to say in pride, and contempt of him . . . , who is the Lord?"[47] Richard Rogers noted regarding the wealthy bishops and clerics of the Anglican church that they "did never seem grossly to have departed from God till they grew in wealth and promotion."[48]

A second reason why riches are dangerous is that they instill reliance on self instead of on God. Richard Baxter was of the opinion that "when men prosper in the world, their minds are lifted up with their estates, and they can hardly believe that they are so ill, while they feel themselves so well."[49] "From rich men's pride in themselves," said John Robinson, "ariseth commonly contempt of others, specially of the poor."[50] Samuel Hieron's model prayer for rich people implies the same point:

Apt I shall be to lift up my heart, to pride myself in my own conceit, to trust unto my wealth, to despise others, to grow in love with this present world . . . , because Thou hast enriched me.[51]

The acquisition of wealth, said the Puritans, also has a way of absorbing so much of a person's time and energy that it draws him or her away from religion and moral concern for others. Richard Mather, in his farewell sermon, said:

Experience shows that it is an easy thing in the midst of worldly business to lose the life and power of religion, that nothing thereof should be left but only the external form, as it were the carcass or shell, worldliness having eaten out the kernel, and having consumed the very soul and life of godliness.[52]

Cotton Mather was equally alarmed by the trend toward materialism in New England society: "Religion begat prosperity and the daughter devoured the mother."[53]

The Puritans also realized that money is dangerous because it generates an appetite that it can never satisfy. Money never keeps its promises, they observed. "Riches are like painted grapes," wrote Henry Smith, "which look as though they would satisfy a man, but do not slake his hunger or quench his thirst. Riches indeed do make a man covet more, and get envy, and keep the mind in care."[54] Thomas Watson concurred:

The soul is a spiritual thing, riches are of an earthly extract, and how can these fill a spiritual substance? . . . How do men thirst after the world, . . . but, alas, it falls short of his expectation. It cannot fill the hiatus and longing of his soul.[55]

"Labor to fill your greatest wants, which worldly wealth will not supply," advised Richard Baxter.[56]

If money is as dangerous as all this, shouldn't a person simply avoid it? Not according to the Puritans. William Ames claimed that "riches . . . are morally neither good nor bad, but things indifferent which men may use either well or ill."[57] Thomas Adams told his city congregation, "We teach you not to cast away the bag, but covetousness."[58]

The antidote to the sins that wealth can bring is to stay clear of devotion to wealth. The Puritans' constant theme in this regard was the inner allegiance of a person's mind and affections. Baxter wrote:

Take heed of this gulf of an earthly mind. . . . Keep these things as thy upper garments, still loose about thee, that thou mayest lay them by whenever there is case: but let God and glory be next thy heart, yea, as the very blood and spirit by which thou livest.[59]

Richard Sibbes had similar advice: "Labour therefore to have the world in its own place, under thy feet."[60]

In short, the way to avoid dangers of money is to put first things first. As Baxter wrote:

> In trade, in farming, or any other profitable enterprise, we are accustomed to say of a man who has grown rich that he has made use of his time; but when heaven and the communion with God in the way, and a life of holy strength and comfort, and death full of joy and hope is to be the gain, how cheerfully should time be redeemed for these?[61]

How Much Is Enough? The Puritan Ideal of Moderation

For the Puritans, the crucial issue was not how large a person's income was but how much money was spent on oneself. The Puritan ideal was moderation. Such an ideal has, of course, appealed to many people besides the Puritans, but the concept of "temperance" was associated with the Puritans in their time.

The Puritans conceived of moderation or temperance as a golden mean between extremes. John Downame wrote that "the mean [median] estate is much to be preferred before the greatest prosperity. . . . The mean estate . . . preserveth us from forgetfulness of God, irreligion, and profaneness."[62] One of William Perkins's answers to the question, "How may a man with good conscience possess and use riches?" was, "We must use specially moderation of mind, in the possessing and using of riches, and be content with our estate."[63] John Cotton spoke in similar terms: "Faith . . . takes all success that befall [a person] in his calling with moderation. . . . Faith frames the heart to moderation."[64]

If moderation is the goal, it needs to be protected against its opposites. One of these is greed for wealth, which is frequently intertwined with covetousness. In a sermon on Matthew 6:19–20, Perkins listed the following as the thing that Christ forbids: "sundry practices of covetousness, whereof the first is excessive seeking of worldly wealth, when men keep no measure or moderation."[65] Richard Steele warned that

> the tradesman ought to watch against covetousness as a sin most repugnant to contentedness. . . . By covetousness I mean here, any insatiable desire of riches, when a man will be rich, or else thinks he cannot be happy.[66]

On the American scene, Cotton Mather denounced people's "insatiable desire after land and worldly accommodations . . . only so that they might have elbow-room in the world."[67]

Another thing that moderation stands opposed to is luxury. The Puritans looked askance at a luxurious lifestyle, no matter what form it took — one's house, clothing, recreation, or eating habits. When Richard Baxter denounced the "wealthy vices," he included a discussion of sensuality, overeating, and overindulgence in sports and recreation.[68] His "directions against prodigality and sinful wastefulness" included comments against "pampering the belly in excess . . . or costliness of meat or drink," "needless costly visits and entertainments," and "unnecessary sumptuous buildings."[69]

Such warnings against luxury were common among the Puritans. Having defined the essence of luxury with the formula "wealth more than necessary for nature and person," William Perkins proceeded to show his negative assessment of it: it is "as a knife in the hands of a child, likely to hurt, if not taken away."[70] Samuel Ward, in his college diary, listed as one of the "sins of the university" that of "excess in apparel."[71]

It would be wrong to conclude that because the Puritans were opposed to luxury they were ascetic. They did not think that denying oneself legitimate indulgences was inherently virtuous. In fact, they were as clear-sighted about the temptations of poverty as they were about the temptations of luxury. Baxter's list of temptations ran like this: "over-much care about their wants and worldly matters," discontent, covetousness, envy of the rich, neglect of spiritual duties, and neglect of "the holy education of their children."[72]

The Puritans found three keys to living moderately. One is to be *content* with a moderate lifestyle. According to one Puritan, we must

> find a contented mind with that which we have already. . . . For if once our affections shall overflow the banks of our own condition, so that in mind we burn with the desire of a better, our doings can never be persuaded [that we have enough].[73]

A second key to moderate living is the ability voluntarily to *set limits* to one's spending and indulgence. "Man may with good conscience desire and seek for goods necessary," wrote Perkins, "but he may not desire and seek for goods more than necessary, for if he doth he sinneth."[74] How does one know what is "necessary"? Obviously we cannot trust our innate desires; in the words of Perkins, "We must estimate sufficiency, not by the affection of covetous men, for them nothing shall ever be sufficient."[75] Perkins admitted that "the Scriptures do not give specific instructions on this subject."[76] But his own suggestion was eminently practical: "we must follow the example of the most sober-minded and the most modest in our social class and of about the same age as ours."[77] In short,

> Things and goods are to be judged necessary and sufficient, not by the affection of the covetous man, which is insatiable, but by two other things: the judgment of wise and godly men, and the example of sober and frugal persons.[78]

A third key to moderation is to *put wealth and possessions in perspective*. According to the Puritan outlook, the spiritual and eternal are more worthy of our time and attention than the physical and temporal. Richard Baxter wrote, "Riches will seem dust and chaff to thee, if thou believe and consider the everlasting state."[79] John Knewstub offered as an antidote to "our corrupt inclination towards the goods of our neighbors" the principle that he called "the remedy of redemption (brought us by Jesus Christ)."[80]

It can be seen, then, that when the Puritans acquired money and property, they sensed a need to be moderate in their self-gratification. While they were not ascetics, they recognized a need for curbs against greed and luxury. Positively, they saw virtue in contentment with a moderate lifestyle and in placing spiritual values over material wealth.

What Is Money For?

The more we explore Puritan attitudes, the more apparent it becomes that the key to everything they said on the topic was their conviction that money is a social good, not a private possession. Its main purpose is the welfare of everyone in society, not the personal pleasure of the person who happens to have control over it.

The genius of Puritanism was its clear-sightedness about what things are *for*, and that genius did not desert them in money matters. Everything depends on how a person uses his or her money. Baxter stated, "The question is how they use that which they labour so hard for, and save so sparingly. If they use it for God, and for charitable uses, there is no man taketh a righter course."[81]

What are the ends or uses of money? The Puritans can speak for themselves on the topic. "Riches may enable us to relieve our needy brethren, and to promote good works for church and state."[82] Money exists "for the glory of God and the good of others."[83] "The more diligently we pursue our several callings, the more we are capacitated to extend our charity to such as are in poverty and distress."[84] "God's children look to the spiritual use of those things which the worldlings use carnally."[85] In none of these comments about the purpose of earning money does one get the impression that income is something people have a right to spend on themselves simply because they have earned it.

William Perkins provides an adequate summary of how the Puritans thought money should be used:

> We must so use and possess the goods we have, that the use and possession of them may tend to God's glory, and the salvation of our souls. . . . Our riches must be employed to necessary uses. These are first, the maintenance of our own good estate and condition. Secondly, the good of others, specially those that are of our family or kindred. . . . Thirdly, the relief of the poor. . . . Fourthly, the maintenance of the Church of God, and true religion. . . . Fifth, the maintenance of the Commonwealth.[86]

Since Calvin has been much maligned on this topic, we should pause to note that his attitude about what money is for is the same as I have ascribed to the Puritans. "If we acquire possessions in gold and silver," he wrote, "it is our duty . . . to do good to our neighbors."[87] Elsewhere Calvin wrote:

> All the rich, when they have property with which they can be of service to others, are here . . . to assist their neighbors. . . . Those to whom God has given much grain and wine are to offer part of these goods to those who are in need of the same.[88]

In a discussion of "the lawful use of riches," Calvin wrote, "For the richer any man is, the more abundant are his means of doing good to others."[89]

The belief that money is a social good is also the key to Puritan views on the taking of interest. The literature on the topic of usury in the sixteenth and seventeen centuries is immense, and I can do no more than summarize the matter here.[90] In the sixteenth century the Puritans were overwhelmingly opposed to the practice of taking interest on money that had been lent. They were opposed to it because of Old Testament prohibitions against it and because of what they felt to be the spirit behind the practice, namely, covetousness and greed. As society changed, becoming less agrarian and more industrial and commercial, Puritans increasingly made a distinction between interest and usury (exploitative interest).

At first glance, the two attitudes seem contradictory, but in fact they are not. Look at what the anti-interest and pro-interest Puritans had in common: they both agreed that money is a social good and that therefore hoarding and exploitation are not permissible. In an increasingly commercial society, the most compassionate act became the willingness to lend money at a modest rate of interest. In Baxter's words, "There is an usury which is against neither justice nor charity," and he went on to describe conditions under which it is charitable.[91]

Why did the Puritans view money as a social good when, as our modern view shows, it is so much more natural to view it as a person's own possession? The Puritan outlook stemmed from a firm belief that people are stewards of what God has entrusted to them. Money is ultimately God's, not ours. In the words of an influential Puritan book, money is "that which God hath lent thee."[92] William Perkins put it thus:

> They which have riches are to consider, that God is not only the sovereign Lord, but the Lord of their riches, and that they themselves are but the stewards of God, to employ and dispense them, according to his will. Yea further, that they are to give an account unto him, both for the having and using of those riches, which they have and use.[93]

According to Baxter, "As we hold our estates under God, as owner, ruler, and benefactor, so we must devote them to him."[94]

This stewardship theory of wealth provides a sure test of whether people are spending their money well or poorly. In the words of Baxter:

> If you desired riches but for the service of your Lord and have used them for him, and can truly give in this account that you laid them not out for the needless pleasure or pride of the flesh, but to furnish yourselves and families and others for his service . . . , according to his will, and for his use, then you may expect the reward of good and faithful servants.[95]

The Puritan Critique of Modern Attitudes Toward Money

Puritans are often charged with having been the origin of modern attitudes toward money. Upon scrutiny, the things ascribed to the Puritans turn out to be secularized versions of something that the Puritans accepted only in a context of supreme allegiance to God and obedience to Christian moral standards. To show the cleavage between Puritan and modern attitudes, I have arranged Puritan views as a series of critiques of modern outlooks.

The Puritan Critique of the Success Ethic. Modern Western culture is based overwhelmingly on the success ethic — the belief that material prosperity is the ultimate value in life and that a person's worth can be measured by material or social standards. By contrast, the Puritan Thomas Watson asserted that "blessedness . . . does not lie in the acquisition of worldly things. Happiness cannot by any art of chemistry be extracted here."[96] Samuel Hieron was far from the success ethic when he prayed:

> Oh, let not mine eyes be dazzled, nor my heart bewitched with the glory and sweetness of these worldly treasures. . . . Draw my affection to the love of that durable riches, and to that fruit of heavenly wisdom which is better than gold, and the revenues whereof do surpass the silver, that my chief care may be to have a soul enriched and furnished with Thy grace.[97]

The Puritan Critique of the Self-Made Person. American culture has been strangely enamored of the image of "the self-made person" — the person who becomes rich and famous through his or her own efforts. The idea of having status handed over as a gift does not appeal to such an outlook. Yet the Puritans denied that there can even be such a thing as a self-made person. Based on an ethic of grace, Puritanism viewed prosperity solely as God's gift. John Preston wrote regarding riches that "it is God that gives them, it is he that dispenseth them, it is he that gives the reward. . . . The care of the work only belongs to us."[98]

The Puritan Critique of Modern Business Ethics. It has become an axiom of modern business that the goal of business is to make as much profit as possible and that any type of competition or selling practice is acceptable as long as it is legal. The Puritans would not agree. For one thing, they looked upon business as a service to society. "We must therefore think," wrote John Knewstub, "that when we come to buying and selling, we come to witness our love towards our neighbor by our well dealing with him in his goods."[99] William Perkins said, "The end of a man's calling is not to gather riches for himself . . . but to serve God in the serving of man, and in the seeking the good of all men."[100]

Nor would the Puritans agree with modern methods of competition or profiteering. When citizens in Boston complained that Robert Keayne charged excessive prices, the magistrates fined him two hundred pounds, and he very nearly found himself excommunicated from the church.[101] John Cotton used the trial as the occasion to lay down some business principles in a public lecture on economics. Cotton denounced as false the following premises:

> That a man might sell as dear [expensively] as he can, and buy as cheap as he can. . . . That he may sell as he bought, though he paid too dear, etc., and though the commodity be fallen, etc. That, as a man may take advantage of his own skill or ability, so he may of another's ignorance or necessity.[102]

In England, John Knewstub showed what a gulf lies between the Puritans and modern commercial practices when he wrote disparagingly of businessmen who

> come to buying and selling as it were to the razing and spoiling of some enemy's city . . . , where every man catcheth, snatcheth and carrieth away whatsoever he can come by. And he is thought the best that carrieth away the most. . . . But the Holy Ghost will bring us to another trial of our love.[103]

The Puritan Critique of the "Simple Life" Philosophy. Modern materialism has produced its own antithesis in the form of people who view affluence and possessions as inherently tainted. The Puritans were closer to such an outlook than to one supporting an affluent lifestyle, but they cannot be fitted comfortably here either. William Perkins wrote, "These earthly things are the good gifts of God, which no man can simply condemn, without injury to God's disposing hand and providence, who hath ordained them for natural life."[104] The Puritans were also wary of a blanket condemnation of people who have a higher standard of living than some other people. In the words of Perkins,

> We must not make one measure of sufficiency of goods necessary for all persons, for it varies according to the diverse conditions of persons, and according to time and place. More things are necessary to a public person than to a private; and more to him that has a charge than to a single man.[105]

The Puritan Critique of Socialism. A final force in modern life of which the Puritans would not approve is socialism, whether in its overt form of governmental ownership or in its subtle form of the welfare state. William Ames wrote, "Ownership and differences in the amount of possessions are ordinances of God and approved by him, Prov. 22:2; 2 Thess. 3:12."[106] John Robinson commented:

> God could, if he would, either have made men's states more equal, or have given every one sufficient of his own. But he hath rather chosen to make some rich, and some poor, that one might stand in need of another, and help another, that so he might try the mercy and goodness of them that are able, in supplying the wants of the rest.[107]

As my discussion has suggested, the Puritans would have shared some of the assumptions of many different groups on the economic scene today. But they would stand aghast at what secularism and self-interest have made of principles that they placed in a Christian context.

Summary

One of the ironies in the history of the Puritans is that their very industriousness and plain living tended to make them relatively affluent. Their virtues produced corresponding temptations. On the one hand, the Puritans held attitudes conducive to the amassing of wealth and property: the view that money and property are good in principle, disbelief that poverty is meritorious in itself, and a conviction that a disciplined and hardworking lifestyle is virtuous.

On the other hand, to curb the potential for self-indulgence that followed in the wake of their lifestyle, the Puritans had an even longer list of cautions: an awareness that God sends poverty as well as riches, an obsession with the dangers of wealth, the ideal of moderation, a doctrine of stewardship in which God is viewed as the ultimate owner of goods, and a view of money as a social good.

FURTHER READING

R. H. Tawney, *Religion and the Rise of Capitalism* (1926).

Max Weber, *The Protestant Ethic and the Spirit of Capitalism* (English ed., 1930).

E. A. J. Johnson, *American Economic Thought in the Seventeenth Century* (1932).

Albert Hyma, *Christianity, Capitalism and Communism: A Historical Analysis* (1937).

Richard B. Schlatter, *The Social Ideas of Religious Leaders, 1660–1688* (1940).

Robert W. Green, ed., *Protestantism and Capitalism: The Weber Thesis and Its Critics* (1959).

H. M. Robertson, *Aspects of the Rise of Economic Individualism* (1959).

M. J. Kitch, ed., *Capitalism and the Reformation* (1967).

Stephen Foster, *Their Solitary Way: The Puritan Social Ethic in the First Century of Settlement in New England* (1971).

Richard L. Greaves, *Society and Religion in Elizabethan England* (1981).

The Puritan home was a center for spiritual and educational activities as well as family life. Here a Puritan father instructs his family in singing. Frontispiece to *The Whole Book of the Psalms;* courtesy of the Folger Shakespeare Library [STC 2431 frontispiece]

Chapter 5

Family

You must live religion as well as talk religion.
— ELEAZAR MATHER

A well-known pastor has made the following observations about the breakdown of the family:

> Nowadays one has more to do with marriage than with all other matters. Because of them we can hardly read, preach, or study.

> I have observed many married couples coming together in such great passion that they were ready to devour each other for love, but after a half year the one ran away from the other.

> I have known people who have become hostile to each other after they had five or six children and were bound to each other not merely by marriage but also by the fruits of their union. Yet they left each other.

The quoted pastor is Martin Luther.[1] His comments stand as a signpost at the very outset of this chapter that the age of the Puritans was no stranger to societal assaults on the Christian family. Faced with the same pressures that confront us today, the Puritans formulated a theory of the family that offers some attractive possibilities for our own age.

What Is a Family For?

The Puritans' thinking about the family was guided throughout by their definition of the purpose of a family. According to the Puritans, the primary purpose of a family is to glorify God. Benjamin Wadsworth theorized that every Christian . . . should do all he can to promote the glory of God, and the welfare of those about him; and the well ordering matters in particular families tends to promote these things.[2]

Richard Baxter applied the same principle to the raising of children when he wrote that "it is no small mercy to be the parents of a Godly seed: and this is the end of the institution of marriage."[3] According to Isaac Ambrose, husband and wife have the task of "erecting and establishing Christ's glorious kingdom in their house."[4]

The Puritans could so confidently view the purpose of a family as being the glory of God partly because they believed that God had established the institution of the family. In the words of William Perkins, "Marriage was made . . . by God himself, to be the fountain . . . of all other sorts and kinds of life in the commonwealth and in the church."[5]

What is important about viewing the purpose of the family as the glory of God? In the long run it determines what goes on in a family. It sets the priorities in a spiritual rather than material direction. It determines what a family does with its time and how it spends its money.

Once the primary purpose of the family had been defined, the Puritans went on to state further goals. They believed that the family was the foundational unit of a godly society. "Such as families are," wrote James Fitch, "such at last the church and commonwealth must be."[6] William Gouge characterized the family as "a school wherein the first principles and grounds of government and subjection are learned," while someone else called the family "a true image of the commonwealth. . . . All will be well with the commonwealth where families are properly regulated."[7]

According to Puritan thinking, the very nature and moral fiber of society depend on what children have picked up — or failed to pick up — in the family. "Well-ordered families," said Cotton Mather, "naturally produce a good order in other societies. When families are under an ill discipline, all other societies [will be] ill disciplined."[8]

Although the Puritans emphasized the family as an institution designed first of all to benefit God and society, they did not neglect the idea that the purpose of a family is also the personal fulfillment of every member of a family. At this level, the common themes are companionship and mutual support. According to Henry Smith, one purpose of marriage is "to avoid the inconvenience of solitariness"; God provided marriage and family "that the infinite troubles which lie upon us in this world might be eased with the comfort and help one of another."[9] William Ames spoke of marriage as "the institution of God which establishes the individual companionship of husband and wife."[10]

Because the Puritans had such a high view of the purpose of the family, they naturally viewed it as a calling — a public good and even a form of social action. According to William Gouge:

> The private vocations of a family and functions appertaining thereto, are such as Christians are called unto by God. . . . This is to be noted for satisfaction of certain weak consciences, who think that if they have no public calling they have no calling at all. . . . A conscionable performance of household duties . . . may be accounted a public work.[11]

The Puritans' high view of what a family exists for resulted in the worth and dignity with which they endowed family roles and activities.

What is a family for? Robert Cleaver provided a succinct summary of all that I have delineated:

> A household is as it were a little commonwealth, by the good government whereof God's glory may be advanced, the commonwealth which standeth of several families benefited, and all that live in that family may receive much comfort and commodity.[12]

The Headship of the Husband/Father

The Puritans' theory of the family was based on a hierarchy of authority. Their attitude can be summarized in a simple formula: they accepted the headship of husband and father as a biblical command and then proceeded to define the nature of that headship in a responsible manner.

Hierarchy in the family means, first of all, that the husband and father is the accountable head for what happens and the one who is finally responsible for seeing that essential matters are happening in a family. Luther and Calvin had established the version of the doctrine that the Puritans accepted. Calvin had written, "Let the husband so rule as to be the head . . . of his wife. Let the woman . . . yield modestly to his demands."[13] Luther had stated that "a wife is indeed to live according to the direction of her husband; what he bids and commands is to be done."[14]

The Puritans similarly believed in the headship of the husband/father. William Perkins wrote that "the husband is he which hath authority over the wife, they twaine being but one flesh, he is also the head over the wife."[15] Thomas Gataker claimed that "the husband is as the head, the wife as the body."[16]

Modeled on Christ's headship of the church, the husband's headship, according to the Puritans, is not a ticket to privilege but a charge to responsibility. It does not entitle a husband to tell others what to do. According to John Robinson, the two things particularly required of the husband are "love . . . and wisdom." His love for his wife must be "like Christ's to his church: holy for quality, and great for quantity."[17] Thomas Gataker used similar terms in saying that "the wife's main duty . . . is subjection, the man's principally love."[18]

Headship did not, for the Puritans, mean tyranny. It was leadership based on love. Benjamin Wadsworth wrote that a good husband will "make his government of her as easy and gentle as possible, and strive more to be loved than feared."[19] According to Samuel Willard, a good husband will so rule "as that his wife may take delight in [his headship], and not account it a slavery but a liberty and privilege."[20]

The Place of the Wife/Mother

In Puritan theory, the counterpart of the husband's headship was the wife's submission. William Ames wrote that the "community of mutual help" that constitutes marriage is "mutual for husband and wife, and should be observed equally in all essential and principal matters, provided that that difference of degree between husband and wife — that the husband govern and the wife obey — be observed in all."[21] The wife's task, said a Puritan preacher, is "to guide the house and not guide the husband."[22]

A common theme in Puritan discussions of the wife's submission was that God commands it in Scripture. According to William Gouge, "Though there seem to be never so little disparity, yet God having so expressly appointed subjection, it ought to be acknowledged."[23] Thomas Gataker wrote that a wife should "acknowledge her husband and her head," while another Puritan pastor claimed that "God . . . appointed to woman to be in subjection to her husband."[24]

What did submission mean in this context? As defined by the Puritans, hierarchy is a matter of function and not of worth, a style of managing a family, not an assessment of personal value. John Robinson theorized that God created man and woman spiritually equal, "neither is she, since the creation more degenerated than he from the primitive goodness." Yet in marriage one of the two must have the final authority, since "differences will arise and be seen, and so the one must give way, and apply unto the other; this, God and nature layeth upon the man."[25] According to Robert Cleaver, the wife should "submit herself unto him, acknowledging him to be her head, that finally they may so agree in one, as the conjunction of marriage doth require."[26]

Submission, of course, is something that a wife must yield at her own initiative. If a husband has to force it, the battle has already been lost. Perhaps this accounts for the frequency with which Puritan preachers appealed to the wife to submit to her husband. Their way of phrasing the appeal varied. John Winthrop said that a Christian wife's submission is "her honor and freedom. . . . Such is the liberty of the church under the authority of Christ."[27] Gataker admonished the wife "in holy wisdom and godly discretion . . . to acknowledge her husband as . . . her head."[28] The emphasis in all such Puritan statements was on the attitude of the wife as the crucial element.

Like Calvin, the Puritans distinguished between spiritual and social equality. Spiritually husband and wife are equal. In the social institution of the family, however, there is a hierarchy of authority. Robert Bolton expressed the spiritual equality by saying that a man's "wife hath as noble a soul as his himself. . . . Souls have no sexes."[29] Robert Cleaver combined spiritual equality with functional hierarchy when he wrote that "the husband and wife are equal in . . . everlasting life" but "unequal as touching the governance and conversation at home."[30]

How the Pattern of Authority Actually Worked

It will be helpful to explore how the theory I have outlined actually worked. The husband's headship did not mean that the wife was his servant. John Downame made this clear when he wrote that God "gave the wife unto the husband to be, not his servant, but his helper, counselor, and comforter."[31] The most customary Puritan term for defining the relationship was to call the wife an assistant. Gataker called the wife "an help, or an assistant; not a mate only, but an helper; not a companion only, but an assistant too."[32]

Nor did the wife's submission mean to the Puritans that women are less intelligent than men. Some Puritans did argue thus, but not all of them. Samuel Torshell wrote that "women are capable of the highest improvement and the greatest glory to which man may be advanced."[33]

Hierarchy did not mean that a wife could not debate an issue with her husband. Samuel Willard expected a husband to be obeyed only if he can support his viewpoint from the Bible, "and lay before her a sufficient conviction of her duty, to comply with him therein; for he hath no authority or compulsion." A wife, he continued, "hath greater liberty of debating the prudence of the thing" than do other subordinates. There is even a duty of mutual admonition: both husband and wife should "choose the fittest seasons to reprove each other, for things which their love and duty calls for."[34]

The Puritans believed that there are spheres of responsibility in a family and that the wife is the authority in some of these spheres. The wife, for example, was, next to the husband/father, the authority over children and household servants. According to Samuel Willard, "She is invested with an authority over them by God; and her husband is to allow it to her. . . . For though the husband be the head of the wife, she is an head of the family."[35] Samuel Sewall recorded in his diary that he had delegated the family finances to his wife for the reason that she had "a better faculty than I at managing affairs."[36]

The principle involved here is that (in the words of John Milton) "particular exceptions" to the husband's authority "may have place, if she exceed her husband in prudence and dexterity, and he contentedly yield, for then a superior and more natural law comes in, that the wiser should govern the less wise, whether male or female."[37] William Gouge said that "there are many things in well governing a family more fit for one to meddle withal than for the other," and he gave examples for both husband and wife.[38]

The practice of hierarchy did not prevent a woman from religious teaching or spiritual admonition of a man. "Women may and must privately and familiarly exhort others," wrote one Puritan writer on the subject; "they may also privately admonish men and reprove them."[39] The Chester minister Nicholas Byfield declared that the wife was not subject to the husband

> in matters of her soul and religion when his will is contrary to God's will. . . . And again, she is not so subject but she may admonish and advise her husband with certain cautions, as if she be sure the thing she speaks against be sinful and hurtful.[40]

Even though the husband was, in the final analysis, the accountable head of the family, in the day-to-day oversight of the family the husband and wife shared the authority for what happened. "In general the government of the family . . . belongeth to the husband and wife and both," wrote William Gouge.[41] William Perkins regarded the husband as the "chief ruler" and the wife as "the associate, not only in office and authority, but also in advice and counsel unto him."[42]

Parental Responsibility to Children

Puritan attitudes toward children were rooted in the conviction that children belong to God and are entrusted to parents as a stewardship. "The children born in our families are born unto God," declared Deodat Lawson; God "put them out to us."[43] According to Cotton Mather, parents "must give an account of the souls that belong unto their families."[44] Thomas Watson believed Christian parents "will endeavor that their children may be more God's children than theirs."[45]

The customary way of expressing this view that parents are responsible to God for their children was the familiar covenant terminology. Benjamin Wadsworth wrote regarding children that God

> calls them his. . . . They belong to him by covenant; they have been solemnly consecrated to his service; and what, will you not bring them up for him, to whom you have thus solemnly consecrated them?[46]

In a similar vein, Thomas Cobbett wrote that

> the greatest love and faithfulness which parents as covenanters can show to God, and to their children, who in and with themselves are joint covenanters with God, is so to educate them, that . . . the conditions of the covenant may be attended by their children, and so the whole covenant fully effected.[47]

The essence of a covenant is the idea of contractual obligation. The framework of covenant theology increased rather than decreased the Puritans' sense of parental responsibility for their children. Some of the most solemn of all Puritan warnings are warnings against parental neglect to train children properly. In the most memorable of these passages, Richard Mather imagined children on the Judgment Day addressing parents who have neglected their training:

> All this that we here suffer is through you: you should have taught us the things of God, and did not; you should have restrained us from sin and corrected us, and you did not; you were the means of our original corruption and guiltiness, and yet you never showed any competent care that we might be delivered from it. . . . Woe unto us that we had such carnal and careless parents, and woe unto you that had no more compassion and pity to prevent the everlasting misery of your own children.[48]

Exactly what is a parent's responsibility to a child? It obviously includes physical provision. "If others in a family suffer want," commented Samuel Willard, "yet the children shall certainly be taken care for, as long as there is anything to be had."[49] New England laws insisting on provision for children were enforced.[50]

As an extension of physical provision, Puritans insisted on the importance of teaching children to work, thereby insuring that children would become productive members of society in their adult years. According to New England laws, every father was required to see that his children were instructed "in some honest lawful calling, labor or employment, either in husbandry, or some other trade profitable for themselves and the commonwealth."[51] Benjamin Wadsworth said that parents should bring children "up to business, some lawful employment," adding that if parents trained their children to be "serviceable in their generation," they did "better for them than if you should bring them up idly, and yet leave them great estates."[52]

For the Puritans, however, the spiritual and moral training of children was no less important than their physical provision. "If you have any compassion for them," said John Hull in a Boston sermon, "take pains that they may know God."[53] Cotton Mather agreed:

> Before all, and above all, tis the knowledge of the Christian religion that parents are to teach their children. . . . The knowledge of other things, though it be never so desirable an accomplishment for them, our children may arrive to eternal happiness without it. . . . But the knowledge of the godly doctrine in the words of the Lord Jesus Christ is of a million times more necessity for them.[54]

One of the most thrilling of all Puritan documents is the 1677 resolution of the members of the church in Dorchester, Massachusetts, to undertake a reformation of their lives. Part of the covenant that they signed was the resolve

> to reform our families, engaging ourselves to a conscientious care to set up and maintain the worship of God in them and to walk in our houses with perfect hearts in a faithful discharge of all domestic duties: educating, instructing, and charging our children and our households to keep the ways of the Lord.[55]

Disciplining Children

The Puritans believed that an important part of the religious training of children consisted of discipline. For the Puritans, moreover, discipline involved the idea of restraining negative inclinations. John Norton claimed that "doctrine and example alone are insufficient; discipline is an essential part of the nurture of the Lord."[56] Cotton Mather's aphorism "Better whipt, than damned" summed up a major tenet of Puritan child-rearing philosophy.[57] John Eliot expressed the same attitude thus:

> The gentle rod of the mother is a very gentle thing, it will break neither bone nor skin: yet by the blessing of God with it, and upon the wise application of it, it would break the bond that bindeth up corruption in the heart.[58]

According to the Puritans, obedience in the spheres of church and state depended on discipline in the home. Wadsworth theorized that

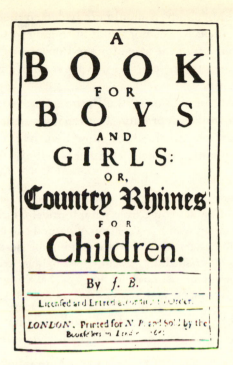

Despite his harried life, John Bunyan found time to write for children. Courtesy of the special collections of the Wheaton College Library

"young persons won't much mind what's said by ministers in public if they are not instructed at home: nor will they much regard good laws made by civil authority if they are not well counseled and governed at home."[59]

To guard against the abuse of breaking a child's spirit in the process of curbing his or her will, the Puritans stressed the need for gentle discipline and adapting the discipline to the temperament of the child. "Diverse children have their different natures," wrote Anne Bradstreet; "those parents are wise that can fit their nurture according to their nature."[60] Samuel Willard advised, "Know their natural inclinations, dispositions [and] use severity as the last means."[61] Richard Greenham claimed that parents should discipline children in an awareness that they themselves might be the source of the child's wayward tendency, and that they should therefore discipline "with the mildest means and with least rigor."[62]

The idea of accountability was deeply ingrained into the Puritan consciousness. Applied to child-rearing, accountability meant not allowing children to grow up without adult guidance and supervision. The

Puritan rule was that "children should not be left to themselves, to a loose end, to do as they please . . . , not being fit to govern themselves."[63] The cost of such discipline was the same for the Puritans as for parents in any age: an enormous outlay of alertness, perseverance, time, and physical and emotional energy.

The theological foundation of the Puritan emphasis on child training was original sin or innate depravity. The Puritans believed that children, if left to themselves, are "inclined to follow their own evil will."[64] In one of the most frequently quoted comments along these lines, John Robinson wrote,

> And surely there is in all children, though not alike, a stubbornness, and stoutness of mind arising from natural pride, which must . . . be broken and beaten down. . . . This fruit of natural corruption and root of actual rebellion against God and man must be destroyed, and no manner of way nourished. . . . For the beating and keeping down of this stubbornness parents must provide . . . that children's wills and wilfulness be restrained and repressed.[65]

The theological premise underlying such statements is that children are lost and in need of conversion. According to one Puritan source:

> The young child which lieth in the cradle is both wayward and full of affections; and though his body be but small, yet he hath a great heart, and is altogether inclined to evil. . . . If this sparkle be suffered to increase, it will rage and burn down the whole house. For we are changed and become good not by birth but by education. . . . Therefore parents must be wary and circumspect. . . ; they must correct and sharply reprove their children for saying or doing ill.[66]

Samuel Willard summed up the paradoxical Puritan attitude toward children when he called them "innocent vipers."[67]

These statements do not accord well with modern sentimental attitudes toward children. Yet we should not let the harshness of the tone and the tactlessness of the statements divert us from the essential issue. Either children are born good and can be allowed to follow their instinctive bent, or they are born sinful and in need of redirection. Our culture generally accepts the former principle, the Puritans the latter.

Some Progressive Puritan Attitudes Toward Child Development

On three crucial issues the Puritans anticipated current theories of child development. One is the importance of early training. John Cotton wrote that "these babes are flexible and easily bowed; it is far more easy to train them up to good things now, than in their youth and riper years."[68] Samuel Willard theorized that since Satan begins his assaults upon children in their infancy, "if you would prevent him, do not delay, but be dropping in instruction as they are able, and as soon as they are able to understand anything."[69]

What generated this Puritan preoccupation with the early spiritual training of children? Mainly their observations. Richard Baxter noted, "I am forced to judge that most of the children of the godly that are ever renewed are renewed in their childhood."[70] The counterpart of this observation is that it is hard to reverse a bad habit that has been picked up in childhood: "If we have been used or accustomed to a course of outward scandalous wickedness, or inward impenitency, hardness of heart, and unbelief, it will be very hard when we come to break off from it."[71]

A second Puritan principle that modern theory credits is that parents teach more through their example than by their words. Richard Greenham wrote, "Experience teacheth us that children like or mislike more by countenance, gesture, and behavior than by rule, doctrine, precept, or instruction."[72] Eleazar Mather wrote:

> Precept without patterns will do little good; you must lead them to Christ by examples as well as counsel; you must set yourselves first, and speak by lives as well as words; you must live religion, as well as talk religion.[73]

Within such a context, the Puritans were particularly concerned about the ability of a bad example to wipe out good instruction. One of them wrote:

> Be sure to set good example before your children. . . . Other methods of instruction probably will not do much good, if you don't teach them by a godly example. Don't think your children will mind the good rules you give them if you act contrary to those rules yourselves. . . . If your counsels are good, and your examples evil, your children will be more like to be hurt by the latter, than benefited by the former.[74]

An English Puritan said something very similar:

> If parents would have their children blessed at church and at school, let them beware they give their children no corrupt examples at home by any carelessness, profaneness, or ungodliness. Otherwise, parents will do them more harm at home than both pastors and schoolmasters can do them good abroad.[75]

In short, parents earn the right to inculcate theory in their children.

A third Puritan principle that we accept today is that effective child training has two sides to it, one negative, one positive. Parents must curb a child's will but foster and encourage his or her spirit. They need to depress impulses toward selfishness and dishonesty and unsociable manners while at the same time building a child's self-image and lovable qualities. The negative task is to "restrain, reprove, correct"; it must be balanced by the parents' resolve to "nourish in themselves a very tender love and affection to their children, and . . . manifest it."[76]

Thomas Cobbett outlined the double task in greater detail:

> When parents by wise observations do perceive the bent and bias of their children, now let them carry it towards them accordingly. If they be strongly bent to some vice more than others . . . admonish them betimes in the evil of it. . . . If children, either by common or saving influences of the Spirit, are more ingenuous spirits, and of better and more hopeful dispositions, oh let parents, as they discern the same, encourage the same all the prudent and pious ways that may be.[77]

Puritan theory steered a middle course between harshness and leniency. According to Samuel Willard, parents "ought to maintain their authority by avoiding extremes of rigor and indulgence. As children are not to be treated either as brutes or slaves, so neither with fondness and letting them enjoy their wills in everything."[78]

Despite their harsh comments about the depraved nature of children, the Puritans actually had an optimistic view of the possibility of children becoming youthful Christians. Thomas Hooker wrote, "Let's bring our children as near to Heaven as we can. . . . It is in our power to restrain them, and reform them, and that we ought to do."[79] Cotton Mather said that "young saints will make old angels; and, blessed be God, there are such young saints in the world."[80] Mather recalled his own childhood thus:

> The great care of my godly parents was to bring me up in the nurture and the admonition of the Lord: whence I was kept from many visible outbreakings of sin which else I had been guilty of; and whence it was that I had many good impressions of the Spirit of God upon me, even from my infancy.[81]

The Spiritualization of the Family

The Puritans' favorite image for the family was a church. Richard Baxter wrote that "a Christian family . . . is a church . . . , a society of Christians combined for the better worshipping and serving God."[82] William Gouge said that the family is "a little church," while William

Puritan children at play. From Johann A. Comenius, *Orbis Sensualium Pictus;* courtesy of the Folger Shakespeare Library [Wing C5525 p. 276]

Perkins wrote, "These families wherein this service of God is performed are, as it were, little churches, yea even a kind of Paradise upon earth."[83]

The Puritans knew that the church can never be a substitute for the religious life of a family. In fact, the health of the church depends on what happens in the family. Richard Greenham claimed that "if ever we would have the church of God to continue among us, we must bring it into our households, and nourish it in our families."[84] William Cartwright insisted that catechizing should be carried on "both at home by the master of the house, and in the church by the minister"; to the question, "Why at home?" he replied, "Because houses are the nurseries of the church."[85]

The picture of the family as a miniature church goes far toward explaining exactly what the Puritans did in their homes. To begin, worship was a regular part of the household routine. Nicholas Byfield advised, "Parents should carefully set up the worship of God in the family that from their cradles [children] may see the practice of piety."[86] Samuel Willard claimed that the church should "look to all the families that they maintain family worship and instruction."[87] Increase Mather's church in Boston made the following commitment:

> We promise (by the help of Christ) that we will endeavor to walk before God in our houses, with a perfect heart; and that we will uphold the worship of God therein continually, according as he in his word requires, both in respect of prayer and reading the Scriptures, that so the word of Christ may dwell richly in us.[88]

In viewing the family as a church, the Puritans made family devotions a standard feature of their life. According to Baxter's *Christian Directory*, family worship should be held twice each weekday:

> It is seasonable every morning to give thanks for the rest of the night past . . . and to beg directions, protection and provisions and blessing for the following day . . . and that the evening is a fit season to give God thanks for the mercies of the day, and to confess the sins of the day, and ask forgiveness, and to pray for rest and protection in the night.[89]

Benjamin Wadsworth spoke in similar terms when he wrote, "We should not (unless some extraordinary matter prevents) suffer one day to pass without reading some portion of the Word of God."[90]

In such a routine, family worship became a major point of family unity. In the words of Thomas Paget, family devotions are appropriate

> because the members of the same family do usually . . . share and partake more or less both in the welfare and in the miseries of one another mutually. And therefore they ought to use the means that God has sanctified and ordained for the mutual good and benefit of one another.[91]

If the church was a center for instruction in Christian doctrine and morals, so was the family, "the little church." John Penry said that fathers were bound to bring children and servants "in instruction and information to the Lord."[92] Thomas Taylor stressed the need "to instruct every one of [a] family in the fear of God."[93]

The technique that the Puritans found most effective in Christian instruction was catechizing. This question-answer format accorded well both with the Puritans' stress on the intellectual content of the faith and their penchant to have matters well-defined. Richard Baxter devoted a section of *The Reformed Pastor* to the topic "the duty of personal catechizing and instructing the flock particularly recommended." The goal of catechizing was not memorization but understanding. Cotton Mather cautioned parents not to let "the children patter out by rote the words of the catechism, like parrots; but be inquisitive how far their understandings do take in the things of God."[94]

Something else that the Puritans did not hesitate to do was to call their own private special religious days. The Puritans rejected the church calendar of Catholicism, with its host of holy days, but they supplemented their Sunday observance with family days of fasting and of thanksgiving.

Families do not automatically become spiritual entities. Someone has to orchestrate the activities. In Puritan thinking, the father was that person. The Geneva Bible stated that "masters in their houses ought to be as preachers to their families, that from the highest to the lowest they may obey the will of God."[95] Another Puritan authority theorized that "God chargeth the master of the family with all in the family."[96]

According to the Puritans, another key to the spiritualization of the family was to guard the spiritual integrity of marriage. Husband and wife, they said, need to stir each other up to high spiritual standards before a family will be strongly Christian. "Virtue and piety," wrote Wadsworth, "are rather to be sought for in an husband or wife than beauty or riches."[97] John Cotton spoke of marriage as something to make a couple "better fitted for God's service, and bring them nearer to God."[98]

Summary

The family provided a good test case for the Puritans to apply their covenantal theology. Covenant meant relationship, first to God and then to other persons. Beginning with the premise that the purpose of a family is to glorify God, the Puritans attempted to make their families a "little church." The family was ideally a place of sanctified relationships and the mutual worship of God.

The idea of a "well-ordered" family also goes a long way toward explaining the Puritan household. In Puritan theory and practice, a well-ordered family was a hierarchical one in which the husband/father was the accountable head, the wife/mother his subordinate with her own spheres of responsibility, and children subject to the discipline and nurture of both parents.

The Puritan theory of child development stressed that children were, like their parents, fallen creatures whose sinful bent needed to be redirected toward God and moral goodness. The threefold foundation of Puritan childbearing was the importance of early training, the influence of example as well as precept, and a balance between restraint and positive support.

FURTHER READING

Charles H. George and Katherine George, *The Protestant Mind of the English Reformation, 1570–1640* (1961).

Christopher Hill, *Society and Puritanism in Pre-Revolutionary England*, chap. 13 (1964).

Edmund S. Morgan, *The Puritan Family: Religion and Domestic Relations in Seventeenth-Century New England* (1944, rev. ed. 1966).

John Demos, *A Little Commonwealth: Family Life in Plymouth Colony* (1970).

Levin L. Schücking, *The Puritan Family: A Social Study from the Literary Sources* (1970).

Lawrence Stone, *The Family, Sex and Marriage in England, 1500–1800* (1977).

Joyce L. Irwin, *Womanhood in Radical Protestantism, 1525–1675* (1979).

Richard L. Greaves, *Society and Religion in Elizabethan England* (1981).

Laurel Thatcher Ulrich, *Good Wives: Image and Reality in the Lives of Women in Northern New England, 1650–1750* (1982).

Steven Ozment, *When Fathers Ruled: Family Life in Reformation Europe* (1983).

The children born in our families are born unto God.

— DEODAT LAWSON

All will be well in the commonwealth where families are properly regulated.

— WILLIAM GOUGE

A Christian family . . . is a church . . . , a society of Christians combined for the better worshipping and serving God.

— RICHARD BAXTER

Preaching was at the vital center of Puritanism. Here New England Puritans walk to hear a sermon at church. Courtesy of the Billy Graham Center, Wheaton College

Chapter 6

Puritan Preaching

There is not a sermon which is heard, but it sets us nearer heaven or hell.

— JOHN PRESTON

To set the stage for my remarks about Puritan preaching, I invite you to accompany me to England near the turn of the sixteenth century. Laurence Chaderton, first Master of Emmanuel College, Cambridge, is preaching in his native Lancashire. This northern shire is Catholic territory. People do not often hear good sermons. Chaderton has preached for two hours. He is about to conclude and says something to the effect "that he would no longer trespass upon their patience."

But the audience will not allow the preacher to stop. "For God's sake, sir, go on, go on," they urge. "Hereat," we are told, "Mr. Chaderton was surprised into a longer discourse, beyond his expectation, in satisfaction of their importunity."[1]

The incident is noteworthy, not because it was rare during the Puritan movement, but because it was common.

If we will look at the English Puritans for a moment through the eyes of their religious opponents, we find that what these antagonists feared most about the Puritans was their preaching. It was through the pulpit that Puritanism made its mark on the English nation in the early seventeenth century. The Anglican Bishop of London complained about Puritan meetings that "the people resort them as in popery they were wont to run on pilgrimage."[2]

That arch defender of Anglicanism, Richard Hooker, grudgingly conceded that Puritan sermons were more popular than Anglican homilies. He noted that "sermons only are observed to prevail so much, while all means else seem to sleep and do nothing," and he described "that singular affection and attention which the people showeth everywhere towards [sermons], and their cold disposition to [homilies]."[3]

Anything that excited the Christian public's devotion to this degree deserves a closer look. How can we account for the appeal of Puritan preaching?

A Portrait of the Puritan Minister

It has been rightly said about the Puritans that "a lifetime spent listening to sermons . . . inevitably produced a knowledgeable and critical laity with definite ideas about preaching and preachers."[4] I suggest, therefore, that we pause to glimpse the Puritan ideal of the minister by listening to some Puritan comments on the subject.

When John Field was suspended from his preaching position in London, his parishioners petitioned for his return, citing his "faithful pains taken amongst us, . . . preaching purely the word of God, and catechizing our youth, teaching obedience to God and our prince, and keeping us in great order."[5] One of the numerous "declarations" that the Puritan movement produced said that the "three parts of a pastor's duty" were "to preach, to minister the sacraments, and to pray."[6]

William Perkins theorized that "every true minister is a double interpreter — God's interpreter to the people by preaching to them from God, and the people's interpreter to God, laying open their wants, confessing their sins, craving pardon and forgiveness."[7] It was said of Richard Greenham that "his masterpiece was in comforting wounded consciences."[8] The collected letters of Rev. Thomas Wilcox were touted as "godly, plain and necessary exhortations and directions for the exercise of godliness."[9]

A survey of parishes made for Parliament in 1584–1585 used such designations as the following to commend pastors of whom the Puritans approved: "honest of conversation," "learned in the tongues," "learned, zealous and godly and fit for the ministry."[10] In America John Cotton considered "that it was his duty to preach with such a plainness, as became the Oracles of God, which are intended for the conduct of men in the paths of Life."[11]

Such commendatory phrases give us an ever-expanding portrait of the ideal Puritan minister. The commonest laudatory epithet, however, was "godly and learned."[12] Why the emphasis on "godly" preachers? It was partly a reaction against abuses in the Anglican church, where many clerics held their positions as a form of patronage.[13] A constant Puritan theme was the scandalous lifestyle of people who held positions in the church but lacked the spiritual qualifications to do so. "How many also," complained Walter Travers, "be there admitted to the government of the church of most wicked life and ungodly behavior."[14]

Given the patronage framework, many Anglican clerics were "in it for the money" and drew salaries in parishes where they did not reside. One Elizabethan bishop, William Hughes of St. Asaph's, held an archdeaconry and sixteen church livings, as well as leasing lands to his wife, children, sisters, and cousins. More typical was Archbishop Bancroft, who held six livings.[15] The lifestyle of many of these clerics was a constant scandal to the Puritans. A church visitation by Puritan surveyors uncovered Anglican rectors and vicars variously characterized as "an alehouse haunter," "consumed by carding, dicing, and gaming," "a drunkard and whoremaster," and a priest whose "chiefest trade is to cure hawks that are hurt or diseased."[16]

In such a context, it is easy to see why Puritans placed such a premium on "godly pastors." Richard Bernard summed up the Puritan attitude by saying that "common people respect more a preacher's life than his learning."[17] William Perkins sounded a similar note: "He must first be godly affected himself who would stir up godly affections in other men."[18] According to a modern scholar, by making the liturgy the central activity of the pastor, the Anglican church created a system in which "the intelligence and morals of the parish priest were of little importance in any ultimate sense," whereas the Puritan emphasis on sermons "required an educated clergy capable of speaking with moral authority."[19]

We can also learn something about how the Puritans viewed the minister by noting the titles by which he was known. The Anglicans retained the Catholic term "priest," with its connotations of professional church status. The Puritans chose the titles "minister" and "pastor." "Minister" names what these men did: they ministered to and helped people with their needs. The term "pastor" or "shepherd" is equally telling: a shepherd is above all someone who feeds and oversees a flock.

What emerges from the foregoing sketch is a multifaceted role that combines teaching, administering the sacraments, nurturing consciences, role modeling the godly life, and counseling.[20] But none of these tasks was primary.

The Puritans were unanimous in saying that the pastor's primary task was preaching. Arthur Hildersham claimed that preaching was "the chief work" of a pastor, while John Owen believed that "the first and principal duty of a pastor is to feed the flock by diligent preaching of the word."[21] William Bradshaw, in his contemporary survey of the Puritan movement, offers us this portrait:

They hold that the highest and supreme office and authority of the pastor is to preach the gospel solemnly and publicly to the congregation, by interpreting the written word of God, and applying the same by exhortation and reproof unto them. They hold that this was the greatest work that Christ and his Apostles did.[22]

The Popularity and Impact of Puritan Preaching

The popularity of Puritan preaching in its day was breathtaking. Henry Smith was so popular and his church so crowded that (in the words of Thomas Fuller) "persons of good quality brought their own pews with them, I mean their legs, to stand upon in the aisles."[23] Christopher Hill has adduced evidence that having a good preacher was an economic asset to a market town because it drew crowds to town to listen to the preacher's market-day lecture.[24] The fame of William Whately as a preacher spread so far that "great wits" and persons of many persuasions from Oxford traveled the twenty miles to Banbury to hear him preach.[25] It is no wonder that Michael Walzer calls the preacher "the hero of sixteenth-century Puritanism."[26]

One of the biggest problems facing the Anglican church became the practice of "gadding to sermons," meaning that laypeople would desert their own parish to attend a neighboring one that had good preaching, which almost invariably meant Puritan preaching. George Walker, a Lancashire-born London preacher, describes in vivid language how the people of his native county

> are ready and willing to run many miles to hear sermons when they have them not at home, and lay aside all care of profit, leaving their labour and work on weekdays to frequent public meetings for prophecy and expounding of God's word.[27]

William Dyke was so popular that

> many absent themselves from their own parish churches on the Sabbath day, yea refuse to hear their own ministers . . . and repair to Dyke to hear him, and many of this gadding people came from far and went home late.[28]

The Puritan pulpit influenced the soul of a nation partly because the Puritan preachers gained the ear of leaders in society, especially young men on the rise. Richard Sibbes "edified the Puritan spirit at Gray's Inn" and his friend John Preston drew crowds at Lincoln's Inn, the two most prestigious law schools in England.[29] When Bishop Scambler of Peterborough complained about people's preference for a preaching service over the Anglican service from the Book of Common Prayer, he noted with alarm regarding the Puritan preachers that "to their purposes they have drawn divers young ministers. . . . In their ways they be very bold and stout, like men that seem not to be without great friends."[30]

The popularity of Puritan preaching was partly the result of the momentousness that Puritans attached to it. John Preston sounded the keynote when he remarked that "there is not a sermon which is heard, but it sets us nearer heaven or hell."[31] We catch the same note in the oft-quoted statement of Richard Baxter that

> it is no small matter to stand up in the face of a congregation, and deliver a message of salvation or damnation, as from the living God, in the name of our Redeemer. It is not easy matter to speak so plain, that the ignorant may understand us; and so seriously that the deadest hearts may feel us; and so convincingly, that contradicting cavillers may be silenced.[32]

The best indication of the value that Puritans attached to preaching is the frequency of their demand for sermons. Puritan ministers preached anywhere from three to five sermons per week, in addition to teaching catechism.[33]

Preaching was momentous because it aimed to be the word of God to people. Someone who sat under John Cotton's preaching was able to pay the following tribute:

> Mr. Cotton preaches with such authority, demonstration, and life that, methinks, when he preaches out of any Prophet or Apostle I hear not him; I hear that very Prophet and Apostle; yea, I hear the Lord Jesus Christ speaking in my heart.[34]

In their own day Puritans were known for their enthusiasm for preaching. Thomas Fuller was able to say of the Puritan era:

> What won them most repute was their ministers' painful ["painstaking; carefully prepared"] preaching in populous places; it being observed in England that those who hold the helm of the pulpit always steer people's hearts as they please.[35]

Modern historians looking back at the era agree. "Preaching, by mouth or by pen, was life for the Puritan," claims John F. H. New, and William Haller speaks of Puritanism's "vital rage for utterance."[36]

The Importance of the Intellect in Preaching

I noted earlier that the Puritan penchant for "godly and learned" pastors was an implied attack on the Anglican clergy. No doubt there are many exceptions to Samuel Johnson's linking of an age of ignorance with an age of ceremony,[37] but it is indisputable that the Anglican practice of reading services from the Prayer Book instead of preaching sermons fostered an alarming ignorance among clergymen. John Hooper's inquiries uncovered 171 (out of 311) Anglican clergymen who could not recite the Ten Commandments, 33 of whom did not know where they were to be found. Thirty could not tell where the Lord's Prayer appears in the Bible, 27 could not name its author, and ten could not recite it.[38]

Such clerical ignorance naturally produced lay ignorance. Josias Nichols, rector of a parish in Kent, found in a survey that scarcely 40 out of 400 parish communicants had any knowledge "of Christ, what he was in his person: what in his office: how sin came into the world: what punishment for sin: what becomes of our bodies being rotten in the graves."[39]

The Puritans responded by making speeches in Parliament that argued "the necessity of preaching and of a learned ministry," and that proposed "that some good course be taken to have a learned ministry."[40] "Of all the miseries wherewith the church is grieved," said Edward Dering in a sermon preached before the queen, "none is greater than this, that her ministers be ignorant and can say nothing."[41]

Puritan zeal for intellectual depth in preaching took several forms. One was a concern for a college-educated clergy. The occasion for the founding of Harvard College only six years after the Puritans' arrival in Massachusetts was the dread of leaving "an illiterate ministry to the churches, when our present ministers shall lie in the dust."[42] This echoed a similar concern in England, where a Puritan document outlined the university reforms that should be instituted for ensuring "a learned and sufficient ministry."[43] A modern authority on the history of Oxford and Cambridge Universities during the centuries of the Reformation has documented how key figures at these universities exercised a formative influence over English Puritanism.[44]

Two distinctly Puritan institutions, "prophesyings" and "lecture-ships," also attest the intellectual respectability of Puritan preaching. *Prophesyings* (eventually stamped out by Queen Elizabeth) were preaching seminars or workshops to upgrade the quality of preaching. They were attended by the ministers of a district. Ministers met at a central church, where up to five of them would preach on a previously agreed-upon text, followed by discussion.[45]

Puritan *lectureships* were a way of improving the laity's grasp of the content of the Christian faith. Puritan lecturers were preachers or speakers who were privately supported by the laity and therefore beyond the direct control of the established church.[46] Christopher Hill calls these lecturers "free-lance clergy," and someone else describes the lecture itself

John Bunyan preaching in his hometown, Bedford, England.
Courtesy of the Trustees of Bunyan Meeting

as "a sort of grand-parent of our modern Bible-study: a preaching service
of considerable length and great depth, usually being attended by pastors
and members from neighboring Puritan congregations."[47]

The Puritan emphasis on religious education for both clergy and
laity resulted in sermons that appealed to the listener's understanding of
doctrinal truth. Puritan preachers assumed the primacy of the intellect as
the channel through which God spoke to people and convicted them of
the truth. Benjamin Whichcote expressed his opinion that "I have always
found that such preaching of others hath most commanded my heart
which hath most illuminated my head."[48] According to William Ames,
"The receiving of the word consists of two parts: attention of mind and
intention of will."[49]

American Puritans agreed. The biographer of Richard Mather noted
that although "his way of preaching was plain and zealous, it was
moreover substantial and very judicious."[50] Such preaching obviously
appealed to the intellect as well as the emotions. A historian of American
education goes so far as to say that "the Puritan clergy came as close to
being an intellectual ruling class — or, more properly, a class of
intellectuals intimately associated with a ruling power — as America has
ever had."[51]

Anyone who takes the time to peruse published Puritan sermons will
sense at once the demands that these sermons placed on the minds of both
the preacher and audience. For one thing, sermons generally lasted an
hour. Thus we find William Cartwright stipulating, "Let there be, if it
may be every sabbath-day, two sermons, and let them that preach always

endeavour to keep themselves within one hour, especially on the week-days."[52]

Puritan preachers prepared their sermons carefully. "Painful preaching" was the ideal, and by it the Puritans meant painstaking, meticulous, carefully prepared sermons. Most ministers preached from notes, but a few wrote their sermons out entirely. Thomas Goodwin declared, "Whereas some men are for preaching only *extempore*, and without study, Paul bids Timothy meditate and study, and give his mind wholly to these things."[53] Richard Baxter read his sermons except when he was too busy to write them out.[54]

On the American scene, John Eliot "liked no preaching but what had been well studied for," and he resolved "by good study" to have "no knots in our sermons left undissolved." Cotton Mather praised John Cotton because his sermons "all smelt of the lamp."[55] Mather also provided an interesting analysis of how writing sermon notes took more preparation than extemporaneous preaching did:

> It is not the want of our abilities, that makes us use our notes; but it's
> a regard unto our work, and the good of our hearers. . . . It is easier
> with us, to preach three sermons without notes, than one with them.[56]

From the annals of Puritan preaching there are, of course, accounts of prodigious feats. When Cromwell wished to test the pulpit powers of John Howe (who became one of Cromwell's chaplains), he altered the text which he had given Howe to expound immediately before the sermon. Howe preached on the text for two hours and was called on to cease only when he was about to turn the hourglass again.[57]

Expository Preaching From the Bible

Despite their bent toward doctrine and theology, the Puritans overwhelmingly favored expository sermons that "opened" the meanings of a specific biblical passage. William Ames paid his disrespect to topical preaching that slighted the announced text from the Bible:

> Ministers impose upon their hearers and altogether forget themselves
> when they propound a certain text in the beginning as the start of the
> sermon and then speak many things about or simply by occasion of
> the text but for the most part draw nothing out of the text itself.[58]

The physical opening of the Bible on the pulpit during the service symbolized the aim of expository preaching, which was to unfold the latent meanings of a specific biblical text.

This aim, in turn, determined the methodology of Puritan preachers, which was to tie the entire sermon to the chosen text in the Bible. William Chappell defined a sermon as "a discourse upon a text of Scripture, disposing its parts according to the order of nature."[59] The Puritans were strong advocates of application in a sermon, as we will see, but it all started with the Bible itself. In the words of William Ames, "First the things contained in the text must be stated. . . . In setting forth the truth in the text the minister should first explain it and then indicate the good which follows from it."[60]

Of the customary three parts of a Puritan sermon, two were closely tied to the Bible itself. According to the *Directory of Public Worship* adopted by the Westminster Assembly,

> In raising doctrines from the text, his care ought to be, First, that the matter be the truth of God. Secondly, that it be a truth contained in, or grounded on, that text that the hearers may discern how God teacheth it from thence.[61]

This conviction about the centrality of the Bible in preaching was reinforced by the practice of largely or exclusively limiting the details of the sermon to biblical material. William Perkins, for example, encouraged the reading of patristic sources in sermon preparation, but also the concealment of this study in the citations made from the pulpit.[62]

The effect of this type of biblical preaching has been well summarized by a modern scholar who studied a century of the St. Paul's Cross sermons preached in London:

> For the Puritans, the sermon is not just hinged to Scripture; it quite literally exists *inside* the Word of God; the text is not in the sermon, but the sermon is in the text. . . . Put summarily, listening to a sermon is being in the Bible.[63]

The Organization of a Puritan Sermon

In their preaching (and in much besides), the Puritans were devotees of methodology. They theorized repeatedly about the form that a sermon should take, and they scrupulously followed those methods in their sermons. The general model was a three-part sermon, though not everyone described the three parts in exactly the same way.

The outline that appears at the end of William Perkins's *The Art of Prophesying* can be taken as the prototype of the organization of a Puritan sermon:

1. To read the text distinctly out of the canonical scriptures.

2. To give the sense and understanding of it being read, by the scripture itself.

3. To collect a few and profitable points of doctrine out of the natural sense.

4. To apply, if he have the gift, the doctrines rightly collected to the life and manners of men in a simple and plain speech.[64]

If we regard reading the biblical text as preliminary to the sermon proper, we end up with the following three parts of the sermon: (1) interaction with the surface meaning of the text, (2) deducing doctrinal or moral principles from the text, and (3) showing how those principles can be applied in daily Christian living.[65] The logic and comprehensiveness of the scheme are impeccable.

When we turn to actual sermons, the tidiness of the "opening — doctrine — uses" scheme is often lost in a maze of details as the basic elements are elaborated. The chief culprit was the second part of the sermon. Finding doctrines in a text was called "dividing" the text. Unrestrained preachers found it easy to multiply these doctrines in hairsplitting ways, and even the responsible ones like John Udall were convinced that "it must needs to be that every sentence of the Holy Scripture containeth in it at least one general doctrine."[66]

Not only did preachers find doctrines in the text, but they felt constrained to proceed to buttress each doctrine with "the examples and testimonies of Scripture, and . . . by the force of reason grounded upon the same."[67] The purpose of such "proof" and "reasons" was to ensure that the doctrine adduced from a specific text had the whole weight of Scripture behind it. John Dod, we are told, would conduct his proofs "not multiplying particulars for oppressing memory, not dwelling so long as to make all truth run through a few texts," and this is no doubt what the best preachers did.[68]

Perry Miller summarizes the standard Puritan sermon thus:

The Puritan sermon quotes the text and "opens" it as briefly as possible, expounding circumstances and context, explaining its grammatical meanings, reducing its tropes and schemata to prose, and setting forth its logical implications; the sermon then proclaims in a flat, indicative sentence the "doctrine" contained in the text or logically deduced from it, and proceeds to the first reason or proof. Reason follows reason, with no other transition than a period and a number; after the last proof is stated there follow the uses or applications, also in numbered sequence, and the sermon ends when there is nothing more to be said.[69]

The Puritan sermon was planned and organized. It may have been long and detailed, but it did not ramble. It was controlled by a discernible strategy and it progressed toward a final goal. The methodology ensured that the content would be tied to Scripture, that the sermon would involve an intellectual grasp of truth, and that theological doctrine would be applied to everyday living.

The Practical Application of Doctrine

One of the most attractive features of Puritan preaching was its emphasis on practical application of doctrine to life. The third part of the sermon explored the "uses" of the doctrine that had been explained and documented from the Bible. The practical bent of Puritanism led preachers to realize that doctrine is lifeless unless a person can "build bridges" from biblical truth to everyday living. "When we read only of doctrines," said Thomas Hooker, "these may reach the understanding, but when we read or hear of examples, human affection doth as it were represent to us the case as our own."[70]

Another way of saying this is that the Puritan sermon was a rhetorical or persuasive art. Its final purpose was to move a listener to right spiritual and moral behavior. Here, too, methodology was crucial, as suggested by the following account from James Durham:

> Application is the life of preaching; and there is no less study, skill, wisdom, authority and plainness necessary in the applying of a point to the conscience of hearers, and in the pressing of it home, than is required in the opening of some profound truth: and therefore ministers should study the one as well as the other. . . . Hence, preaching is called persuading, testifying, beseeching, entreating, or requesting, exhorting, etc. All which import some such dealing in application.[71]

The appeal to the hearer's conscience was how the Puritans often conceived of application. William Ames was typical:

> They sin . . . who stick to the naked finding and explanation of the truth, neglecting the use and practice in which religion and blessedness consist. Such preachers edify the conscience little or not at all.[72]

As the statement suggests, the aim of the application was to stir the individual Christian to a change of behavior wherever it was needed by awakening the conscience. For the Puritans, preaching was a subversive activity. Its goal was "holy reformation" of character and action — to "reform the life from ungodliness," as William Perkins put it.[73]

This application was the responsibility of the person in the pew as well as the preacher. In fact, it fostered good listening. "The doers of the Word are the best hearers," said Thomas Manton.[74] Samuel Ward admonished himself in his diary to "remember always at the hearing of God's word to be applying the things delivered always to thyself, and so bythoughts will take less place."[75]

The need for personal application was one of many reasons the Puritans gave for rejecting the prescribed homilies of the Anglican liturgy. The homilies failed to meet the conditions of a local situation. Richard Baxter argued, for example,

> If I know my hearers to be most addicted to drunkenness, must I be tied up from preaching or reading against that sin, and tied to read and preach only against covetousness or the like?[76]

To suggest something of the methodology of Puritan preachers in applying Christian doctrine, I wish to take one more excursion into Perkins's *Art of Prophesying*. Perkins divided "the ways of application" into seven categories, depending on the conditions of the listeners:

> I. Unbelievers who are both ignorant and unteachable. . . . II. Some are teachable, but yet ignorant. . . . III. Some have knowledge, but are not as yet humbled. . . . IV. Some are humbled. . . . V. Some do believe. . . . VI. Some are fallen. . . . VII. There is a mingled people. . . .

Furthermore, "application is either mental or practical." Practical application "is that which respecteth the life and behaviour: and it is instruction and correction." Each of these is further subdivided.[77]

It is obvious that Puritan preachers knew what they wanted to achieve with their preaching. They were goal-oriented. The ultimate goal was holy living; doctrinal truth was a means to that end. "That knowledge is best," wrote Thomas Manton, "which endeth in practice. . . . The hearer's life is the preacher's best commendation."[78]

Affective Preaching

Puritan sermons placed immense demands on the intellect, but this emphasis on the rational understanding of truth was balanced by an appeal to the heart and will. The Puritan sermon was *affective:* it aimed to *affect* the listener. Baxter stated the theory very well:

> As man is not so prone to live according to the truth he knows except it do deeply affect him, so neither doth his soul enjoy its sweetness, except speculation do pass to affection. The understanding is not the

whole soul, and therefore cannot do the whole work. . . . The understanding must take in truths, and prepare them for the will, and it must receive them and commend them to the affections; . . . the affections are, as it were, the bottom of the soul.[79]

We can catch the Puritan spirit on this point best by paying attention to the typical imagery that writers used when stating the theory. It was said of Richard Mather that he aimed "to shoot his arrows not over people's heads but into their hearts and consciences."[80] Thomas Cartwright said, "As the fire stirred giveth more heat, so the Word, as it were, blown by preaching, flameth . . . in the hearers."[81] Baxter wrote, "If our words be not sharpened, and pierce not as nails, they will hardly be felt by stony hearts."[82] This imagery of active attack and physical contact with the recipient captures exactly the Puritan ideal of affective preaching.

The affective power of preaching resided, not in the manipulation of the audience by the preacher, but in the action of the Holy Spirit. "The preaching of God's holy word," said Richard Sibbes, "is the ministry of the Spirit."[83] Thomas Hooker said that "the work of the spirit doth always go with . . . the Word."[84]

The Puritan practice of affective preaching meant that listening to a sermon was not a spectator sport but an active involvement. Critiques of sermons by liturgical advocates, in the Puritan era or today, misunderstand the dynamics of good sermon listening. For the Puritans, listening to a sermon was an active exercise that required the full attention of the listener. Several Puritan practices show exactly *how* active the person in the pew was.

One of these practices was the notetaking that became a standard feature of Puritan church services. We read about Comenius, visiting England from the Continent, watching with admiration as London congregations took shorthand notes of sermons.[85] John Brinsley, Puritan educator, advised, "For the Sabbaths and other days when there is any sermon, cause everyone to learn something at the sermons. The very lowest [youngest] to bring some notes."[86]

A second Puritan practice was further meditation on a sermon by the listener after it had been heard. Edmund Calamy said that sermons were like food on the table: "you must eat it; and not only eat it, but concoct it, and digest it. . . . One sermon well digested, well meditated upon, is better than twenty sermons without meditation."[87]

Such meditation was naturally aided by memory. William Ames criticized preachers whose sermon outlines make it difficult for their hearers to remember. . . . Their hearers cannot commit the chief heads of the sermon to memory so that they may afterwards repeat it privately in their families; and when this cannot be done, the greatest part of the fruit, which would otherwise be made available to the church of God through sermons, is lost.[88]

We should note that Ames assumes that the major impact of a sermon will occur outside of the church and after the service is over.

Notetaking and an active memory were given impetus by yet another Puritan practice, "repeating the sermon" with the assembled family at home. A contemporary of the Puritans observed that what the Puritan "heard in public" he "repeated in private, to whet it upon himself and family."[89] The practice of Theophilus Eaton was in every way typical of Puritan families. He assembled his whole family on Sunday evenings, "and in an obliging manner conferred with them about the things with which they had been entertained in the house of God, shutting up all with a prayer for the blessing of God upon them all."[90]

In short, the Puritan theory of preaching went hand in hand with the ideal of a religiously educated laity. The sermon was expected to serve as a stimulus to a whole range of daily activities at a personal and family level. In the words of A. G. Dickens,

> Puritans thought that the future of the Church lay with a clergy distinguished . . . by a new fervour, a superior intellectual equipment, a power to communicate. . . . The main purpose of the new cleric was to impart zeal to laymen, making them able to join in selecting their own ministers, to examine their own spiritual lives, to lead family prayers, to read godly books and take part in ecclesiastical administration.[91]

The purpose of preaching, in other words, was judged, not by what went on in the church, but by the effect of the sermon outside the church.

The Plain Style of Preaching

Virtually everything that I have said thus far provides a context for the plain style of preaching about which the Puritans had so much to say. Preaching as a popular activity that appealed to the cross section of society, the belief that sermons must convey God's truth to every listener, the desire to be practical and to stimulate further thought — all these combined to produce a sermon style in which the preacher viewed himself as Wordsworth described the poet: a person speaking to other persons.

This simple prose style was a means to the end of clarity. William Perkins theorized that preaching "must be plain, perspicuous, and evident. . . . It is a by-word among us: *It was a very plain sermon:* And I say again, *the plainer, the better.*"[92] Richard Sibbes claimed that

> truth feareth nothing so much as concealment, and desireth nothing so much as clearly to be laid open to the view of all: when it is most naked, it is most lovely and powerful.[93]

And Henry Smith said that "to preach simply is not to preach rudely, nor unlearnedly, nor confusedly, but to preach plainly and perspicuously that the simplest man may understand what is taught, as if he did hear his name."[94]

Plain preaching was defined by what it lacked as well as by what it contained. What it avoided was such things as the "heaping up citations of Fathers, and repeating words of Latin or Greek."[95] What the Puritans did not want was a pastiche of quotations or an embellished style that called great attention to its own ostentatiousness. For Samuel Torshell it was a sign of bad preaching to "tell you how many Fathers we have read, how much we are acquainted with the schoolmen, what critical linguists we are or the like. It is a wretched ostentation."[96]

Why did the Puritans dislike the high style in sermons? For one thing, they felt that it diverted attention from the content of the sermon to the preacher, for whom the occasion became, in modern parlance, an "ego trip." In the ostentatious style, said Perkins, "we do not paint Christ, but . . . our own selves."[97] Robert Bolton said that such preaching was "for self praise, and private ends."[98]

Other principles also underlie the prevailing plainness of Puritan style. One was sociological: the Puritan preachers aimed to reach the whole of society. It was said about John Dod that

> poor simple people that never knew what religion meant, when they had gone to hear him, could not choose but talk of his sermon. It mightily affected poor creatures to hear the mysteries of God . . . brought down to their own language and dialect.[99]

Even more memorable is the tribute that Thomas Fuller paid to Perkins, who was said to preach in such a way that "his sermons were not so plain but that the piously learned did admire them, nor so learned but that the plain did understand them."[100]

The plain style also rested on the premise that the final purpose of a sermon was not aesthetic excellence but spiritual edification. Prefaces to published Puritan sermons typically expressed the intention "to edify more than to please, any further than pleasing is a means to edification" (as one preface put it).[101] The only art that Increase Mather was interested in displaying was "that one art of being intelligible."[102]

The hero of the Puritan movement was
the preacher, who mobilized lay opinion
into an effective agency for church reform
and social action. From an edition of Bunyan's
Pilgrim's Progress; courtesy of the special collections
of the Wheaton College Library

Obviously, too, Puritan style was based on the premise that the
content of a sermon is more important than its form. John Flavel
theorized that "words are but servants to matter. An iron key, fitted to
the wards of the lock, is more useful than a golden one that will not open
the door to the treasures."[103] For the Puritans, language was a means to
an end — something "useful" — not an end in itself.

John Cotton preached in both styles during his Cambridge days,
and therein lies an interesting anecdote. As one of the ostentatious
preachers at Cambridge University, he preached to large audiences "after
the mode of the University at that time, which was to stuff their sermons
with as much quotation and citing of authors as might possibly be." But
after he came under conviction of his pride in the matter, Cotton
determined to give his next sermon "after the plain and profitable way, by

raising of doctrines, with propounding the reasons and uses of the same." The scholars who attended the lecture expecting to be entertained by a literary performance pulled their hats over their eyes, "thereby to express their dislike of the sermon." John Preston, future Master of Emmanuel College, joined those who pulled their hats over their eyes, but he was convicted by the message in spite of himself, and he "was so affected that he was made to stand up again and change his posture, and attend to what was spoken."[104] For the Puritans, the purpose of a sermon was to serve as a means of grace.

There is a simplicity that dignifies as well as a simplicity that diminishes. The biblical style belongs to the first category, and the Puritans aspired to model their own style on it. In the words of Benjamin Keach, "There simplicity is joined with majesty, commanding the veneration of all serious men; more than the elaborate flourishes and long-winded periods of Tully."[105]

Summary

To summarize the Puritan theory of preaching, I can do no better than to let some Puritan preachers speak for themselves:

> I preached what I felt, what I smartingly did feel. . . . Indeed I have been as one sent unto them from the dead. I went myself in chains to preach to them in chains; and carried that fire in my own conscience that I persuaded them to beware of.[106]

> I preached, as never sure to preach again,
> And as a dying man to dying men.[107]

> The word preached is a means of health, a chariot of salvation. . . . The preaching of the Word is that lattice where Christ looks forth and shows himself to his saints.[108]

> Heaven itself cannot show forth a more excellent creature than a faithful preacher. . . . Yea, heaven itself is not more glorious than a small village having a Peter, a Paul, to preach in it.[109]

> Preaching, therefore, ought not to be dead, but alive and effective so that an unbeliever coming into the congregation of believers should be affected and, as it were, transfixed by the very hearing of the word so that he might give glory to God.[110]

> Indeed, preaching is the ordinance of God, sanctified for the begetting of faith, for the opening of the understanding, for the drawing of the will and affections to Christ.[111]

FURTHER READING

John Brown, *Puritan Preaching in England* (1900).

Caroline Francis Richardson, *English Preachers and Preaching, 1640–1670* (1928).

W. Fraser Mitchell, *English Pulpit Oratory from Andrews to Tillotson* (1932).

Perry Miller, *The New England Mind: The Seventeenth Century*, chap. 12 (1939).

Babette May Levy, *Preaching in the First Half Century of New England History* (1945).

Winthrop S. Hudson, "The Ministry in the Puritan Age," pp. 180–206 in *The Ministry in Historical Perspectives*, ed. H. Richard Niebuhr and Daniel D. Williams (1956).

Christopher Hill, *Society and Puritanism in Pre-Revolutionary England*, chaps. 2 and 3 (1964).

Irvonwy Morgan, *The Godly Preachers of the Elizabethan Age* (1965).

Paul S. Seaver, *The Puritan Lectureships: The Politics of Religious Dissent, 1560–1662* (1970).

David D. Hall, *The Faithful Shepherd: A History of the New England Ministry in the Seventeenth Century* (1972).

Peter Lewis, *The Genius of Puritanism* (1977).

I preached . . . as a dying man to dying men.
— RICHARD BAXTER

The receiving of the word consists of two parts: attention of mind and intention of will.   — WILLIAM AMES

It is a by-word among us: It was a very plain sermon: *And I say again,* the plainer, the better.
— WILLIAM PERKINS

Here is the essence of Puritan worship: simple, plain, luminous, distrustful of ritual and human diversion, built around the preaching of the Word. Photograph by Douglas R. Gilbert

Chapter 7

Church and Worship

I am of the opinion that all things in the church should be pure, simple, and removed as far as possible from the elements and pomps of this world.

— RICHARD COX

Puritanism began as a movement of "divers Godly and learned" people "which stand for and desire the Reformation of our church in discipline and ceremonies according to the pure Word of God and the law of the land."[1] As that Puritan platform suggests, the very name *Puritan* first denoted a desire to purify the established Church of England from Catholic vestiges in worship and church government. Yet paradoxically the goal of church reform is the one thing that the English Puritans ultimately failed to achieve.

In America, where the Puritans were free to set up their own churches, Puritanism never constituted a separate denomination. From the time of the Reformation it has been possible to speak of the Lutheran Church and the Reformed Church, but never of a Puritan Church. The Puritans were a scattered presence in a broad expanse of affiliations. Whatever we might mean by Puritan ecclesiology, therefore, it does not involve a unified denomination.

Most English Puritans remained within the Anglican church. Many of them, unable to conform sufficiently, left or found themselves ejected from the Church of England. This was nearly inevitable, given the state church situation in which the English government acknowledged only

111

one official church. The more frequently the Puritans were thus removed from the established church, the more accurately we can think of them as separatists. During certain eras of the movement Puritans identified themselves as Presbyterians, and in fact many American Puritans did so. And while many American Puritans theoretically tried to remain Anglican, in practice they became Congregational in church polity.

There was, to be sure, a theoretical Puritan consensus on most issues involving worship and the theory of what a church is. Puritanism also bequeathed at least one permanent legacy, the phenomenon of a "gathered church" separate from the state and with an accompanying proliferation of independent churches. But at the outset it is important to be aware that in church affiliation the Puritans present a chaotic picture compared with the relatively defined situation of Lutheran, Reformed, and Presbyterian denominations.

The Biblical Basis for Determining Church Policy

The logical starting point for exploring what the Puritans believed about the church is to note where they got their ideas. Faced with the extravagance and ceremony that the church had accumulated during the Catholic centuries, the Puritans resorted to the strongest control at their disposal, the Bible. They vowed to limit all church policy and worship practices to what could be directly based on statements or procedures found in the Bible, except in "things indifferent" (though even here the Puritans required a loose biblical sanction).

Luther, although he did not press the principle of biblical warrant as rigorously as the Puritans were to do, had written:

> There is an amazing confusion of religions and forms of religious worship in the world. This came about because all . . . proceeded without the Word of God, according to the opinion of their own heart. . . . God does not want to be worshipped in any other way than that which He Himself prescribed.[2]

Calvin had similarly made the comment that "no form of government is to be drawn up in the Church by human judgment, but that men must wait for the command of God."[3]

The Puritans operated on the same principle of seeking biblical warrant for church practices. Thus when the English exiles in Geneva composed an order of worship, it was

> a form and order of a reformed church limited within the compass of God's Word, which our Saviour hath left unto us as only sufficient to govern all our actions by; so that what so ever is added to this Word

> by man's device, seem it never so good, holy, or beautiful, yet before
> our God . . . it is evil, wicked, and abominable.[4]

Even more of a Puritan landmark were Thomas Cartwright's lectures at Cambridge University on the first two chapters of Acts in 1570. Cartwright used the early Christian church as the model for what the church should be like in all subsequent ages. The appeal to the apostolic norm had far-reaching implications, for it allowed the Puritans to reject Catholic and Anglican practices such as vestments and extravagant rituals as based on Old Testament models that had been abrogated in the New Testament dispensation.[5]

Following Continental precedents and Cartwright's influence, the Puritans made the appeal to biblical authority for church policy a major theme, especially in their official platforms and petitions. The authors of the Waldegrave Prayer Book asked that their work be tried "only by the touchstone of his word."[6] *An Admonition to the Parliament* asked Parliament to institute "in God's church those things only which the Lord himself in his word commandeth."[7] In any absolute sense, we can now see, it is impossible to avoid either being influenced by traditions of worship or bequeathing them to subsequent generations. The Puritans did, however, make a decisive break with both Catholic and Anglican precedents by disallowing extrabiblical tradition as a foundation for church practices.

The Puritans' attitude was a logical outgrowth of their view of biblical authority. For the Puritans, as for Calvin, the Bible was a complete and sufficient authority for all of life, not simply in matters pertaining to personal salvation. William Ames sounded the keynote:

> The Scripture is not a partial, but a perfect rule of faith and manners:
> neither is there anything that is . . . to be observed in the Church of
> God, which depends either upon tradition, or upon any authority
> whatsoever, and is not contained in the Scriptures.[8]

In a similar vein, Henry Jacob said that "the New Testament is absolutely perfect [complete] for delivering the whole manner of God's worship," and John Owen was confident that "scripture contains all things necessary to be . . . practised in the worship of God."[9]

Puritan insistence on biblical warrant for church practices was part of their larger critique of tradition as an adequate authority for religious belief. In their written statements, in fact, the Puritans frequently combined their appeal to scriptural sanction with an attack on Catholic and Anglican practices based on tradition. A "Supplication" addressed to the king in 1605 asked for permission to assemble together somewhere publicly to the service and worship to God, to use and enjoy peaceably among ourselves alone the whole exercise of God's worship and church government . . . without any tradition of man whatsoever, according only to the specification of God's written word.[10]

Above all, acceptance of biblical and especially apostolic precedence for church policy involved a rejection of Catholic/Anglican ritual, ceremony, and wealth. John Bale argued the point with particular thoroughness. Christ, he said,

> never allowed their ceremonies. He never went in procession with cope, cross, and candlestick. . . . He never said mass, matins nor evensong. . . . He never hallowed church nor chalice, ashes nor palms, candles nor bells. He never made holy water nor holy bread, with such like. But such dumb ceremonies not having express commandment of God he called leaven of the Pharisees and damnable hypocrisy.[11]

Not all Puritans were equally rigid in applying the principle of scriptural warrant, a situation that produced some of the internal divisions within Puritanism. Although (as John Hooper put it) even "things indifferent must have their origin and foundation in the Word of God," such warrant might simply be a general principle deduced from the Bible, not a specific regulation.[12] Thomas Cartwright outlined four scriptural criteria by which the details of worship must be measured:

I Cor. x.32	The first, that they offend not any, especially the church of God.
I Cor. xiv. 40	The second is . . . that all be done in order and comeliness.
I Cor. xiv. 26	The third, that all be done to edifying.
Rom. xiv. 6-7	The last, that they be done to the glory of God.[13]

In practice, this meant (to quote again from Cartwright) that "certain things are left to order of the church, because they are of that nature which are varied by times, places, persons, and other circumstances, and so could not at once be set down and established for ever."[14]

In summary, William Bradshaw's codification of English Puritanism in 1605 accurately describes the principle of scriptural warrant that I have delineated:

> They hold and maintain that the word of God contained in the writings of the Prophets and Apostles is of absolute perfection, given by Christ the Head of the Church, to be unto the same the sole canon and rule of all matters of religion, and the worship and service of God

whatsoever. And that whatsoever cannot be justified by the said word is unlawful.[15]

In case this seems unnecessarily restrictive, we must remember the context within which the Puritans were operating. They were trying to reform an existing church structure. They needed a spiritual authority by which to reform something that in their view had gotten out of hand by following human tradition. In such a context, it was perfectly logical to "desire the reformation of our church in discipline and ceremonies according to the pure Word of God."[16] As Horton Davies has noted, "Reformed theology perforce meant liturgical reform," and acceptance of biblical authority was the very foundation of Reformed theology.[17]

The Church as a Spiritual Reality

The greatest of all Puritan legacies in regard to ecclesiastical theory was also the most revolutionary in its time. It was the notion that the church is a spiritual reality. It is not impressive buildings or fancy clerical vestments. It is instead the company of the redeemed.

The Puritans repeatedly showed their acceptance of Luther's dictum that "the church is a spiritual assembly of souls. . . . The true, real, right, essential church is a matter of the spirit and not of anything external."[18] For William Gouge the church consists of those who "inwardly and effectively by the spirit . . . believe in Christ."[19] John Hooper denied that the church consists of "bishops, priests and such other," affirming rather that it is "the company of all men hearing God's word and obeying unto the same."[20] Richard Baxter agreed: the church is "a holy Christian society for ordinary holy communion and mutual help in God's public worship and holy living."[21]

Implicit in these definitions of the church is a Puritan preference for the invisible church over any type of institutional structure. The church is emphatically not the professional clergy and their rituals. "What understand you by the church?" asked John Ball's Catechism. The answer: "By the church, we understand not the pope. . . ; nor his bishops and cardinals met in general council. . . ; but the whole company of believers."[22] If the church is essentially invisible rather than institutional, its head is obviously not a pope or church council, but Christ. The Puritans reiterated this again and again, as when Gouge spoke of "that church whereof Christ is properly the head."[23]

Another corollary of viewing the church as essentially spiritual is that it becomes dissociated from any particular place, whether a shrine or cathedral or church building. An early advocate of this view was William Tyndale:

God is a spirit and will be worshipped in spirit; that is, though He is present everywhere, yet He dwelleth lively and gloriously in the minds . . . and hearts of men that love His laws and trust in His promises. And wheresoever God findeth such a heart, there He heareth prayer in all places indifferently. So that outward place neither helpeth or hindereth. . . .[24]

The most memorable statement along these lines is that by George Gillespie:

unto us Christians no land is strange, no ground unholy; every coast is Jewry, every house is Sion; and every faithful company, yea, every faithful body a Temple to serve God in.[25]

The delocalizing of the church had profound effects on the very concept of worship. Worship was no longer confined to something that the priest did in a specific holy place. Worship became something that all Christians did wherever they might happen to be during the course of a day. Patrick Collinson summarizes Puritan theory and practice by saying that

the life of the puritan was in one sense a continuous act of worship, pursued under an unremitting and lively sense of God's providential purposes and constantly refreshed by religious activity, personal, domestic and public.[26]

If the church is not a professional clergy or a building, what are its visible signs? In Puritan ecclesiology, the visible signs of the church are defined chiefly in terms of certain *activities* and in *relationships* or fellowship among believers.

A true church is visible in its activities. Richard Sibbes, following John Calvin, held that these activities were "sound preaching of the Gospel, right dispensation of the sacraments, prayer religiously performed, and evil persons justly punished."[27] *An Admonition to the Parliament* declared:

The outward marks whereby a true Christian church is known are preaching of the word purely, ministering of the sacraments sincerely, and ecclesiastical discipline.[28]

The basic core of activities among virtually all the Puritans was preaching, sacraments, and discipline, with individual writers adding such things as prayer and giving of alms.

Such a definition of the visible church contrasted with the Catholic and Anglican churches, as the Puritans were quick to observe:

> If we behold the face of the popish church, Lord, how it glistereth, and gorgeous it is in comparison of Christ's true church! which is discerned in these days but by the word of God truly preached, the sacraments purely ministered, and some discipline.[29]

The visible manifestations of the church consisted secondly in the relationships among Christians. The definition of the church in John Davenport's creed, for example, stressed relationships:

> It is a company of faithful and holy people, or persons called out of the world to fellowship with Jesus Christ, and united in one congregation to him as members to their head, and one with another, by a holy covenant for mutual fellowship in all such ways of holy worship of God, and of edification of one towards another.[30]

This was more revolutionary than it may at first appear, for although the Puritans could not have foreseen all of the consequences, it implied a voluntary church membership instead of the enforced uniformity of a state church. In answer to the question, "How was such a church to be constituted?" Henry Jacob's catechism replied, "By a free mutual consent of believers joining and covenanting to live as members of a holy society together."[31]

We find here the seeds of one of the most enduring of Puritan ideals, the practice of voluntary church membership based on the church preference of the member. As Collinson notes, the Puritans quickly established a situation that "pointed unmistakably to voluntarism and independency."[32]

The Puritan devaluing of the institutional church in deference to spiritual activities and fellowship was accompanied by a doctrine of the fallibility of the institutional church. "Not to be capable of errors," said John Preston, "is the inseparable attribute of God himself . . . which cannot be said of any creature."[33] "All visible churches upon earth . . . are subject to apostasy," said William Perkins, and John Owen asserted that "the church in no sense is absolutely freed in this world from . . . errors."[34]

It is within the context that I have delineated that we can begin to grasp the much misunderstood topic of Puritan iconoclasm (tearing down physical images from churches). If, as Milton put it, God "dost prefer / Before all Temples the upright heart and pure,"[35] then it is both illogical and spiritually misguided to lavish attention on the external accouterments of worship.

The Puritans called their churches "meeting houses" in an effort to divert attention from the physical place to the spiritual activities that were the true core of church worship. For anyone who believes that the church's "beauty indeed is all inward, . . . outwardly being but simple," keeping visual images out of churches is the only possible practice.[36] There were, as we shall see, other reasons for Puritan iconoclasm (chiefly an aversion to idolatry), but belief in the primacy of the spiritual in their doctrine of the church was a key reason.

The Elevation of the Laity

Another revolutionary element in the Puritan doctrine of the church was the elevation of the layperson's role in church and worship. This too is a topic that keeps expanding in its implications.

The changing role of the laity can be seen, first of all, in Puritan attitudes toward church government. Thomas Cartwright, in his lectures on Acts that cost him his position at Cambridge University, had argued for a Presbyterian form of church government in which congregations would elect their own ministers and determine church policy. Cartwright's preference for a Presbyterian form of state church eventually gained many advocates among the Puritans. Even Puritans who stopped short of rejecting the Episcopalian form of government would have agreed on the principle that the local congregation should hold the most authority in such matters as choosing the minister and determining the details of worship. Someone has described the Puritan ideal in this regard as "a nice combination of clerical leadership and lay responsibility."[37]

In America, the power of the congregation to control local church policy and elect the minister became the established practice, under a polity that was largely Congregational. Although the English Puritans failed to achieve as much, the laity did in fact find ways of wresting power from the church hierarchy. For a time they hired their own preaching lecturers. They used the House of Commons to force concessions. Lay objection to clerical vestments was so strong that many ministers were virtually forced to abandon them.[38]

The enlarged role of the laity was seen even more clearly in the home meetings, or "conventicles," that became a standard feature of Puritan life in England (and for which many Puritans were hauled into church courts). In the Diocese of Chester, for example, the court records include accounts of charges such as the following: an assembled company "conferred together of such profitable lessons as they had learned that day at a public catechising"; twelve Puritans were charged "for keeping a private fast upon Christmas day last in the house of Waring Croxton"; a small group was charged with having "assembled and met in divers houses" for religious purposes; an individual "for having a private meeting at his house of men and women but not known to what end"; several people "for having private meetings in their houses."[39]

Patrick Collinson's book *The Elizabethan Puritan Movement* includes an important chapter on "The Meetings of the Godly" that surveys the remarkable range of ways in which the Puritan laity took initiative in finding spiritual sustenance, often in defiance of harassment from the state and the established church.[40] Thus was born one of the noblest of all Puritan practices, the "church within the church," that is, the spiritual fellowship within the bigger institutional church by those who were serious about the Christian life.

The increasing power of the laity also transformed public worship. Continuing a trend from the early Reformation, services were in English rather than Latin. The plain style of preaching insured that every person in the congregation could understand what was said. Whereas Catholics and Anglicans had used clerical vestments on the principle that "the clergy should be . . . clothed on all occasions as to be easily distinguishable from laymen,"[41] the Puritans destroyed the external marks of distinction between clergy and laity. The Puritans permanently changed church architecture from the two-room principle, in which members were onlookers as the clergy performed the liturgy, to a one-room sanctuary.

Laypeople were even encouraged to critique ministers' sermons by comparing their content with Scripture. Edward Reynolds wrote:

> The people are hereby taught, first, to examine the doctrines of men by the rule and standard of the Word; . . . for though the judgment of interpretation belong principally to the ministers of the Word, yet God hath given all believers a judgment of discretion, to try the spirits and to search the Scriptures, whether the things which they hear be so or no.[42]

There can be no mistaking the revolutionary narrowing of the gap between clergy and laity that occurred with the Reformation. The movement toward equalizing the stature of clergy and laity rested on the principle of the priesthood of all believers. This doctrine had the double effect of removing the church as a necessary intermediary between people and God for salvation and of generally raising the spiritual status of the ordinary person. "Are we not all a royal priesthood?" asked Edward Reynolds; "capable is the poorest member in Christ's church, being grown to maturity of years, of information in the faith."[43]

Simplifying the Worship Service

If we are looking for a principle that will unify the various facets of the public worship services of the Puritans, the idea of simplicity will suffice. Given the context of Catholic/Anglican extravagance in public

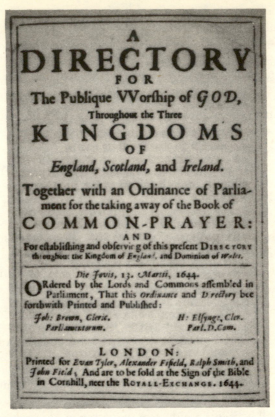

Puritan concern for proper worship found its
supreme expression in the Westminster Assembly's
Directory for Public Worship

worship, the whole thrust of Puritan worship was toward getting rid of
the clutter and focusing on the essential, which for them was summarized
by the ideal of edification. What, then, was the corporate worship of the
Puritans like?

To begin, it was *orderly and clearly organized*. It steered a middle course
between the excessive proliferation of ceremony in a high church service
and the pietistic pattern of preliminaries plus the sermon. Despite their
objections to the Anglican Book of Common Prayer, the Puritans did not
reject the idea of service books or directories of worship. In fact, they
produced their share of them.[44] A typical order of worship in such service
books looked like this:

1. A Confession of sins
2. A Prayer for pardon
3. A metrical Psalm

4. A Prayer for illumination

5. Scripture Reading

6. Sermon

7. Baptisms and publication of Banns

8. Long Prayer and Lord's Prayer

9. Apostles' Creed (recited by the Minister)

10. A metrical Psalm

11. The Blessing (Aaronic or Apostolic)[45]

Secondly, Puritan worship *curbed ceremony and ritual*. Compared with Catholic/Anglican services, it could accurately be called anti-ceremonial. Anglican Archbishop Bancroft had said that "there is no religion where there are no ceremonies," while the Puritan minister Richard Greenham claimed, "The more ceremonies, the less truth."[46]

The Puritans accordingly got rid of clerical vestments, which they disliked for many reasons.[47] One Puritan, the botanist William Turner of Wells, even trained a pet dog to leap up and snatch the square caps from the heads of conforming clerics![48] For the Catholic/Anglican schedule of saints' days and holy days, the Puritans simply substituted Sunday worship; in the words of Richard Greenham, "Our Easter day, our Ascension day, our Whitsuntide is every Lord's day."[49]

To sense the simplicity that resulted from Puritan rejection of ceremony, we can turn to John Foxe's satiric catalog of what went on in a liturgical service. Foxe wondered how anyone could keep from laughing upon seeing the priests'

> turning, returning, half turning and whole turning, such kissing, blessing, crouching, becking, crossing, knocking, ducking, washing, rinsing, lifting, touching, fingering, whispering, stopping, dripping, bowing, licking, wiping, . . . shifting, with a hundred things more.[50]

A Puritan service without such ceremony would have struck any contemporary as distinctly simplified.

Thirdly, the Puritans *simplified church architecture and furnishings*. They took images and statues out of the churches. They replaced stone altars with communion tables. The multiroom floor plan became a single, rectangular room. The walls were painted white. The physical objects that would have caught one's eye upon entering a Puritan church were a high central pulpit with a winding stairway to it, a Bible on a cushion on a ledge of the pulpit, a communion table below the pulpit, and an inconspicuous baptismal font.

All this simplicity should not be interpreted as an attempt to avoid symbolism. It *was* the symbol of Puritan worship, and it was a richly multiple symbol. Here in visual form was the Puritan aversion to idols and human intervention between God and people. Here was a sign of humility before God and His Word. Here was a symbol of the essentially inward and spiritual nature of worship. Here was a reminder that God cannot be confined to earthly and human conceptions, that he is transcendent and sovereign. By calling their buildings "meeting houses," moreover, Puritans stressed the domestic aspect of worship as a spiritual family meeting with their heavenly Father.

This triumph of simplicity was not necessarily unaesthetic. The simple is a form of beauty as well as the ornate. Horton Davies calls the simple beauty of Puritan church architecture "a study in black and white etching, rather than the coloured and multi-textured appearance of Anglican . . . churches."[51] A study of Puritan vocabulary shows that "naked" was one of their positive words when applied to worship. In the Puritan church, the individual worshiper stood "naked" before the light and purity of God's Word and presence. An authority on church architecture writes about Puritan churches, "Clean, well-lighted, they concentrated on the essentials of Puritan worship, the hearing of God's Word, with no distractions."[52]

Fourthly, Puritan worship *simplified church music*. It eliminated complex polyphonic compositions, obscure Latin songs, and professional musicians. The Puritans removed organs from their churches (but kept them in their homes). All these were replaced with congregational singing of psalms.[53]

The Puritans also *simplified the sacraments*. They reduced the number of sacraments from the Catholic seven to two, the Lord's Supper and baptism. They scaled down the definition of the efficacy of the sacraments by denying that their exercise by the ordained clergy is indispensable in imparting God's grace and affirming instead that the sacraments are signs and seals of God's saving grace. The Puritans simplified the liturgy of the Communion service and even learned to make creative use of silence during the service.[54] A perusal of E. Brooks Holifield's study in *The Covenant Sealed: The Development of Puritan Sacramental Theology* leaves one with the impression that the Puritans accorded the sacraments the place they hold in the New Testament — significant elements of Christian worship but not nearly as important as Catholicism, high church Anglicanism, and theological controversialists through the centuries have made them.

Finally, the relative simplicity of Puritan worship is evident in their *clearly defined goals for worship*. Richard Baxter's formulation can serve as a good specimen: the ends of worship are "the honor of God; the edification of believers; the communicating of spiritual knowledge, holiness, and delight to others; and the increase of God's actual kingdom in the world."[55]

If we pay attention to the typical vocabulary of Puritan writers on the topic of worship, a whole mindset comes into focus, as summarized by the key words I have italicized in the following statements:

I am of the opinion that all things in the church should be *pure, simple, and removed as far as possible from the elements and pomps of this world.*[56]

If the religion be *pure, spiritual, simple and lowly,* as the Gospel most truly is, such must the face of the ministry be.[57]

Our principal care and desire is to administer . . . the ordinances of Christ himself . . . in their *native purity and simplicity, without any dressing or painting of human inventions.*[58]

Congregational Participation in the Worship Service

One innovation of Puritan worship was the involvement of the whole congregation in the worship service. To sense the change, we must recall the Catholic service as it existed before the Reformation. The Catholic Mass had been a Latin service. Music, whether instrumental or choral (with words in Latin), was performed by professionals or trained musicians and was unintelligible to the ordinary person. The "choir" (the part of an English church where the choir stands or sits) was screened off from the main sanctuary where the congregation sat. The chancel and various side rooms likewise divided people from each other and from the altar where the host was elevated. All these factors conspired to make the worship service a spectacle at which the lay congregation remained passive.

What did the Puritans do to make the lay worshipers participants in the service? They began by changing the interior arrangement of the church. They removed the screens and made the sanctuary or nave an auditory in which everyone could see and hear the entire service. The communion table was taken out of the chancel and placed close to the congregation.

Music underwent a similar transformation in the interests of congregational participation, in changes that have already been described.[59] In the place of instrumental music and polyphonic choral music, Puritans instituted their great favorite, congregational singing of metrical psalms in the English language. Increase Mather, writing a preface for his son's *Accomplished Singer,* stated, "I would encourage especially our younger people to learn the skill by which they may sing regularly, that so this part of divine worship may be more beautifully carried on, and more generally delighted in."[60]

Congregational singing was as important to the Puritan movement as it was to Lutheranism in Germany. A contemporary recorded its effectiveness thus:

> The practice of joining in church music has very much helped us. For as soon as they had once begun singing in public, in only one little church in London, immediately not only the churches in the neighborhood, but even in the towns far distant began to vie with each other in the same practice. You may sometimes see at St. Paul's Cross, after the service, six thousand persons, old and young, of both sexes, all singing together and praising God.[61]

In short, the Puritans restored the right of the common people to join in the praise of God.

The Puritan worship service culminated in the sermon, and this may seem to us today to contradict the idea of congregational participation. But the Puritans emphatically did not regard the sermon as a spectator activity. According to the Jesuit William Weston, who witnessed the outdoor preaching exercises at Wisbech, the people who attended had their Bibles open on their laps and looked up the texts cited by the preachers. After the sermon "they held arguments also, among themselves, about the meaning of various Scripture texts, all of them, men and women, boys and girls, laborers, workmen and simpletons."[62] Notetaking at sermons and repetition of the sermon at home also attest how active the Puritans expected listeners of the sermon to be. By comparison, it would have been easier to remain mentally passive while reading the words from a prayer book service.

The Primacy of the Word

The Protestant Reformation, whether Continental or Puritan, stood for a word-based piety. Beginning with a conviction that the Bible was where a person encountered God most directly, religion became in significant ways a literary experience. The acts of worship emphasized by the Reformers and Puritans were overwhelmingly literary acts: reading the Bible, meditating on its meaning, listening to sermons, and talking to others about one's grasp of the doctrine based on these. The Puritans displayed excitement, even a sense of the mystical, when reading and talking about the sacred text.

This emphasis on the word (broadly defined to include the Bible but much besides) provides the context for understanding why the Puritans made the reading and exposition of Scripture the primary event in the worship service. There can be no doubt that for these worshipers the Word became a verbal sacrament (even though they would not have used that term to describe it). A sacrament is a means of grace in which the individual believer encounters the real presence of God in a uniquely powerful way. In the public worship of the Puritans,

> the Word is made flesh — not to sight, as in images; not to taste, as in the bread and wine; not to smell, as in the fumes of incense; but to hearing, and dwells among us. Preaching is a sacrament.[63]

The Puritans expected the verbal imagination to do the work that Catholic/Anglican worship had placed on the visual and aural imagination. In this, Puritan worship resembles the plays of Shakespeare. Shakespeare was content with the scantiest of stage props and built scenery and imagery into the texts of the plays themselves. In a similar way, the Puritans got rid of the "stage scenery" of Catholic/Anglican worship and relied on *verbal* imagery and symbolism, most of it based on the Bible.

Recent literary scholarship has begun to document the richness of the Puritan imagination — its reliance on master images, its figurative profusion, its allusions to the Bible.[64] Puritan sermons participated in this imagistic matrix. They were not as exclusively abstract, theological, and propositional as we tend to think. Once we grant the validity of the verbal image, it becomes clear that the Puritan worship service did not starve the imagination or even the senses of the worshiper. Allusions to the Bible carried immense imaginative and emotional voltage for a person to whom the Patriarchs were like neighbors and Mary and Martha like their own sisters.[65]

Puritan worship services, therefore, were far from being devoid of images and symbols. These were simply embodied in the sermon instead of visible to the eye in the church sanctuary. To test that thesis, I once randomly opened three books of Puritan sermons that a student had just brought into my office. Here are the specimens that greeted me:

> The sinner is a bramble, not a fig tree yielding sweet fruit. . . . A wicked man, like Jehoram, has "his bowels fallen out" (2 Chronicles 21:19). Therefore he is compared to an adamant (Zechariah 7:12) because his heart does not melt in mercy. Before conversion the sinner is compared to a wolf for his savageness, to a lion for his fierceness (Isaiah 11:6). . . .[66]

> Adam's posterity has not been so numerous as his sins. A little cloud, no bigger than a man's hand — so it seems at first — grows and spreads to cover the whole hemisphere. The water that at first seemed little

and shallow, swells more and more from the ankles to the knees, from the knees to the loins, from there to the head until it grows into such a great river that it cannot be passed over. In this way grows sin. . . . It is as a snowball that grows bigger by rolling in the snow.[67]

The law may chain up the wolf, but it is the Gospel that changes the wolfish nature; the one stops the stream, the other heals the fountain.[68]

No worship service that includes such appeals to the imagination can be said to be excessively abstract.

There was, of course, another reason why the Puritans made the sermon central to the worship service, and that was their passion for doctrinal truth. They expected worship to include an appeal to the understanding. The Puritans were preoccupied with religious truth because they lived in an age of religious upheaval and doctrinal controversy. What C. S. Lewis says about the poet Edmund Spenser's decision to make Truth rather than Grace the guide to Holiness in Book I of *The Faerie Queene* is equally applicable to the Puritan movement:

Spenser is writing in an age of religious doubt and controversy when the avoidance of error is a problem as pressing as, and in a sense prior to, the conquest of sin: a fact which would have rendered his story uninteresting in some centuries, but which should recommend it to us.[69]

The sacramental effect of the spoken word, combined with a conviction that religious understanding is important, explains why the Puritans insisted (as Luther had) that preaching must accompany the administration of the two sacraments. William Cartwright argued that since "the life of the sacraments dependeth on the preaching of the Word of God, there must of necessity the Word of God be, not read, but preached unto the people."[70] Dudley Fenner said that preaching was so necessary to Communion that "if it be omitted, it destroyeth the Sacrament."[71]

Puritan worship services reached their climax in the sermon. When Puritan preaching became popular, the Anglican establishment made numerous attempts to limit the role of preaching in the worship service.[72] The Puritans refused to be quelled, for the reasons I have sketched: they had too high a regard for the Bible as God's authoritative Word to them, they experienced that Word as a verbal sacrament in which they encountered God's real presence, their imaginations were satisfied by the imagistic richness of the sermons, and they were intent on having an adequate intellectual understanding of Christian truth.

Keeping Worship Creative and Fresh

A main concern of Puritan worship was the attempt to keep it from becoming a routine that lost its power through sheer repetition. This was at the heart of Puritan hostility to the Anglican Book of Common Prayer.

Instead of repeating the same words each week in the Sunday service, Puritans opted for prayers in the preacher's own words and for a new sermon. One of the best indictments of repeating the same words each week came from the great antagonist of the Puritans, Richard Hooker. In theorizing about why sermons were so popular with the people, Hooker acknowledged "a custom which men have to let those things carelessly pass by their ears, which they have oftentimes heard before, or know they may hear again whensoever it pleaseth themselves." By contrast, sermons have a natural ability "to procure attention . . . in that they come always new."[73] The Puritans themselves could not have said it better.

The Puritans were the foes of laziness and hypocrisy in worship. Mindlessly "going through the motions" held no appeal for them. Richard Baxter wrote regarding the hard work involved in worship:

> If it were only the exercise of the body, the moving of the lips, the bending of the knee, then it were an easy work indeed. . . ; yea, if it were to spend most of our days in numbering beads, and repeating certain words and prayers. . . , yet it were comparatively easy. . . . But it is a work more difficult than all this."[74]

The Puritans also wanted to keep an element of spontaneity in their worship. They protected the preacher's right and duty to choose a sermon topic suited to the needs of the local congregation and prompted by the Holy Spirit instead of printed homilies prescribed in a service book. They disliked "stinted" prayers read from a prayer book (though they did not reject the practice of writing out one's own prayer for use in public). A contemporary said of the Puritans that they "esteem that manner of prayer best where, by the gift of God, expressions were varied according to the present wants and occasion; yet . . . did not account set forms unlawful."[75]

For the Puritans, praying from a prayer book was equivalent to greeting family members at the breakfast table by reading the greetings from a book. Horton Davies comments that "they had learned in the love of Christ to speak to God as a Father."[76] The Puritans yearned for freedom and chafed under confinement. Milton wrote that "to imprison and confine by force, into a pinfold [pen for cattle] of set words, those two most unimprisonable things, our prayers and that Divine Spirit of utterance that moves them, is a tyranny."[77]

The creativity of Puritan worship is perhaps best seen in their acts of worship beyond the church building. Such worship took two main forms. One was the practice of private daily devotions that is virtually synonymous with Puritanism. As part of this private devotional emphasis, the Puritans produced a genre of aids-to-meditation, the best known of which, Baxter's *Saints' Everlasting Rest*, is a classic to this day.[78]

In addition to encouraging private worship, the Puritans fostered creativity in worship in their homes. Some of this worship was family worship, while some of it involved neighbors and friends. Puritan families organized their own thanksgiving days and fast days.[79] A specimen entry in a diary catches some of the flavor of such gatherings initiated by individual families:

> We had a solemn day of thanksgiving at my house for my wife's and son's recovery; my son Eliezer began, Mr. Dawson, John proceeded, I concluded with preaching, prayer; we feasted 50 persons and upwards, blessed be God.[80]

Thomas Paget, Lancashire divine, encouraged home meetings as an enlargement of family devotions:

> It is not only lawful and expedient but also useful and necessary that the governor of a family sometimes, as extraordinary occasions require . . . do call for and crave the company and assistance of some godly brethren and Christian neighbors, for the more solemn performance of religious duties together.[81]

It has become a scholarly commonplace to see home worship as a hallmark of Puritanism. Christopher Hill has written about "the spiritualization of the household" that occurred under the Puritans.[82] Lawrence Stone speaks of the "general tendency to substitute the household for the church" and concludes that "the essence of Puritanism was a family church."[83] William Perkins, we might recall, spoke of the family as "a little church."[84]

The Puritan Sabbath

The issue of Sunday observance is an immense topic that requires brief mention here because of its relevance to Puritan worship. I will content myself with summarizing the main points of the Puritan doctrine of the Sabbath, which have been copiously documented in several excellent studies.[85]

Although Sabbatarianism became a distinguishing mark of Puritanism, the issue of Sunday observance *extended far beyond the Puritan segment of society.* It was as much a political and social issue as a church issue. In the sixteenth century, some Anglicans were as concerned to establish Sabbath policies as were the Puritans. The history of the subject reveals that the desire to keep Sundays free from work was a form of social action as well as a religious act. The Puritans provided the theological basis for Sunday observance. Thus, although all Puritans were Sabbatarians, not all Sabbatarians were Puritans.

The Puritans formulated *a multiple biblical basis for Sabbath observance.* Resting on one day of the week was a memorial to God's creation of the world and (on the basis of Gen. 2:1–3) a creation ordinance. The fourth commandment of the Decalogue made sanctifying one day in seven a moral command. The New Testament Lord's Day makes Sunday a memorial to Christ's resurrection and accounts for the shift from the seventh (the Jewish Sabbath) to the first day of the week. Because Sunday is a day of cessation from earthly labor and a time of worship, it is an experience that prefigures the believer's eternal bliss in heaven.

By basing their theory of Sunday observance partly on the fourth commandment, Puritans accepted a continuity between the Old Testament Sabbath and the New Testament Lord's Day. In doing so, however, they *distinguished between the Old Testament Sabbath as a ceremonial law and as a moral law.* Such facets of the Old Testament Sabbath as its being observed on the seventh day and its extreme prohibitions of work and activity were ceremonial laws that had been abolished after the coming of Christ. But the moral principle that one day in seven should be a day of rest and worship was regarded as a "natural, moral and perpetual" principle.[86] One Puritan theorist identified the permanent moral portion of Sabbath observance as the command "to have one day in the seven to serve the Lord generally in," and the ceremonial portion, abolished by Christ, "to have precisely the Saturday, and to rest so strictly from all labour as they did."[87]

Following the principle stated in the fourth commandment, part of Sunday observance was *rest from ordinary work.* As such it was an antidote to worldliness. Arthur Hildersham said that Sabbath observance was especially necessary for hardworking people who were in danger of having their hearts "corrupted and glued to the world."[88] Nicholas Bownde used similar language in arguing that "we cannot attend God's business if we are encumbered with worldly business."[89] According to William Ames, the specific types of activity that are inappropriate to Sunday are "those which concern our wealth and profit."[90]

Whatever its motivation, Sabbatarian rest from work was *a form of humanitarian social action.* One reason why national and local governments were so zealous in passing and enforcing Sabbath laws was that without it some employers would have forced people to work seven days a week. The Sabbatarians protected the employees who (in Baxter's words) "would be left remediless under such masters as would both oppress them with labour, and restrain them from God's service."[91] Richard Byfield defended the rights of servants to refuse to work on Sundays.[92] Christopher Hill suggests further that it was not only employees who needed this type of protection, but employers as well: "In the seventeenth-century there was only one way in which the industrious sort could be protected from themselves: by the total prohibition of Sunday work, and of travel to and from markets."[93]

In the eighteenth century, Joseph Addison looked back at the Sunday observance that the Puritans had brought to England and concluded:

> If keeping holy the seventh day were only a human institution, it would be the best method that could have been thought of for the polishing and civilizing of mankind: . . . a stated time in which the whole village meet together with their best faces and in their cleanliest habits, to converse with one another upon indifferent subjects, hear their duties explained to them, and join together in adoration of the Supreme Being.[94]

We can catch here the notes of a secular attitude to Sabbath observance, but it serves to remind us of the social dimension of it.

Part of the moral dimension of Sunday observance became a stress on *works of mercy to those in need*. Milton spoke of using the day "to quicken withal the study and exercise of charity," and George Wither of "the charity we owe to our neighbours."[95]

The Puritans went far beyond the utilitarian defense of Sunday that I have been discussing. Their distinctive contribution to Sabbatarianism was to insist that *the main purpose of Sunday was religious worship*. "The principal end then of rest," wrote Nicholas Bownde, "is that we might wholly in soul and body . . . attend upon the worship of God."[96] Peter Bayley admonished:

> Let no man think that a bare rest from labour is all that is required of him on the Lord's Day, but the time which he saves from the works of his calling he is to lay out on those spiritual duties.[97]

John Field's catalog of Sunday duties is typical: God's people should be occupied "in hearing his Word, in giving themselves to prayer, in receiving his sacraments, in meditating of his wonderful works, and putting in practice of holy duties."[98]

If the Puritan Sabbath required rest from work, it was at the same time *opposed to making Sunday a day of idleness.* The Puritan Sunday was emphatically not a day of inactivity. One Puritan wrote:

> He that keeps the Sabbath only by resting from his ordinary work, keeps it but as a beast; but rest on this day is so far forbidden as it is an impediment to the outward and inward worship of Almighty God.[99]

Unless we grasp the underlying religious principle of Sunday observance, some of the Puritans' prohibitions may strike us as silly. The heart of Sabbath observance was *the sanctification of the day to God.* Anything that got in the way of such sanctifying had to go, whether it was work or its opposites, such as sports or idleness. William Ames got to the heart of the matter when he wrote:

> The correct observance of the day requires two things: rest and the sanctification of that rest. . . . Sanctification of this rest, as of the day itself, is in our special devotion to the worship of God. . . . Contrary to the observance of the day are all business, trade, feasts, sports, and other activities which draw the mind of man away from the exercises of religion.[100]

When people work on Sunday, claimed Richard Greenham, it is simply evidence that "they have not been taught to sanctify it."[101]

Because the vital core of the Puritan Sabbath was the sanctification of the day to the worship of God and service to others, the Puritans vigorously *rejected recreation as a worthy Sunday pursuit.* William Perkins wrote:

> It is a notable abuse of many to make the Lord's Day a set day of sport and pastime, which should be a day set apart for the worship of God and the increase in the duties of religion.[102]

Richard Baxter theorized in this regard that people who were physically overworked during the week were not tired in mind but in their bodies, "and therefore there is no recreation so suitable to them as the ease of the body, and the holy and joyful exercise of the mind upon their Creator and their Redeemer and their everlasting rest."[103] For people who claimed that Sunday was the only day on which working people could play, Puritans like Baxter, Dod, and Cleaver had a very humanitarian reply: employers should allow laborers time for recreation during the week.[104]

To view the practice of Sunday observance outlined above as a dreary, joyless experience is a caricature by an irreligious age. Puritans who practiced it had a clear conscience before God and their fellow citizens, and they liked it that way. John Preston spoke of the day as "kept with delight."[105] George Wither talked about "a sanctified pleasure" and "a rectified conscience" as rewards of the day.[106] As for the popularity of Sabbath observance, Thomas Fuller has this portrait:

> It is almost incredible how taking this doctrine was, partly because of its own purity, and partly for the eminent piety of such persons as maintained it; so that the Lord's day . . . began to be precisely kept.[107]

In conclusion, I offer the winsome question of Thomas Hooker: "Is not the sanctification of the Sabbath day better than the profanation of it?"[108]

The Church as a Fellowship

Virtually everything that I have said about Puritan views of the church touches sooner or later on the concept of fellowship. By deemphasizing the institutional church with its clerical hierarchy and fixed ceremonies, the Puritans created a dynamic, fluid church in which fellowship among saints in the worship of God became the central reality.

The focus on fellowship is seen in Puritan definitions of the church. William Ames, for example, defined the church as "a society of believers joined together in a special bond for the continual exercise of the communion of saints among themselves."[109] Another New England Puritan defined it as "a company of people combined together by holy covenant with God, and one with another."[110]

In place of the state church system, in which the local parish mechanically determined the composition of the church, the Puritans increasingly practiced the ideal of a church "gathered" out of society by the voluntary choice of the members. This spirit of freedom breathes through Governor William Bradford's description of the Plymouth church: "the Lord's free people joined themselves (by a covenant of the Lord) into a church estate, in the fellowship of the gospel."[111]

One thing that made it easy to stress fellowship as a feature of church life was the more democratic spirit that prevailed in Puritan congregations as compared with hierarchical conceptions of church order. Several years ago when I visited the church that John Bunyan attended as a youth, the guide pointed out the side door near the front of the originally Catholic church that the clergy had used to avoid contact with the laity as much as possible. We can contrast such a situation with Richard Sibbes's picture of the church as a hospital:

> The church of Christ is a common hospital, wherein all are in some measure sick of some spiritual disease or other; that we should all have ground of exercising mutually the spirit of wisdom and meekness.[112]

I noted earlier that the Puritans stressed the spiritual identity of the church. One consequence of this was that spiritual kinship, and not institutional membership, became the true bond among believers. The spiritual communion of Christians was one of the great Puritan themes. According to Oliver Cromwell's kinsman William Hooke, "the same thread of grace is spun through the hearts of all the godly under heaven."[113] Thomas Watson used the same metaphor: "God's children are knit together with the bond of love, as all the members of the body are knit together by several nerves and ligaments."[114] It is no wonder that Richard Sibbes considered that withdrawing from Christian fellowship was "a grand enormity."[115]

No doubt this extreme valuing of union was fostered by the Puritans' cultural situation in which they were an often-persecuted minority (or in New England a people on the edge of the wilderness). They were virtually forced into pursuing a church-within-a-church. Like other minorities, they formed close relationships in their loyalty to a common cause. Thomas Case wrote from prison, "Oh how amiable are the assemblies of the saints and the ordinances of the Sabbath, when we are deprived of them."[116] Thomas Doolittle noted that "Christ's sheep are sociable creatures" who "love to be with sheep, but not with wolves."[117]

Part of the Puritan concept of fellowship was the belief that Christians can exert a beneficial influence on each other. Mutual spiritual support became a major Puritan ideal. Sibbes praised "that sweet communion of saints . . . to strengthen and encourage one another in the ways of holiness," and he spoke of the ability of Christians to "allure and draw on others to a love . . . of the best things."[118] "Associate with sanctified persons," suggested Thomas Watson; "they may, by their counsel, prayers, and holy example, be a means to make you holy. As the communion of saints is in our creed, so it should be our company."[119]

It is within this framework of wishing the best for other believers that Puritan thinking about exhortation and discipline should be understood. Samuel Ward wrote in his *Diary:*

> Pity men when thou seest them run with full stream to sin, bewail their case, insult not over them. Seek by all gentle means to reclaim them, use not rough words to provoke any man.[120]

Robert Coachman claimed that "it is no small privilege . . . to live in such a society, as where the eyes of their brethren are so lovingly set upon them, that they will not suffer them to go on in sin."[121]

The Puritan ideal of the church as a fellowship of those committed to Christ and to each other awakened some of the Puritans' deepest feelings. Richard Mather pictured the church as a company of Christians, called by the power and mercy of God to fellowship with Christ, and by his providence to live together, and by his grace to cleave together in the unity of faith and brotherly love, and . . . bind themselves to the Lord and one to another, to walk together by the assistance of his Spirit, in all such ways of holy worship in him, and of edification one towards another.[122]

Summary

The Puritans never formed a separate denomination. Their lone institutional legacy was that they laid the foundation for denominational pluralism by making churches increasingly independent from state control.

But even more important than this institutional legacy are the principles for which the Puritans stood. The Puritans based church polity on the authority of the Bible. They viewed the church as a spiritual reality and expanded the role of the laity. They simplified worship, encouraged congregational participation, honored the power of God's Word, and fostered creativity in worship. They also sanctified Sunday for worship and reveled in the fellowship that the church afforded them.

FURTHER READING

Percy A. Scholes, *The Puritans and Music in England and New England* (1934).

Nathaniel Micklem, ed., *Christian Worship: Studies in Its History and Meaning* (1936).

Horton Davies, *The Worship of the English Puritans* (1948).

Patrick Collinson, *The Elizabethan Puritan Movement* (1967).

James H. Nichols, *Corporate Worship in the Reformed Tradition* (1968).

Horton Davies, *Worship and Theology in England: From Cranmer to Hooker, 1534–1603* (1970).

E. Brooks Holifield, *The Covenant Sealed: The Development of Puritan Sacramental Theology in Old and New England, 1570–1720* (1974).

Horton Davies, *Worship and Theology in England: From Andrewes to Baxter and Fox, 1603–1690* (1975).

Winton U. Solberg, *Redeem the Time: The Puritan Sabbath in Early America* (1977).

Paul D. L. Avis, *The Church in the Theology of the Reformers* (1981).

Charles E. Hambrick-Stowe, *The Practice of Piety: Puritan Devotional Disciplines in Seventeenth-Century New England* (1982).

The more ceremonies, the less truth.

— RICHARD GREENHAM

Is not the sanctification of the Sabbath day better than the profanation of it? — THOMAS HOOKER

The church of Christ is a common hospital, wherein all are in some measure sick of some spiritual disease or other; that we should all have ground of exercising mutually the spirit of wisdom and meekness. — RICHARD SIBBES

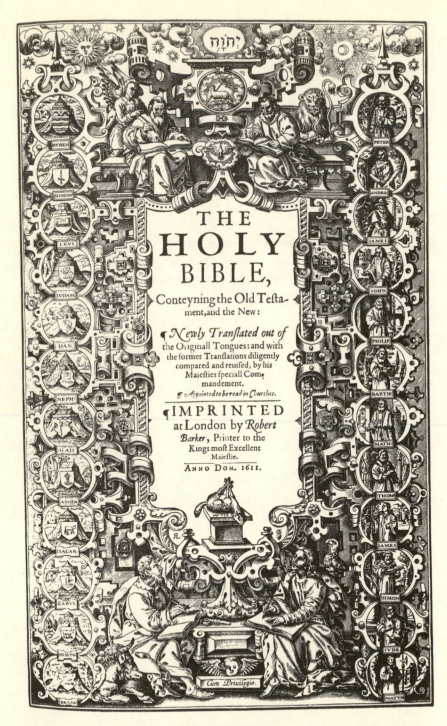

Title page of the 1611 King James Bible. Courtesy of the Huntington Library

Chapter 8

The Bible

There is not a condition into which a child of God can fall but there is a direction and rule in the Word, in some measure suitable thereunto.

— THOMAS GOUGE

What can possibly remain to be said about Puritan attitudes toward the Bible? We all know that the Protestant Reformation championed the Bible as the sole final authority for religious belief. So I theorized as I dutifully resigned myself to including the present chapter in this book.

As it turned out, my research turned up much that is far from familiar. In addition to casting light on current issues, an inquiry into Puritan views on Scripture provides an explanation of where evangelical Protestantism originally got many of its foundational principles. In other areas, the Puritans were champions of ideas about the Bible that modern Christians have neglected to their own impoverishment. In short, Puritan attitudes toward the Bible include much that is of current relevance, historical significance, and corrective value to Christians today.

The Laity's Right of Access to the Bible

The English Reformation was a biblically based movement that took as its motto the right of each Christian to read and interpret the Bible in one's native language. Luther had first given this theory its definitive expression: "We have never yet desired anything else . . . than the liberty to have the Word of God, or the Holy Scriptures, to teach and to practice it."[1]

English Protestants echoed the sentiment. Whereas the Catholic

Erasmus had expressed the wish that the farmer and weaver would be able to recite parts of the Bible at their work, the Puritan William Tyndale was more ambitious. He told a Gloucestershire priest that "if God spare my life, ere many years pass, I will cause a boy that driveth the plough shall know more of the Scriptures than thou dost."[2] In answer to the question, "Doth the knowledge of the Scriptures belong unto all men?" John Ball's Catechism replied, "Yes, all men are not only allowed, but exhorted and commanded, to read, hear, and understand the Scripture. . . . The Scriptures . . . ought to be translated into known tongues and interpreted."[3]

Backed by this conviction that individual Christians should have access to the Bible in their own language, the Puritans, hand in hand with other English Protestants, set about the task of translating the Bible into English. The story begins with William Tyndale, an ardent Reformer and a linguistic genius competent in seven languages. Because of resistance to Bible translation in Catholic England, Tyndale went to the Continent in 1524 to work on his translation of the New Testament. The first printed copies of Tyndale's English New Testament reached England in 1526 amid violent opposition from the Catholic authorities. Tyndale was led to the stake before he translated much of the Old Testament. Just before his death he uttered an eloquently brief statement that would reverberate through several generations of Puritans: "Lord, open the King of England's eyes."

If we are looking for a specifically Puritan contribution to Bible translation, we should look to the Geneva Bible of 1560. Produced by the English-speaking colony in Calvin's Geneva, it became the favorite Bible for several generations of Puritans, as well as the Bible used by Shakespeare and Spenser. It was printed with marginal notes containing Puritan and Calvinistic interpretations of passages. Of more long-term importance were several innovations that set the standard for future English Bibles. It divided the text into numbered verses, making the Bible an easy reference tool. It was printed in Roman type instead of black letter, making it readable by ordinary people. Words that had no precise equivalent in the original were printed in italics to indicate that they had been supplied for the sake of understanding.

The Geneva Bible quickly became the cheap, popular version of the Bible. For more than half a century it was the Bible most read by English people and most often reprinted. In Scotland it was from the beginning the version appointed for used in the churches. Cromwell's *Soldier's Pocket Bible*, issued in 1643 for the use of the parliamentary army, contained selected passages from the Geneva Bible. Perhaps the highest tribute that we can pay to it is to note that it contributed more than any other version to the King James Bible of 1611.

The climax of a century of English Bible translation, and the greatest of all English Bibles, was the version produced under the sanction of King James and the Church of England. It was partly a product of the Puritans. It originated at the Hampton Court Conference, which was held in January 1604. At this conference the Puritans made a number of proposals to King James, one of which was the suggestion that a new translation of the Bible be undertaken.

The proposal was moved by John Reynolds, president of an Oxford college and a leader of the Puritan side of the Church of England. The king was no friend of the Puritans — in fact he had already threatened to "harry them out of the land, or yet do worse" — yet, by a strangely perverted logic he gave impetus to the famous Bible that ironically bears his name. "I profess," he said at the conference, "I could never yet see a Bible well translated in English; but I think that, of all, that of Geneva is the worst."[4]

And so, to spite the Puritans, King James set up the committee of fifty-four scholars who carried out the translation. One historian concludes that the translators were about evenly divided between Anglican and Puritan parties.[5] The resulting Bible, while making use of all the English versions that had preceded it, used more from the Geneva Bible than from any other.

The Bible, of course, does not become a personal possession just because there is an English version of it in the home or pew. Did the presence of English versions of the Bible mean that the Puritans took advantage of the increasing accessibility of Scripture?

There can be little doubt that serious Christians of the Reformation era knew the Bible better than their evangelical counterparts today. They displayed what can truly be called an appetite for the Word. "FEED upon the WORD," John Cotton told his congregation.[6] Richard Baxter begged his readers to "love, reverence, read, study, obey and stick close to the Scripture."[7] As a young man, John Milton's father was put out of his parental home and permanently disinherited when his Catholic father found him reading an English Bible in his room.[8] John Winthrop recorded his "unsatiable thirst after the word of God" after his conversion.[9]

The availability of the Bible quickly produced some familiar Puritan practices. One was daily Bible reading in the home. "Let not a day ordinarily pass you," wrote Cotton Mather, "wherein you will not read some portion of it, with a due meditation and supplication over it."[10] Puritans also began holding Bible studies and prayer meetings, secretly in the late or early hours to avoid harassment from Anglican officials.

Biblical preaching also flourished with the advent of the English

Bible. In fact, when the young Henry Newcome began his first pastorate, an older preacher advised him that his sermons contained too much history and not enough Scripture. "The people came with Bibles," he was reminded, and "expected quotations of Scripture."[11]

Ultimately the most significant result of Bible translation was that it ended the clergy's monopoly on the knowledge and interpretation of the Bible. The Catholic Thomas More rebuked the laity for "meddling" with Scripture and urged them to "say to the preachers appointed thereto, as the people saith unto Moses, 'Hear you God, and let us hear you.'"[12] By contrast, William Ames declared that "the duty of inquiry is laid on men; the gift of discerning truth both publicly and privately is bestowed upon them."[13]

What this right of access actually produced is well summed up in the example of Robert Pasfield, an illiterate servant of John Bruen. According to a biographer of Bruen, Pasfield was "a man utterly unlearned being unable to read a sentence or write a syllable." Yet he "was so well acquainted with the history of the Bible, and the sum and substance of every book and chapter, that hardly could any ask him where such a saying or sentence were, but he would with very little ado tell them in what book and chapter they might find it."[14]

The Nature and Scope of Biblical Authority

Basic to religious belief is the question of what constitutes the authority for belief. Historically there have been three main views of what constitutes the ultimate authority: the Bible, church tradition, and human reason, either alone or in combination. The Puritans, following the lead of the Continental Reformers, claimed Scripture alone as the final authority for religious belief. "The rule according to which conscience is to proceed," wrote Cotton Mather, is "what God has revealed in the Sacred Scriptures."[15] "This is the glory and sure friend of a church," added John Lightfoot, "to be built upon the Holy Scriptures. . . . The foundation of the true church of God is Scripture."[16]

To claim Scripture as the only final authority is, of course, to reject the other options. This is exactly how the Puritans understood the issue. According to Joseph Caryl, the truth or falsity of religious statements cannot be tried "by that which is usually called Antiquity: but by that which transcends all human antiquity, customs, counsels, and traditions (though all those may contribute some help), the Word of God."[17] "Pin not your faith upon men's opinions," wrote John Owen; "the Bible is the touchstone."[18] How important was this view of *sola Scriptura* to the Puritans? The "popish error of tradition," wrote Robert Baillie, "shakes not one or two, but all the ground-stones of Protestant reformation."[19]

The Puritans rested on the Bible alone as the final authority because they believed it to be the inspired Word of God. In a sense different from what could be claimed for any other book, God the Holy Spirit was regarded as the author of the Bible. "Think in every line you read that God is speaking to you," said Thomas Watson.[20] John Eliot, minister and missionary to the Indians from the church of Roxbury, Massachusetts, asserted that "the writings of the Bible are the very words of God."[21] For John Owen, "The whole authority of the Scripture . . . depends solely on its divine original origin. . . . The Scripture hath all its authority from its Author."[22]

If God is the author of the Bible, theorized the Puritans, it is a reliable guide that cannot deceive a Christian. Edward Reynolds spoke of the entire Bible as "being written by the Spirit of truth, which cannot lie nor deceive."[23] John Lightfoot asserted, "All that the holy writers have recorded is true (and no falsehood in the Scripture, but what is from the error of scribes and translators)."[24]

The Puritans' line of reasoning on biblical authority is impeccable: if God is the author of Scripture, it cannot lie, and if it does not deceive, it must be inerrant and infallible. The Puritans did not hesitate to apply either word to the Bible. In keeping with Luther's view that "Scripture . . . has never erred" and Calvin's conviction that the Bible is "the infallible rule of . . . truth,"[25] Samuel Rutherford declared, "The Word of God . . . is infallible."[26] "Only those could set down the rule of faith and conduct," stated William Ames, "who . . . were free from all error because of the direct and infallible direction they had from God."[27] According to Richard Baxter, the apostles wrote "without errors," and for John Owen the Bible was "a stable, infallible revelation of [God's] mind and will."[28]

It is customary in Christian circles today to ascribe the inerrancy of the Bible to the original manuscripts only and to acknowledge the presence of scribal errors in the Bibles that we possess. This distinction can be traced back at least as far as the early Protestants. According to Richard Capel, for example,

> The translators and transcribers might err, being not . . . indued with that infallible spirit in translating, or transcribing. The Scriptures in their translated copies are not free from all possible corruptions.[29]

John Lightfoot stated that "no error or contradiction is in it, but what is in some copies, by the failing of preservers, transcribers, printers, or translators."[30]

It is not hard to determine where the Puritans stood on the question of inerrancy that has so preoccupied twentieth-century apologetics.

Believing the Bible to be God's Word, the Puritans naturally regarded it as being without error. But to say that the Bible is infallible does not end the matter, as the current debate over limited inerrancy has shown. In what areas is the Bible authoritative? Only in matters that speak directly to salvation? Or does the Bible speak infallibly to all of life? The Puritans made it clear how far they extended the authority of the Bible.

To begin, Scripture is the authoritative standard for testing religious truth. It is "the touchstone that trieth all doctrines," "the judge and determiner of all questions and controversies in religion," "the rule according to which we must believe."[31] Thomas Cartwright believed that the Bible teaches "all things pertaining to the kingdom of Heaven, whether in matters of doctrine or government," while for John Gough it was a "touchstone to try all doctrines by."[32]

The Puritans extended biblical authority to matters of morality as well. They viewed Scripture as "sufficient to govern all our actions by," "the perfect system or frame of laws to guide all the moral actions of man."[33] "To me it is a wonder," exclaimed Samuel Rutherford in the heat of debate, "that the Old and New Testament, which containeth an exact system and body of all morals . . . , should not be the only rule of all morals."[34] William Ames called the Bible "a perfect rule of faith and morals."[35]

According to the Puritans, the Bible also governs ecclesiastical issues. Thomas Cartwright started a revolution in the Church of England when he declared that "the Word of God containeth the direction of all things pertaining to the church."[36] William Fulke asserted that "the church of God . . . ought to be directed in all things according to the order prescribed . . . in his holy word."[37] William Ames made it clear that "no observance can be continually and everywhere necessary in the church of God . . . unless it is contained in the Scriptures."[38]

To say that the Puritans regarded the Bible as an infallible guide in the areas of doctrine, ethics, and church practice is to state what everyone probably expects of them. The controversial issue in our day is whether the inerrancy and authority of the Bible extend any further than this. For the Puritans, to limit the authority of the Bible to narrowly "religious" issues would violate the principle that all of life is religious.

When the Puritans spoke about the authority of the Bible, they made it open-ended instead of constantly limiting it to matters pertaining to salvation. "There is not a condition into which a child of God can fall," wrote Thomas Gouge, "but there is a direction and rule in the Word, in some measure suitable thereunto."[39] Richard Sibbes concurred:

> There is not anything or any condition that befalls a Christian in this
> life but there is a general rule in the Scripture for it, and this rule is
> quickened by example, because it is a practical knowledge.[40]

For Cartwright the Bible "contains the direction of . . . whatsoever things
can fall into any part of man's life."[41]

Within such a framework, it is not surprising that the range of issues
to which the Puritans applied biblical principles and proof texts is an
ever-expanding list. According to William Perkins, the Bible "compre-
hendeth many holy sciences," and when he began to list them, they
included "ethics . . . , economics (a doctrine of governing a family) . . . ,
politics (a doctrine of the right administration of a common weal) . . . ,
academy (the doctrine of governing schools well)."[42] According to
another source, the Bible is so broad in its application that all subjects "in
schools and universities" can be related to it.[43]

In thus applying Scripture to all of life, the Puritans did not
simplistically expect to find specific rules that they could literally or
directly follow. What they found was general principles that could be
translated into contemporary situations or applied in general ways to
various disciplines of thought. George Gillespie conceded that for many
of his beliefs "no express Scripture will prove it," but he believed that the
principle underlying a given belief was a "necessary consequence" of
biblical data.[44]

Ultimately the best index to how the Puritans viewed biblical
authority is to observe how they actually applied Scripture. They quoted
proof texts and biblical models on virtually every topic — economics,
government, family, church, life, sex, nature, education, and many
others. Did the Puritans embrace limited or full inerrancy? Their
practice, as well as their theory, made Scripture the rule for all of life.

For people who do not share this conviction that the Bible is an
infallible authority, the perennial charge has always been "bibliolatry."
The charge is actually frivolous. *Everyone* claims *some* authority for his or
her beliefs. To hold the Bible as the ultimate authority did not mean that
the Puritans worshiped the Bible. Increase Mather wrote, "But though
we ought to reverence the blessed Bible above all other books, yet we
may not worship it, but the author of it only."[45]

Principles of Biblical Interpretation

The principles of interpretation espoused by the Puritans will strike
most readers as the standard Protestant way of reading the Bible. This is
no accident. We have the early Protestants to thank for our basic tools of

THE BIBLE

AND

HOLY SCRIPTVRES

CONTEYNED IN

THE OLDE AND NEWE

Testament.

TRANSLATED ACCOR=
ding to the Ebrue and Greke, and conferred With
the best translations in diuers langages.

WITH MOSTE PROFITABLE ANNOTA-
tions vpon all the hard places, and other things of great
importance as may appeare in the Epistle to the Reader.

FEARE TE NOT. STAND STIL, AND BEHOLDE
the saluacion of the Lord, which he wil shewe to you this day. Exod. 14, 13.

AT GENEVA.
PRINTED BY ROVLAND HALL.
M.D.LX.

The Geneva Bible, published in Geneva in 1560, was the standard Puritan Bible until the King James Bible gradually supplanted it. It contributed more to the King James Bible than any other predecessor. *Courtesy of the Huntington Library* biblical analysis. If the territory I am about to cover seems familiar, we need to remind ourselves that these principles were revolutionary when the Reformers first established them.

The Nonallegorical Interpretation of Scripture. The logical starting place is the Puritans' belief that the Bible must ordinarily be interpreted literally or historically, not arbitrarily allegorized. To understand why the Puritans made so much of the literal or single interpretation of Scripture, we need to know something about the centuries-long Catholic practice of attributing allegorical interpretations to virtually all of Scripture.

Catholic interpreters, for example, claimed that in the story of Rebekah, Rebekah's drawing water for Abraham's servant really means that we must daily come to the Bible to meet Christ.[46] The six water pots at the marriage in Cana refer to the creation of the world in six days.[47] The woman's comment in the Song of Solomon that "my beloved is to me a bag of myrrh, that lies between my breasts" was interpreted as meaning the Old and New Testaments, between which stands Christ. Another commentator found the breasts to denote the learned teachers of the church, and yet another thought the verse referred to the crucifixion of Christ, which the believer keeps in eternal remembrance between his breasts, that is, in his heart.[48]

To the Puritans, such allegorizing was ridiculous and unreliable. "The Scripture hath but one sense," claimed Tyndale, "which is the literal sense, and that literal sense is the root and ground of all, and the anchor that never faileth."[49] Thomas Gataker agreed: "Sir, we dare not allegorize the Scriptures, where the letter of it yields us a clear and proper sense."[50]

We should pause to note what the Puritans did *not* mean when they insisted on the literal or plain interpretation of Scripture. They did not mean that the Bible is literal rather than figurative. William Bridge, for example, commented that "though the sense of the Scripture be but one entire sense, yet sometimes the Scripture is to be understood literally, sometimes figuratively and metaphorically."[51] The Puritans did not even deny that there were allegorical passages in the Bible. James Durham wrote, "There is great difference betwixt an allegoric exposition of Scripture, and an exposition of allegoric Scripture."[52] He then proceeded to differentiate between biblical passages intended by their author to be interpreted allegorically and ones in which the allegory is supplied by the interpreter contrary to the intention of the text.

The Clarity of Scripture. Within the context of literal or plain interpretation, two additional Puritan principles fall naturally into place. One of these is the belief that the Bible is clear to any reader on all matters essential to salvation and Christian morality. Given our modern awareness of how variously people interpret the Bible, we are not inclined to make sweeping claims for the clarity of Scripture. The early Protestants, however, were operating in quite a different context. They were at pains to rescue the Bible from the obscurity with which the Catholic clergy had surrounded the Bible with their allegorical interpretations.

Richard Capel linked clarity with literal interpretation when he wrote, "Of the Word of God there is but one sense: it is the easier found out because there is but one sense."[53] "Scripture is so framed," wrote John Arrowsmith, "as to deliver all things necessary to salvation in a clear and perspicuous way."[54] According to John Owen, "All necessary truth is plainly and clearly revealed in the Scripture."[55]

This emphasis on the clarity of Scripture was an outworking of the Puritan belief in the priesthood of all believers, as John Milton made clear when he wrote:

> The very essence of Truth is plainness, and brightness. . . . The Scriptures [protest] their own plainness and perspicuity, calling to them to be instructed, not only the wise and learned, but the simple, the poor, the babes.[56]

The Illumination of the Holy Spirit. The priesthood of all believers also helps to explain what the Reformers had in mind with their constant theme that the Holy Spirit illumines the mind of any Christian as he or she reads the Bible. "Every godly man hath in him a spiritual light," declared John White, "by which he is directed in the understanding of God's mind revealed in his word."[57] Thomas Goodwin said with equal confidence that

> the same Spirit that guided the holy apostles and prophets to write it must guide the people of God to know the meaning of it; and as he first delivered it, so must he help men to understand it.[58]

What are we to make of this confidence that the Holy Spirit guides us in understanding the Bible? We must realize that Catholic allegorizing of the Bible had obscured Scripture, in effect making "the Pope the doorkeeper of Scripture, not the Holy Spirit."[59] Set in the context of ingenious Catholic allegorizing in which the Bible's message was decipherable only by the professional clergy, the Puritan belief in the illumination of the Holy Spirit put the Bible back within the grasp of every reader. Thus John Ball could write:

> We are not necessarily tied to the exposition of Fathers or Councils for the finding out of the sense of Scripture. Who is the faithful

interpreter of the Scripture? The Holy Ghost speaking in the Scripture is the only faithful interpreter of the Scripture.[60]

Interpreting Passages in Context. The Puritans were as insistent as good scholars today that a given passage in the Bible must be interpreted in its context. One of them wrote, "It is the best rule to come to the understanding of the phrases of Scripture, to consider in what sense they were taken in that country, and among the people, where they were written."[61] William Bridge added, "If you would understand the true sense . . . of a controverted Scripture, then look well into the coherence, the scope and context thereof."[62] William Perkins's stock questions for a passage were: "Who? to whom? upon what occasion? at what time? in what place? for what end? what goeth before? what followeth?"[63]

It is obvious that the picture of a Puritan preacher arbitrarily pouncing on a text and applying it without understanding what it meant in context is a travesty foisted on us by the debunkers of the Puritans.

The Unity of Scripture. No principle of interpretation was more crucial to the Puritans than the belief that the Bible is unified. This unity implied, first of all, that the Bible as a whole does not contradict itself. *The Scots Confession* affirmed that "the Spirit of God, who is the Spirit of unity, cannot contradict himself."[64] Richard Mather asserted, "The Word is never contrary to itself."[65]

The phrase that the Puritans most often used when talking about the unity of the Bible was "the analogy of faith." It is an awkward phrase, based on a misinterpretation of Romans 12:6.[66] What the Reformers meant by the phrase was that Scripture makes up a coherent system of doctrine and that any specific passage, including an obscure one, must be interpreted in harmony with what we know about Christian doctrine generally.

John Owen provided one of the best definitions of the concept when he wrote:

> In our search after truth our minds are greatly to be influenced and guided by the analogy of Faith. . . . There is a harmony, an answerableness, and a proportion, in the whole system of faith, or things to be believed. Particular places are so to be interpreted as that they do not break or disturb this order.[67]

William Perkins is also helpful on the subject:

> The analogy of faith is a certain abridgement or sum of the scriptures, collected out of most manifest and familiar places. The parts thereof are two. The first concerneth faith, which is handled in the Apostles' Creed. The second concerneth charity or love, which is explicated in the Ten Commandments.[68]

To see how this analogy of faith works in practice, we can note an example from Thomas Gataker. Gataker refuted an Antinomian interpretation of a passage with the comment that "this cannot be the meaning of the place, because it evidently crosseth the main tenor of the story and the truth of God's Word." In then offering his own interpretation of the passage, Gataker argued that it "well agreeth, both with the truth of the story, and the analogy of faith . . . and receiveth further confirmation . . . from the collation of other Scriptures."[69]

In its practical outworking, this theory meant that a given passage was interpreted by the Bible itself by being placed in the broader context of the Bible as a whole. Alexander Henderson stated that "Scripture cannot be authentically interpreted but by Scripture."[70] Someone else called Scripture "ever the sure expositor of itself."[71] The analogy of faith also meant that obscure passages were interpreted in the light of clear ones. John Owen stated as a rule that "we affix no sense unto any obscure or difficult passages of Scripture but what is . . . consonant unto other expressions and plain texts."[72] In a variety of ways, then, the analogy of faith acted as a safeguard against eccentric interpretations based on isolated passages in the Bible and at the same time ensured a concern with the broad sweep of biblical doctrine.

Law and Gospel. J. I. Packer has said that "with Luther, the Reformers saw all Scripture as being, in the last analysis, either law or gospel — meaning by 'law' all that exposes our ruin through sin and by 'gospel' everything that displays our restoration through faith."[73] This framework, when applied flexibly, helps to organize virtually any passage in Scripture. The Bible as a whole asserts a double theme, one negative, the other positive.

Although the Puritans did not always use Luther's terms *law* and *gospel*, they interpreted the Bible within a similar framework. William Tyndale wrote:

> The scripture containeth . . . first, the law, to condemn all flesh; secondarily, the gospel, that is to say, promises of mercy for all that repent and acknowledge their sins.[74]

William Perkins articulated the same twofold framework when discussing how to conduct the application part of a sermon:

> The foundation of application is to know whether the place propounded be a sentence of the law or of the gospel. . . . For the law is thus far effectual as to declare unto us the disease of sin and by accident to exasperate and stir it up, but it affords no remedy. Now the gospel, as it teacheth what is to be done, so it hath also the efficacy of the Holy Ghost adjoined with it. . . .[75]

George Gillespie spoke of "the general scope" of the Bible as being "to abase man and to exalt God."[76] The most customary Puritan terms for what I have been describing were the "promises" and "threatenings" of God.[77]

The Bible as Literature

The twentieth century has popularized the phrase "the Bible as literature." The irony of that fact, as C. S. Lewis notes,[78] is that the concept became fashionable only after most English-speaking people ceased to believe in the Bible as a sacred book. Our own age has perpetuated an unfortunate dichotomy between unbelievers who read the Bible only as literature and believing Christians who are largely oblivious to the fact that, in its genres and style of writing, the Bible is much closer to an anthology of literature than to a theology book. For the synthesis that sees the Bible as both a sacred book and a work of literature, we need to go back to the Puritan era.

What does it mean that the Bible is partly literary in nature? Primarily three things: the Bible often takes concrete human experience as its subject, it frequently shows a perfection of style and technique that can only be called artistic, and it consists heavily of literary forms or genres rather than expository writing. In all three aspects the Puritans had a grasp of the literary nature of the Bible.

At the level of subject matter, literature takes actual human experience as its focus. It *presents* human experience instead of talking abstractly *about* it. It appeals to our imagination — to our image-making and image-perceiving capacity. William Ames, the archlogician among the Puritans, surprises us by stating, as well as I have ever seen it stated, how literature works:

> In form of expression, Scripture does not explain the will of God by universal and scientific rules, but rather by stories, examples, precepts, exhortations, admonitions, and promises. This style best fits the common usage of all sorts of men and also greatly affects the will by stirring up pious motives, which is the chief end of theology.[79]

Richard Sibbes was equally clear about the fact that the Bible is not content to present truth abstractly and intellectually: "After God hath revealed spiritual truths, and faith hath apprehended them, then imagination hath use while the soul is joined with the body."[80] Henry Lukin summarized the point by saying, "Hence it is that examples are of greater force than precepts, and do in a sort compel."[81]

The Puritans also showed an awareness of the artistry with which Scripture expresses its truth. Thomas Gataker was particularly clear-sighted on the topic:

> Among the rest of Psalms, some of them there are about which the Holy Ghost's pleasure was that the penmen thereof should take more pains than usual, and more art than ordinary should be showed, in the framing and contriving of them: and where he useth more art, we may well expect more excellence.[82]

George Wither called the Psalms the "most excellent lyric poetry that ever was invented," and Milton believed that the poetic parts of the Bible "not in their divine argument alone, but in the very . . . art of composition" are "incomparable" over all extrabiblical poetry.[83]

Did God inspire the forms of the Bible, or only the content? The Puritans not only asked the question but implicitly answered it by saying that the forms of the Bible are worthy of our attention and admiration. They spoke repeatedly of what one of them called "the majesty of the style" of the Bible.[84]

Approaching the Bible as literature also means being sensitive to its literary forms or genres, and here too the Puritans are a reliable guide. The two dominant genres in the Bible are narrative, or story, and poetry. The basic premise of narrative is that the storyteller speaks *with* characters and events, not in the form of logical arguments. Narrative embodies the meaning in a concrete example or situation.

This was exactly how the Puritans viewed biblical narrative. William Perkins, after dividing the Old Testament books into the three categories of historical, dogmatic, and prophetic, commented that the historical books (Genesis through Job) are "stories of things done, for the illustration or confirmation of that doctrine which is propounded in other books."[85] Richard Rogers explained his purpose in a commentary on Judges this way:

> I intended . . . to benefit students and preachers . . . so they may learn how to make use of the historical part of the Bible and learn to draw doctrine and instruction out of the examples thereof.[86]

The result of this interest in biblical narrative as a source of theological truth was a whole body of Puritan preaching and exegesis that treated biblical characters and events as examples of general principles that were relevant to people in any age.

The other major category of biblical literature is poetry. The important principle here is that poetry uses a special idiom comprised of images and figures of speech. Poetry is based on a kind of indirection.

Puritans were people of the Book. Here a character in Bunyan's *Pilgrim's Progress* reads the Bible. Courtesy of the special collections of the Wheaton College Library

Like narrative, therefore, it calls for interpretation. The Puritans had a great deal to say about the figurative language of the Bible.

The most general rule for interpreting poetry was stated by John Ball as the need to determine "whether the words be spoken figuratively or simply."[87] Thomas Hall similarly asserted the necessity to pay attention to the "metaphors, metonymies, synecdoches, etc." in the Bible, adding that "ignorance of rhetoric is one ground of many errors" in biblical interpretation.[88] Wither spoke of the "similes, metaphors, hyperboles, comparisons" in the Psalms, and Richard Sibbes was equally sensitive to how "God hath condescended to represent heavenly things to us under earthly terms."[89]

Virtually every Puritan commentator showed similar familiarity with the forms of poetry. A modern literary scholar has shown how seventeenth-century Protestants believed in "the centrality of figurative language to theological truth." They viewed poetic language not as ornament but as a vehicle for divine truth: "the governing assumption . . . was that the poetic language of scripture in itself . . . is a vehicle of truth, validated by God himself who chose such forms for his revelation."[90]

To summarize, Puritan commentators handled the Bible with sensitivity to its literary forms and style. They recognized the Bible's tendency to embody truth in concrete images and literary genres such as story and poetry. They also admired its stylistic excellence.

The Affective Power of the Bible

For the Puritans, the Bible was a book of information and theology, but it was also more than that. It was an affective book — a book with more-than-ordinary ability to move and influence a person.

A key principle underlying the Puritan experience of the Bible was the belief that the Bible is perpetually relevant and up-to-date. William Ames wrote:

> Although various parts of the Scripture were written upon a special occasion and were directed to particular men or assemblies, in God's intention they are equally for the instruction of the faithful of all ages, as if specially directed to them.[91]

Isaac Ambrose believed that the content of the Bible is "daily verified in others and in my own self," and the advice of Thomas Gouge regarding the commands and warnings of the Bible was, "So apply them to thy self as if God by name had delivered the same unto thee."[92] Regarding the details in the Bible as open-ended in their application, the Puritans produced a wealth of sermons, histories, and diaries in which they read their own experiences in terms of the history and characters of the Bible.

Convinced that the Bible spoke to their own situations, the Puritans championed the idea of daily reading of the Bible. John Preston spoke for most Puritans when he wrote, "If though wouldest abound in grace, . . . study the Scriptures, much attend to them, much meditate in them day and night."[93] Richard Greenham advised, "Evermore be musing, reading, hearing, and talking of God's word."[94]

The Puritans knew that there is nothing magical about reading the Bible. Bible reading does not produce any effects automatically, the way the ground absorbs the rain. Everything depends on how the individual mind and will act upon the Word. The Puritans looked upon contact with the Bible as a springboard to action. Such a process began with the assent of the will to the content of the Bible. John Bunyan found "his soul and Scripture . . . to embrace each other, and a sweet correspondency and agreement between them."[95] Mere head knowledge was never the goal of Puritan Bible reading. Nicholas Udall defended biblical translation on the ground that it led people "not to be curious searchers of the high mysteries, but to be faithful executors and doers of God's biddings."[96]

The key to allowing the Bible to be a spur to action was, according to the Puritans, to view it as personally applicable. Robert Harris said that "we must be careful to read it, hear it, lodge it in our hearts, apply it close to our consciences, and then it will heal our hearts."[97] Cornelius Burges wrote:

> It is the great fault of too many, when they read in Scripture of wonderful protections and deliverances, they behold them only to admire the acts done, but not to roll themselves by virtue thereof upon God for the like.[98]

Increase Mather noted that the Bible "reaches ye very thoughts of ye heart," while Henry Lukin commented that

> in reading any command or prohibition in Scripture we must make particular application of it to ourselves, as if God had directed it to us in particular or had spoken to us by name or sent a special message from heaven to us.[99]

Because the Puritans viewed contact with the Bible as dynamic rather than static, they had enormous faith in the affective power of Scripture. Edward Reynolds wrote, "Though men were as hard as rocks, the Word is a hammer which can break them; though as sharp as thorns and briers, the Word is a fire which can devour and torment them."[100] George Gillespie spoke of "the irresistible power over the conscience" that the Bible possesses, while Nicholas Udall called Scripture "the consuming fire of God's word."[101] John Goodwin observed that

> the world now for many generations together hath had a full experiment [experience] of this great power we speak of, breaking out of the Scriptures in the ministry of them, like fire or lightening out of the cloud, by which their hearts and souls have been revived, quickened, and raised, as it were, from the dead.[102]

The English equivalent to the moment when Martin Luther stood at his trial and declared, "I am bound by the Scriptures," was the trial of John Rogers in 1555. At Rogers' trial before the High Commission on charges of heresy, Bishop Stephen Gardiner, Queen Mary's Lord Chancellor, asserted, "No, no, thou canst prove nothing by the Scripture, the Scripture is dead: it must have a lively expositor." To which Rogers replied, "No, the Scripture is alive."[103] It was, indeed, the unstated motto of two centuries of Puritans.

Summary

The Puritans were people of a Book. They made the Bible accessible to everyone by translating it into English. They regarded the Bible as a trustworthy guide for all of life. For the Puritans, moreover, the Bible was a living book, uniquely powerful to affect a person's behavior and destiny.

The Puritans also bequeathed the principles of biblical interpretation that still stand — an emphasis on the plain level of meaning rather than arbitrary allegorizing, a reliance on the illumination of the Holy Spirit for any true seeker after the truth of Scripture, attention to the context of a passage, a confidence in the unity of the Bible, a distinction between law and gospel as the dominant biblical themes, and sensitivity to the literary dimension of the Bible.

What did the Bible mean to the Puritans? The preface to the Geneva Bible is an apt summary: the Bible is "the light to our paths, the key of the kingdom of heaven, our comfort in affliction, our shield and sword against Satan, the school of all wisdom, the glass wherein we behold God's face, the testimony of his favor, and the only food and nourishment of our souls."

FURTHER READING

Benjamin B. Warfield, *The Westminster Assembly and Its Work* (1931).

J. I. Packer, in *A Goodly Heritage* (1958), pp. 18–26.

U. Milo Kaufmann, *The Pilgrim's Progress and Traditions in Puritan Meditation* (1966).

Jack B. Rogers, *Scripture in the Westminster Confession* (1967).

Derek Wilson, *The People and the Book: The Revolutionary Impact of the English Bible, 1380–1611* (1976).

Barbara K. Lewalski, *Protestant Poetics and the Seventeenth-Century Religious Lyric* (1979).

Allen Carden, "The Word of God in Puritan New England: Seventeenth-Century Perspectives on the Nature and Authority of the Bible," *Andrews University Seminary Studies*, 18 (Spring 1980): 1–16.

John R. Knott, Jr., *The Sword of the Spirit: Puritan Responses to the Bible* (1980).

Think in every line you read that God is speaking to you.
— THOMAS WATSON

The foundation of the true church of God is Scripture.
— JOHN LIGHTFOOT

The scripture containeth . . . first, the law, to condemn all flesh; secondarily, the gospel, that is to say, promises of mercy for all that repent and acknowledge their sins.
— WILLIAM TYNDALE

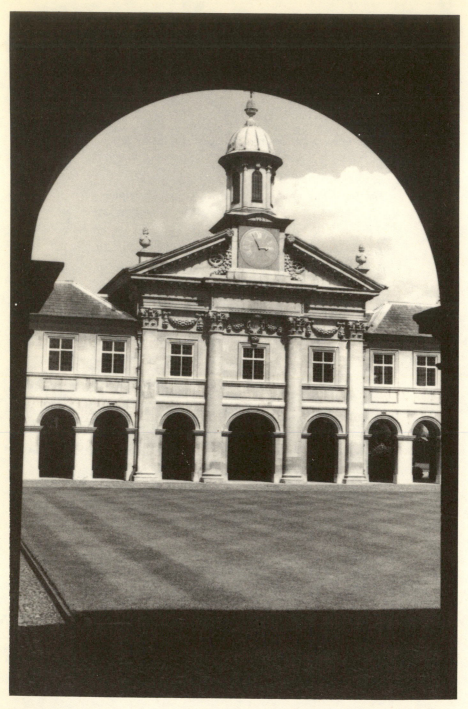

Puritanism was an educated movement. Especially influential was Emmanuel College, Cambridge University.

Chapter 9

Education

"Truth comes from God, wheresoever we find it, and it is ours."
— RICHARD SIBBES

T. S. Eliot once observed that "we must derive our theory of education from our philosophy of life. The problem turns out to be a religious problem."[1] The Puritans would have agreed. There has never been a better example of education growing out of a philosophy of life than the one provided by the Puritans.

The theory of education that I am about to outline is a corrective not only to secular education today but to much Christian education as well. Some spokesmen for Christian education today who assume that they stand within the Reformation tradition are in fact outside it.

The Puritans as Advocates for Education

Before looking at the Puritan philosophy of education, we can profitably note a few facts and statistics regarding Puritan involvement in education. This historical sketch will show that Puritan zeal for education was one of the most noteworthy aspects of the movement.

In America no other English-speaking colonizers established higher education as soon after their arrival as did the Puritans. Only six years after their arrival in Massachusetts Bay, the General Court voted four hundred pounds "toward a school or college."[2] Thus established, Harvard College was kept alive during its early years partly through the sacrifice of farmers, who contributed wheat to support teachers and students.[3]

In the famous document of American Puritanism entitled *New*

England's First Fruits (1643), we read this account of what lay behind the founding of Harvard College:

> After God had carried us safe to New England, and we had builded our houses, provided necessaries for our livelihood, reared convenient places for God's worship, and settled the civil government, one of the next things we longed for and looked after was to advance learning and perpetuate it to posterity.[4]

Cotton Mather called that act "the best thing that ever New England thought upon," adding that the Puritans "were willing to let the richer colonies, which retained the ways of the Church of England, see 'how much true religion was a friend unto good literature.' "[5]

Founding schools became a hallmark of American Puritanism. "Lord, for schools everywhere among us!" prayed John Eliot at a synod of the Boston churches in their early days; "Oh, that our schools may flourish! That every member of this assembly may go home and procure a good school to be encouraged in the town where he lives."[6] A 1647 law of Massachusetts ordered the establishment of schools, and Connecticut did the same three years later. The New Haven Code of 1655 ordered all parents and masters to provide means for teaching their children and apprentices.[7]

This respect for education was equally characteristic of English Puritanism. The number of grammar schools doubled in England while the Puritans were in the ascendancy.[8] John Knox had the boldness to admonish the Great Council of Scotland that "your Honours be most careful for the virtuous education and godly upbringing of the youth of this realm."[9] An English Puritan told Parliament:

> That God who is abstract wisdom and delights that his rational creatures should search after it, and that his ministers should study to propagate it, will expect that you should be foster-fathers of knowledge.[10]

Oliver Cromwell was personally responsible for establishing a college at Durham.[11]

Modern historians of education credit the Puritans with great educational accomplishments. One of them says that "in several respects the Commonwealth was a period when university studies reached a peak."[12] Between 1640 and 1660 the Puritan authorities took an active role in regulating the nation's schools and establishing new schools. The Propagation Act of 1641 was instrumental in founding more than sixty free schools in Wales, all of which disappeared after the Restoration.[13] Cromwell "founded or re-founded scores of elementary schools, and he also directed that commissioners be sent throughout the country to ascertain educational needs."[14]

Puritan Defenses of Learning Against Anti-Intellectualism

Education has always needed defense against anti-intellectual forces in society and within the church. In the seventeenth century, radical Protestants in England known as "sectaries" kept up a running attack on the Puritans and others who extolled the value of education and the importance of reason. Their counterparts in America, known as "the antinomians," created such a disturbance that the Puritans finally banished them to Rhode Island. One of the antinomians asserted his preference in preaching with the comment, "I had rather hear such a one that speaks from the mere motion of the spirit, without any study at all, than any of your learned scholars, although he may be fuller of Scripture."[15]

The Puritans overwhelmingly defended the cause of learning and the faculty of reason against such attacks on the mind. For the Puritans, zeal was no substitute for knowledge. John Preston declared, "I deny not but a man may have much knowledge and want grace, but on the other side, . . . you cannot have more grace than you have knowledge."[16] Richard Baxter believed that "education is God's ordinary way for the conveyance of his grace, and ought no more to be set in opposition to the Spirit than the preaching of the Word."[17] John Cotton claimed that although "knowledge is no knowledge without zeal," yet "zeal is but a wild-fire without knowledge."[18]

The sectaries and antinomians pictured faith and reason as antagonists. The Puritans rejected the perennial attempt to belittle reason in religious matters. "Faith is grounded upon knowledge," said Samuel Willard; "though God be . . . seen by an eye of faith, yet he must be seen by an eye of reason too: for though faith sees things above reason, yet it sees nothing but in a way of reason."[19] John Preston wrote that divine grace

> elevateth reason, and makes it higher, it makes it see further than reason could, it is contrary indeed to corrupt reason, but to reason that is right reason it is not contrary, only it raiseth it higher: and therefore faith teacheth nothing contrary to sense and reason.[20]

John Cotton called reason "an essential wisdom in us," and William Hubbard, "our most faithful and best councilor."[21]

The Puritans' faith in the authority of the Bible did not lead them to belittle reason as unimportant. Cotton Mather made the profound comment that "Scripture is reason in its highest elevation."[22] Harvard's first college laws required that students be able not only to read the Scriptures, but also "to resolve them logically."[23] A hint of what this entailed is suggested by Richard Baxter's description of instances when Christians must use their reason:

> We must use our best reason . . . to know which are the true Canonical Scriptures . . . , to expound the text, to translate it truly . . . , to gather just and certain inferences from Scripture assertions; to apply general rules to particular cases, in matters of doctrine, worship, discipline, and ordinary practice.[24]

William Bridge sounded the authentic Puritan note when he wrote that "reason is of great use, even in the things of God."[25] Thomas Hooker was eulogized by his colleague Samuel Stone for making "the truth appear by light of reason."[26]

Given the forces of anti-intellectualism at work in their own religious milieu, the Puritans could have slipped into a disparagement of reason. Instead they remained defenders of reason and knowledge.

Puritan Aversion to Ignorance

The Puritans' defense of learning and reason had as its counterpart an unusual aversion to ignorance, especially in religious matters. The impulse behind the Puritans' founding of Harvard College was their "dreading to leave an illiterate ministry to the churches, when our present ministers shall lie in the dust."[27] Ebenezer Pemberton, in a funeral sermon delivered on the death of the Honorable John Walley, declared that "when ignorance and barbarity invade a generation, their glory is laid in the dust."[28] Thomas Hooker exclaimed regarding the English people of his day, "It is incredible and unconceivable, what ignorance is among them," while William Perkins was of the opinion that "where ignorance reigneth, there reigns sin."[29]

To say that the Puritans treasured an educated mind is not to imply that they found that ideal easy to attain. The obstacles to it were the same then as now: mental laziness, the complacency and snobbery of ignorance, the pressures of time, and the temptation to amass money instead of paying for an education.

Puritan leaders, at least, valued an educated mind over material riches. Cotton Mather admonished his congregation with the comment, "If your main concern be to get the riches of this world for your children, and leave a belly full of this world unto them, it looks very suspiciously as if you were yourselves the people of this world, whose portion is only in this life."[30] John Milton paid this moving tribute to his father as he neared the completion of his college education:

> Father, you did not enjoin me to go where the broad way lies open, where money slides more easily into the hand, and the golden hope of piling up wealth shines bright and sure . . . , desiring rather that my mind should be cultivated and enriched. . . . What greater wealth could a father have given . . . , though he had given all things except heaven?[31]

Setting the right priority of values has been the hidden agenda for every generation of Christians. In a day of relatively modest material means, many Puritans showed by their actions that they valued learning above possessions.

The Christian Purpose of Education

Albert Einstein once remarked that we live in a day of perfect means and confused goals. The Puritans did not make that mistake. The strength of their educational theory was that they knew what education was *for*. Their primary goal was Christian nurture and growth.

The statutes of Emmanuel College, the most Puritan college at Cambridge University, stated, "There are three things which above all we desire all the Fellows of this college to attend to, to wit, the worship of God, the increase of the faith, and probity of morals."[32] John Knox exhorted the Council of Scotland to be "most careful for the virtuous education and godly upbringing of the youth of this realm," for "the advancement of Christ's glory."[33]

American Puritans voiced the same religious goals for education. The immediate occasion for founding Harvard College was religious, as we have already seen. One rule observed at the new college was this:

> Let every student be plainly instructed and earnestly pressed to consider well the main end of his life and studies is to know God and Jesus Christ which is eternal life, John 17:3, and therefore to lay Christ in the bottom, as the only foundation of all sound knowledge and learning.[34]

When his son entered Harvard as a student, Thomas Shepard wrote to him, "Remember the end of your life, which is coming back again to God, and fellowship with God."[35]

The religious goal of education was evident in the most famous educational act ever passed in America. It is known as "Ye Old Deluder

Act" and it established free public education in Massachusetts in 1647. The reason that the General Court of Massachusetts gave for the establishment of a reading school was this: it is "one chief project of ye old deluder, Satan, to keep men from the knowledge of the Scriptures."[36] The way to foil Satan, according to the Puritans, was to educate people to read and study the Bible.

It is obvious that the Puritans would be shocked by secular education devoid of religious purpose. In their view, such an education would lack the most essential ingredient. Cotton Mather expressed it thus:

> Before all, and above all, tis the knowledge of the Christian religion that parents are to teach their children. . . . The knowledge of other things, though it be never so desirable an accomplishment for them, our children may arrive to eternal happiness without it. But the knowledge of the godly doctrine in the words of the Lord Jesus Christ is a million times more necessity for them.[37]

The English preacher Thomas Gataker saw things the same way:

> Let parents learn here what to aim at in the education of their children . . . : not study only how to provide portions for them . . . but labor to train them up in true wisdom and discretion.[38]

It is important to note in passing that Puritan writers on the subject address most of their remarks about the Christian goal of education to parents, not to educators. In the Puritans' view, Christian education begins at home and is ultimately the responsibility of parents. Schools are only an extension of parental instruction and values, not a substitute for them.

The Centrality of the Bible in the Curriculum

Given this religious conception of education, the Puritans naturally made the study of the Bible and Christian doctrine central in their curriculum. This practice can be traced to Luther, who had insisted, "Above all, the foremost reading for everybody, both in the universities and in the schools, should be Holy Scripture. . . . I would advise no one to send his child where the Holy Scriptures are not supreme."[39]

The Puritans agreed. At Cambridge University, the statutes of Emmanuel College established the Bible as central to the curriculum:

> It is an ancient institution in the church . . . that schools and colleges be founded for the education of young men in all piety and good learning and especially in Holy Writ and theology, that being thus instructed they may thereafter teach true and pure religion.[40]

At Harvard College the rule was that

> every one shall so exercise himself in reading the Scriptures twice a
> day that he shall be ready to give such an account of his proficiency
> therein . . . as his tutor shall require, . . . seeing the entrance of the
> word giveth light, it giveth understanding to the simple, Psalm
> 119:130.[41]

The Puritans' aim in the classroom was to measure all human
knowledge by the standard of biblical truth. Although Milton's proposed
curriculum contained both classical and Christian readings, the works of
writers like Plato and Plutarch were subjected finally to "the determinate
sentence of David and Solomon, or the evangels and apostolic scriptures."[42] Thomas Hall wrote that "we must . . . bring human learning
home to divinity to be pruned and pared with spiritual wisdom."[43] A
stipulation at Rivington School, one of many grammar schools founded
by Puritans in Lancashire, England, was that the instruction must be in
accord with "that which is contained in the holy Bible."[44]

Milton's Definition of Christian Education

The classic statement of the Christian goal of education appears in
Milton's famous treatise *Of Education*, where he wrote:

> The end then of learning is to repair the ruins of our first parents by
> regaining to know God aright, and out of that knowledge to love him,
> to imitate him, to be like him.[45]

Milton here defines education in terms of what it is designed to
accomplish. There may be many ways to achieve a Christian education,
but in the meantime we had better not lose sight of what it *is*.

In Milton's view, education is not what people so often reduce it
to — completing a certain number of courses, writing the required
number of papers, "getting a requirement out of the way," or acquiring a
degree (though perhaps not an education). Milton the educator is less
interested in how much a person knows than in the kind of person he or
she is in the process of becoming.

The goal of education, in Milton's definition, focuses on a person's
relationship to God. Properly conducted, a person's education makes him
or her a better Christian. Milton even describes education as a process of
sanctification when he writes that the aim is "to know God aright, and out
of that knowledge to love him, to imitate him, to be like him." We
customarily limit sanctification to moral and spiritual progress; for
Milton, becoming like God can mean coming to share God's love of truth
and beauty as well as his holiness.

The Puritans kept the religious goal of education clearly in view. They had big expectations for Christian education, which they conceived very broadly. While our society today is preoccupied with marketable skills, the Puritans were busy talking about becoming like God.

The Liberal Arts Ideal

The Puritan emphasis on the Christian element in education will surprise no one. That emphasis, however, is only half of the picture. The other half is not nearly so well known. While the aim of Puritan education was religious, its *content* was the liberal arts. Puritan colleges were established primarily to provide an educated clergy, but this did not mean that they were seminaries or Bible colleges. They were Christian liberal arts colleges.

This concern for a broad education in all subjects was influenced by the Continental Reformers, especially Luther and Calvin. Luther had written to the councilmen of Germany:

> If I had children and could manage it, I would have them study not only languages and history, but also singing and music together with the whole of mathematics. . . . The ancient Greeks trained their children in these disciplines; . . . they grew up to be people of wonderous ability, subsequently fit for everything.[46]

"Fit for everything": this has always been the goal of liberal education, as distinct from vocational training.

The person fit for everything was also a Puritan ideal. Robert Cleaver theorized that no matter what profession a person entered,

> the more skill and knowledge he hath in the liberal sciences, so much the sooner shall he learn his occupation and the more ready . . . shall he be about the same.[47]

In the Dorchester, Massachusetts, regulations of 1645, the master of the school was required to instruct his pupils "both in humane learning and good literature," with the latter phrase denoting the humanities as distinct from a vocational education.[48]

We might expect that as the early American settlers struggled with the wilderness for their survival they would have been indifferent to the liberal arts, but the reverse is true. Cotton Mather praised President Charles Chauncy of Harvard not only for "how constantly he expounded the Scriptures to them in the college hall" but also "how learnedly he . . . conveyed all the liberal arts unto those that sat at his feet."[49] The ministerial students at Harvard not only learned to read the Bible in its original languages and to expound theology, but also studied mathematics, astronomy, physics, botany, chemistry, philosophy, poetry, history, and medicine. One authority describes the initial tradition at Harvard as one in which "there was no distinction between a liberal and a theological education, and its two sources were first, Calvinism, and second, Aristotle."[50]

For the Reformers and their heirs the Puritans, no education was complete if it included only religious knowledge. Samuel Rutherford said, for example, "It is false that Scripture only, as contradistinguished from the law of nature, can direct us to Heaven: for both concurreth in a special manner, nor is the one exclusive of the other."[51] The General Court of Massachusetts went on record as believing that "skill in the tongues and liberal arts" was "beyond all question not only laudable but necessary for educated people."[52] Here again we can see the Puritan unwillingness to set up a division between the spiritual and the natural.

To this day, ministers in the Reformed and Puritan traditions are expected to have a college education plus seminary training, not simply a religious education as in some pietistic traditions. This practice is part of the Puritan heritage. "What art or science is there which a divine shall not stand in need of?" asked Richard Bernard; "grammar, rhetoric, logic, physics, mathematics, metaphysics, ethics, politics, economics, history, and military discipline" are all useful to the minister.[53]

In America, President Chauncy of Harvard said that "as far as it concerns a minister to preach all profitable and Scripture truths, the knowledge of arts and sciences is useful and expedient to him to hold them forth to his hearers."[54] Cotton Mather's writings show his acquaintance with more than three hundred authors, including Aristotle, Cato, Livy, Homer, Ovid, Plutarch, Virgil, and Tacitus.[55] Matthew Swallow praised his pastor, John Cotton, for excelling "in the knowledge of the arts and tongues, and in all kind of learning divine and human," adding, "Neither did he feed his people with the empty husks of vain discourses."[56]

The Puritans' endorsement of the liberal arts is easily explainable if we keep in mind that in England the Puritan era was also the age of the Renaissance. The Renaissance was a rebirth of the humanistic values of classical culture. It was based on a recovery of classical written texts, and it led to humanism — the striving to perfect all human possibilities. Although in our century the term "humanism" is sometimes used to denote purely human knowledge, in the sixteenth and seventeenth centuries most humanists were *Christian* humanists. They valued human knowledge within a context of God-centered Christianity.

It would be a great mistake to set up Puritanism and the classical

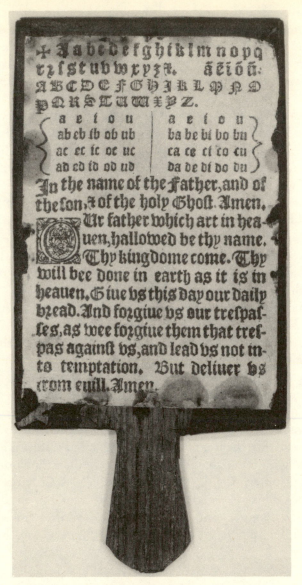

This hornbook used by Puritan school children reminds us of how important education was in the Puritans' daily life. It also suggests the essential thrust of Puritan education: mastery of the tools of culture for Christian ends. *Courtesy of the Folger Shakespeare Library* [STC 13813.5]

Renaissance as opposites. They shared much in common, including a repudiation of medieval Catholicism, a desire to return to a more distant past, and a preoccupation with ancient written texts as the key to constructive change. That is why C. S. Lewis can write that "there was no necessary enmity between Puritans and humanists. They were often the same people, and nearly always the same sort of people: the young men in the Movement, the impatient progressives demanding a 'clean sweep.'"[57] The first translators of classical texts into English were radical Protestants or Puritans.[58] Both the humanistic Renaissance and Puritanism shared a zeal for education as the best means by which to change the consciousness and values of their culture.[59]

The Puritan ideal was a comprehensive study of human knowledge in all its branches within a context of biblical revelation. Such an integration of human knowledge with the Bible is captured in a Harvard thesis of 1670 that described the seven liberal arts as "a circle of seven sections of which the center is God."[60] Puritans of such a mind looked on piety and learning as complementary, not as opposites. The phrases they used when speaking about schools speak volumes: "seed plots of piety and the liberal arts"; "piety, morality, and learning"; "knowledge and godliness"; "progress in learning and godliness"; "that fit persons of approved piety and learning may . . . employ themselves in the education of children in piety and good literature."[61]

All Truth Is God's Truth

The Puritan commitment to humanistic knowledge was based on the conviction that God is the ultimate source of all truth. All truth is God's truth. Richard Sibbes asserted that

> truth comes from God, wheresoever we find it, and it is ours, it is the church's. . . . We must not make an idol of these things, but truth, wheresoever we find it, is the church's; therefore, with a good conscience we may make use of any human author.[62]

Charles Chauncy said in a commencement sermon, "It cannot be denied that all truth, whosoever it be that speaks it, comes from the God of truth."[63]

The doctrinal framework that allowed the Puritans to affirm both religious and human knowledge was the idea that God had revealed his truth in two "books"—the Bible and nature. In England, Edward Reynolds refuted the sectaries' attack on human learning with the comment:

> there is a knowledge of God *natural* in and by his works: and a knowledge *supernatural* by revelation out of the Word; and though this be the principal, yet the other is not to be undervalued.[64]

On the other side of the Atlantic, Thomas Shepard wrote to his son at Harvard:

> Remember that not only heavenly and spiritual and supernatural knowledge descends from God, but also all natural and human learning and abilities; and therefore pray much, not only for the one but also for the other from the Father of Lights and mercies.[65]

Believing in God's general revelation in nature as well as his special revelation in the Bible, the Puritans fully embraced the scientific study of the physical world. Whether they actually produced the rise of modern science is a question of great scholarly debate, but that they were favorable to that movement is indisputable.[66] Richard Baxter wrote:

> Our physics, which is a great part of human learning, is but the knowledge of God's admirable works; and hath any man the face to call himself God's creature, and yet to reproach it as vain human learning?[67]

Alexander Richardson wrote that "the world and the creatures therein are like a book wherein God's wisdom is written, and there must we seek it out."[68] For John Cotton, "To study the nature and course and use of all God's works is a duty imposed by God upon all sorts of men."[69]

The Puritans embraced the study of the arts as fully as science. In the Dorchester regulations of 1645 the master was required to instruct his pupils "both in human learning and good literature," which meant the humanities and the classics.[70] Increase Mather went so far as to tell the legislature that "some have well and truly observed that the interest of religion and good literature hath risen and fallen together."[71]

Buttressing the Puritan acceptance of the liberal arts was the doctrine of common grace, which has always been prominent in Calvinism. The doctrine of common grace asserts that God endows all people, believers and unbelievers alike, with a capacity for truth, goodness, and beauty. Calvin described common grace thus:

> In reading profane authors, the admirable light of truth displayed in them should remind us that the human mind, however much fallen and perverted from its original integrity, is still adorned and invested with admirable gifts from its Creator. If we reflect that the Spirit of God is the only fountain of truth, we will be careful . . . not to reject or condemn truth wherever it appears.[72]

A firm grip on the doctrine of common grace allowed most Puritan educators to accept the validity of pagan learning.[73] Increase Mather noted that "some among the heathen have been notable moralists, such as Cato, Seneca, Aristides, etc."[74] Based on such a view of common grace,

Mather could encourage people to "find a friend in Plato, a friend in Socrates and . . . in Aristotle."[75] Charles Chauncy wrote, "Who can deny but that there are found many excellent and divine moral truths in Plato, Aristotle, Plutarch, Seneca, etc.?"[76] The English Puritan Richard Sibbes believed that since "truth comes from God," we "may read heathen authors."[77]

Since all truth is God's truth, it is ultimately one. The Puritans thus had a foundation for seeing the interrelatedness of all academic subjects. Samuel Mather commented that

> all the arts are nothing else but the beams and rays of the Wisdom of the first Being in the creatures, shining and reflecting thence upon the glass of man's understanding; and as from Him they come, so to Him they tend. Hence there is an affinity and kindred of arts. One makes use of another, one serves to another, till they all reach and return to Him.[78]

Someone has rightly said that "in view of the Puritans' belief in the unity of all knowledge, to surrender any of the arts and sciences . . . was unthinkable."[79]

A Complete and Generous Education

The Puritan ideal in learning was liberal arts education. Its goal was a capable and qualified person. No statement of that ideal can rival Milton's in his treatise *Of Education:*

> I call therefore a complete and generous education that which fits a man to perform justly, skilfully, and magnanimously, all the offices, both private and public, of peace and war.[80]

The heart of Milton's definition is that a complete education is one that frees a person to perform "all the offices, both private and public." A liberal education is comprehensive. It prepares a person to do well all that he or she may be called to do in life.

Learning a certain amount of information will not by itself constitute a liberal education. Such knowledge becomes worthwhile only as it is instrumental in forming a qualified person. The effects of a good education, according to Milton, are twofold: education influences people in their personal lives, and it makes them productive members of society.

Education in our day often focuses on a single public role, that of job or vocation, which is increasingly defined in economic terms only. Milton's phrase "public offices" covers much more than that, however. It includes being a good church member and a positive contributor to the community.

In thus stressing the social purpose of education, Milton was typically Puritan. John Knox had exhorted parents to educate their sons "to the profit of the church and to the commonwealth."[81] On the American scene, the Roxbury Act of 1645 established education "as a means for the fitting of instruments for public service in church and commonwealth."[82]

And what are the "private offices" that Milton mentioned? They included being a good friend, roommate, spouse, or parent, and they include the most personal world of all — the inner world of the mind and imagination. One of the best tests of whether a person is generously educated is what he or she does with leisure time. Many Puritans were not offended at the idea that knowledge is its own reward, even when it is not directly useful. Richard Baxter spoke of a person taking "comfort of his learning and wisdom" by "making discoveries in arts and sciences which delight him . . . by the very acting."[83] Edward Reyner defended the study of natural philosophy partly on the ground that it "is a very pleasant study."[84]

If Milton and the Puritan tradition within which he wrote were right, we should not ask first of all, "What can I do with a Christian liberal arts education?" but rather, "What can a Christian liberal arts education do with and for me as a person?"

Summary

The Puritan theory of education was a wonderfully unified and integrated whole. It combined God's special and natural revelations, the Bible and human knowledge, faith and reason. The curriculum included both theology and the arts and sciences, both the Bible and the classics.

The goals of education were similarly comprehensive. They included both piety and knowledge, both becoming like God and preparing to do all things well in daily life in the world.

Puritan education aimed to educate the whole person. Samuel Willard summed up the ideal by asserting:

The Word of God and rule of religion teach us, not to destroy, but to improve every faculty that is in us . . . to the glory of God who gave them to us.[85]

All this integration was possible ultimately because of the Puritans' view of truth. In their view, God was the source and end of all truth. There is thus no dichotomy between religious and human or natural truth. Samuel Willard's description once again serves as a fitting conclusion:

All streams do naturally lead down to the ocean; and all divine truths do as certainly carry us home to God himself, who is the essential truth. As truth comes from God, so it leads back to God.[86]

FURTHER READING

Ellwood P. Cubberly, *Readings in the History of Education* (1920) and *A Brief History of Education* (1922).

Samuel Eliot Morison, *Harvard College in the Seventeenth Century* (1936).

Perry Miller and Thomas H. Johnson, ed., *The Puritans* (1938; rev. ed. 1963). See especially the editors' introduction.

Perry Miller, *The New England Mind: The Seventeenth Century* (1939; rev. ed. 1954).

Richard B. Schlatter, *The Social Ideas of Religious Leaders, 1660–1688* (1940).

Earle E. Cairns, "The Puritan Philosophy of Education," *Bibliotheca Sacra* 104 (1947): 326–36.

J. W. Ashley Smith, *The Birth of Modern Education: The Contribution of the Dissenting Academies, 1660–1800* (1954).

Mark H. Curtis, *Oxford and Cambridge in Transition, 1558–1642* (1959).

Richard L. Greaves, *The Puritan Revolution and Educational Thought: Background for Reform* (1969).

————. *Society and Religion in Elizabethan England,* chap. 8 (1981).

The statue of Oliver Cromwell that stands today in front of the Houses of Parliament is a reminder of how significantly Puritanism has influenced the social conscience and institutions of England and America.

Chapter 10

Social Action

Love towards God cannot consist without . . . charity towards our neighbor.
— WILLIAM AMES

To study Puritanism is to explore what it means to maintain a paradoxical balance between poles of thought. Puritan doctrine is a vast equilibrium of potential opposites held in harmonious tension. Some examples include faith and reason, intellect and feeling, law and grace, the contemplative and active lives, this world and the eternal world, theory and practice, optimism and pessimism.

Puritan thinking on the individual in society was perhaps the most paradoxical of all. Their theory of the Christian's relationship to society as I outline it in this chapter will combine such dichotomies as the individual and the community, personal rights and social duties, the traditional and the radical, private and social sins, public and personal piety, the voluntary and the authoritarian, equality and hierarchy.

Social Involvement as a Christian Calling

The Puritans were not obscurantists. They accepted society as something ordained by God and the arena within which they were expected to make Christian principles prevail. In England the Puritans became strong enough to wield the dominant influence in the government for nearly two decades in the middle of the seventeenth century. In colonial Massachusetts and Connecticut they took an even more active role in shaping social and governmental policy.

The Puritans were comfortable with such social involvement because they regarded society as part of God's order for life in this world. "The orderly ruling of men over men . . . is from God, in its root," declared John Davenport in an election day sermon of 1669.[1] The idea of calling, so central to Puritan thought, found a definite place for politics as a calling. Thomas Adams viewed "the government of men" as "the highest and busiest vocation."[2]

Cultural involvement was one of the things that set the Puritans apart from other religious groups in America. One study has shown that the first families of Puritan Boston contributed many more descendants to the intellectual and political leadership of the nation than their counterparts in Quaker Philadelphia.[3] The Catholic tradition had elevated to the status of saint the person who withdrew from society, but the Puritan Samuel Willard eulogized the merchant John Hull with the comment that "he was a saint upon earth," not in withdrawal but "in the midst of all outward occasions and urgency of business."[4]

Basic to all Puritan involvement in culture was their ideal of a Christian society. The means to that end varied widely among the Puritans themselves, but the goal itself was never in doubt. That goal was, in the words of a title of one of Richard Baxter's books, a holy commonwealth. Even more famous is John Winthrop's comment about the Puritan experiment in America: "For we must consider that we shall be as a city upon a hill, the eyes of all people are upon us."[5] The early English Puritan Thomas Cartwright stated that

> the commonwealth must be made to agree with the church [that is, with Christian principles]. . . . As it is the foundation of the world, it is meet that the commonwealth, which is builded upon that foundation, should be framed according to the church.[6]

More than a century later, the American John Barnard declared, "The ultimate and supreme ends of government are the same with the last end of all creatures, and all their actions: that God in all things may be glorified."[7]

Seeking the Common Good

Puritan concern for the health of society was based partly on an ethic of responsibility for the common good. We have heard the charge of "rugged individualism" directed against the Puritans so often that we are in for a shock when we find out what the Puritans actually believed about communal life.

In Puritan New England, single men and women were forced to live with families. In 1636 Connecticut passed a law that "no young man that is neither married nor hath any servant . . . shall keep house by himself, without consent of the town where he lives."[8] Plymouth enacted similar legislation in 1669.[9] During the years 1669–1677, Massachusetts took action against sixty people for living alone.[10] The strong introspective streak in the Puritans, evident in their diaries and practices of meditation, was, in the words of one scholar, "less unhealthy than it seems because people lived much closer together three centuries ago."[11]

The Puritans did not share the confidence of our century that social cohesion depends on governmental structures. Rather, they understood the crucial role played by the *spirit* of community, whatever the governmental arrangement. They also understood that the essential ingredients of community spirit are selflessness and mutual concern. "Neighbour is a word of love," wrote William Tyndale, "and signifieth that a man should ever be nigh, and at hand, and ready to help in time of need."[12] "When once we are in Christ," said Richard Sibbes, "we live for others, not for ourselves."[13] A good society is one in which "each part" is "so contiguous" to the others "as thereby they do mutually participate with each other, both in strength and infirmity, in pleasure and pain."[14]

One of the noblest of all Puritan statements of social unity is John Winthrop's sermon *A Model of Christian Charity*, delivered to passengers on the *Arbella* en route to New England. "The care of the public must oversway all private respects," said Winthrop, "for it is a true rule that particular estates cannot subsist in the ruin of the public." He went on to say:

> We must be knit together in this work as one man, we must entertain each other in brotherly affection . . . , we must uphold a familiar commerce together in all meekness, gentleness, patience and liberality, we must delight in each other, make others' conditions our own, rejoice together, mourn together, labor and suffer together, always having before our eyes our commission and community in the work, our community as members of the same body, so shall we keep the unity of the spirit in the bond of peace, the Lord will be our God and delight to dwell among us.[15]

It is no wonder that a modern commentator has said that the spirit of the sermon leans more toward socialism than toward capitalism, though its spirit is closer still to Paul's description of the church as the body of Christ.

In the Puritan view, society is a whole network of interdependent people. This was exactly how Thomas Lever pictured it in a sermon preached at Paul's Cross:

> The merchant by buying and selling, and the craftsman by his occupation, must provide unto the commonwealth the necessary

wares and sufficient supplies for all. The landlord, by leasing lands at a moderate price must furnish fields to the tenants, and also homes at low rates of rent. The husbandman must till the soil with proper diligence, and so produce the necessary crops, rents, and provisions for himself and the community at large.[16]

The motivation for such community spirit, said the Puritans, is a strong commitment to the public or common good over purely personal interests. According to William Perkins,

He abuseth his calling, whosoever he be that . . . employs it for himself, seeking wholly his own, and not the common good. And that common saying, Every man for himself and God for us all, is wicked.[17]

Richard Baxter claimed that a holy commonwealth is one in which things are done for "the common good, and the glory and pleasing of God."[18] "Go forth, every man that goeth, with a public spirit," exhorted John Cotton to the departing colonists in 1630, and look "not on your own things only, but also on the things of others."[19] Samuel Willard said that "every man in his place owes himself to the good of the whole; and if he doth not so devote himself, he is unjust."[20]

It is obvious that such a conception of community spirit is strongly moral, rooted in the Old Testament Law and Prophets, as well as the New Testament Epistles' exhortations to mutual caring and Paul's metaphor of believers as a single body. The Puritans' favorite way of picturing the individual's participation in society was the covenant or contract. "All civil relations are founded in covenant," said John Cotton.[21] Thomas Hooker added that any person who chooses to enter a society "must willingly bind and engage himself to each member of that society to promote the good of the whole."[22]

The idea of society as a contract among persons, and between the individual and the state, goes a long way toward explaining the balance that the Puritans found between personal and public interests. A contract includes rights as well as duties. It confers promises as well as imposing obligations. Social cohesion has been called "the Puritans' greatest achievement,"[23] but it was not a cohesion exacted at the cost of a reasonable amount of individual freedom. The Puritans possessed a balanced viewpoint that allowed William Perkins to assert in a single statement that we may work in order to "maintain our families" and also that "the true end of our lives is to do service to God, in serving of man."[24]

Puritan Social Action

The Puritans were prototypes of evangelical social action. Concern for the poor is virtually the first thing that comes into our minds when we use the phrase "social action," and it is a good place to begin a discussion of the Puritans' social conscience. One repository of data is a large body of exhortations in sermons and tracts.

According to one of these sources, "One main end of all our civil actions, political employments, or corporeal endeavors in our particular callings, must be to give to the poor."[25] An anonymous treatise called *St. Paul the Tent-Maker* asserted that "the more diligently we pursue our several callings, the more we are capacitated to extend our charity to such as are in poverty and distress."[26] William Perkins was of the opinion that any earnings above a fair maintenance of estate must go directly to "the good of others, ... the relief of the poor, ... the maintenance of the church."[27] Thomas Lever said in a sermon that "rich men should keep to themselves no more than they need, and give to the poor as much as they need."[28]

But talk is cheap in such matters. What did the Puritans actually do to help the poor? The Anglican divine Lancelot Andrewes noted in 1588 that the Calvinist refugee churches in London were able "to do so much good as not one of their poor is seen to ask in the streets," and he regretted that "this city, the harborer and maintainer of them, should not be able to do the same good."[29] W. K. Jordan has assembled an enormous quantity of data about patterns of philanthropy in England during the Reformation era.[30] He contrasts the Catholic Middle Ages, which "were acutely sensitive to the spiritual needs of mankind while displaying only scant, or ineffectual, concern with the alleviation" of poverty, misery, and ignorance, with the impressive private donations in England from 1480–1660. "A very large proportion [of the donors] were Puritans," concludes Jordan, and he lists as one of "the great moving impulses" behind the growth of voluntary charity "the emergence of the Protestant ethic."[31]

It is worthy of note that Puritan preachers, themselves often relatively poor, were particular models of Christian charity to the poor. Samuel Ward recorded "how good a man Mr. Chadderton is, who hath such a living affection to the poor, which is certain token of a sound Christian."[32] John Foxe wrote of seeing in John Hooper's house at Worcester "a table spread with good store of meat and beset full of beggars and poor folk"; upon inquiry, Foxe learned that Hooper made it a regular practice to feed the poor.[33] Richard Greenham worked out a scheme of cooperative purchasing in his parish to help the poor buy cheap corn in time of crisis.[34]

In this woodcut illustration from John Bunyan's *Pilgrim's Progress,* Mercy clothes the poor.
Courtesy of the special collections of the Wheaton College Library

The Puritans showed equal concern for the unemployed. A century after Calvin had appeared before the city council of Geneva to urge the magistrates to find work for the unemployed,[35] Samuel Hartlib, the Puritan utopian, suggested that a clear distinction be made between the incorrigibly idle and the involuntarily unemployed. The "comfortless poor," he said, "wait for a reformation, as the thirsty ground for rain . . . and there is . . . great need for the Parliament to find out ways and means to preserve people from poverty."[36]

The Puritans also encouraged public action against certain forms of social injustice. They were, for example, capable of taking action against exorbitant prices. Sometimes Puritan preachers used the pulpit to influence prices. In 1673 the New England Puritan Urian Oakes spoke out against the much "gripping, and squeezing, and grinding of the faces of the poor."[37] Increase Mather exhorted his parishioners thus:

> A poor man cometh amongst you and he must have a commodity whatever it cost him, and you will make him give whatever you please, and put what price you please upon what he hath to give . . . , without respecting the just value of the thing.[38]

178

Then there is the celebrated case of Robert Keayne of Boston. According to Winthrop's journal, Keayne was a merchant who "was notoriously above others observed and complained of" because he charged excessive prices. "The cause being debated by the church, some were earnest to have him excommunicated; but the most thought an admonition would be sufficient."[39] Keayne was fined two hundred pounds by the magistrates, even though his defense of himself in his last will and testament leaves one with the impression that the Puritan society had been overly zealous in protecting consumer rights.[40]

In England, Richard Baxter showed a similar concern about economic abuses in society at large. Included in a list of business practices that he disallowed to Christians were taking more for goods than they are worth, making a product seem better than it is, concealing flaws in a product, asking a price as high as one thinks he can get, and taking advantage of another's necessity.[41]

The Puritan social conscience was not limited to Christians in need but extended to the whole of society. Baxter said that "such is the tenderness of a godly eye that it hath tears to shed even for enemies."[42] John Preston, in answering the question, "Would you have us to love none but the saints?" replied, "We ought to love all others with a love of pity, we should show abundance of this love to all mankind."[43] And Thomas Doolittle told his fellow Puritans in plague-ridden London to "have a fellow-feeling of the miseries that others are urged with . . . and this regardless of their spiritual condition."[44]

The common caricature of the Puritans as concerned only with private sins and unconcerned about social sins is inaccurate. When William Perkins preached in the field at Sturbridge Fair some time around 1592, he denounced the sins of his culture. The resulting list included both personal and social sins: "ignorance of God's will and worship," "contempt of Christian religion," "blasphemy," "profanation of the Sabbath," "unjust dealing in bargaining betwixt man and man," "murders, adulteries, usuries, briberies, extortions."[45]

The Moral and Theological Basis for Christian Social Action

What lay behind this Puritan stand for social action? The answer is both moral and theological. On the moral side, the Puritans were convinced that Christians are responsible for those in need. Their social action was rooted in a Christian moral conscience. "True morality, or the Christian ethics," wrote Baxter, "is the love of God and man, stirred up by the Spirit of Christ, through faith; and exercised in works of piety, justice, charity, and temperance."[46] Elsewhere Baxter exhorted, "Take heed that you lose not that common love which you owe to mankind."[47] For William Ames, "To profit or benefit others is a duty belonging to all men. . . . Love towards God cannot consist without this charity towards our neighbor . . . neither can any true religion."[48]

There was also a theological side to the Puritans' social involvement. In contrast to Catholic views of good works as something that helps to secure salvation, the Puritans believed that the New Birth results in social concern. Genuine piety produces good works, which are acts of gratitude, not of merit. Cotton Mather said of his father:

> A noble demonstration did he give that they who do good works because they are already justified will not come short of those who do good works that they may be justified; and that they who renounce all pretense to merit by their good works will more abound in good works than the greatest merit-mongers in the world.[49]

This theme of piety producing morality was one of the commonest topics among the Puritans. "Precept without patterns will do little good," wrote Eleazar Mather; "you must . . . speak by lives as well as words; you must live religion, as well as talk religion."[50] William Ames concurred: "Inward obedience is not sufficient by itself because the whole man ought to subject himself to God. Our bodies are to be offered to God."[51]

Personal Rather Than Institutional Social Action

The Puritans had much more confidence in personal social responsibility than in governmental or social agencies. For them, effective social action began with the individual. Richard Greenham wrote:

> Surely if men were careful to reform themselves first, and then their own families, they should see God's manifold blessings in our land and upon church and commonwealth. For of particular persons come families; of families, towns; of towns, provinces; of provinces, whole realms.[52]

Such a statement is an implicit rejection of the modern liberal position that the way to combat social ills is to multiply social agencies. That individual people are fallen the Puritans knew as well as we, but they also knew that institutions did not escape the effects of the Fall and are, in fact, the product of fallen people. M. M. Knappen summarizes the Puritan theory well when he writes:

When Puritanism is compared with modern collectivistic systems, its individualism also appears. The sixteenth-century thinkers put no faith in the state as such. The correctness of a system would save nobody. Correctness there must be, but there must also be personal cooperation and personal responsibility.[53]

The Puritans were equally individualistic in their approach to financial aid. They were opposed to indiscriminate charity and insisted that aid be given only to those in genuine need. William Perkins may be taken as typical of Puritan thought on the subject of beggars and vagabonds. Perkins said that they "are (for the most part) a cursed generation," "plagues and banes" to both church and state.[54] "It is the good law of our land," he added, "agreeable to the law of God, that none should beg that are able to labor."[55] Paul's injunction that "if any one will not work, let him not eat" (2 Thess. 3:10) was one of the most regularly quoted texts among the Puritans.

Christopher Hill summarizes the Puritan attitude as a matter of thinking that "indiscriminate charity . . . was a social menace. It prevented the poor from realizing their responsibilities and seriously looking for employment."[56] As a result, many Puritans preferred that the churches take care of the poor in their own parishes, where they could judge between genuine and fraudulent need.

The Puritans' positive counterplan to the dole was putting people to work and making them productive members of society. Richard Stock claimed that

> this is the best charity, so to relieve the poor as we keep them in labour. It benefits the giver to have them labour; it benefits the commonweal to suffer no drones, nor to nourish any in idleness; it benefits the poor themselves.[57]

When Hugh Peter returned to England from America, he told Parliament in a sermon, "I have lived in a country where in seven years I never saw beggar, nor heard an oath, nor looked upon a drunkard: why should there be beggars in your Israel where there is so much work to do?"[58] Richard Baxter, pastor at Kidderminster, undertook a successful program for qualifying the poor to work in the clothing industry there.[59]

The Puritans were deeply concerned for the quality of their society. Increase Mather summed up their viewpoint when he said that the purpose of the Bible is to show us "how we must serve God, and how we must serve the generation wherein we live."[60] Serving the generation wherein we live: this has always been the motto of Christians who are concerned with living out their faith in the world.

No Little People: The Trend Toward Equality in Puritanism

Despite all its emphasis on community, Puritanism is also known as a movement that championed individualism. The theological basis of that individualism was the priesthood of every believer. This individualism was not the humanistic individualism of the Renaissance, which was a form of self-fulfillment based on the inherent goodness of every person. It was instead an "individualism . . . for the common man."[61]

This individualism can be seen in the Puritans' "leveling" impulse to treat all people as equals before God and to protect the significance of every individual. To illustrate, consider the following representative statements covering a range of situations:

> The most despised person in the realm ought to be treated as if he were the king's brother and fellow-member with him in the kingdom of God and of Christ. Let the king, therefore, not think himself too good to do service to such humble people.[62]

> The poorest ploughman is in Christ equal with the greatest prince.[63]

> No man is to stand upon his gentility, or glory in his parentage for nobility and great blood, but only rejoice in this, that he is drawn out of the kingdom of darkness.[64]

> A people are not made for rulers, but rulers for a people.[65]

> All Christians . . . are made priests alike unto God; and so there is among them no clergy or laity, but the ministers are such who are chosen by Christians . . . ; they have no right nor authority at all to this office but by the consent of the church.[66]

All these statements tend in the direction of putting people on an equal footing, especially in spiritual matters. They all challenge centuries of thinking in which society had automatically handed over certain privileges and power to an exalted elite. Lawrence Stone has written about "the effect of the Puritan conscience in sapping respect for rank and title at all levels of the social hierarchy."[67] One result of this tendency was to exalt the dignity and worth of every individual. A modern scholar believes that "the deepest bond between Puritanism and democracy was their common respect for the human individual irrespective of his place in any ecclesiastical, political, economic, or other institution."[68] This is not to claim, of course, that the Puritans could have envisioned the democratic institutions that would eventually stem from their thinking.

The Puritans were well aware that there was something revolutionary in their emphasis on the common person. Cromwell organized the New Model Army on the basis of merit rather than status; he wrote, "The officers are of no better family than the common soldiers."[69] Another Puritan wrote:

> The voice of Jesus Christ reigning in his church comes first from . . . the common people. . . . God used the common people and the multitude to proclaim that the Lord God Omnipotent reigneth. . . . You that are of the meaner rank, common people, be not discouraged; for God intends to make use of the common people in the great work of proclaiming the kingdom of his Son.[70]

According to John Benbrigge, an essential mark of a true convert is that he or she "prizeth the poorest man or woman who is rich in Christ," and he went on to denounce people who prefer "rich worldlings before poor Christians."[71]

Such attitudes about equality were inherent in Reformed theology. By ascribing primacy to spiritual rather than external matters, the Puritans opened the door to a weakening of any privilege based solely on birth or position. This in turn was coupled with the doctrine of the priesthood of every believer. In such a climate of thinking, every saint becomes equal to every other one and superior to people whose only claim to status is social or institutional. According to William Dell, it is a rule in the church

> to keep equality between Christians. For though according to our first nativity . . . there is great inequality, . . . yet according to our new or second birth, whereby we are born of God, there is exact equality, for here are none better or worse, higher or lower.[72]

Thomas Hooker made a similar claim:

> Take the meanest saint that ever breathed on the earth, and the greatest scholar for outward part and learning . . . ; the meanest ignorant soul, that is almost a natural fool, that soul knows and understands more of grace and mercy in Christ than all the wisest and learnedst in the world, than all the greatest scholars.[73]

Lest we think that this is simply the ignorant person's bias, we can match it with a statement from the most learned of all English poets, John Milton: "A plain unlearned man that lives well by that light which he has is better and wiser and edifies others more towards a godly and happy life" than a clergyman trained at the universities.[74] Underlying all these statements is the principle that Christianity introduces a whole new set of criteria by which to judge a person's worth.

The most obviously "democratic" direction that Puritan thinking took was a new emphasis on rule by the consent of those who are governed. In the seventeenth century, people increasingly assumed that they had a right to reject the rule of magistrates or church officials whose decisions did not enjoy the support of a majority of the people. Wherever the Puritans gained an upper hand, congregations had a voice in choosing their ministers.

In the political realm, John Winthrop theorized that people should not be brought under anyone's rule except "according to their will and covenant," and he regarded as illegitimate any situation "where a people have men set over them without their choice or allowance."[75] John Davenport said in an election sermon that the people consent to a ruler "conditionally . . . so as, if the condition be violated, they may resume their power of choosing another."[76] In England, John Milton defended the deposition of the king on exactly the same ground:

> Since the king or magistrate holds his authority of the people . . . , then may the people, as oft as they shall judge it for the best, either choose him or reject him, retain him or depose him . . . , merely by the liberty and right of freeborn men to be governed as seems to them best.[77]

These democratic aspirations were not necessarily based on scriptural or theological grounds. In a treatise that bears the telling title *The Throne Established by Righteousness*, John Barnard denied that any political institution by itself guarantees the success of a society:

> I know of no particular form of civil government that God himself has, directly and immediately, appointed by any clear revelation of his mind and will to any people whatever.[78]

Were the Puritans responsible for the rise of modern democracy? Their whole political situation was so different from our own that it is difficult to answer that question. At the very least, they produced a climate of thought and practice that made the development of democracy possible. Someone has said about New England Puritanism that

> few societies in Western culture have ever depended more thoroughly or more self-consciously on the consent of their members than the allegedly repressive "theocracies" of early New England. . . . Every aspect of public life in New England demanded the formal assent of the public. Church members elected their ministers, town meetings their selectmen, freemen their deputies and magistrates, and militiamen their officers.[79]

Surely the *spirit* of democracy was inherent in Puritan thought.[80]

Summary

The Puritans were social thinkers and social activists. Given the state church situation, even the freedom to practice their specifically religious convictions required that they enter the political arena.

Puritan social action was based on a covenant theology that required people to pursue the common good of the community and that viewed good works as an inevitable act of gratitude for God's salvation. One aspect of Puritan social action was a concern to help the needy in society. Another was the denunciation of public or social sins as well as private ones. Puritan social action was primarily voluntaristic and personal rather than governmental or institutional.

Puritan emphasis on the community was balanced by a concern for the freedom and dignity of every individual. The Puritans challenged privilege based on rank or birth and encouraged a spirit of equality. They also articulated and practiced a theory of rule by the consent of the governed.

FURTHER READING

Margaret James, *Social Problems and Policy During the Puritan Revolution, 1640–1660* (1930).

Richard B. Schlatter, *The Social Ideas of Religious Leaders, 1660–1688* (1940).

Helen C. White, *Social Criticism in Popular Religious Literature of the Sixteenth Century* (1944).

A. S. P. Woodhouse, ed., *Puritanism and Liberty* (1951).

John Dykstra Eusden, *Puritans, Lawyers, and Politics in Early Seventeenth-Century England* (1958).

Michael Walzer, *The Revolution of the Saints: A Study in the Origins of Radical Politics* (1965).

Edmund S. Morgan, ed., *Puritan Political Ideas, 1558–1794* (1965).

T. H. Breen, *The Character of the Good Ruler: A Study of Puritan Political Ideas in New England, 1630–1730* (1970).

Stephen Foster, *Their Solitary Way: The Puritan Social Ethic in the First Century of Settlement in New England* (1971).

The statue of John Bunyan that stands today in Bedford, England, suggests some of the ambivalence that many people today feel toward the Puritans. We find it easy to admire their courage, their faithfulness to God and the Bible, their effectiveness in changing the course of history. But we also sense their remoteness from us, their somewhat foreboding austerity, their rigidity, and their tendency to be looking for an argument.

Chapter 11

Learning From Negative Example: Some Puritan Faults

They harangue long and very learnedly. . . . Their longsomeness is woeful.
— ROBERT BAILLIE

This chapter on Puritan faults is essential to the purposes of the book in two important ways. My aim has been to present the truth about what the Puritans thought and practiced. The Puritans were far from perfect, and their failings, too, are part of the truth about them.

Secondly, I am interested in what the Puritans can teach us. In exploring Puritan faults, I have not lost sight of that purpose. Puritan failings highlight important issues and can serve as a picture of what we should avoid.

Criticism is of course a subjective activity. What I call Puritan faults will occasionally seem like virtues to others. I am also certain to have omitted items that others would consider important failings of the Puritans.

Some Preliminary Cautions

It can be a risky business to criticize people from the past. A lot of mischief has been done by debunkers of the Puritans who do not inquire into the *context* of certain Puritan practices. For example, when we hear that some Puritans were opposed to the celebration of Christmas, we do not stop to ask exactly *what* they opposed. We assume that our own Christmas observances are what Christmas has always been and that the Puritans were fanatical for rejecting such a wholesome thing.

We cannot afford such historical naïveté. Governor William Bradford did not allow New Englanders to celebrate Christmas day as they had been accustomed (simply as a holiday), but he was not opposed to Christmas in principle. He wrote in his Log-Book, "If they made the keeping of it a matter of devotion, let them keep [it in] their houses, but there should be no gaming or revelling in the streets."[1] A genuinely religious Christmas was obviously not objectionable.

What, then, were the Christmas practices to which the Puritans objected? An English observer painted this picture of the activities practiced under the Lord of Misrule at Christmas time:

> Then march this heathen company towards the church and church-yard, their pipers piping, drummers thundering, . . . and in this sort they go into the church (though the minister be at prayer or preaching), dancing and swinging their handkerchiefs over their heads . . . with such a confused noise that no man can hear his own voice. Then the foolish people, they look, they stare, they laugh, they . . . mount upon forms and pews to see these goodly pageants.[2]

Before we criticize the Puritans, therefore, we had better inquire into the details of their historical situation.

We also need to be aware that the Puritans are sometimes attacked for things that were not distinctive to them but were shared with others in their culture. When one travels in England today, he or she is told about how "the Puritans" removed art from the churches and whitewashed over murals on the walls of churches. But these practices were also the work of Anglicans. An injunction of Queen Elizabeth in 1559 stipulated:

> Also they shall take away, utterly extinguish and destroy, all shrines, coverings of shrines, all tables, candlesticks, trindals and rolls of wax, pictures, paintings and all other monuments of feigned miracles, pilgrimages, idolatry and superstition; so that there remain no memory of the same in walls, glass windows or elsewhere within their churches or houses.[3]

Puritan armies used churches and cathedrals as barracks and horse stables, but so did the Royalist armies that included Anglicans.[4]

Something else that we would do well to get straight as quickly as possible is that Nathaniel Hawthorne's story *The Scarlet Letter* is *not* a historically accurate picture of the Puritans. In the preface to the novel,

Hawthorne describes discovering the scarlet letter that Hester wears in the story as punishment for her adultery while working in a Salem custom house. Hawthorne's account is purely fictional; he never ran across such a letter in real life. Furthermore, Hawthorne (who wrote two centuries after the original Puritans) used the Puritans in his story for *satiric* purposes, and it is a convention of satire to exaggerate the negative features of the thing being attacked. It is a great tragedy that the only picture many people have of the Puritans comes from works of literary satire that make no pretense of being sources of accurate history.

A final preliminary note that I need to make is that I began this study of the Puritans thinking that their attitudes toward art, music, and literature would find a place in this chapter on Puritan failings. My research did not confirm this prejudice, and I have listed some sources that interested readers can pursue.[5] The Puritans' removal of art from churches and cathedrals is almost totally irrelevant in this regard, since their objection was to Catholic worship practices rather than to art. In fact, Puritans sometimes bought the organs and paintings at auctions for use in their homes.

An Inadequate View of Recreation

The Puritan attitude toward leisure has always left me uneasy. A recent survey of Puritan views on recreation uncovered a more positive picture than we had generally been led to expect.[6] The modern stereotype that the Puritans were opposed to all recreation is based on a misreading of the evidence: Puritan disapproval of all sports *on Sundays* and of *selected sports* at all times (sports such as gambling, cock fighting, bear baiting, and games of chance, including card playing) has been wrongly interpreted to mean that they were against sports in principle.[7]

John Downame wrote that people should moderately partake of such pastimes as

> walking in pleasant places, conferences which are delightful without offence, poetry, music, shooting, and such other allowable sports as best fit with men's several dispositions for their comfort and refreshing.[8]

William Burkitt wrote in a similar vein:

> It being impossible for the mind of man to be always intent upon business, and for the body to be exercised in continual labors, the wisdom of God has therefore adjudged some diversion or recreation . . . to be both needful and expedient. . . . A wise and good man . . . is forced to . . . let religion choose such recreations as are healthful, short, recreative, and proper, to refresh both mind and body.[9]

A parliamentary act of 1647, when the Puritans were in control, decreed that every second Tuesday of the month was to be a holiday when all shops, warehouses, and so forth were to be closed from 8 A.M. until 8 P.M. for the recreation of workers.[10]

On the American scene, Thomas Shepard advised his son at college, "Weary not your body, mind, or eyes with long poring on your book. . . . Recreate yourself a little, and so to your work afresh."[11] John Winthrop once cut back on his recreations in order to concentrate more wholeheartedly on his religious endeavors. He reported that he

> grew unto great dullness and discontent; which being at last perceived, I examined my heart, and finding it needful to recreate my mind with some outward recreation, I yielded unto it, and by a moderate exercise herein was much refreshed.[12]

What, then, was wrong with the Puritan play ethic? For one thing, the defense of play was a *utilitarian* theory of recreation. Instead of valuing recreation for its own sake, or as celebration, or as an enlargement of one's human spirit, the Puritans tended to look upon play as something that made work possible:

> Recreation belongs not to rest, but to labor; and it is used that men may by it be made more fit to labor.[13]

> The true end of recreation is the refreshing of the mind and recreating of the body, to make them the fitter for the service of God, in the duties of our general and particular callings.[14]

> In commanding labour, [God] alloweth the means to make us fit for labor. And therefore . . . he admitteth lawful recreation, because it is a necessary means to refresh either body or mind that we may the better do the duties which pertain to us. . . . And therefore recreation . . . serveth only to make us more able to continue in labour.[15]

Someone has correctly observed of the Puritans that "they wrote about recreation with the gravity of a modern sociologist."[16]

This utilitarian play ethic was a result of the Puritans' overemphasis on work. Realistically speaking, how much recreation can we expect from a mindset that thinks like the following?

> Let your business engross most of your time. 'Tis not now and then an hour at your business that will do. Be stirring about your business as early as 'tis convenient. Keep close to your business, until it be convenient you should leave it off.[17]

> Be wholly taken up in diligent business of your lawful callings when you are not exercised in the more immediate service of God.[18]

In addition to making recreation an appendage to their work ethic, the Puritans surrounded their affirmations of recreation with a highly developed legalism that drastically dampened their theoretic endorsement of recreation. Richard Baxter affirmed "lawful sport or recreation" and then proceeded to list eighteen rules for determining whether a given recreation was "lawful!"[19] William Perkins endorsed recreations and promptly set up four "rules" that they must meet.[20]

The Puritans found a place for recreation as necessary to their work ethic, but they were unable to rise to a genuine theory of leisure and pastime. They were too fearful of idleness to do so. Baxter equated "pastimes" with "time wasting" and rejected the very word as "infamous."[21] His advice was:

> Keep up a high esteem of time and be every day more careful that you lose none of your time. . . . And if vain recreation, dressings, feastings, idle talk, unprofitable company, or sleep be any of them temptations to rob you of any of your time, accordingly heighten your watchfulness.[22]

Michael Walzer has suggested that the Puritans "discovered a utopia . . . without leisure."[23] A glorious exception among them was Milton, who wrote, "We . . . have need of some delightful intermissions, wherein the enlarged soul . . . may keep her holidays to joy and harmless pastime."[24]

Too Many Rules

The Puritans were strict in lifestyle, and they also liked matters to be well-defined. These virtues, when carried to an extreme, produce a legalistic lifestyle that becomes stifling with too many rules. At their worst, the Puritans practiced this vice with enthusiasm.

We can see this, for example, in their Sabbath observance. Theoretically the Puritans made a distinction between Sabbath observance as a perpetual moral law and as an Old Testament ceremonial law whose strictness was abrogated for New Testament Christians. But in practice they were often as strict as the laws of Moses had been.

In New England, two young lovers were tried for "sitting together on the Lord's Day under an apple tree in Goodman Chapman's orchard." Someone else was publicly reproved "for writing a note about common business on the Lord's Day, *at least in the evening somewhat too soon*" (italics mine). Elizabeth Eddy of Plymouth was fined "for wringing and hanging out clothes," and a New England soldier for "wetting a piece of an old hat to put in his shoe" to protect his foot.[25]

Of course such legalism produced false guilt and a loss of

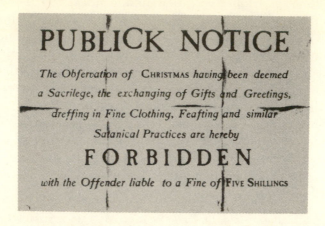

A public notice that offers the gist of a New England statute of 1660.

discrimination about what constituted a serious sin. At the age of sixteen, Nathaniel Mather wrote in his diary,

> When very young I went astray from God. . . . Of the manifold sins which then I was guilty of, none so sticks upon me as that . . . *I was whittling on the Sabbath Day;* and for fear of being seen, I did it behind the door. A great reproach of God! a specimen of that atheism that I brought into the world with me.[26]

The case of John Bunyan is even more famous. Playing a game of "cat" on a Sunday afternoon after the morning sermon had focused on Sabbath observance, Bunyan suddenly became stricken with guilt between the first and second strike of the wood. Momentarily transfixed, he concluded that he was too great a sinner to be forgiven and "went on in sin with great greediness of mind."[27]

Throughout this book I have had occasion to praise the Puritans for the things they affirmed — work, sex, the physical world, education, and much besides. But Puritan theorists on these subjects had a way of surrounding their affirmations with so many qualifying rules that a person could scarcely practice these activities without a sense of guilt creeping in. I have already observed the legalism with which they surrounded recreational activities.

Something similar emerges from Puritan affirmations of marital sex. Having argued that sex is a necessary part of marriage, the Puritans then proceeded to talk at length about the possibility that marital sex might be illegitimate lust after all. A whole literature grew up on the subject of the dangers of committing adultery with one's spouse (a theme that can be traced back to the patristic writers).[28] Writers in this tradition made dark denunciations of "sensual and brutish love" in marriage, "immoderate, intemperate, excessive sex," "unnatural sex," and sex that was not "modest and chaste." Whatever legitimate principle might underlie this elaborate theory of adultery with one's spouse, for me its effect is to dampen the Puritans' endorsement of marital sex.

The Puritan seemed never to tire of creating lists of rules to which a given activity had to measure up. They did it for work, for worship, for duties within a family, for choosing a spouse, and many other activities.

Too Many Words

Prolixity, the vice of being long-winded and verbose, was one of the Puritans' most salient traits. Many Puritans lacked the type of self-criticism that let them know when enough had been said. They certainly failed to realize the power of leaving some things unstated and only suggested.

Consider some of the accounts that come to us from the history of Puritan preaching. Cotton Mather reported that at his ordination he prayed for an hour and a quarter, after which he preached for an hour and three quarters.[29] In 1625 members of the House of Commons were subjected to seven hours of preaching in a service that "continued full nine hours, during all which time it was observed that not any one man of their company fainted."[30]

Anthony Burgess preached 145 sermons on John 17 and a preacher named Manton 190 sermons on Psalm 119. George Trosse spent several years preaching a marathon series on the attributes of God. Another Puritan preacher preached for four months on Joseph's coat of many colors.[31] Here is the description of what transpired on a Puritan fast day:

> Dr. Twisse having commenced the public service with a short prayer, Mr. Marshall prayed in a wonderful pathetic and prudent manner for two hours. Mr. Arrowsmith then preached an hour, then they sung a psalm, after which Mr. Vines prayed nearly two hours. Mr. Henderson then spoke of the evils of the time and how they were to be remedied, and Dr. Twisse closed the service with a short prayer.[32]

The Puritans had a way of talking things to death. Scottish representatives to the English Parliament in 1643 soon grew weary of the long debates on church matters. "They harangue long and very learnedly," wrote Robert Baillie, but "their longsomeness is woeful at this time." The assembly spent two or three sessions discussing the duties of widows in the church, "not that we needed to stay so long on that subject," complained Baillie, "but partly because every thing that comes to the assembly must be debated, and none of their debates are short." After several months of this, the Scottish patience wore thin. Baillie complained of "the unhappy and unamendable prolixity of this people," adding that "we are vexed and overwearied with their ways."[33]

The Puritan glut of words is evident in their style of writing. In choosing quotations for this book I repeatedly had to omit redundancies from passages. The characteristic Puritan style, I quickly concluded, is to take at least twice as many words as necessary to express a thought. Like the poets of the Bible (but without their poetic conciseness and artistry), the Puritans seemed to search for ways to say everything at least twice in different words. A random specimen of such redundancy is this one:

> God hath placed us in the world to do him some work. This is God's
> working place; he hath houses of work for us: now, our lot here is to
> do work, to be in some calling . . . to work for God.[34]

Looking back over his life, Richard Baxter concluded, "And concerning almost all my writings I must confess that my own judgment is that fewer well studied and polished had been better."[35] That judgment can appropriately be extended to the Puritan movement as a whole.

Too Much Pious Moralizing

The Puritans exempted no part of life from their religion. That was their strength. They were not content, however, to let Christian principles be simply the general framework within which they conducted their affairs. Some of them seem to have felt that an activity could not be conducted for God's glory without dragging in a bit of Christian moralizing.

Consider some of their expressions of romantic love. Edward Taylor apparently did not feel comfortable with expressing his love to his beloved ("a golden ball of pure fire," he called it) without piously adding that "it must be kept within bounds, too. For it must be subordinate to God's glory."[36] John Winthrop addressed his fiancée as "the happy and hopeful supply (next Christ Jesus) of my greatest losses," and after marriage wrote to her that she was "the chiefest of all comforts under the hope of salvation."[37] The Puritans seem to have kept their noses to the theological grindstone at all times.

Puritan habits of child rearing provide an even clearer example of pious moralizing. When Cotton Mather's children fell sick, he would remind them of "the analogous distempers of their souls" and instruct them "how to look up unto their great Saviour for the cure of those distempers." When he saw his children playing, he would suggest to them "those pious instructions which the circumstances of their play may lead them to think upon."[38] Mather also made it a rule "rarely to let one of my children to come near me, and never to sit any time with them, without some explicit contrivance and endeavor to let fall some sentence or other that shall carry an useful instruction with it."[39]

The Puritans believed that their physical bodies had been given them by God so that as creatures they might glorify their Creator. Not content to allow this to remain a general principle, Cotton Mather

> would anatomically and particularly consider every part of my body, . . . on what method I may serve my glorious Lord with them. . . . These considerations must be accompanied by consecrations, . . . entreating the Lord that he would accept my body . . . in these applications.[40]

Stricken by an awareness of his physical similarity to dogs, Mather resolved to get the better of the brutes by "shaping in my mind some holy, noble, divine thought" every time he went to the toilet.[41]

At every turn, Puritan preachers and writers show a tendency to moralize about the topic at hand. No matter what human activity they discussed, they believed it their duty to add a reminder that it must be done to the glory of God and that it must be "lawful." Their theology on these occasions was impeccable, but their style leaned in the direction of what today we would call "overkill."

Male Chauvinism

At its most enlightened, the Puritan theory of the headship of the husband and the subordination of the wife was a defensible Christian position. But the terms in which the Puritans frequently couched their theory of marital hierarchy are an embarrassment and offense in a day of sensitivity to women's feelings and dignity.

After describing the male's mental and physical superiority to females, Robert Bolton added that the wife "hath as noble a soul as himself" and that "souls have no sexes." But the way in which he then clinched the point shows his chauvinism: "In the better part they are both men."[42] John Robinson claimed that "experience teacheth how inconvenient it is if the woman have but a little more understanding . . . than her husband hath."[43] According to William Gouge, "a wife must be mild, meek, gentle, obedient, though she be matched with a crooked, perverse, profane, wicked husband."[44]

Benjamin Wadsworth thought that a good husband would "strive more to be loved than feared, though neither is to be excluded."[45] Richard Baxter listed twenty disadvantages of marriage for ministers, one of which centered on "the natural imbecility of the female sex," by which he apparently meant "weakness."[46]

John Winthrop had an interesting theory about why the wife of Governor Hopkins of Connecticut went insane. She read too much and dabbled in intellectual matters where she had no business:

> For if she had attended her household affairs, and such things as belong to women, and not gone out of her way . . . to meddle in such things as are proper for men, whose minds are stronger, etc., she had kept her wits and might have improved them usefully and honorably in the place God had set her.[47]

Thomas Parker wrote a public letter to his sister in which he told her, "Your printing of a book, beyond the custom of your sex, doth rankly smell."[48] And John Knox, in *The First Blast of the Trumpet Against the Monstrous Regiment of Women*, let the world know how he felt about a woman on the throne of England:

> To promote a woman to bear rule . . . above any realm . . . is repugnant to nature, contumely to God, a thing most contrarious to his revealed will and approved ordinance; and finally, it is the subversion of good order, and all equity and justice.[49]

This type of paternalism sometimes extended to the father's dominance over his children as well. Cotton Mather's way of training his children included the following procedure:

> I first beget in them an high opinion of their father's love to them, and of his being best able to judge what shall be good for them. Then I make them sensible, 'tis a folly for them to pretend any wit and will of their own; they must resign all to me, who will be sure to do what is best; my word must be their law.[50]

The picture I have drawn here should not be allowed to obscure what was positive about Puritan contributions to marriage and the place of women. Modern scholars generally agree that the status of women rose with the progress of the Reformation.[51] But by modern standards there is far too much male chauvinism in Puritan writing on these matters.

Partisan Spirit

M. M. Knappen has written that "the curse of partisanship was another evil heritage from the early Reformation struggle."[52] Such partisanship was characteristic of *all* groups at the time. I should note, too, that the type of partisan spirit I am about to explore was a hallmark of Puritan polemical or controversial writing much more than writing that was removed from direct combat with opponents.

The most unfortunate result of Puritan partisanship was that many Puritans overreacted in rejecting things that were religiously indifferent. Because church organs were associated with Catholic ritual and doctrine, the Puritans ripped them out of churches, sometimes smashing them to pieces in the process, but also, as mentioned earlier, sometimes placing them in their own homes. When the Puritans built their meeting houses in New England, they originally built them without bell towers and steeples because these were regarded as "popish."[53]

We should perhaps not be too hasty to judge the Puritans in these instances. In their own historical context, many things *did* carry meanings that have disappeared with time. But with the luxury of historical distance at our disposal, we should not follow Puritan example in such matters.

The Puritans' total rejection of things that had been subject to abuse has exacted a heavy toll from them in our own day. It has been all too easy for debunkers to discredit the Puritans by pointing out their closing of the theaters, their hostility to fiction and recreational reading (especially of romances), their rejection of Christmas celebrations, and their objection to the use of wedding rings.

Given the state church situation in which only one religious allegiance was allowed, it was perhaps inevitable that the Puritans would have developed an all-or-nothing outlook. Understandable as it may be, it is nonetheless a fault that needs to be recognized. Its most customary form was to take the view that if something failed to measure up to Puritan doctrine, it must be *completely* wrong.

Consider, for example, the following well-known repudiation of the Anglican Prayer Book:

> We must needs say . . . that this book is an imperfect book, culled and picked out of that popish dunghill, the mass book full of all abominations. For some and many of the contents therein be such as are against the word of God.[54]

Even if "many" of the contents were heretical, logic tells us that "many" must also have been biblical. For the Puritans, there was rarely any acknowledgment of a middle ground between total acceptance and total rejection. It was one thing for William Whittingham to call the Bible the "only sufficient" guide and to deny ultimate authority to "whatsoever is added to this Word by man's device"; but it was quite another thing to denounce all such human standards as "evil, wicked and abominable."[55]

Puritan style in these matters was characterized by an unpleasant cantankerousness that is one of their most unattractive traits. Like their opponents, the Puritans made little attempt to treat other religious viewpoints with respect. In the Diocese of Chester, for example, Puritans did such things as the following:

1. Ralph Hickock interrupted the baptism of his child by telling "the minister not to use the sign of the cross and calling him doting fool and unmannerly fellow."

2. Numerous Puritans kept their hats on during church services to show their disrespect for the Anglican church.

3. Thomas Constable, hauled into church court for failing to attend the Anglican communion, claimed, "I will never kneel at the communion while I live."[56]

This cantankerous spirit infected Puritan relations among themselves as well. The Puritans found it almost impossible to agree on policy and never represented a truly united front. Or consider the account of the Jesuit William Weston regarding the outdoor preaching services that he observed among the Puritans at Wisbech. The people listened to the sermon with their Bibles open. Afterward "they held arguments also among themselves about the meaning of various Scripture texts." It all sounds ideal until we read that "these discussions were often wont, as it was said, to produce quarrels and fights."[57]

One manifestation of partisan spirit among the Puritans was the conviction, especially prominent in America, that the Puritans were God's elect nation — the answer to the world's problems. Peter Bulkeley wrote that the people of New England "are as a city set upon an hill, in the open view of all the earth, . . . because we profess ourselves to be a people in covenant with God." Their function, he added, was to live in such a way that the nations would say, "Only this people is wise, an holy and blessed people."[58] John Cotton said that in New England "the order of the churches and of the commonwealth was so settled . . . that it brought to . . . mind the New Heaven and New Earth, wherein dwells righteousness."[59] Seen from the perspective of three centuries' distance, such claims seem unrealistically idealistic and naïve.

Insensitivity to the Religious Feelings of Other Groups

Today it is considered a mark of reasonable people that they respect and tolerate viewpoints other than their own. The Puritans generally failed to rise to such an ideal. Their whole cultural situation, of course, did not provide them with models for toleration. This failure to cope with the phenomenon of pluralism in society was especially acute in New England, where the Puritans were the dominant force and where they developed coercive strategies for denying freedom of conscience to dissenters.

For people who had suffered as much persecution as the Puritans, it is difficult to believe that they could have been so oppressive when they themselves came into power. Like others in their day, the Puritans did not conceive of the possibility of a pluralistic society in which everyone had the privilege of believing and living as his or her conscience directed. In Puritan New England, people with unorthodox viewpoints were simply banished from the town, with Anne Hutchinson and Roger Williams being the most notorious instances of such intolerance. Reading in George Fox's *Journal* about how the Puritans treated the Quakers during the Protectorate in England is as heartrending as the accounts of how the Puritans fared under the English monarchs and bishops.

We might expect that since the Puritans themselves were deeply religious people, they would have respected the feelings of other religious groups in *their* religious practices. But I look in vain for much evidence that this was so. Given the Puritans' understanding of what constituted the proper worship of God, they cannot be faulted for removing images from churches and cathedrals. What is distressing is *how* they went about their iconoclasm (destruction of images in churches) in total insensitivity to people for whom those images were religiously important.

The information about Puritan destruction of church organs comes from a biased Royalist-Anglican source, but presumably there is truth in the account. Here is a typical instance of how parliamentary soldiers conducted demolitions of churches and cathedrals: In Exeter

> they brake down the organs, and taking two or three hundred pipes with them in a most scornful and contemptuous manner, went up and down the streets piping with them; and meeting with some of the choristers of the church, whose surplices they had stolen before, and employed them to base servile offices, scoffingly told them, "Boys, we have spoiled your trade, you must go and sing hot pudding pies."[60]

At Westminster Abbey the soldiers "put on some of the singing-men's surplices, and in contempt of that canonical habit ran up and down the church; he that wore the surplice was the hare, the rest were the hounds."[61]

For the Puritans, no place was more sacred than any other, but this does not excuse their disrespect for English cathedrals. Anyone who has been moved by the beauty and sanctity of them is surely pained to think of their being used for horses and weapon stockpiles.

Puritan Extremism

The Puritans often suffered from a lack of proportion about things. They are in this regard a frequent embarrassment to people who believe that they generally had the right viewpoint on issues.

As Exhibit A, we can consider the Puritan conviction that children are fallen creatures who stand in need of God's grace to save them. There is obviously a right and a wrong way to state this truth. The Puritans often chose the wrong way:

> Laugh not with thy son, lest thou have sorrow with him and lest thou gnash thy teeth in the end. Give him no liberty in his youth and wink not at his follies. Bow down his neck while he is young, and beat him on the sides while he is a child.[62]

> Their hearts naturally are a mere nest, root, fountain of sin and wickedness; an evil treasure from whence proceed evil things. . . . Their hearts . . . are unspeakably wicked, estranged from God.[63]

> Surely there is in all children, though not alike, a stubbornness and stoutness of mind arising from natural pride, which must . . . be broken and beaten down. . . . For the beating must provide carefully for two things: first that children's wills and wilfulness be restrained and repressed.[64]

One of the Puritans' strengths was their consciousness of God's presence in all of life. They were acutely aware of God's providence in their daily lives and kept diaries that prove it. But surely it is possible to carry such religious introspection and reading of God's providence too far. When Samuel Sewall got up in the middle of the night to urinate in a pot whose bottom fell out and wet the bed, he explained the accident on the ground that he had been too tired that night to say his prayers.[65] When Cotton Mather had a toothache, he looked for a moral cause: "Have I not sinned with my teeth? How? By sinful, graceless, excessive eating, and by sinful speeches."[66]

Extremism also produced the passages of self-loathing that are anthologized today and are therefore the only picture of Puritanism that many people have. That people are fallen creatures with an inclination toward evil is biblical doctrine. But some of the Puritans' attitudes toward themselves were not. Cotton Mather, upon seeing a dog urinate at the same time he was urinating, concluded, "What mean and vile things are the children of men in this mortal state! How much do our natural necessities abase us and place us in some regard on the same level with the very dogs!"[67]

During the course of an illness, Michael Wigglesworth wrote in his diary:

> Look down and see my plague sores which I spread before thee, my
> savior, wounds and old putrified sores which provoke the Lord, stink
> in his nostrils, and poison the peace and comfort of my own soul.[68]

"Behold I am vile," he wrote, "when thou showest me my face I abhor
myself. Who can bring a clean thing out of filthiness?"[69]

I know of no group that has been more victimized by what today we
would call its "lunatic fringe" than the Puritans. I refer to individuals
whose aberrations made them a liability to the movement or good people
whose blunders have been paraded through the years to the discredit of
the Puritans. Throughout subsequent history, anyone wishing to discredit
the Puritans has found it easy to find material, which is usually far from
the norm for Puritanism generally.

Summary

We can learn from Puritan failings by practicing the following:

— Value leisure and recreation as good in themselves for purposes
  of rest, celebration, and human enrichment.
— Be on guard against multiplying the rules that we add to our
  foundational moral principles.
— Practice the art of conciseness, leave some things unstated,
  choose quality of words over their quantity, and respect the
  attention span of an audience.
— Beware of overkill through too much moralizing.
— Avoid thinking in terms of male superiority.
— Rise above party spirit by differentiating between the principle
  of a thing and its abuse.
— Respect the religious feelings of people whose viewpoint we
  reject.
— Remember that accuracy of expression is better than overstate-
  ment, that mildness of expression gains more respect than
  belligerence, and that a good thing when carried too far becomes
  ridiculous.

FURTHER READING

It is difficult to suggest specific sources on the subject of Puritan failings. I
have found wholesale attacks on the Puritans to be unreliable in their facts. The
unattractive features of the Puritans are something that one picks up piecemeal
in an extensive study of them. With this qualification in mind, I offer the
following sources as quick ways to get a taste of Puritan failings:

— In the process of defending the Puritans against a host of charges, Percy Scholes, *The Puritans and Music*, alerts the reader to a wide range of things for which the Puritans have been attacked, not always justifiably.

— One of the best entries into the subject of Puritan failings is simply to start reading in a modern anthology of Puritan primary sources. It is not long before one encounters viewpoints with which a modern reader will disagree. Examples of such anthologies include *The Puritans*, ed. Perry Miller and Thomas H. Johnson, rev. ed. (1963), 2 vols.; and *Womanhood in Radical Protestantism, 1525–1675*, ed. Joyce L. Irwin (1979).

— For an illustration of the Puritan tendency to be nearly interminable, and of an especially constipated Puritan prose style, the complete *Magnalia Christi Americana* of Cotton Mather will suffice.

— The *Journal* of Quaker founder George Fox will give a feel for how one Protestant group fared under the Puritans.

— For a quick dose, the verse of Michael Wigglesworth is an old standby (excerpts can be found in Miller/Johnson, 2:585–630).

These discussions were often wont . . . to produce quarrels and fights. — WILLIAM WESTON

When very young I went astray from God. . . . Of the manifold sins which then I was guilty of, none so sticks upon me as that . . . I was whittling on the Sabbath Day. . . . *A great reproach of God!* — NATHANIEL MATHER

Laugh not with thy son, lest thou have sorrow with him and lest thou gnash thy teeth in the end. Give him no liberty in his youth and wink not at his follies. Bow down his neck while he is young, and beat him on all sides while he is a child. — THOMAS BECON

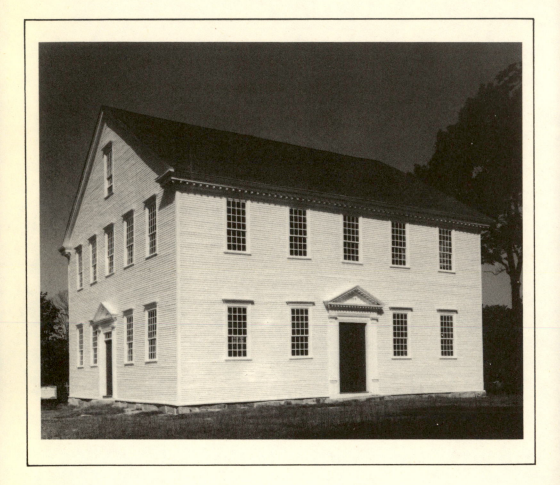

As their architecture attests, the Puritans valued honesty, openness, and the simplicity that dignifies. Photograph by Douglas R. Gilbert

Chapter 12

The Genius of Puritanism: What the Puritans Did Best

Have you forgot ... the milkhouse, the stable, the barn, and the like, where God did visit your soul?

— JOHN BUNYAN

The customary way to conduct a survey of a movement is to explore what spokesmen of the movement said on various topics. But an equally revealing approach is to undertake an anatomy of underlying principles that cut across those categories.

Consider, for example, the Puritan affirmation of the created physical order as good in principle. This is a principle that influenced Puritan thinking on such topics as work, sex, politics, social action, family, and money.

Preceding chapters in this book have taken a topical approach. In this concluding chapter I attempt an anatomy of underlying principles. Since each of these applies to a whole cluster of earlier topics, I trust that the chapter will serve to integrate the entire book into a unified final impression.

The God-centered Life

The Puritans' sense of priorities in life was one of their greatest strengths. Putting God first and valuing everything else in relation to him was a recurrent Puritan theme.

The Puritans knew that only God can satisfy people permanently and at the deepest level. John Winthrop wrote that "only the fruition of Jesus Christ and the hope of heaven can give us true comfort and rest."[1] He accordingly "resolved by the grace of God . . . not to suffer my heart to delight more in anything than in the comfort of my salvation."[2]

Thomas Shepard wrote to his son at college, "Remember the end of your life, which is coming back again to God and fellowship with God."[3] Having identified God as "the great and ultimate object of religion," Samuel Willard went on to conclude that "the knowledge of him is the first thing necessary to be sought after."[4] In such a hierarchy of values, the great mistake that a person can make is to "neglect his precious soul."[5]

For the Puritans, spiritual reality was the great *sine qua non* in life, the ultimately important factor. Samuel Willard wrote:

> The generality of men take their measures from the observation of outward providence: if there be outward peace and plenty, they call them happy days; of outward distress and trouble, they call them evil. But we have a better rule, and more safe for Christians. . . . The more of Christ that a people enjoy, the happier are they, and the less he is known and acknowledged in his great design of mediatorship, the greater is the infelicity of such a people.[6]

Francis Higginson said about Salem village that "our greatest comfort and means of defense above all others is that we have here the true religion and holy ordinances of Almighty God among us."[7]

Delight in God's presence was what the Puritans sought and found. Baxter's parting advice to his parishioners at Kidderminster was to "be sure to maintain a constant delight in God."[8] Cornelius Burges preached that every person should "lift up his soul to take hold of God, to be glued and united to him, . . . to be only his forever."[9] For Thomas Watson, one of the signs of being a child of God "is to delight to be much in God's presence."[10]

John Winthrop's account of his life after his conversion sounded the authentic Puritan note:

> I was now grown familiar with the Lord Jesus Christ; he would oft tell me he loved me. I did not doubt to believe him; if I went abroad, he went with me, when I returned, he came home with me. I talked

with him upon the way, he lay down with me, and usually I did awake with him: and so sweet was his love to me, as I desired nothing but him in heaven or earth.[11]

According to William Perkins, the reward of conversion is that "then shalt thou rejoice in God's presence in the world, and delight to think of God, to speak of God, to pray unto Him, to meet Him in His Word and Sacraments."[12]

For the Puritans, the God-centered life meant making the quest for spiritual and moral holiness the great business of life. "In a divine commonwealth," wrote Baxter, "holiness must have the principal honor and encouragement, and a great difference be made between the precious and the vile."[13] Ralph Venning concluded a book-length treatise on sin by challenging his readers to "an heroic resolution to be strict and circumspect, to walk in an exact and geometrical holiness in the midst of a crooked and perverse generation."[14]

The Puritan vision was not simply theocentric (as is sometimes claimed) but was specifically Christocentric. William Perkins concluded his treatise on preaching with the statement, "The sum of the sum: preach one Christ by Christ to the praise of Christ."[15] When Oliver Cromwell's daughter was approaching her marriage, he wrote to her:

Dear heart, . . . let not anything cool thy affections after Christ. . . . That which is best worthy of love in thy husband is that of the image of Christ he bears. Look on that and love it best, and all the rest for that.[16]

Samuel Ward wrote, "O Lord, give us grace to consider how that all our night watching and all ought to tend to this end, to the winning of Christ."[17] And Richard Sibbes wrote:

Christ himself is ours. In the dividing of all things, some men have wealth, honours, friends and greatness, but not Christ . . . : but a Christian hath Christ himself. . . . Therefore what if he wants those . . . lesser things, he hath the main, . . . the spring, the ocean, him in whom all things are.[18]

The character of Puritanism was determined by its spiritual priorities. It is to the credit of the Puritans that they were concerned with the great matters — the glory of God, the renewal of the human soul in Christ, the forgiveness of sins, the life everlasting, the friendship of God, and holy living.

All of Life Is God's

Puritanism was impelled by the insight that all of life is God's. The Puritans lived simultaneously in two worlds — the invisible spiritual world and the physical world of earthly existence. For the Puritans, both worlds were equally real, and there was no cleavage of life into sacred and secular. *All* of life was sacred.

Thomas Goodwin wrote that when he was converted, "the glory of the great God was set up in my heart, as the square and rule of each and every particular practice."[19] John Cotton theorized:

> Not only my spiritual life, but even my civil life in this world, all the life I live, is by the faith of the Son of God: he exempts no life from the agency of his faith.[20]

According to Thomas Gouge, Christians should "so spiritualize our hearts and affections that we may have heavenly hearts in earthly employ-ments."[21] Puritanism had as one of its main effects restoring a sense of wholeness to life.

C. S. Lewis has written enthusiastically of "the beautiful, cheerful integration of [William] Tyndale's world. He utterly denies the medieval distinction between *religion* and secular life."[22] Someone else has said that "the Puritan was determined to make earthly things divine, not by forbidding them, but by infusing them with holiness."[23] No area of life was exempt from such infusion.

It reached to the family, for example: "If ever we would have the church of God to continue among us, we must bring it into our households and nourish it in our families."[24] The Christian life also extended to one's daily work: George Swinnock said that the pious tradesman will know that "his shop as well as his chapel is holy ground," while Richard Steele was sure that a Christian can exercise "grace in his calling."[25] Politics was also part of the Christian life: according to Richard Sibbes, it is "an abominable conceit to distinguish religion from policy and government, as if the reasons of religion were one and the reasons of state were another."[26]

Godliness in every phase of a person's life was the Puritan goal. One Puritan spoke of Christianity as a "universal habit of grace" in which "the whole creature is resigned . . . to the obedience and glory of its maker."[27] "If God be God over us," wrote Peter Bulkeley, "we must yield him universal obedience in all things. He must not be over us in one thing, and under us in another, but he must be over us in every thing."[28]

The Puritans' zest for life and culture is suggested by this flute that John Bunyan carved from a chair leg while in prison for preaching. Courtesy of the Trustees of Bunyan Meeting

Seeing God in the Commonplace

A logical extension of the principle that all of life is God's was the Puritan emphasis on seeing God in the ordinary events of life. It is one of the Puritans' most attractive traits. For the Puritans, everything in life became a pointer to God and carrier of grace. They viewed life through the wide-angle lens of God's sovereignty over all of life.

The sanctity of the common was a constant Puritan theme. John Bunyan asked in the preface to *Grace Abounding*, "Have you forgot . . . the milkhouse, the stable, the barn, and the like, where God did visit your soul?"[29] "Canst not thou think on the several places thou hast lived in and remember that they have each had their several mercies?" asked Richard Baxter.[30] Walter Pringle told his children the exact places at which certain things happened to him: his first experience of prayer came "at the north-east of Stitchel Hall," and years later he committed his newly born son to God "at the plum tree on the north side of the garden door."[31]

In such a framework, there are no "trivial" events. Nathaniel Mather claimed that even the simplest activities, such as "a man's loving his wife or child," become "gracious acts . . . of great account in the eyes of God."[32] God "sanctified" John Winthrop's "dangerous hot malignant fever" in such a way that Winthrop "never had more sweet communion with him than in that affliction."[33] For the Puritans, anything in life might become a channel of God's grace. The young Robert Blair looked out of the window one day to see "the sun brightly shining, and a cow with a full udder"; he remembered that the sun was made to give light and the cow to give milk, which made him realize how little he understood the purpose of his own life.[34]

The Puritan view of the sanctity of the common rested partly on an extraordinary awareness of God's providence. This, in turn, produced the Puritan practice of keeping diaries. "If we were well read in the story of our own lives," said Richard Sibbes, "we might have a divinity of our own, drawn out of the observations of God's particular dealing toward us."[35] John Bartlet advised Christians to "meditate on the experience you have had of God's faithfulness, and [the] goodness you have had in all his providences. . . . To help you herein, you shall do well to make a catalogue and keep a diary of God's special providences."[36] Isaac Ambrose used the provocative phrase "a sanctified memory" in urging the same practice.[37]

If the doctrine of providence led the Puritans to see God in the commonplace, so did the doctrine of nature as God's creation. Thomas Taylor said that "the voice of God is in all the creatures and by them all speaketh unto us always and everywhere."[38] "There is not a fly, but what may confute an atheist," claimed Cotton Mather.[39] Thomas Shepard asked, "Can we, when we behold the stately theater of heaven and earth, conclude other but that the finger, arms, and wisdom of God hath been here?"[40]

In sum, there was no place where the Puritans could not potentially find God. They were always open to what Richard Baxter called "a drop of glory" that God might allow to fall upon their souls.[41]

The Momentousness of Life

It is an easy step from the sanctity of the common to the Puritan awareness that life is momentous. No matter what the activity, the Puritans were alive to its tremendous potential. Richard Baxter advised, "Write upon the door of thy shop and chamber, 'I must be in heaven or hell for ever,' or 'this is the time upon which my endless life dependeth.'"[42]

Along with the potential of life for good (already seen in the Puritan comments about the sanctity of the common), there was an awareness of the dangerousness of life. Baxter asked, "Will it not awaken us to compassion to look on a languishing man and to think that within a few days his soul will be in heaven or hell?"[43] Samuel Willard showed that there is no reason for complacency within Christian circles when he said, "There are none upon the face of the earth that stand upon more dangerous precipices than the children of the covenant."[44] The dangerousness of life prompted Richard Sibbes to write that

> they are scoffing atheists that trifle with religion, as if it were no great matter what it be. . . . Therefore the temper of the true professor is to be earnest . . . to advance his religion. . . . In the course of Christ, in the course of religion, he must be fiery and fervent.[45]

If life is this momentous, virtually any daily event can become a "teachable moment." Richard Greenham wrote:

> Because we know not who is the man, what is the time, where is the place, which is the sermon that God hath appointed to work on us, let us in all obedience attend on the ministry of every man, watch at all times, be diligent in every place, and run to every sermon which we can conveniently, because though the Lord touch us not by this man, in this place, at this time, through such a sermon, yet he may touch us by another.[46]

In such a climate of thinking, the story of Thomas Goodwin's conversion emerges as "vintage Puritanism." As a Cambridge University student, Goodwin was on his way "to be merry with my companions" when he heard a funeral bell toll. A fellow student urged him to attend the sermon, but Goodwin "was loathe to go, for I loved not preaching . . . , which I thought to be dull stuff." Goodwin decided to listen to the sermon, which turned out to be about "deferring repentance, and of the danger of doing so." Goodwin's own account of what followed is matchless:

> So God was pleased on the sudden . . . to alter the whole course of his former dispensation towards me, and said . . . to my soul, Yea, live. . . . And as he created the world . . . by a word, so he created and put a new life and spirit into my soul. . . . This speaking of God to my soul, although it was but a gentle sound, yet it made a noise over my whole heart, and filled and possessed all the faculties of my whole soul.[47]

John Bunyan's teachable moment came on a day when his work took him to Bedford. As he passed through one of the streets, he overheard "three or four poor women sitting at a door in the sun, and talking about the things of God." Bunyan's own account of what followed tells the story best:

> I drew near to hear what they said, for I was now a brisk talker . . . in the matters of religion; but I may say, I heard but understood not. . . . Their talk was about a new birth, the work of God on their hearts . . . ; they talked how God had visited their souls with His love in the Lord Jesus. . . . They were to me as if they had found a new world. . . . At this I felt my own heart began to shake . . . ; for I saw that in all my thoughts about religion and salvation, the new birth did never enter into my mind, neither knew I the comfort of the word and promise.[48]

Living in a Spirit of Expectancy

One of the things that makes reading the Puritans so therapeutic and refreshing is the sense of expectancy that breathes through their writing. The Puritans were exhilarated with hopes of what lay around the corner.

They lived in an awareness that the new age had arrived. Edward Johnson said about the New England experiment, "The winter is past, the rain is changed and gone, . . . fear not because your number is but small, gather into churches, and let Christ be your king."[49]

This sense of excitement about enlarging horizons was evident in the Puritans' attitude toward institutions such as the church and the state. Thomas Becon said about developments in his time that

> all false religion is extirpated and plucked up by the roots. The miserable captivity wherewith we were oppressed in the pope's kingdom is turned into delectable liberty. Our consciences are restored to their old freedom.[50]

American Puritanism was equally buoyant: William Bradford wrote regarding the new church at Salem, "as one small candle may light a thousand, so the light kindled here hath shone unto many, yea in some sort of our whole nation."[51] It was Samuel Willard's conviction that "there are better times coming on," while Milton thought he saw in his mind "a noble and puissant nation rousing herself like a strong man after sleep."[52]

When the Puritans defined the purpose of various activities or institutions, they thought so ambitiously that they take our breath away. The overall vision of the Puritans, we should never forget, was nothing less than a totally re-formed society based on biblical principles. When Milton defined the aims of education, he spoke about becoming like God and learning to do everything that a person might be called to do "justly, skilfully, and magnanimously."[53] The purpose of a family, according to the Puritans, is to glorify God. Preaching has as its aim equally ambitious results: it is "sanctified for the begetting of faith, for the opening of the understanding, for the drawing of the will and affections to Christ."[54]

At a more personal level, the Puritan temperament was marked by an expectant openness to what God would send next. Nicholas Lockyer, Cromwell's chaplain, asked, "What have I of God? how might I have more? more of his love, more of his power working in my soul?"[55] John Robinson, addressing the Pilgrims on the eve of their voyage to America, claimed that he was "very confident the Lord had more truth and light yet to break forth out of his holy Word."[56]

The sheer energy of the Puritans is impressive. They were activists to the very core of their being. This active spirit profoundly influenced how they conceived of the Christian life. Samuel Rutherford wrote in a letter that "without running, fighting, sweating, wrestling, heaven is not taken."[57] In a letter to the Speaker of the House of Commons, Cromwell crossed out the words "wait on" and made the statement read "who have *wrestled with* God for a blessing."[58] At the Day of Judgment, according to Bunyan, people will not be asked, "Did you believe?" but, "Were you doers, or talkers only?"[59]

"You must not think to go to heaven on a feather-bed," claimed Thomas Hooker; "if you will be Christ's disciples, you must take up his cross; and it will make you sweat."[60] "The way to grow in any grace is the exercise of that grace," said John Preston.[61] Henry Hall believed that "those that would put in for a share in his kingdom . . . must not be dull and sluggish, but earnest and violent in pursuance of it."[62] And according to Richard Sibbes, the sanctified person displays "a holy violence in the performing of all duties."[63]

The spectacle of an effortless Christian life held no appeal for the Puritans. It did not correspond to what they knew about life in a fallen world. In a famous passage in *Areopagitica*, Milton wrote:

> I cannot praise a fugitive and cloistered virtue, unexercised and unbreathed, that never sallies out and sees her adversary, but slinks out of the race. . . . That which purifies us is trial, and trial is by what is contrary.[64]

John Knox wrote in a letter, "I see the battle shall be great, for Satan rageth even to the uttermost; and I am come (I praise my God) even in the brunt of the battle."[65] Richard Baxter was of the same temperament:

> Christianity is not a sedentary profession or employment, nor doth it consist in mere negatives. . . . Sitting still will lose you heaven, as well as if you run from it. . . . If the way to heaven be not far harder than the world imagines, then Christ and his apostles knew not the way, or else have deceived us.[66]

The Practical Impulse in Puritanism

Part of the genius of Puritanism was its urge to be practical. For the Puritans, the mark of true Christianity was that it made a difference in how people actually live. According to Eleazar Mather, Christians must "speak by lives as well as words; you must live religion, as well as talk religion."[67] John Owen claimed that "our happiness consisteth not in the *knowing* the things of the gospel, but in the *doing* of them."[68] "The soul of religion is the practical part," wrote John Bunyan.[69]

This practical impulse permeated Puritan thinking in many areas. In preaching sermons, for example, William Ames insisted that it was not enough to state the truth; the preacher must also show "the use, goodness, or end" of Christian doctrines.[70] In urging Christians to meditate on how they can serve God and society, Cotton Mather stipulated, "Consider it till you have *resolved* on something. Write down your resolutions."[71]

The Puritans wanted things to be useful. Cotton Mather again sounded the keynote: "There is a virtuous Epicurism in usefulness. No Epicure can swim in such delights as the man that is useful wherever he comes."[72] It is no wonder that a comparison of early Boston and early Philadelphia shows a contrast between "the *doing* tradition of Puritanism" and "the *being* tradition of Quakerism."[73]

The practical bent of the Puritans led them to emphasize the experiential nature of the Christian faith. Intellectual assent to Christian doctrine was not enough. One of the customary Puritan terms was *experimental*, meaning "experiential." Thomas Shepard wrote:

> Saints have an experimental knowledge of the work of grace, by virtue of which they come to know it as certainly . . . as by feeling heat, we know that fire is hot; by tasting honey, we know it is sweet.[74]

"Experience is the life of a Christian," said Richard Sibbes, while Tyndale spoke of "feeling faith" as contrasted to "historical faith."[75]

Getting Back to Basics

The Puritans had a knack for getting to the root of a matter. They were profoundly distrustful of elaborate externalities and placed their confidence instead in the inner heart of a person or issue. They knew that the inner story that people tell to God and themselves is more indicative of what they truly are than the outward story they tell to the world.

The result was an emphasis on "heart religion" as distinct from external rituals. "A Christian's great care should be to keep the heart pure," wrote Thomas Watson, "because it is the heart that sanctifies all we do. If the heart be holy, all is holy — our affections holy, our duties holy."[76] Surely we get to the heart of the matter when we read that "the best work of man is the believing and doing of God's Word and will."[77]

The concern with heart religion gave people a new ethic in which the inner motive was what made an action moral or immoral. John Preston thus wrote:

> You might meddle with all things in the world and not be defiled by them, if you had pure affections, but when you have an inordinate lust after anything, then it defiles your spirit.[78]

The same outlook transformed attitudes toward work: "The meanness of the calling doth not abase the goodness of the work: for God looketh not at the excellence [external dignity] of the work but at the heart of the worker."[79]

The dignity of human work has never stood higher than it did with the Puritans. From Jost Amman, *Book of Trades;* courtesy of the British Library

The preference for inner reality rather than external appearances was also applied to church and worship. "Christ's true church," theorized John Bradford, is something "whose beauty indeed is all inward, . . . outwardly being but simple."[80] A person's individual worth was put on the same foundation: "No man is to stand upon his gentility or glory in his parentage," wrote Perkins, "but only rejoice in this, that he is drawn out of the kingdom of darkness."[81]

In short, the Puritans would have agreed with Richard Baxter that "fundamentals in religion are the life of the superstructure."[82] In Puritan thinking, this urge to get rid of superfluous details and get down to basics meant returning to the primitive biblical past. A. G. Dickens makes the provocative comment that "one who has never felt this nostalgia, this desire to sweep away the accretions, to cross the centuries to the homeland, can understand little of the . . . real successes achieved by Protestantism."[83] "We seek the Old Way, and the best way," said Richard Sibbes, while John Owen spoke of returning Christianity to "its primitive liberty" and restoring "the old, glorious, beautiful face of Christianity."[84]

The Balanced Christian Life

Perry Miller has said that "the Puritans lived on intimate, if not always comfortable, terms with paradox."[85] This means that they were willing to embrace both halves of apparently contradictory concepts. Thomas Gataker wrote that many things "to a mere natural man will seem to be strange paradoxes, which yet every good Christian, having duly weighed, will easily acknowledge . . . to be agreeable to truth."[86] The Puritans were adept at taking a comprehensive view of Christian theology. In the process, they achieved balance among various aspects of the Christian faith that throughout history have often been split apart.

Consider, for example, the Puritan blend of "head and heart" in Christian experience. The Puritans valued an intellectual grasp of Christian doctrine, but at the same time they preserved the emotional side of religious experience. Cotton Mather praised William Ames for his combination of "a scholastical wit joined with a heart warm in religion."[87] On one side we find Puritans saying that "to raise the affections without informing the mind is a fruitless, unprofitable labor, and serves to make zeal without knowledge."[88] On the other side, Richard Baxter would conduct his catechism sessions by first examining his pupils' understanding of the doctrine and then urging them "with all possible . . . vehemency to answerable affection and practice."[89]

Closely akin to the balance between head and heart in religion was the Puritan equilibrium between theory and practice. William Perkins insisted that "ministers be godly men as well as good scholars: and their lives be inoffensive as well as their doctrine sound."[90] According to the preface to the Geneva Bible, the Christian life has a double thrust: it "chiefly is attained by the knowledge and practicing of the word of God."[91]

Puritan attitudes toward this world were shot through with paradox. They both accepted and rejected this world. It was simultaneously God's world in which Christians were called to make the divine will prevail *and* the temporal, evil realm that could sidetrack people from their eternal spiritual life. On the one hand, "God hath placed us in the world to do him some work. This is God's working place."[92] But on the other hand, the Puritans were convinced that

> where the world hath got possession in the heart, it makes us false to God and false to man . . . false to religion itself. Labor therefore to have the world in its own place, under thy feet.[93]

The strength of the Puritan outlook was the ability to live as a citizen of two worlds: "The life of a Christian is wondrously ruled in this world, by the consideration and meditation of the life of another world."[94]

The active and contemplative aspects of the Christian life have often threatened to pull apart. In the Middle Ages they *did* divide. The Puritans reintegrated them. Puritans devoted major attention to private Bible reading, prayer, meditation, and introspection. But they were also activists, backed by a work ethic that assured them that God approved of their daily employment. The Puritan ideal was the person who both "walks with God, . . . loves to be much retired from the world" and at the same time can "follow his occasions in the world . . . in obedience unto God."[95]

The tension between human works and God's grace, between law and gospel, is perennial in Christian theology. Puritan doctrine was wide enough to encompass both poles. William Perkins found two types of people reprehensible — those "that would have nothing but mercy, mercy" and those that "have nothing in their mouths but the law, the law, and justice, justice."[96] Richard Baxter similarly wrote that "our righteousness, which the law of works requireth, . . . is wholly in Christ, and not one grain in ourselves. . . . But yet ourselves must personally fulfil the conditions of the new covenant and so have a personal evangelical righteousness."[97]

In their social theory, Puritans likewise walked a middle path between such dichotomies as rights and duties, individual freedom and the good of the community, idealism about the possibility of improving social institutions and a cynicism about the corruption of those institutions. The Puritans saw no need to choose *between* personal holiness and social action; in their view, the Bible shows us both "how we must serve God and how we must serve the generation wherein we live."[98]

Much of what I have suggested about the Puritans' balance in the Christian life is summarized in Everett Emerson's description of American Puritanism:

> It emphasized church fellowship. . . . But it demanded that man probe, privately but profoundly, his own soul. . . . It was highly intellectual and put a premium on education, but it also taught that what really motivates man is the heart, the affections. Puritanism was an activist, this-worldly kind of religion that denied the ultimate value of anything material. It was profoundly pessimistic about the nature of man, but it encouraged a forwardlooking attitude towards America.[99]

A Simplicity That Dignifies

In significant ways Puritanism was a quest for simplicity. At their best, the Puritans chose the simplicity that exalts, not the simplicity that diminishes.

In worship this impulse resulted in a streamlined church service with everything unified around the Word of God. Puritan architecture was a triumph of tasteful simplicity. In personal lifestyle, the Puritan ideal of moderation and thrift tended toward a similar pattern. Lucy Hutchinson's description of her Puritan husband's appearance is well-known:

> He was wonderful neat and cleanly and genteel in his habit [dress], and had a very good fancy in making good clothes, but he left off very early the wearing of anything that was costly, yet in his plainest . . . habit [dress] appeared very much a gentleman.[100]

Because theology is so often synonymous with speculative thought, I remember how refreshed I felt when I first read the opening of William Ames's *Marrow of Theology:* "Theology is the doctrine of living for God." Equally attractive is William Perkins's formulation: "Theology is the science of living blessedly forever."[101] When seen against the background of the gallons of ink that theologians have spilled arguing about the sacrament of Communion, Thomas Watson's description stands out resplendent in its clarity: "In the Word preached the saints hear Christ's voice; in the sacrament they have his kiss."[102]

The simplicity that dignifies is also attractively illustrated by the Puritan gift for aphorism — the clear and concise statement of a truth, so striking that it not only expresses an idea but compels insight and assent. To illustrate, consider the following specimens:

The time of our loathing was the time of God's loving.[103]

Were earthly comforts permanent, who would look for heavenly?[104]

Consider that no sin against a great God can be strictly a little sin.[105]

Religion begat prosperity and the daughter devoured the mother.[106]

Truth may be lost by weakness as well as wickedness.[107]

This gift for aphorism, when coupled with the Puritan impulse to define things precisely, produced some of the memorable Puritan definitions:

Man's chief end is to glorify God and enjoy him forever.[108]

The preaching of the Word is that lattice where Christ looks forth and shows himself to his saints.[109]

[Faith is] a persuasion of my heart that God hath given his son for me, and that he is mine, and I his.[110]

By Christianity I intend that universal habit of grace which is wrought in a soul by the regenerating spirit of God, whereby the whole creature is resigned up into the divine will and love, and all its actions designed to the obedience of that for the glory of its maker.[111]

A Sure Foundation

No structure is stronger than its foundation. It is appropriate to conclude this survey of Puritan strengths with a reminder that Puritanism was not simply a human movement comprised of people with good ideas and unusual courage. The Puritans were people of confidence, even in defeat, because they knew that they were part of something much bigger than themselves.

Puritan convictions on every topic were rooted in the Bible as God's reliable revelation of truth. It is impossible to overstate how much difference it makes in a person's life when he or she views the Bible as "a perfect and absolute rule" for life.[112] Stop to consider how many questions are resolved once a person accepts William Perkins's beginning axiom that

the word of God must be our rule and square whereby we are to frame and fashion all our actions; and according to direction received thence, we must do the things we do, or leave them undone.[113]

Of course there remain the usual problems of interpreting and applying the Bible, but the important boundaries for determining truth and action have already been established. Puritan confidence is at the opposite pole from the modern mentality that thinks it has to take a Gallup poll in order to determine what the truth of an issue is.

The character of God was also a foundation of Puritan thought and action. God's justice and mercy, holiness and love, provided the poles between which Puritan theology moved. Of the two, God's love was the more prominent in Puritan preaching. The justice of God gave the Puritans their conviction of sin and the sense of self-limitation that ran strong in their thinking. But it was on the bedrock of God's love that the Puritans lived their spiritual lives in the world. Richard Baxter sounded the keynote:

> Is it a small thing in thine eyes to be beloved of God? . . . Christian, believe this and think on it. Thou shalt be eternally embraced in the arms of that love which was from everlasting and will extend to everlasting.[114]

A corollary of such conviction about the love of God was Puritan reliance on the atonement of Christ as the groundwork of justification. The Puritans reveled in the freedom of knowing that their salvation did not depend on their own efforts. "We are justified and saved by the very righteousness of Christ, and no other," wrote John Flavel, adding, "He wrought it, though we wear it."[115] An experiential awareness of personal salvation was the basis of Puritan identity. When Thomas Goodwin was converted at a funeral service, "God took me aside, and as it were privately said unto me, Do you now turn to me, and I will pardon all your sins."[116] A strong sense of personal identity — of knowing who they were in Christ — was a hallmark of the Puritans.

Literary and historical scholars today speak of the "story" that people tell about themselves and in terms of which they live their lives. The Puritans viewed themselves as pilgrims on a journey to God and heaven. That journey led through this world and was not an escape from it. The Puritans were protagonists in a great spiritual battle between good and evil, God and Satan. As warfaring and wayfaring Christians, they were assured of victory because they were on God's side. This theology of hope was stronger than the theology of suffering that was equally a part of the Puritan consciousness. And it accounts for the courage with which the Puritans were willing to face persecution for their faith.

Summary

We live at a moment in history when evangelical Protestants are looking for "roots." One of the foibles that some would foist on them is that the only traditions from the past to which they can return are the Catholic and Anglo-Catholic traditions. Like Nicodemus, who was a teacher in Israel but did not know about the New Birth, evangelical Protestants tend to be strangers to what is best in their own tradition.

Puritanism can give us a place to stand. The Puritans believed that all of life is God's. This enabled them to combine personal piety with a comprehensive Christian world view. Beginning with the premise that the Bible is a reliable repository of truth, the Puritans had a basis from which to relate their Christian faith to all areas of life — to work, family, marriage, education, politics, economics, and society.

The Puritans' zestful approach to life in the world was fed by the spiritual springs of the new life — prayer, Christian fellowship, meditation, preaching, and contact with the Bible. In Puritanism, a theology of personal salvation was wedded to an active life in the world.

FURTHER READING

To get a taste of the strength and attractiveness of Puritanism, there is no substitute for reading the Puritans at firsthand. The best series of modern reprints of Puritan primary sources is that published by the Banner of Truth Trust, and I much commend it. The works of John Bunyan and John Milton are also excellent starting points.

Some of my most positive impressions of Puritanism have come from book-length studies of individuals. I have in mind books like these: N. H. Keeble, *Richard Baxter: Puritan Man of Letters* (1982); Ernest B. Lowrie, *The Shape of the Puritan Mind: The Thought of Samuel Willard* (1974); Derrick Sherwin Bailey, *Thomas Becon and the Reformation of the Church in England* (1952).

Puritan autobiographies and books on meditation frequently offer an attractive entry into Puritanism. A good secondary source is Owen C. Watkins, *The Puritan Experience: Studies in Spiritual Autobiography* (1972). For a picture of Puritanism at its best, I recommend Lucy Hutchinson's portrait of her husband in her preface ("To My Children") to *Memoirs of the Life of Colonel Hutchinson* (available in a modern reprint by Oxford University Press, 1973); here, in a dozen pages or so, is the Puritan ideal.

This detail from John Bunyan's tomb reminds us that the Puritan image of the pilgrim burdened by a weight of sin is not the most cheering view of human experience, but it is truest to the facts.

Notes

The documentation of sources has been based on these procedures: (1) for any item that appears in incomplete form, the reader must refer to the bibliography that follows the notes for the complete information about publication; (2) all items enclosed in brackets are either the secondary source or the scholarly modern edition from which I have quoted a Puritan primary source.

FOREWORD

[1] Cited from Wakefield, *Puritan Devotion*, p. x.

[2] George Whitefield, *Works* (London, 1771), 4:306–7.

[3] Wakefield, *Puritan Devotion*, p. x. One cannot help thinking of the married lady who came to tell D. L. Moody that she thought she was called to be a preacher. "Have you got any children at home?" Moody asked. "Yes, six." "There's your congregation; off you go!"

CHAPTER 1

[1] H. L. Mencken, as quoted in Perry, p. 239.

[2] Quoted by C. S. Lewis, "Donne and Love Poetry in the Seventeenth Century," in *Seventeenth Century Studies Presented to Sir Herbert Grierson* (Oxford: Oxford University Press, 1938), p. 74. Although the term *Puritan* was not yet used in More's day, it is common for historians to consider Tyndale the founder of what later became known as Puritanism. William A. Clebsch, *England's Earliest Protestants, 1520–1535* (New Haven: Yale University Press, 1964), writes, "Tyndale founded English Puritanism as the theological, religious, and moral system that univocally regarded scripture as God's law for everyman" (p. 317).

[3] Lewis, "Donne and Love Poetry," p. 75.

[4] Langdon Mitchell, as quoted in Perry, p. 240.

[5] *Journal* (London: J. M. Dent and Sons, 1924), p. 151.

[6] C. S. Lewis, *Studies in Medieval and Renaissance Literature* (Cambridge: Cambridge University Press, 1966), p. 121.

[7] Christopher Hill, *The Intellectual Origins of the English Revolution* (Oxford: Oxford University Press, 1965), p. 293.

[8] A. G. Dickens, "The Ambivalent English Reformation," in *Background to the English Renaissance*, ed. J. B. Trapp (London: Gray-Mills, 1974), p. 47.

[9] William Gouge, *Of Domestical Duties* [Frye, p. 155; Schücking, p. 38].

[10] William Perkins, *Christian Economy* [Breward, p. 424].

[11] Richard Baxter, *The Saints' Everlasting Rest*, p. 182.

[12] Richard Bernard, *The Isle of Man* [Haller, *Rise of Puritanism*, p. 139].

[13] Richard Rogers, *Seven Treatises* [Irvonwy Morgan, p. 143].

[14] Richard Sibbes, *Bowels Opened* [George, p. 114].

[15] *A Wife in Deed* [Lerner, p. 112].

[16] *The Work of William Tyndale* [Derek Wilson, p. 48]. M. M. Knappen, *Tudor Puritanism*, writes, "Where Puritan ascetic regulations did appear, . . . they were . . . ancillary rather than primary. They were designed to clear the ground of underbrush. . . . Happiness itself was not under fire, but only such aspects of the lesser species as interfered with the attainment of the greater kind. It was the old story of the good being the enemy of the best" (p. 428).

[17] Scholes, p. 105.

[18] Quoted in Scholes, p. 105.

[19] Demos, pp. 53–54. See also the portrait in Louis B. Wright, *Life in Colonial America*, p. 162.

[20] Hans-Peter Wagner, *Puritan Attitudes Towards Recreation in Early Seventeenth-Century New England* (Frankfurt: Verlag Peter Lang, 1982).

[21] Richard Sibbes, *Works* [Foster, p. 106].

[22] Quoted in Stone, *Crisis*, p. 331.

[23] *A Christian Directory*, p. 50.

[24] *God's Bounty* [McNeill, p. 41].

[25] The best source to consult on this subject is Percy A. Scholes, *The Puritans and Music in England and New England*.

[26] Ibid., p. 6.

[27] Ibid., p. 5.

[28] Ibid.

[29] Ibid. In the Puritan era music passed "from public institutional culture to domestic and voluntary practice" (Watson, p. 532).

[30] *The Saints' Everlasting Rest* [Kaufmann, p. 250].

[31] *A Sermon Preached to the Honorable House of Commons* . . . [Rogers, p. 247].

[32] *Studies in Medieval and Renaissance Literature*, p. 121.

[33] Quoted in Pearson, p. 242.

[34] Bishop Scambler to Burghley [Babbage, p. 11]. Another Anglican official complained in a letter about the "new orators . . . rising up from among us, foolish young men, who . . . are seeking the complete overthrow and rooting up of our whole ecclesiastical polity" (*Zurich Letters* [Derek Wilson, p. 135]).

[35] Collinson, pp. 373–74.

[36] Gooch, p. 44. Gooch calls the incident "typical." A Continental reformer wrote in 1554, "English youths have come over to us in great numbers within these few days, partly from Oxford, and partly from Cambridge, whom many godly merchants are bringing up to learning" (J. Strype, *Ecclesiastical Memorials* [Derek Wilson, p. 121]).

[37] *Autobiography* [Wagner, p. 46].

[38] *The Marrow of Theology*, p. 236.

[39] Samuel Clarke, *The Saint's Nosegay* [McGee, p. 47].

[40] Baxter, *The Saints' Everlasting Rest*, p. 142.

[41] Richard Sibbes, *The Saint's Cordials* [Stannard, p. 26].

[42] Jordan's books are entitled *The Development of Religious Toleration in England;* the first volume is subtitled *From the Beginning of the English Reformation to the Death of Queen Elizabeth,* and the second *From the Accession of James I to the Convention of the Long Parliament (1603–1640).* The phrases quoted in my text come from the first volume, pp. 32, 260–61.

[43] Ashley, pp. 144–45.

[44] William Perkins wrote, "In the very midst of the Roman Papacy, God hath always had a remnant which have in some measure truly served him" (*Works* [George, p. 380]). Thomas Adams said, "I believe that many of our forefathers went to Heaven, though through blindness" (*Works* [George, p. 370]).

[45] Quoted in *Eminent Persons,* ed. Clarke [Porter, *Reformation and Reaction,* p. 229].

[46] *The Diary of Samuel Ward,* in *Two Elizabethan Puritan Diaries,* ed. Knappen.

[47] Quoted in Seaver, p. 37.

[48] *The Mourner's Cordial Against Excessive Sorrow* [Lowrie, p. 225].

[49] Quoted by Schlatter, p. 16.

[50] Hayward, p. 347.

[51] *Sermons on Fast Days, 1678–1684* [Miller, *Nature's Nation,* p. 29]. William Stoughton criticized "empty outside custom-born Christians" whose faith "hath run itself out of breath and broke its neck" (*New-England's True Interest* [Miller, *Nature's Nation,* p. 26]).

[52] *The Beatitudes* (Edinburgh: Banner of Truth Trust, 1977), p. 172. Watson added, "Civility does but wash a man, grace changes him. . . . Civility is but strewing flowers on a dead corpse. A man may be wonderfully moralized, yet but a tame devil" (p. 175).

[53] *Morality Not to Be Relied on for Life* [Lowrie, p. 230]. Increase Mather denounced those "who give out, as if saving grace and morality were the same" (*Some Important Truths Concerning Conversion* [Miller, *Nature's Nation,* p. 26]).

[54] *Diary of Cotton Mather* [Greven, *Protestant Temperament,* p. 67].

[55] Samuel Willard, *Complete Body of Divinity* [Greven, *Protestant Temperament,* p. 203]. Willard distinguished between "sinful self-love" and "regular self-love."

[56] Davies, *Worship and Theology . . . 1534–1603,* p. 285.

[57] Baltzell, p. 247. Max Weber agrees with this assessment: "The great men of the Puritan movement were thoroughly steeped in the culture of the Renaissance. . . . Perhaps no country was ever so full of graduates as New England in the first generation of its existence" (*The Protestant Ethic and the Rise of Capitalism,* p. 168).

[58] *Worship of the English Puritans,* p. 9.

[59] Davies, *Worship and Theology . . . 1534–1603,* writes that "the flexibility and unity of Puritanism are best preserved if I describe their subdivisions as conforming or nonconforming Puritans, or even better, as patient and impatient Puritans" (p. 44).

[60] Dickens, p. 319. Knappen's influential book *Tudor Puritanism* comes to the same conclusion: "Puritanism was primarily a religious movement. This fact cannot be too often repeated in any discussion of its social and economic teaching" (p. 401).

[61] Major-General Harrison, letter to Oliver Cromwell [Micklem, p. 186]. Samuel Willard gave a religious interpretation of the founding of the Massachusetts Bay Colony that the letters from the first settlers back to England bear out: "The main errand which brought your fathers into this wilderness was, not only that they might themselves enjoy, but that they might settle for their children, and leave them in full possession of the free, pure, and uncorrupted liberties of the covenant of grace" (Quoted in Lowrie, p. 167).

[62] Knappen, *Tudor Puritanism,* comments that for the Puritans "all acts were moral. At no moment was one exempt from ethical considerations" (p. 342).

[63] *Works* [George, p. 109].

[64] Preface to Queen Elizabeth in the Geneva Bible [Trinterud, p. 211]; Solemn League and Covenant of 1643 [Warfield, p. 24]; *Records of the First Church in Dorchester* [Edmund Morgan, *Puritan Family,* p. 140].

[65] William Perkins, *The Art of Prophesying* [Breward, p. 343].

[66] Seaver, p. 44.

[67] *Society and Religion*, p. 234. Davies, *Worship and Theology . . . 1534–1603*, comments that Puritanism "was a new and vigorous movement of protest against the dead hand of tradition" (p. 285).

[68] *Tudor Puritanism*, p. 102. McGee writes that "Puritans were extremely conscious of their membership in an international brotherhood of saints. They had long thought of the churches of Geneva, the Rhineland, and other centers of advanced Protestantism on the Continent as the models of the reformation they sought for England" (p. 255). Rogers notes that, in contrast to the separatists, "Puritans sought the advice of the leaders of Continental Reformed theology, although they often felt that they could not heed it because of the peculiarity of the English situation" (p. 67). W. K. Jordan contrasts the international flavor of Puritanism to Anglicanism as well, noting that foreign contacts increasingly became the concern of the Puritan wing alone of the English church (vol. 2, pp. 130–31).

[69] Dickens, p. 333.

[70] Seaver, p. 290. Seaver notes regarding the minority status of Puritanism in England, "That Puritanism as a movement commanded the allegiance of only a minority of Englishmen is undoubtedly true, but it is also largely beside the point, for there is little reason to suppose that the majority gave the Established Church . . . more than their lukewarm acquiescence" (p. 293).

[71] Information about persecution of the Puritans can be gained from a number of sources, including the following: W. H. Frere, *The English Church in the Reigns of Elizabeth and James I* (1904); C. E. Whiting, *Studies in English Puritanism from the Restoration to the Revolution, 1660–1688* (1931); W. K. Jordan, *The Development of Religious Toleration in England* (companion volumes in 1932 and 1936); Gerald R. Cragg, *Puritanism in the Period of the Great Persecution, 1660–1688* (1957); Horton Davies, *Worship and Theology in England: From Andrewes to Baxter and Fox, 1603–1690* (1975), pp. 437–54; Patrick McGrath, *Papists and Puritans under Elizabeth I* (1967); R. C. Richardson, *Puritanism in North-West England* (1972); Samuel R. Gardiner, *The First Two Stuarts and the Puritan Revolution, 1603–1660* (1876; reprint 1970).

[72] Trinterud, p. 166. Trinterud writes further, "The Reformation emerges . . . as an anticlerical movement. It was the large-scale revolt of a newly self-conscious laity against clerical prerogatives that gave to some reform-minded religious leaders an opportunity . . . to work toward the changes they regarded as desirable."

[73] *Works*, 14:247.

[74] Derek Wilson, p. 132.

[75] Stone, *Crisis*, comments, "It was this infiltration of the universities which turned Puritanism from the sectional eccentricity of a few great households in the countryside and groups of artisans and small traders in the towns into a nation-wide movement affecting all classes of society" (pp. 740–41).

[76] *Collections of the Massachusetts Historical Society* [Schlatter, p. 54].

[77] Curtis, p. 197. E. Harris Harbison has written that "the Protestant Reformation began in a scholar's insight into the meaning of Scripture. It was to a large extent a learned movement, a thing of professors and students" (*The Christian Scholar in the Age of the Reformation* [New York: Scribner, 1956], p. vi).

[78] Haller, *Rise of Puritanism*, p. 258.

[79] Quoted in Lowrie, pp. 171–72.

[80] Quoted in Seaver, p. 8.

[81] *Collected Works* [Seaver, p. 8].

[82] Bailey, *Thomas Becon*, p. 120.

[83] James Johnson writes that "the doctrine of social covenant set out by federal theologians in both Englands provides a way of transferring what had been solely an individualistic ethic into one having social relevance as well" (p. 20).

[84] George Swinnock, *The Christian Man's Calling* [Schlatter, p. 189].

85 *A Christian Directory* [Lewalski, p. 165].

86 *A Man in Christ* . . . [Daly, p. 74].

87 John Bunyan, *Grace Abounding to the Chief of Sinners* [Watkins, p. 64].

88 The study of Puritan vocabulary and the Puritan imagination is a largely uncultivated field that holds great promise. A preliminary study of Puritan vocabulary is M. van Beek, *An Enquiry into Puritan Vocabulary* (Groningen: Wolters-Noordhoff, 1969).

89 *The Complete Body of Divinity* [Greven, *Protestant Temperament*, p. 179].

90 *The Saints' Everlasting Rest*, p. 33.

91 *Works* [Norman Pettit, *The Heart Prepared: Grace and Conversion in Puritan Spiritual Life* (New Haven: Yale University Press, 1966), p. 48].

92 *The Reformed Pastor*, p. 115. John Goodwin similarly wrote that "there is no sight so lovely as naked truth" (*Certain Brief Observations and Antiquaries* . . . [Haller, *Liberty and Reformation*, p. 147]).

93 *Works* [Haller, *Rise of Puritanism*, p. 140].

94 *The Christian's Two Chief Lessons* [McGee, p. 247].

95 *Works* [Haller, *Rise of Puritanism*, p. 140].

96 Rogers, *Diary* [Knappen, *Two Elizabethan Puritan Diaries*, p. 64]; Mather, *John in the Wilderness* [John Eusden, introduction to Ames's *Marrow of Theology*, p. 3].

97 *Diary* [Knappen, *Two Elizabethan Puritan Diaries*, p. 119].

98 *The Saints' Everlasting Rest*, p. 125.

99 *Covenant-Keeping the Way to Blessedness* and *A Complete Body of Divinity* [Lowrie, p. 230].

100 Regulations of the Lewisham Grammar School [Watson, pp. 131–32].

101 *Massachusetts Laws of 1672* [Edmund Morgan, *Puritan Family*, p. 149].

102 Collinson, p. 371.

103 *Suffolk Court Records* [Edmund Morgan, *Puritan Family*, p. 148].

104 Ibid.

105 *Colonial Society of Massachusetts Publications* [Edmund Morgan, *Puritan Family*, p. 141].

106 Ibid.

107 *Winthrop Papers* [McGee, p. 244]. An English Puritan had a similar experience upon coming to London: "When I came out of the country hither to the city, methinks I came into another world, even out of darkness into light; for here the Word of God is plentifully preached" (Edward Bush, *A Sermon Preached at Paul's Cross* [Hill, *Change*, p. 4]).

108 Seaver, p. 39. Seaver comments, "That a sermon inflicted on an aristocratic wedding party should be regarded as a source of pleasure demonstrates the power of Puritanism to modify traditional modes of behavior."

109 Thomas Doolittle defined Christian conference as conversation in which "believers build up one another in faith" (*Rebukes for Sin by God's Burning Anger* [McGee, p. 196]).

110 Knappen, *Two Elizabethan Puritan Diaries*, p. 63.

111 *Winthrop Papers* [McGee, p. 196].

112 John Robinson, *Observations of Knowledge and Virtue* [Reinitz, p. 67].

113 *Winthrop Papers* [Irvonwy Morgan, p. 122].

114 Benjamin Wadsworth wrote a book entitled *The Well-Ordered Family*, and Cotton Mather wrote one entitled *A Family Well-Ordered*.

115 *The Child's Portion* [Miller/Johnson, 2:369].

116 Stone, *Family*, p. 141.

117 Dickens, pp. 316, 318.

¹¹⁸Stone, *Crisis*, pp. 733–34.

¹¹⁹Hunt, p. 252.

CHAPTER 2

¹Quoted in Joachim Jeremias, *Rediscovering the Parables* (New York: Scribner, 1966), p. 113.

²*Demonstratio Evangelica* [Forrester, p. 42]. Forrester comments, "The sacred and secular on this view differed not merely in degree but in kind. Within the monastery or convent, the 'religious' who had a 'vocation' aimed at perfection, devoted themselves largely (though not exclusively) to contemplation, while outside in the family, in the market-place, in the field and on the seas, the others kept the wheels of the work of the world running, at the cost of condemning their souls to a second-best spiritual life" (p. 45). As Forrester shows, there were individual attempts by churchmen (notably Francis of Assisi) to sanctify ordinary work, but these attempts never became the dominant position of medieval Catholicism.

³Luther claimed, for example, "When a maid cooks and cleans and does other housework, because God's command is there, even such a small work must be praised as a service of God far surpassing the holiness and asceticism of all monks and nuns" (*Works* [Forrester, p. 148]). Again, household work "has no appearance of sanctity; and yet these very works in connection with the household are more desirable than all the works of all the monks and nuns. . . . Seemingly secular works are a worship of God and an obedience well pleasing to God" (Commentary on Gen. 13:13). Further, "Your work is a very sacred matter. God delights in it, and through it he wants to bestow his blessing on you" (Exposition of Ps. 128:2 [Plass, 3:1493]).

⁴Calvin wrote such things as this: "It is an error that those who flee worldly affairs and engage in contemplation are leading an angelic life. . . . We know that men were created to busy themselves with labor and that no sacrifice is more pleasing to God than when each one attends to his calling and studies to live well for the common good" (Commentary on Luke 10:38).

⁵*The Parable of the Wicked Mammon* [Louis B. Wright, *Middle-Class Culture*, p. 171]. Thomas Shepard wrote, "Seeing yourself thus working in worldly employments for [Christ], you may easily apprehend that . . . you honor God . . . more by the meanest servile worldly act, than if you should have spent all that time in meditation, prayer, or any other spiritual employment" (*Works* [Edmund Morgan, *Puritan Family*, pp. 70–71]).

⁶*Works* [Davies, *Worship and Theology . . . 1534–1603*, p. 66]. Perkins also wrote, "Hereby is overthrown the condition of monks and friars, who challenge to themselves that they live in a state of perfection, because that they live apart from the societies of men in fasting and prayer: but contrariwise, this monkish kind of living is damnable; for besides the general duties of fasting and prayer, which appertain to all Christians, every man must have a particular and personal calling that he may be a good and profitable member of some society and body" (*A Treatise of the Vocations or Callings of Men* [Edmund Morgan, *Political Ideas*, p. 52]).

⁷*The Third Sermon Upon the Lord's Prayer* [Louis B. Wright, *Middle-Class Culture*, p. 174]. Luther had expressed the opinion that if we would look upon all work as a form of service to God, "the entire world would be full of service to God, not only the churches but also the home, the kitchen, the cellar, the workshop, and the field of townsfolk and farmers" (Sermon on Matt. 6:24–34 [Plass, 2:560]).

⁸*A Godly Form of Household Government* [Walzer, p. 214].

⁹*Christian Calling* [Miller/Johnson, 1:322–23]. "Our Savior Christ was a carpenter," preached Latimer; "therefore let no man disdain . . . to follow him in a . . . common calling and occupation" (*Sixth Sermon Preached before King Edward VI* [Green, p. 70]).

¹⁰*Treatise of the Vocations . . .* [Edmund Morgan, *Political Ideas*, p. 51]. Elsewhere Perkins noted that "God looketh not at . . . the work, but at the heart of the worker," and therefore common tasks, "howsoever gross they appear outwardly, yet are they sanctified" (*Works* [George, pp. 138, 139]).

¹¹*A Sermon . . .* [Elliott, p. 179].

¹²*The Tradesman's Calling* [Tawney, p. 245]. Calvin had said that "there is no part of our life or conduct, however insignificant which should not be related to the glory of God" (Commentary on 1 Cor. 10:31).

13 Steele, *The Tradesman's Calling* [Kitch, p. 115].

14 *Sermons* [Kitch, p. 155].

15 *Christian Calling* [Miller/Johnson, 1:319].

16 *A Christian at His Calling* [McGiffert, p. 124].

17 Quoted in Hill, *Society and Puritanism*, p. 136.

18 *The Tradesman's Calling* [Tawney, pp. 240, 321].

19 Edmund Morgan, *Political Ideas*, pp. 36, 51.

20 *A Christian at His Calling* [McGiffert, p. 123].

21 *Christian Calling* [Miller/Johnson, 1:319].

22 John Dod and Robert Cleaver, *Ten Sermons* . . . [Davies, *Worship and Theology* . . . 1534–1603, p. 66].

23 *The Tradesman's Calling* [Tawney, p. 245].

24 *Treatise of the Vocations* . . . [Edmund Morgan, *Political Ideas*, p. 37].

25 *Christian Calling* [Miller/Johnson, 1:322].

26 *A Christian at His Calling* [McGiffert, p. 127]. This is reminiscent of Luther's comment in his sermon on Matthew 6: "Be content with the fact that your Father up there in heaven sees it. . . . The life of all Christians is intended for the eyes of God alone. . . . It is enough that our action is intended to satisfy and to glorify the One who sees it" (Sermon on Matt. 6:16–18 [Plass, 1:241]).

27 *A Christian at His Calling* [McGiffert, p. 127]. Contentment in one's calling had been a major theme of both Luther and Calvin. Luther wrote, "Nothing is so bad . . . but what it becomes sweet and tolerable if only I know and am certain that it is pleasing to God" (*The Estate of Marriage* [Luther, *Works*, 45:49]). Calvin wrote thus about the contentment that comes from an awareness of God's calling: "In all our cares, toils, annoyances, and other burdens, it will be no small alleviation to know that all these are under the superintendence of God. . . . Every one in his particular mode of life will, without repining, suffer its inconveniences, cares, uneasiness, and anxiety, persuaded that God has laid on the burden. This, too, will afford admirable consolation in following your proper calling. No work will be so mean and sordid as not to have a splendor and value in the eye of God" (*Institutes of the Christian Religion*, 3.10.16).

28 *The Tradesman's Calling* [Kitch, p. 158].

29 These suggestions came from, in order, William Ames, *The Marrow of Theology*, pp. 322–23; Richard Steele, *The Tradesman's Calling* [Kitch, p. 158]; Thomas Dudley to John Woodbridge [Foster, p. 100].

30 John Cotton, *The Way of Life* [Edmund Morgan, *Puritan Family*, p. 72]. Samuel Willard told his Old South Church, "God doth never call any to service but he fits them for it, hence we have a rule to judge our calling" (Boston Sermons [Edmund Morgan, *Puritan Family*, p. 72]).

31 *Commonplace Book* [*CPW*, 1:405].

32 *The Tradesman's Calling* [Tawney, p. 241]. Tawney comments, "The calling is not a condition in which the individual is born, but a strenuous and exacting enterprise, to be undertaken, indeed, under the guidance of Providence, but to be chosen by each for himself, with a deep sense of his solemn responsibilities" (p. 241).

33 *Christian Calling* [Miller/Johnson, 1:320].

34 *Works* [George, p. 135]. Calvin had written that "each should be content with his calling, and persist in it, and not be eager to change to something else," adding that Paul in 1 Corinthians 7:20 "wishes to correct the thoughtless eagerness which impels some to change their situation without any proper reason" and to condemn "the restlessness which prevents individuals from remaining contentedly as they are" (Commentary on 1 Cor. 7:20). Luther likewise castigated "fickle, unstable spirits" who "cannot continue in their calling" (Sermon on 1 Peter 4:8–11 [Plass, 3:1497]).

35 *A Christian at His Calling* [McGiffert, p. 127].

36 *Christian Calling* [Miller/Johnson, 1:326].

[37] *The Tradesman's Calling* [Kitch, p. 115]. Luther had similarly theorized that "work should . . . be done to serve God by it, to avoid idleness, and satisfy his commandments" (Sermon on the Fourth Petition of the Lord's Prayer [Plass, 3:1494]). Calvin said that "we know that men were created to busy themselves with labor . . . for the common good" (Commentary on Luke 10:38).

[38] *Treatise on the Vocations* . . . [Edmund Morgan, *Political Ideas*, pp. 56–57]. William Tyndale said that a person should "refer his craft and occupation unto the common wealth, and serve his brethren as he would do Christ himself" (*The Parable of the Wicked Mammon* [Louis B. Wright, *Middle-Class Culture*, p. 172]).

[39] *The New Covenant* [George, p. 137].

[40] *A Christian Directory* [Perry, pp. 307, 315]. Richard Steele asserted that people have been given a calling "both for their own and the common good" (*The Tradesman's Calling* [Tawney, p. 240]).

[41] *Two Brief Discourses* [Perry, p. 312].

[42] *A Christian at His Calling* [McGiffert, p. 122].

[43] *Christian Calling* [Miller/Johnson, 1:320]. A group of ministers meeting in Boston in 1699 agreed that no occupation "is lawful but what is useful unto human society" (Cotton Mather, *Magnalia Christi Americana* [Edmund Morgan, *Puritan Family*, p. 71]).

[44] *A Christian Directory* [Green, p. 72].

[45] Ibid., p. 60

[46] Ibid., p. 59.

[47] *Treatise of the Vocations* . . . [Edmund Morgan, *Political Ideas*, p. 39]. Luther had similarly spoken slightingly of people who "do not use their talents in their calling or in the service of their neighbor; they use them only for their own glory and advantage" (Sermon on 1 Peter 4:8–11 [Plass, 3:1497]).

[48] *Treatise of the Vocations* . . . [Edmund Morgan, *Political Ideas*, p. 56].

[49] *A Sermon* . . . [Louis B. Wright, *Middle-Class Culture*, p. 174].

[50] Commentary on Psalm 127:2. Luther, in commenting on the same text, wrote, "You must, of course, labor — but the effort is futile if you do nothing but labor and imagine that you are supporting yourself. . . . Labor you should, but supporting and providing for you belongs to God alone" [Plass, 3:1496].

[51] Commentary on Luke 17:7. Luther wrote in a similar vein, "When riches come, the godless heart of man thinks: I have achieved this with my labors. It does not consider that these are purely blessings of God, blessings that at times come to us through our labors and at times without our labors, but never because of our labors; for God always gives them because of His undeserved mercy" (Exposition of Deut. 8:17–18 [Plass, 3:1495]).

[52] *Sober Sentiments* [Perry, p. 312].

[53] *A Sermon* . . . [Greaves, *Society and Religion*, p. 549].

[54] *The Christian Man's Calling* [Schlatter, p. 200].

[55] *Society and Religion*, p. 550.

[56] Robertson, *Aspects of the Rise of Economic Individualism*, presents evidence for a thesis that would be widely held in scholarly circles today — that what people mistakenly call "the Puritan work ethic" is a secular development that set in with the eighteenth century. Robertson writes, "The doctrine of the 'calling' did not breed a spirit of capitalism. The spirit of capitalism was responsible for a gradual modification and attrition of the Puritan doctrine; and this attrition had barely begun in England before the Restoration" (p. 27).

[57] *The Catechizing of Families* [Hill, *Society and Puritanism*, p. 139]. Luther had been equally vivid on the subject of idleness: "God . . . does not want me to sit at home, to loaf, to commit matters to God, and to wait till a fried chicken flies into my mouth. That would be tempting God" (Exposition of Exod. 13:18 [Plass, 3:1496]).

[58] *Works* [George, p. 130]. Dalby Thomas believed that "only industrious and laborious people are the riches of any nation" (*An Historical Account of the Rise and Growth of the West India Colonies* [Hill, *Society and Puritanism*, p. 136]).

[59] Hill, *Society and Puritanism*, p. 139.

[60] Ibid., p. 124.

[61] *A Christian Directory* [Tawney, p. 262]. On the subject of viewing the necessity to work as a command of God, Calvin had written, "How few are to be found who, were it left to their own choice, would desire to live by their own labor. . . . The Prophet therefore bids the fearers of God be content with . . . the assurance that having God for their foster-father they shall be suitably maintained by the labor of their own hands" (Commentary on Ps. 128:2).

[62] *The Beatitudes*, p. 257. Richard Bernard wrote that to refuse to work is "contrary to God's injunction that men should labor, contrary to the practice of all the godly. . . . Let him or they whosoever, which think themselves religious indeed, make conscience to take pains in some calling and beware of living idly" (*Ruth's Recompense* [Hill, *Society and Puritanism*, p. 140]).

[63] *Works* [George, p. 132]. Luther had the same idea: "How much more perfect [work] would have been in that garden in the state of innocence. But it is appropriate here also to point out that man was created not for leisure but for work, even in the state of innocence" (Exposition of Gen. 2:14 [Plass, 3:1494]).

[64] *Observations of Knowledge and Virtue* [Reinitz, p. 66].

[65] *A Christian Directory* [Kitch, p. 156].

[66] Quoted in Tawney, p. 245.

[67] Quoted by Miller, *Seventeenth Century*, p. 44. Baxter held the same view: to neglect work "and say, 'I will pray and meditate,' is as if your servant should refuse your greatest work, and tie himself to some lesser, easy part" (*A Christian Directory* [Tawney, p. 242]).

[68] *The Saint's Qualification* [George, p. 172].

[69] *The Anatomy of the Abuses in England* [Tawney, p. 216].

[70] Quoted in Tawney, p. 238. Such self-accusations became common among the Puritans. Foster rightly claims that as long as the Puritans "continued to denounce themselves, as long as they were sure they had deserted their ideal, they were faithful to it. When they *stopped* bemoaning their worldliness and no longer felt a sense of guilt, at least one part of the Protestant ethic had finally given way to the spirit of capitalism" (p. 125).

[71] *The Tradesman's Calling* [Tawney, p. 244].

[72] Quoted in Miller, *Seventeenth Century*, p. 42. Luther had a similar ideal of the golden mean: "The right middle way is not to be lazy and indolent or to rely on one's own work and doing but to work and act and yet expect all success from God alone" (Exposition of Ps. 147:13 [Plass, 3:1495]).

[73] Quoted in Miller, *Seventeenth Century*, p. 42.

[74] J. M. Evans, *Paradise Lost and the Genesis Tradition* (Oxford: Oxford University Press, 1968), p. 249.

[75] *Paradise Lost*, bk. 4, lines 618–20. Max Weber draws an interesting contrast between the ending of the Catholic poet Dante's *Divine Comedy* (which ends with the protagonist transfixed by the beatific vision of God in heaven) and the ending of Milton's Puritan epic (which ends with Adam and Eve leaving Paradise with the world "all before them"): "One feels at once that this powerful expression of the Puritan's serious attention to this world, his acceptance of his life in the world as a task, could not possibly have come from the pen of a medieval writer" (pp. 87–88).

CHAPTER 3

[1] Chad Powers Smith, *Yankees and God* (New York: Hermitage House, 1954), p. 11.

[2] William Gouge, *Of Domestical Duties* [Frye, p. 153].

[3] Edmund Morgan, *Puritan Family*, p. 63.

[4] Quoted in Hunt, pp. 242–43.

[5] Ulrich, *Good Wives*, p. 221.

[6] The quoted excerpts come from two separate sources, *The Application of Redemption* and *A Comment Upon Christ's Last Prayer* [Edmund Morgan, *Puritan Family*, pp. 61–62].

[7] Schücking, p. 37.

[8] The details that I cite in my survey of medieval Catholic teaching on sex are commonplace in any survey of the subject, and I have accordingly not documented the sources of my information. Good brief surveys include Robert Briffault, *The Mothers*, vol. 3 (New York: Macmillan, 1927), pp. 372–75; Maurice Valency, *In Praise of Love: An Introduction to the Love-Poetry of The Renaissance* (New York: Macmillan, 1958), pp. 19–24; and Oscar E. Feucht, ed., *Sex and the Church* (St. Louis: Concordia, 1961), pp. 41–73. More detailed studies include E. C. Messenger, *The Mystery of Sex and Marriage* (Westminster, Md.: Newman, 1948); Derrick Sherwin Bailey, *Sexual Relation in Christian Thought* (New York: Harper and Brothers, 1959), pp. 19–166; William G. Cole, *Sex in Christianity and Psychoanalysis* (New York: Oxford University Press, 1966), pp. 43–99.

[9] According to Briffault, who cites Justin and Origen as sources, numerous others had the same surgery performed (p. 372). The church officially condemned the practice.

[10] *A Dialogue of Comfort Against Tribulation* [C. S. Lewis, *English Literature in the Sixteenth Century Excluding Drama* (Oxford: Oxford University Press, 1944), p. 34].

[11] Quoted by C. S. Lewis, "Donne and Love Poetry in the Seventeenth Century," in *Seventeenth Century Studies Presented to Sir Herbert Grierson* (Oxford: Oxford University Press, 1938), p. 74.

[12] *Works* [George, p. 265].

[13] *The Spiritual Man's Aim* [G. F. Sensabaugh, "Platonic Love and the Puritan Rebellion," *Studies in Philology* 37 (1940): 469].

[14] *A Good Wife* [George, p. 169]. Luther had written, "Now it is certainly obvious that these human laws forbidding the marriage of priests are really not the laws of man but of the devil" (critique of the spiritual order of pope and bishops [Plass, 2:890]).

[15] Erasmus, *Modest Means to Marriage* [Frye, p. 152]; Cotton, *A Meet Help* [Edmund Morgan, *Puritan Family*, pp. 62–63].

[16] *Works* [George, p. 266].

[17] William Perkins, *Christian Economy* [James Johnson, p. 67].

[18] Thomas Becon, *The Christian State of Matrimony* [Lerner, p. 111].

[19] Thomas Gataker, *A Wife Indeed* [Schnucker, pp. 139–40].

[20] *A Good Wife God's Gift* [Emerson, *English Puritanism*, p. 210].

[21] *Works* [George, p. 268].

[22] Christopher Niccholes, *A Discourse of Marriage and Wiving* [James Johnson, p. 116].

[23] *A Christian Directory* [Halkett, p. 20].

[24] *The Gift of God* [Davies, *Worship and Theology . . . 1534–1603*, p. 318].

[25] *Of Domestical Duties* [Frye, p. 155].

[26] *Tetrachordon* [*CPW*, 2:606–7].

[27] *Conscience with the Power and Cases Thereof* [James Johnson, p. 64]. Both Luther and Calvin had prepared the way for the Puritan affirmation of married sex. Calvin, for example, had written that "conjugal intercourse is a thing that is pure, honorable and holy, because it is a pure institution of God" (*Commentary on First Corinthians* [Cole, p. 120]).

[28] *Christian Economy* [Halkett, p. 11].

[29] Robert Cleaver, *A Godly Form of Household Government* [Halkett, p. 11].

[30] *Of Domestical Duties* [Schücking, p. 38].

[31] *The Office of Christian Parents* [Frye, pp. 155–56].

[32] *Discourse of Marriage and Wiving* [James Johnson, p. 23].

[33] *The Lover: or, Nuptial Love* [Schnucker, p. 307]. Gouge frequently disparaged what he called "Stoical abstinence," calling it at one point "a disposition no way warranted by the Word" (*Of Domestical Duties* [Frye, p. 154]).

34 Milton, *Tetrachordon* [*CPW*, 2:597].

35 Whately, *A Care-Cloth* [James Johnson, p. 115]; Perkins, *Works* [George, p. 268].

36 *A Godly Form of Household Government* [James Johnson, p. 56].

37 *A Bride-Bush* [Frye, p. 156].

38 See Schnucker, pp. 340–42, for examples.

39 Henry Smith, *Sermons* [Schnucker, p. 341]; Gouge, *Of Domestical Duties* [Schnucker, pp. 341–42].

40 *Christian Economy* [James Johnson, p. 70].

41 *Commonplace Book* [Edmund Morgan, "The Puritans and Sex," p. 5]. Some of the best comments about sex as natural appear in Martin Luther, who wrote, for example, "If a girl is not sustained by great and exceptional grace, she can live without a man as little as she can without eating, drinking, sleeping, and other natural necessities. Nor, on the other hand can a man dispense with a wife. The reason for this is that procreating children is an urge planted as deeply in human nature as eating and drinking" (critique of the spiritual order of pope and bishop [Plass, 2:889]).

42 *Works* [George, p. 268].

43 *A Godly Form of Household Government* [James Johnson, p. 56].

44 *Tetrachordon* [*CPW*, 2:598].

45 *Christian Economy* [James Johnson, p. 67].

46 *A Care-Cloth* [Schnucker, p. 364].

47 *A Preparative to Marriage* [Frye, p. 155].

48 *A Bride-Bush* [Frye, p. 155].

49 *Of Domestical Duties* [Schnucker, p. 302].

50 *The Well-Ordered Family* [Edmund Morgan, *Puritan Family*, p. 63].

51 *A Bride-Bush* [Frye, p. 155].

52 For examples, see Frye, pp. 156–57; and Schnucker, pp. 344–45.

53 *Of Domestical Duties* [Schnucker, p. 345].

54 Ibid., p. 306.

55 *The Marrow of Theology*, p. 318.

56 The quoted description of Spenser's picture of chastity comes from Graham Hough, *A Preface to the Faerie Queene* (New York: Norton, 1962), p. 170.

57 James Johnson, p. 114. Johnson also notes that "exalting companionship over procreation does not mean for the Puritans that procreation has less place in marriage. Rather a Christian marriage is expected to produce offspring as a result of companionable life" (p. 116).

58 *Christian Economy* [James Johnson, p. 68].

59 *The Doctrine and Discipline of Divorce* [*CPW*, 2:235]. Luther had similarly written, "Propagation is not in our will and power, for no parents are able to foresee whether they . . . will bring forth a son or a daughter. My father and mother did not consider that they wanted to bring a Dr. Martin Luther into the world. Creation is of God alone and we are not able to perceive it" (*Tischreden* [Roland Bainton, *What Christianity Says About Sex, Love, and Marriage* (New York: Association, 1957), p. 79]). Lawrence Stone, *Family*, concludes that "Protestant theologians of all persuasions had long since identified mutual comfort and endearment as two of the purposes of the sexual act within marriage" (p. 625).

60 *A Godly Form of Household Government* [Schnucker, p. 302].

61 *A Godly and Learned Exposition of Christ's Sermon in the Mount* [Schnucker, p. 360].

62 *Tetrachordon* [*CPW*, 2:608–9].

63 *Matrimonial Honour* [Haller, "The Puritan Art of Love," p. 264].

64 *Works* [George, p. 268].

[65] *Life and Letters of John Winthrop* [Edmund Morgan, *Puritan Family*, p. 50]. Edward Taylor, after claiming that "conjugal love ought to exceed all other," added that human love "must be kept within bounds too. For it must be subordinate to God's glory" (*History of Norwich, Connecticut* [Edmund Morgan, *Puritan Family*, p. 50]).

[66] *Paradise Lost*, bk. 8, lines 589–92.

[67] *A Good Wife God's Gift* [James Johnson, p. 96].

[68] *Practical Commentary Upon John* [Edmund Morgan, *Puritan Family*, p. 48].

[69] *A Good Husband and a Good Wife* [Halkett, p. 38].

[70] *Book of Matrimony* [Powell, pp. 126–27].

[71] Quoted in Edmund Morgan, *Puritan Family*, p. 50.

[72] *The Probate Records of Essex County* [Ulrich, *Good Wives*, p. 108].

[73] *Prototypes* . . . [Schnucker, p. 302].

[74] *Life and Letters of John Winthrop* [Edmund Morgan, *Puritan Family*, p. 60].

[75] *Sermons* [Halkett, p. 65].

[76] *Of Domestical Duties* [Lerner, p. 121].

[77] *A Good Wife God's Gift* [Lerner, p. 121].

[78] *Matrimonial Honour* [James Johnson, p. 110].

[79] Haller, "The Puritan Art of Love," p. 265.

[80] "Donne and Love Poetry in the Seventeenth Century," p. 75. For commentary on the influence of the Protestant ethic of wedded romantic love on literature, see also Laurence Lerner, *Love and Marriage: Literature and Its Social Context;* and Leven L. Schücking, *The Puritan Family: A Social Study from the Literary Sources.*

[81] Herbert Richardson, p. 67. Richardson claims that "the rise of romantic marriage and its validation by the Puritans . . . represents a major innovation within the Christian tradition" (p. 69).

[82] *A Bride-Bush* [James Johnson, p. 107].

[83] *The Well-Ordered Family* [Edmund Morgan, *Puritan Family*, p. 54]. Gataker said that marriage "must needs bind the husband not only to love, but to love his wife with a love above all other love" (*Marriage Duties* [Schnucker, p. 105]).

[84] *The Crown Conjugal* [Schnucker, p. 104]. This is similar to Gouge's comment that "nor friend nor child nor parent ought to be so loved as a wife; she is termed, *the wife of his bosom*, to show that she ought to be as his heart in his bosom" (*Of Domestical Duties* [Schnucker, p. 105]).

[85] Bremer, p. 177.

[86] Thomas Thatcher, Boston Sermons [Edmund Morgan, *Puritan Family*, pp. 51–52].

[87] Ibid., p. 52.

[88] Ibid.

[89] Bailey, *Sexual Relation*, p. 61. The correspondence between attitudes toward sex and women is illustrated by the misogyny (hatred of women) that prevailed during the Catholic Middle Ages. Someone who made a study of misogyny concluded that "while a condemnation of sex does not necessarily entail misogyny, there is an obvious connection between them: abhorrence of sex leads to abhorrence of the sexual object" (Katharine M. Rogers, *The Troublesome Helpmate: A History of Misogyny in Literature* [Seattle: University of Washington Press, 1966], p. 8).

[90] Ulrich, *Good Wives*, believes that the Puritan view of the wife "was based on a doctrine of creation which stressed the equality of men and women" (p. 109). Roberta Hamilton, *The Liberation of Women* (London: Allen and Unwin, 1978), writes, "While basic spiritual equality between men and women is a fundamental Christian tenet, the Protestants took special pains to emphasize it. It proceeded logically from the doctrine of the priesthood of all true believers" (p. 66). The Georges concluded that "the whole emphasis upon companionship between husband and wife . . . contributes to this view of the wife as a coadjutor of her husband" (p. 287).

[91] *Matrimonial Honour* [Powell, p. 139].

92 *A Godly Form of Household Government* [Irwin, p. 76].

93 Rogers, *Matrimonial Honour* [Frye, p. 159].

94 *A Meet Help* [Edmund Morgan, "The Puritans and Sex," p. 41].

95 *A Godly Form of Household Government* [Irwin, p. 76].

96 Stone, *Family*, p. 14.

97 *A Complete Body of Divinity* [Ulrich, *Good Wives*, p. 8].

98 *Tetrachordon* [*CPW*, 2:589].

99 *A Wedding Ring* [Ulrich, *Good Wives*, p. 107].

100 *Matrimonial Honour* [Stenton, p. 150].

101 *Of Domestical Duties* [Irwin, p. 98].

102 *Paradise Lost*, bk. 4, lines 741–49.

103 Ibid., lines 750–61.

CHAPTER 4

1 The Weber thesis has been in decline for some time, and with good reason: see the critiques by Hyma, *Christianity, Capitalism and Communism*; Robertson, *Aspects of the Rise of Economic Individualism*; various authors in *Protestantism and Capitalism: The Weber Thesis and Its Critics*, ed. Robert W. Green; and Walzer, *The Revolution of the Saints*, pp. 304–7.

2 Commentary on Matthew 19:24 [Hyma, p. 182].

3 *The High Esteem Which God Hath of the Death of His Saints* [Miller, *Nature's Nation*, p. 38].

4 *A Christian Directory* [Kitch, p. 113].

5 *A Complete Body of Divinity* [Foster, p. 111].

6 Quoted in Emerson, *Puritanism in America*, pp. 141–42.

7 *Works* [Kitch, pp. 108–9].

8 *A Christian Directory* [Harkness, pp. 184–85].

9 *Works* [Hyma, p. 233].

10 *Observations of Knowledge and Virtue* [Reinitz, p. 73].

11 *The Saints' Cordials* [George, p. 125].

12 Proponents of the Weber thesis have centered their attack especially on Calvin, claiming that he made money-making the sign that one was elect. Yet Calvin denied that prosperity has any necessary connection with virtue. He stated, for example, "We must recognize this as a general principle, that riches come not at all to men through their own virtue, nor wisdom, nor toil, but only by the blessing of God" (Sermon on Deut. 8:14–20 [Harkness, p. 217]). In his commentary on Psalm 127:2, Calvin wrote, "Solomon affirms that neither living at a small expense, nor diligence in business will by themselves profit anything at all."

13 *Sober Sentiments* [Perry, p. 312]. Calvin had written that "men in vain wear themselves out with toiling, and waste themselves by fasting to acquire riches, since these also are a benefit only by God" (Commentary on Ps. 127:2).

14 *Observations of Knowledge and Virtue* [Reinitz, p. 73].

15 A standard source is H. G. Wood, "The Influence of the Reformation on Ideas Concerning Wealth and Property," pp. 141–77 in *Property: Its Duties and Rights* [no editor] (New York: Macmillan, 1922).

16 *Conscience with the Power and Cases Thereof* [Miller, *Nature's Nation*, p. 34].

17 *The Marrow of Theology*, p. 323.

18 Hull, *Diaries* [Miller, *Nature's Nation*, p. 37].

[19] *Winthrop Papers* [McGee, p. 45]. This accords with Luther's view that "no one is rich, be he emperor or pope, except the man who is rich in God" (Exposition of Exod. 20:5 [Plass, 3:1438]).

[20] *The Gospel-Covenant; or the Covenant of Grace Opened* [McGiffert, pp. 36–37].

[21] Knappen, *Two Elizabethan Puritan Diaries*, p. 73.

[22] *The Beatitudes*, p. 259. Luther had stated the case even more decisively: "God may fill the coffers of a rascal. But it does not follow from this that the fellow is pious. . . . On the other hand, he may let a pious man have a hard and bitter lot" (Sermon on Exod. 20:2 [Plass, 1:434]).

[23] *Christian Calling* [Miller/Johnson, 1:324]. Elsewhere Cotton theorized that "no man can certainly discern the love or hatred of God to himself or others by their outward events or estates" (*A Brief Exposition on Ecclesiastes* [Foster, p. 128]).

[24] *A Complete Body of Divinity* [Foster, p. 128]. Willard claimed that wealth and poverty are "things [that] in themselves make men neither better nor worse; and are equally improvable for eternal salvation."

[25] "A Prayer Fit for One Whom God Hath Enriched with Outward Things" [Emerson, *English Puritanism*, p. 182]. Luther had called "utterly nonsensical" the "delusion" that led people to conclude that if someone "has good fortune, wealth, and health . . . , behold, God is dwelling here" (Exposition on Gen. 19:2–3 [Plass, 3:1436]).

[26] *Conscience with the Power and Cases Thereof*, p. 253.

[27] *The Saints' Everlasting Rest*, pp. 62–63.

[28] *The True Bounds of Christian Freedom*, p. 175.

[29] *The Beatitudes*, p. 251.

[30] *Conscience with the Power and Cases Thereof*, pp. 252–53.

[31] Thomas Watson's discussion of "evangelical poverty" in a sermon on the Beatitudes is typical: We must distinguish, he wrote, "between poor in an evangelical sense and poor in a popish sense. The papists give a wrong gloss upon the text. By 'poor in spirit' they understand those who, renouncing their estates, vow a voluntary poverty, living retiredly in their monasteries. But Christ never meant these. He does not pronounce them blessed who make themselves poor, leaving their estates and callings, but such as are evangelically poor" (*The Beatitudes*, p. 41).

[32] *A Christian Directory* [Kitch, p. 114].

[33] *A Sermon Preached at Paul's Cross* [Hyma, p. 182].

[34] *Sixth Sermon Preached Before King Edward VI* [Green, p. 70].

[35] *The Fifth Sermon on the Lord's Prayer* [Tawney, p. 262].

[36] *Observations of Knowledge and Virtue* [Reinitz, p. 73].

[37] *A Sermon Preached Before the King* [Hyma, p. 181].

[38] *Diary* [Knappen, *Two Elizabethan Puritan Diaries*, p. 81].

[39] *A Christian Directory* [Hyma, p. 224].

[40] Quoted in Miller, *Seventeenth Century*, p. 473.

[41] *The Saints' Cordials* [George, p. 125].

[42] "The Puritan Ethic and the American Revolution," in McGiffert, p. 185.

[43] *Works* [Kitch, p. 108; George, p. 172].

[44] *Grave Counsels and Godly Observations* [White, p. 228].

[45] Ibid.

[46] *The Beatitudes*, p. 25.

[47] *Observations of Knowledge and Virtue* [Reinitz, p. 73].

[48] *Diary* [Knappen, *Two Elizabethan Puritan Diaries*, p. 79].

[49] *The Practical Works* [Hyma, pp. 224-25].

[50] *Observations of Knowledge and Virtue* [Reinitz, p. 74].

[51] "A Prayer Fit for One Whom God Hath Enriched with Outward Things" [Emerson, *English Puritanism*, p. 181].

[52] *A Farewell Exhortation to the Church and People of Dorchester in New-England* [Miller, *Colony*, p. 4].

[53] *Magnalia Christi Americana* [Foster, p. 121].

[54] *Works* [Irvonwy Morgan, p. 109].

[55] *The Beatitudes*, pp. 26, 28–29.

[56] *A Christian Directory* [Hyma, p. 224].

[57] *Conscience with the Power and Cases Thereof*, p. 253.

[58] *Works* [Hill, *Change*, p. 96].

[59] *The Saints' Everlasting Rest*, p. 124.

[60] *The Saints' Cordials* [George, p. 125].

[61] *A Christian Directory* [Hyma, p. 224].

[62] *The Plea of the Poor* [George, p. 162].

[63] *The Whole Treatise of the Cases of Conscience* [White, p. 263].

[64] *Christian Calling* [Miller/Johnson, 1:324].

[65] *Works* [Kitch, p. 109].

[66] *The Tradesman's Calling* [Kitch, p. 116].

[67] *Magnalia Christi Americana* [Hyma, p. 250].

[68] *Chapters from A Christian Directory*, ed. Jeannette Tawney (London: G. Bell and Sons, 1925), pp. 55–57.

[69] Ibid., pp. 157–63.

[70] *Of the Cases of Conscience* [Hyma, p. 235].

[71] Knappen, *Two Elizabethan Puritan Diaries*, p. 122.

[72] *Chapters from A Christian Directory*, pp. 43–46.

[73] John Knewstub, *Ninth Lecture on the Twentieth Chapter of Exodus* [Trinterud, p. 357].

[74] *Works* [Hill, *Change*, p. 96]. Elsewhere Perkins added, "Subjects in kingdoms should content themselves if they have as much as will provide them food and raiment" (*Works* [Kitch, p. 107]).

[75] *Works* [Kitch, p. 107].

[76] *Works* [Hyma, p. 233].

[77] Ibid. Elsewhere the model was said to be "the example and judgment of the godly and grave men and women of our estate and order" (*Works* [Kitch, p. 107]).

[78] *Works* [Hyma, p. 234].

[79] *A Christian Directory* [Kitch, p. 114].

[80] *Ninth Lecture on the Twentieth Chapter of Exodus* [Trinterud, p. 377].

[81] *A Christian Directory* [Kitch, p. 114].

[82] Ibid., p. 113.

[83] Edward Browne, *A Rare Pattern of Justice and Mercy* [Hill, *Society and Puritanism*, p. 137]. John Hooper wrote that people should not trust in riches, "nor keep them otherwise than their use or keeping should serve to the glory of God" (*Early Writings of John Hooper* [Hyma, p. 180]).

[84] *St. Paul the Tent-Maker* [Hill, *Society and Puritanism*, p. 136].

[85] Richard Greenham, *Works* [Hill, *Change*, p. 96].

86 *Works* [Kitch, p. 108].

87 Sermon on 1 Timothy 6:9 [Hyma, p. 82].

88 *Works* [Hyma, p. 82].

89 Commentary on 1 Timothy 6:18.

90 Sources on interest/usury include these: Kitch, pp. 117–43; Harkness, p. 204–9; Hyma, *passim;* Robertson, pp. 111–32; Baxter, *Chapters from A Christian Directory,* ed. Tawney, pp. 118–31; Benjamin Nelson, *The Idea of Usury,* 2d ed. (Chicago: University of Chicago Press, 1969). The last source includes an extensive bibliography.

91 *Chapters from A Christian Directory,* pp. 125–29. William Ames allowed some forms of interest but opposed "such usury which is commonly practised by usurers and bankers," which he regarded as "deservedly condemned of all: because it is a catching art, and no regard of charity or equity being had, lies in waiting for other men's goods" (*Conscience with the Power and Cases Thereof* [Hyma, p. 218]).

92 John Dod and Robert Cleaver, *A Godly Form of Household Government* [Hill, *Change,* p. 96].

93 *The Whole Treatise of the Cases of Conscience* [White, p. 263].

94 *Chapters from A Christian Directory,* p. 157.

95 *A Christian Directory* [Kitch, pp. 114–15].

96 *The Beatitudes,* p. 25.

97 "A Prayer Fit for One Whom God Hath Enriched with Outward Things" [Emerson, *English Puritanism,* pp. 182–83]. In contrast to the modern practice of naming buildings after wealthy donors, Baxter spoke slightingly of people who "wouldst fain leave behind thee some monument of thy worth, that posterity may admire thee when thou are dead and gone" (*The Saints' Everlasting Rest,* p. 127).

98 *The New Covenant* [George, pp. 137–38]. Luther had long since established the same viewpoint: "When riches come, the godless heart of man thinks: I have achieved this with my labors. It does not consider that these are purely blessings of God, blessings that at times come to us through our labors and at times without our labors, but never because of our labors; for God always gives them because of his undeserved mercy" (Exposition of Deut. 8:17–18 [Plass, 3:1495]).

99 *Ninth Lecture on the Twentieth Chapter of Exodus* [Trinterud, p. 351].

100 *Of the Cases of Conscience* [Hyma, p. 235].

101 Winthrop's *Journal* contains the account [McGiffert, pp. 115–16].

102 Winthrop, *The History of New England* . . . [McGiffert, pp. 115–16].

103 *Ninth Lecture on the Twentieth Chapter of Exodus* [Trinterud, p. 351]. Arthur Dent made a catalogue of the economic "oppression" of his era, denouncing such practices as usury, rackrenting, and "hiring poor men's houses over their heads" (*The Plain Man's Path-way to Heaven* [George, p. 150]). William Tyndale commanded, "Let Christian landlords be content with their rent and old customs; not raising the rent or finds and bringing up new customs to oppress their tenants" (*Obedience of a Christian Man* [Knappen, *Tudor Puritanism,* p. 405]).

104 *Works* [George, p. 123]. William Ames similarly believed that riches "are rightly called the gifts and blessings of God" (*Conscience with the Power and Cases Thereof,* p. 253).

105 *Works* [Hyma, p. 234].

106 *The Marrow of Theology,* p. 323. Calvin had already established the same critique of socialism: "The poor . . . have no right to pillage the wealthy. . . . God has distributed this world's goods as He has seen fit, and even the richest of all people . . . shall not be robbed of their possessions by those in direct need" (*Works* [Hyma, p. 82]).

107 *Observations of Knowledge and Virtue* [Reinitz, p. 73]. Dudley Fenner, replying to the socialist theory that everyone is entitled to the same income and quantity of possessions, stated, "There may be a diversity of rewards given, so long as none have too little nor any too much" (*A Counter-Poison, Modestly Written for the Time* [Knappen, *Tudor Puritanism,* p. 403]).

CHAPTER 5

[1] Sermon on Matthew 19:10–12; remark recorded by J. Airifaber [Plass, 2:899–900].

[2] *The Well-Ordered Family* [Wilson Smith, p. 41]. In elaborating what characterizes a family that exists for the glory of God, Wadsworth stated, "A family wherein the true worship of God, good pious instruction and government are upheld, is beautiful in the eyes of God himself; he delights to bless such."

[3] *A Christian Directory* [Halkett, p. 20]. Luther was of the same opinion: "The best thing in married life, for the sake of which everything ought to be suffered and done, is the fact that God gives children and commands us to bring them up to serve Him. To do this is the noblest and most precious work on earth, because nothing may be done which pleases God more than saving souls" (Sermon on married life [Plass, 2:907]).

[4] *Works* [R. C. Richardson, p. 105].

[5] *Works* [George, p. 268].

[6] *An Explanation of the Solemn Advice* [Edmund Morgan, *Puritan Family*, p. 143]. Other Puritan writers called the family "the root whence church and commonwealth cometh," "the foundation of all societies," "the nurseries of all societies" (all three sources quoted in Morgan, p. 143).

[7] Gouge, *Works* [George, p. 275]; J. Bodis, *Six Books of the Commonwealth* [Hill, *Society and Puritanism*, p. 459].

[8] *A Family Well-Ordered* [Edmund Morgan, *Puritan Family*, p. 143]. Richard Baxter agreed: "The life of religion, and the welfare and glory of both the church and state, depend much on family government and duty. If we suffer the neglect of this, we shall undo all" (*The Reformed Pastor*, p. 100).

[9] *Sermons* [Davies, *Worship and Theology . . . 1534–1603*, pp. 318–19].

[10] *The Marrow of Theology*, p. 319.

[11] *Works* [George, p. 276].

[12] *A Godly Form of Household Government* [James Johnson, p. 25].

[13] Commentary on Matthew 19:5 [Harkness, p. 153].

[14] Sermon on 1 Peter 3:7 [Plass, 2:903].

[15] *Works* [George, p. 277].

[16] *Marriage Duties* [George, p. 277].

[17] *Works* [Demos, p. 91].

[18] *Marriage Duties* [James Johnson, p. 105].

[19] *The Well-Ordered Family* [Edmund Morgan, *Puritan Family*, p. 46].

[20] *A Complete Body of Divinity* [Edmund Morgan, *Puritan Family*, p. 46].

[21] *The Marrow of Theology*, p. 320.

[22] Boston Sermons, September 30, 1672 [Edmund Morgan, *Puritan Family*, p. 43].

[23] *Of Domestical Duties* [Irwin, p. 98].

[24] Gataker, *Marriage Duties* [George, p. 279]; Christopher Goodman, *How Superior Powers Ought to be Obeyed* [R. C. Richardson, p. 107].

[25] *Works* [Demos, p. 83].

[26] *A Godly Form of Household Government* [Irwin, p. 81].

[27] *The History of New England from 1630 to 1649* [McGiffert, p. 39]. Samuel Willard said that "the wife ought to carry it so to her husband, as he may take content in her" (*Complete Body of Divinity* [Edmund Morgan, *Puritan Family*, p. 46]).

[28] *Marriage Duties* [George, p. 279]. Robinson urged wives to display "a reverent subjection" (*Works* [Demos, p. 83]).

29 *Works* [George, p. 282]. Gataker called husband and wife "copartners in grace" (*Marriage Duties* [James Johnson, p. 98]). Johnson comments on the Puritan theory that "receiving God's grace here and now does not destroy the natural order, which is itself a gift of God" (p. 99).

30 *A Godly Form of Household Government* [Irwin, p. 78].

31 *The Plea of the Poor* [George, p. 285].

32 *A Good Wife* [George, p. 287].

33 *The Woman's Glory* [R. C. Richardson, p. 106].

34 *A Complete Body of Divinity* [Ulrich, "Vertuous Women Found," pp. 221–22].

35 *A Complete Body of Divinity* [Edmund Morgan, *Puritan Family*, pp. 45–46].

36 *Diary* [Edmund Morgan, *Puritan Family*, p. 43]. When Richard Mather's wife died, he thought the affliction "the more grievous, in that she being a woman of singular prudence for the management of affairs, had taken off from her husband all secular cares" (Increase Mather, *The Life and Death of That Reverend Man of God, Mr. Richard Mather* [Morgan, p. 43]).

37 *Tetrachordon* [*CPW*, 2:589].

38 *Of Domestical Duties* [Irwin, p. 95].

39 Samuel Torshell, *The Woman's Glory* [R. C. Richardson, p. 106]. The New England churches followed Paul's command that women not speak in the church services, yet Cotton Mather claimed that women "speak by what we see in them, such things as we ought certainly to take much notice of," and he praised Abiel Goodwin for having taught him much about salvation (Quoted in Ulrich, "Vertuous Women Found," p. 225).

40 *Commentary Upon the Three First Chapters . . . of St. Peter* [R. C. Richardson, p. 106].

41 *Works* [George, p. 186]. Gouge elaborated his point with the comment that "though there be a difference betwixt father and mother in relation to one another, yet in relation to their children they are both as one, and have a like authority over them" (Ibid.).

42 *Works* [George, pp. 286–87].

43 *The Duty and Property of a Religious Householder* [Edmund Morgan, *Puritan Family*, p. 91].

44 *Small Offers Towards the Service of the Tabernacle in This Wilderness* [Stannard, p. 51].

45 *The Beatitudes*, p. 235.

46 *The Well-Ordered Family* [Edmund Morgan, *Puritan Family*, p. 91].

47 *A Fruitful and Useful Discourse* [Edmund Morgan, *Puritan Family*, p. 91].

48 *Farewell Exhortation* [Edmund Morgan, *Puritan Family*, p. 92].

49 *The Child's Portion* [Stannard, p. 52].

50 Edmund Morgan, *Puritan Family*, pp. 65–66.

51 Ibid., p. 66.

52 *The Well-Ordered Family* [Wilson Smith, p. 48].

53 Boston Sermons, August 31, 1679 [Edmund Morgan, *Puritan Family*, p. 140].

54 *Cares About the Nurseries* [Edmund Morgan, *Puritan Family*, p. 90].

55 *Records of the First Church in Dorchester* [Edmund Morgan, *Puritan Family*, p. 140].

56 *Abel Being Dead Yet Speaketh* [Edmund Morgan, *Puritan Family*, p. 103]. Cotton Mather wrote of his brother Nathaniel that "he wanted not the cares of his father to bestow a good education on him, which God blessed for the restraining him from the lewd and wild courses by which too many children are betimes resigned up to the possession of the devil" (*Magnalia Christi Americana* [Morgan, p. 94]).

57 *Help for Distressed Parents* [Edmund Morgan, *Puritan Family*, p. 103].

58 *The Harmony of the Gospels* [Edmund Morgan, *Puritan Family*, p. 103].

59 *The Well-Ordered Family* [Edmund Morgan, *Puritan Family*, p. 139].

60 *Works* [Edmund Morgan, *Puritan Family*, pp. 107–8].

61 Boston Sermons [Edmund Morgan, *Puritan Family*, p. 108].

62 *The Works* [Emerson, *English Puritanism*, p. 151].

63 Benjamin Wadsworth, *The Well-Ordered Family* [Wilson Smith, p. 49].

64 Samuel Willard, *A Complete Body of Divinity* [Edmund Morgan, *Puritan Family*, p. 92]. Wadsworth theorized about children that "their hearts naturally are a mere nest, root, fountain of sin and wickedness; an evil treasure from whence proceed evil things. . . . Indeed, as sharers in the guilt of Adam's first sin . . . their hearts . . . are unspeakably wicked, estranged from God" (*A Course of Sermons on Early Piety* [Morgan, p. 93]).

65 *The Works of John Robinson* [Stannard, p. 49].

66 Robert Cleaver and John Dod, *A Godly Form of Household Government* [Walzer, p. 190]. Thomas Hooker stated the same idea thus: "Parents, mourn for your children that are natural. When thou lookest upon thy child whom thou dearly lovest, and who perhaps hath good natural parts and is obedient unto thee in outward respects, when thou beholdest this child of thine, . . . then this may pierce thee to the very heart. Then thou mayest burst out and say, woe is me that this child of mine was ever born, for he is in a natural condition and therefore a child of the devil" (Quoted in Emerson, *English Puritanism*, p. 223).

67 *The Mourner's Cordial Against Excessive Sorrows* [Stannard, p. 52].

68 *Practical Commentary Upon John* [Edmund Morgan, *Puritan Family*, p. 96].

69 *Useful Instructions for a Professing People* [Edmund Morgan, *Puritan Family*, p. 96]. Cotton Mather's answer to the question, "When should we begin to teach our children the knowledge of the Holy Scriptures?" was, "BETIMES! BETIMES! Let the children have the early knowledge of the Holy Scriptures" (*Corderious Americanus* [Morgan, p. 96]).

70 *Works* [Watkins, p. 53].

71 Benjamin Wadsworth, *Exhortations to Early Piety* [Edmund Morgan, *Puritan Family*, p. 94].

72 *The Works* [Emerson, *English Puritanism*, p. 152].

73 *A Serious Exhortation to the Present and Succeeding Generation in New England* [Edmund Morgan, *Puritan Family*, p. 102].

74 Benjamin Wadsworth, *The Well-Ordered Family* [Wilson Smith, p. 52].

75 Richard Greenham, *The Works* [Emerson, *English Puritanism*, pp. 151–52].

76 Benjamin Wadsworth, *The Well-Ordered Family* [Wilson Smith, pp. 49, 46].

77 *A Fruitful and Useful Discourse* [Edmund Morgan, *Puritan Family*, p. 108].

78 *A Complete Body of Divinity* [Greven, *Protestant Temperament*, p. 161].

79 *The Application of Redemption* [Edmund Morgan, *Puritan Family*, p. 95].

80 *Early Religion Urged* [Edmund Morgan, p. 96]. Deodat Lawson wrote, "For although there is a corrupt nature in every child in its infancy . . . yet care and education will much prevail to keep under the corrupt principle, and promote better inclinations in them" (*The Duty and Property of a Religious Householder* [Morgan, p. 95]).

81 *Parentator* [Edmund Morgan, *Puritan Family*, p. 95].

82 *Works* [Davies, *Worship and Theology . . . 1603–1690*, p. 123].

83 Gouge, *Works;* Perkins, *Works*, both quoted in George, p. 275. John Geree observed as a characteristic of the typical Puritan father that "his family he endeavoured to make a church" (*Character of an Old English Puritan* [Collinson, p. 375]).

84 *Works* [Hill, *Society and Puritanism*, p. 443]. John Angier wrote, "The more we worship God in secret, the fitter shall we be for family worship, and the more we worship God in our families, the fitter shall we be for public worship" (*Help to Better Hearts for Better Times* [R. C. Richardson, p. 91]).

85 *Cartwrightiana* [Hill, *Society and Puritanism*, p. 454].

86 *Commentary Upon the Three First Chapters of the First Epistle General of St. Peter* [R. C. Richardson, p. 91]. Robert Cleaver said that the head of the family "must set an order in his house for the service of God" (*A Godly Form of Household Government* [James Johnson, p. 30]).

87 Boston Sermons, Oct. 14, 1677 [Edmund Morgan, *Puritan Family*, p. 139].

88 *Returning Unto God the Great Concernment* [Edmund Morgan, *Puritan Family*, p. 140].

89 *A Christian Directory* [Davies, *Worship and Theology . . . 1603–1690*, p. 123]. Elsewhere Baxter commented that "experience proveth that family sins are daily committed, and family mercies daily received, and family necessities daily do occur" (*A Christian Directory* [Davies, *Worship of the English Puritans*, p. 279]).

90 *Exhortations to Early Piety* [Edmund Morgan, *Puritan Family*, p. 89].

91 *Demonstration of Family Duties* [R. C. Richardson, p. 93].

92 *Three Treatises* [Hill, *Society and Puritanism*, p. 455].

93 *Works* [Hill, *Society and Puritanism*, p. 455].

94 *Cares About the Nurseries* [Edmund Morgan, *Puritan Family*, p. 98]. On pages 98–100 Morgan has similar comments by other writers.

95 Marginal note to Genesis 17:23.

96 John Dod and Robert Cleaver, *The Ten Commandments* [Hill, *Society and Puritanism*, p. 443]. Tyndale had earlier claimed that "every man ought to preach in word and deed unto his household, and to them that are under his governance" (*Expositions and Notes on . . . the Holy Scriptures* [Hill, *Society and Puritanism*, p. 465]).

97 *The Well-Ordered Family* [Edmund Morgan, *Puritan Family*, p. 80]. A New England synod of 1680 approved the statement that "it is the duty of Christians to marry in the Lord" (Cotton Mather, *Magnalia Christi Americana* [Morgan, p. 182]).

98 *Practical Commentary Upon John* [Edmund Morgan, *Puritan Family*, p. 48].

CHAPTER 6

1 The account comes from Thomas Fuller, *The Worthies of England* [Davies, *Worship and Theology . . . 1603–1690*, p. 315].

2 Quoted in Babbage, p. 11.

3 *The Laws of Ecclesiastical Polity* [Davies, *Worship of the English Puritans*, p. 186].

4 Seaver, p. 43.

5 *The Second Part of a Register* [Seaver, p. 37].

6 *A Brief and Plain Declaration Concerning the Desires of All Those Faithful Ministers . . .* [Trinterud, p. 270].

7 *The Calling of the Ministry* [Brown, p. 74].

8 Thomas Fuller, *The Church History of Britain* [Collinson, p. 128].

9 The letters were described thus by Roger Morrice [Collinson, p. 128].

10 Collinson, pp. 280–81.

11 *Cottonus Redevivus* [Mitchell, p. 116].

12 As early as 1547, for example, Thomas Becon called for a ministry of "learned and godly preachers" (*The Jewel of Joy* [Bailey, *Thomas Becon*, p. 60]).

13 Hudson describes the patronage system thus: "The decision as to qualifications for ordination had been taken from the bishops by the State, while the right of nomination to a parish post, after ordination, was largely controlled by lay patrons, and the bishops were forced to induct the nominee if he met the most meager requirements. About the only test of the fitness of the man to be inducted that the bishop was permitted to impose was political. He was directed to admit men who would take the oath of supremacy and agree to read the service book, and he was instructed not to make too close an inquiry at other points" (p. 202).

14 *A Full and Plain Declaration of Ecclesiastical Discipline* [George, p. 329]. Edward Dering spoke of the "idle, profane, unlettered, and unskillful pastors" who afflicted the Church of England" (*Works* [George, p. 329]).

15 These figures come from Emerson, *English Puritanism*, p. 19, who states further that "in 1603 close to four thousand of the slightly more than nine thousand ecclesiastical livings in England were in the hands of impropriators; that is, the revenue went not into the hands of the parson but largely to the Crown, the nobility, bishops, university colleges, and cathedral deans and chapters."

16 Collinson, pp. 290–91.

17 *The Faithful Shepherd* [Haller, *Rise of Puritanism*, p. 138].

18 *Works*, [Hudson, p. 205].

19 Seaver, p. 43.

20 Much of the counseling took the form of sermons and writings on "cases of conscience." Peter Lewis, *The Genius of Puritanism*, surveys part of this immense body of pastoral counsel. Hudson notes that Richard Baxter opened his home on Thursday evenings as "a clinic for group therapy" (p. 99); the group assembled to "repeat" the previous Sunday's sermon.

21 Hildersham, *CLII Lectures Upon Psalm LI* [Lewis, p. 35]; Owen, *Works*, 16:74. Richard Sibbes claimed similarly that preaching "is the gift of all gifts. . . . God esteems it so, Christ esteems it so, and so should we esteem it" (*Works* [Lewis, p. 36]).

22 *English Puritanism* . . . [Davies, *Worship of the English Puritans*, p. 183].

23 *The Church History of Britain* [Hudson, p. 185].

24 *Society and Puritanism*, pp. 98–99.

25 Stenton, p. 108.

26 Walzer, p. 119. Walzer describes the Puritan preachers as "educated (or self-educated) and aggressive men who wanted a voice in church government, who wanted a church, in effect, open to talent" (p. 120).

27 *An Exhortation for Contributions to Maintain Preachers in Lancashire* [R. C. Richardson, p. 84]. Walker also described how "hardly can a preacher travel through their towns and lodge there on any day in the week but they will by importunity obtain a public sermon from him and in great troops suddenly and upon short warning assembled they will gladly and cheerfully hear him with all reverence and attention."

28 Contemporary source quoted in Collinson, p. 373. Puritan preachers also had ready access to the leaders of government both in England and America.

29 Haller, *Rise of Puritanism*, pp. 160–64.

30 Letter to Burghley, *Lansdowne MSS* [Babbage, p. 11].

31 *A Pattern of Wholesome Words* [Hill, *Society and Puritanism*, p. 46].

32 *The Reformed Pastor* [Davies, *Worship and Theology* . . . *1603–1690*, p. 162].

33 Davies, *Worship of the English Puritans*, pp. 200–201.

34 Roger Clap, *Memoirs of Captain Roger Clap* [Vaughan and Bremer, p. 70]. Davies writes, "The preaching of the Word was neither a moral homily nor a philosophical disquisition; it was the authoritative declaration of the Blessed God. Therein lay its supreme significance" (*Worship of the English Puritans*, p. 185).

35 *The Church History of Britain* [Hudson, p. 185].

36 New, p. 71; Haller, *Rise of Puritanism*, p. 258.

37 *A Journey to the Western Islands* [Hill, *Change and Continuity*, p. 101].

38 Knappen, *Tudor Puritanism*, p. 100. John Stockwood, preaching at Paul's Cross in 1579, claimed that only one parish in twenty had an able teacher and concluded, "No marvel therefore if there dwell in the people such horrible and wonderful ignorance" (*A Very Fruitful Sermon* . . . [Hill, *Society and Puritanism*, p. 52]). Hill cites some statistics about the low percentage of preaching ministers (e.g. 1 out of 12, 58 out of 288, 20 out of 220, etc.) in various regions of England (pp. 52–53). Derek Wilson also cites some numbers and suggests why the relatively few Puritan preachers were able to gain so much influence: "at least once a month a sermon had to be preached in every parish church and on these occasions the non-preaching clergy sometimes had to call upon their Puritan colleagues" (p. 135).

[39] *The Plea of the Innocent* [Hill, *Society and Puritanism*, p. 56]. For more on Anglican ignorance on religious matters, see Hill, *Society and Puritanism*, pp. 250–51; and George, p. 336.

[40] Collinson, pp. 312, 315.

[41] *A Sermon Preached Before the Queen's Majesty* . . . [Trinterud, p. 159]. The Anglican defender Richard Hooker could not understand what all the bother was about. He was aghast at what he regarded as the wasted labor represented by a sermon, speaking disparagingly of "sermons [not] read. . . , but sermons without book, sermons which spend their life in their birth, and may have public audience but once" (*The Laws of Ecclesiastical Polity* [Davies, *Worship of the English Puritans*, p. 185]).

[42] *New England's First Fruits* [Miller/Johnson, 2:701].

[43] Quoted in Curtis, p. 190.

[44] Curtis, *Oxford and Cambridge in Transition, 1558–1642*, ch. 7. Although the Puritan influence was stronger at Cambridge, Curtis modifies the conventional picture of Oxford as being largely devoid of Puritan influence.

[45] Davies, *Worship of the English Puritans*, pp. 188–89. Trinterud calls prophesyings "a pre-Puritan device for the improvement of preaching" (p. 191).

[46] The most complete source is Paul S. Seaver, *The Puritan Lectureships*. Seaver describes the situation thus: "If an incumbent minister could not or would not preach the number and kind of sermons demanded, the laity could hire another minister, the lecturers, to preach at times when the church was not being used for regular services. If the regular parochial income was too small to attract a preaching incumbent, the laity could supplement it by adding a lectureship. The success of this institutional device was due in part to its very simplicity, for it was infinitely adaptable to local circumstances" (p. 6).

[47] Hill, *Society and Puritanism*, p. 80; Lewis, pp. 61–62.

[48] *Sermons* [Brown, p. 121].

[49] *The Marrow of Theology*, p. 254.

[50] Increase Mather, *The Life and Death of . . . Richard Mather* [R. C. Richardson, p. 43].

[51] Richard Hofstadter, *Anti-Intellectualism in American Life* (New York: Knopf, 1963), p. 59.

[52] Quoted in Davies, *Worship of the English Puritans*, p. 193.

[53] *Works* [Davies, *Worship of the English Puritans*, p. 194].

[54] *Sheet Against the Quakers* [Davies, *Worship of the English Puritans*, p. 194].

[55] The quotations from Eliot and Mather appear in Miller, *Seventeenth Century*, p. 352. Thomas Shepard is recorded as saying, "God will curse that man's labours that lumbers up and down in the world all the week, and then upon Saturday in the afternoon goes to his study; when as God knows, that time were little enough to pray in and weep in and to get his heart in frame" (Quoted in Babette May Levy, *Preaching in the First Half Century of New England History* [1915; reprint New York: Russell and Russell, 1967], p. 82). Shepard spent three days per week in sermon preparation.

[56] *Magnalia Christi Americana* [Mitchell, p. 22].

[57] Davies, *Worship of the English Puritans*, p. 193.

[58] *The Marrow of Theology*, p. 191.

[59] Quoted in Miller, *Seventeenth Century*, p. 340.

[60] *The Marrow of Theology*, p. 191. Ames also wrote, "Since . . . the will of God is to be set forth out of the word, no one is fit for the ministry who is not greatly concerned with the Holy Scripture, even beyond ordinary believers" (p. 191).

[61] Davies, *Worship of the English Puritans*, p. 191. William Haller, *Elizabeth I and the Puritans* (Ithaca: Cornell University Press, 1964), says regarding the Puritan preachers that "their method was to start with a text — that is to say a particular episode, character, or case, drawn from the Scriptures — to explain its meaning in its immediate context, to relate it to other supposedly relevant texts, to deduce the appropriate lesson or doctrine" before proceeding to application (p. 36).

[62] *The Art of Prophesying* [Breward, p. 345].

⁶³Millar Maclure, *The Paul's Cross Sermons, 1534–1642* (Toronto: University of Toronto Press, 1958), p. 165.

⁶⁴*The Art of Prophesying* [Breward, p. 349].

⁶⁵Davies, *Worship and Theology . . . 1534–1603*, writes, "The structure took the form of the exposition of a passage of Scripture, . . . by collecting lessons (or 'doctrines') from each verse and adding the moral applications (or 'uses') of them" (p. 304).

⁶⁶*Commentary Upon the Lamentations of Jeremy* [Emerson, *English Puritanism*, p. 112].

⁶⁷Ibid.

⁶⁸Samuel Clarke, *General Martyrologie* [Haller, *Rise of Puritanism*, pp. 134–35]. William Ames in effect urged moderation in the multiplying of proofs when he wrote, "The discussion of a doctrine consists partly in proofs, if it be questioned by the hearers (it is foolish to go to any length to confirm what all acknowledge), and partly in illustration of the things already well proved" (*The Marrow of Theology*, p. 192).

⁶⁹Miller, *Seventeenth Century*, pp. 332–33. This accords with the following description by a contemporary of William Bourne: "He seldom varied . . . the method of preaching, which after explication of his text was doctrine, proof of it by scripture [and] by reason, answering one or more objections and then the uses. . . . And lastly consolation" (Richard Hollingsworth, *Mancuniensis* [R. C. Richardson, p. 43]). Richard Baxter's biographer paints a similar picture: "Beginning with a careful 'opening' of the text, he proceeded to the clearance of possible difficulties or objections; next, to a statement of the 'uses'; and lastly to a fervent appeal for acceptance by conscience and heart" (F. J. Powicke, *A Life of the Reverend Richard Baxter* [Davies, *Worship of the English Puritans*, p. 192]).

⁷⁰Quoted in Miller, *Seventeenth Century*, p. 356.

⁷¹*A Commentary Upon the Book of Revelation* [Lewis, p. 49].

⁷²*The Marrow of Theology*, p. 192. Ames defines "use" as that "which shows the use, goodness, or end" of doctrine.

⁷³*The Art of Prophesying* [Breward, p. 343]. Davies, *Worship and Theology . . . 1534–1603*, writes, "What was perhaps most interesting about the structure of the Puritan sermon was that it was streamlined in the direction of changing man's mind with a view to improving his behaviour. There was little interest in speculative thought or even speculative divinity. Of paramount concern was the godliness which desires to know the will of God in order to follow it" (p. 305).

⁷⁴*Complete Works* [Lewis, p. 48].

⁷⁵*Diary* [Knappen, *Two Elizabethan Puritan Diaries*, p. 108].

⁷⁶*Five Disputations* [Davies, *Worship of the English Puritans*, p. 188].

⁷⁷*The Art of Prophesying* [Breward, pp. 342–43].

⁷⁸*Complete Works* [Lewis, p. 48].

⁷⁹*The Saints' Everlasting Rest*, p. 142. What John Knott says about Richard Sibbes is equally true of the Puritan preachers in general: "Until recently most discussion of Puritan sermons, following the influential lead of Perry Miller, has emphasized their rationality. . . . Whatever truth there may be in Miller's characterization, it . . . does not allow for the skill of a Sibbes in playing on the affections of his hearers" (p. 46).

⁸⁰Samuel Clarke, *Lives of Sundry Eminent Persons in This Later Age* [Haller, *Rise of Puritanism*, p. 132].

⁸¹Quoted in Davies, *Worship of the English Puritans*, p. 186.

⁸²*The Reformed Pastor*, p. 117.

⁸³*Works* [Rooy, p. 37].

⁸⁴Quoted in Emerson, *English Puritanism*, p. 45.

⁸⁵See R. C. Richardson, p. 101; and Hill, *Society and Puritanism*, p. 65.

⁸⁶*Ludus Literarius* [Mitchell, p. 32]. Brinsley further prescribed that those who took notes were supposed to write down "1. The text, or a part of it. 2. To mark as near as they can, and set down every doctrine, and what proofs they can, the reasons and the uses of them" (p. 33).

[87] *The Art of Divine Meditation* [Kaufmann, p. 119].

[88] *The Marrow of Theology*, p. 192.

[89] John Geree, *Character of an Old English Puritan* [Collinson, p. 377].

[90] Cotton Mather, *Magnalia Christi Americana* [Edmund Morgan, *Puritan Family*, p. 102]. Nicholas Bownde's influential *Doctrine of the Sabbath* regarded family repetition of the sermon as a necessary part of Sunday activities (Collinson, p. 377).

[91] *The English Reformation*, p. 320.

[92] *Works* [George, p. 338].

[93] *Works* [Haller, *Rise of Puritanism*, p. 140].

[94] Quoted in Brown, p. 85.

[95] Richard Baxter, *The Practical Works* [Mitchell, p. 104]. Perkins wrote, "Neither the words of arts, nor Greek and Latin phrases and quirks must be intermingled in the sermon" (*Works* [George, p. 339]).

[96] *Three Questions* . . . [R. C. Richardson, p. 42].

[97] *Works* [George, p. 338].

[98] Ibid., p. 339.

[99] Samuel Clarke, *General Martyrology* [Haller, *Rise of Puritanism*, p. 58]. Martin Luther had voiced a similar concern: "I see that the ambition of preachers is growing. . . . They neglect the simple and plain people. A sincere preacher must consider the young people, the servants, and maids in the church, those who lack education" (Lauterback-Weller, *Nachschriften* [Plass, 3:1130]).

[100] *The Holy State* [Davies, *Worship and Theology . . . 1534–1603*, p. 305].

[101] Quoted from a preface in Miller, *Seventeenth Century*, p. 358.

[102] Ibid.

[103] *The Works of John Flavel* [Lewis, p. 48].

[104] Miller, *Seventeenth Century*, p. 331.

[105] *Tropologia* [Knott, p. 48].

[106] John Bunyan, quoted in Brown, p. 146.

[107] Richard Baxter, *Poetical Fragments* [Keeble, p. 12].

[108] Thomas Watson [*The Beatitudes*, p. 251].

[109] Richard Heyricke, Worsley MSS [R. C. Richardson, p. 71].

[110] William Ames, *The Marrow of Theology*, p. 194.

[111] Richard Sibbes, *Works* [Rooy, p. 63].

CHAPTER 7

[1] Heading to *A Part of a Register* [Holifield, p. 33].

[2] Commentary on Isaiah 10:10–11 [Plass, 3:1548].

[3] *Commentary on Hebrews* [Avis, p. 114].

[4] *The Form of Prayers and Ministration of Sacraments, etc., Used in the English Congregation at Geneva* [Knappen, *Tudor Puritanism*, p. 140].

[5] William Turner, for example, wrote, "But the Evangelists and Apostles have made no mention of the Pope's ceremonies, laws, and traditions; therefore they are not necessary for Christ's church" (*The Second Course of the Hunter* . . . [Knappen, *Tudor Puritanism*, p. 69]).

[6] Quoted in Davies, *Worship of the English Puritans*, p. 2.

[7] *Puritan Manifestoes*, p. 8.

[8] *The Marrow of Sacred Divinity* [Davies, *Worship of the English Puritans*, p. 5].

[9] Jacob as quoted in Davies, *Worship of the English Puritans*, p. 77; Owen, *Works*, 14:84.

[10] Davies, *Worship of the English Puritans*, p. 79. Samuel Rutherford wrote, "All additions to God's Word are unlawful" (*The Divine Right of Church-Government* . . . [Rogers, p. 352]).

[11] *Yet a Course at the Romish Fox* [Knappen, *Tudor Puritanism*, p. 66].

[12] John Hooper, *The Regulative Principle and Things Indifferent* [Murray, p. 55].

[13] *The Works of John Whitgift* [Coolidge, p. 5].

[14] Ibid., p. 6.

[15] *English Puritanism* . . . [Davies, *Worship and Theology* . . . *1534–1603*, p. 70].

[16] Heading to *A Part of a Register* [Holifield, p. 33].

[17] *Worship of the English Puritans*, p. 15. Rogers comments that "opposition to religious ceremonialism emerged as a consequence of the Puritan acceptance of the Bible as the guide for all church doctrine and practice" (p. 60).

[18] Debate with Alveld [Plass, 1:272].

[19] *Works* [George, p. 316].

[20] *Later Writings* [Knappen, *Tudor Puritanism*, p. 101].

[21] *A Christian Directory* [Rooy, p. 92]. Haller, *Rise of Puritanism*, comments that the Puritans "identified the true church not with society nor with the nation but with an exclusive congregation of saints" (p. 176).

[22] *A Short Treatise* . . . [Warfield, p. 182]. Edward Dering wrote, "The house of God is neither in Rome, nor in the capitol of Rome, . . . but in every nation and in every country; the men that fear God and work righteousness, they are the Church" (*Works* [George, p. 379]). The Georges note that "the whole of English Protestantism is characterized by this movement away from the institutional and toward a more spiritual concept of the church" (p. 317).

[23] *Works* [George, p. 316].

[24] *Works* [Campbell, p. 98]. Luther repeatedly stressed the same theme: "Therefore not stonework, not good construction, not gold and silver embellish or make sacred a church, but the Word of God and sound preaching. For where the goodness of God is commended and revealed to men and souls are lifted up so that they may rely on God and call on the Lord in times of trouble, there you truly have a grand temple" (Commentary on Gen. 13:4 [Plass, 1:297]).

[25] *Dispute Against the English Popish Ceremonies* [Davies, *Worship and Theology* . . . *1603–1690*, pp. 21–22].

[26] Collinson, p. 356.

[27] *Works* [Rooy, p. 33].

[28] *Puritan Manifestoes*, p. 9.

[29] John Bradford, *The Hurt of Hearing Mass* [Murray, p. 17].

[30] Printed in John Cotton's *The Covenant of God's Free Grace* [H. S. Smith, p. 112].

[31] *Principles and Foundations of Christian Religion* [H. S. Smith, p. 83].

[32] Collinson, p. 381.

[33] *Sermons* [George, p. 318].

[34] Perkins, *Works* [George, p. 318]; Owen, *Works*, 14:30.

[35] *Paradise Lost*, bk. 1, lines 16–17. Cf. Davies's comment, *Worship and Theology* . . . *1603–1690*, that "for Quakers and Puritans . . . consecrated people alone were God's true temples" (pp. 19–20).

[36] John Bradford, *The Hurt of Hearing Mass* [Murray, p. 17].

[37] Knappen, *Tudor Puritanism*, p. 92. Luther had already provided a model for the Puritans: "No bishop is to install anyone without the choice, will, and call of the congregation; but he is to confirm him who has been chosen and called by the congregation" (Treatise of 1523 [Plass, 2:925]).

[38] Collinson, pp. 94–97, collects the evidence. He notes that for Puritans who had witnessed the Marian burnings, the clerical vestments were "the uniform of an oppressive class," not unlike the Nazi uniforms of a more recent era. See also R. C. Richardson, pp. 74–75, for evidence that the clergy feared to offend the laity on the vestment question.

[39] R. C. Richardson, pp. 86–88. Richardson concludes that "conventicles . . . provide one of the surest indications of the existence of organised lay puritanism."

[40] Collinson, pp. 372–82. Charles Hambrick-Stowe, *The Practice of Piety*, pp. 137–43, shows that small group meetings were also a feature of American Puritanism.

[41] Knappen, *Tudor Puritanism*, p. 38.

[42] *An Explication of the Fourteenth Chapter of the Prophet Hosea* [Rogers, p. 383].

[43] *The Life of Christ* [Rogers, p. 384]. Miller, *Seventeenth Century*, concludes that the Puritans "went as far as mortals could in removing intermediaries between God and man: the church, the priest, the magical sacraments, the saints and the Virgin" (p. 45). Davies, *Worship of the English Puritans*, states that "the Puritans, . . . by their democratic form of ecclesiastical government, as opposed to the monarchical government of the Established Church, expressed their belief in the doctrine of election and the priesthood of all believers. The inevitable result was that their ministry was not regarded as a priestly hierarchy" (p. 22).

[44] For a survey, see Davies, *Worship of the English Puritans*, pp. 115–61.

[45] *The Form of Prayers and Ministration of the Sacraments, etc., Used in the English Congregation at Geneva* [Davies, *Worship of the English Puritans*, p. 119].

[46] Both quoted in Hill, *Change*, pp. 88–89.

[47] The Puritan case against vestments included these arguments: infringement on religious liberty; association with Roman Catholicism; signs of pomp and grandeur instead of Christlike humility; cleavage between clergy and laity.

[48] Collinson, p. 73.

[49] *Works* [Greaves, *Society and Religion*, p. 421].

[50] *Acts and Monuments* [Davies, *Worship and Theology . . . 1534–1603*, p. 74].

[51] Davies, *Worship and Theology . . . 1603–1690*, p. 11.

[52] James F. White, *Protestant Worship and Church Architecture* (New York: Oxford University Press, 1964), p. 107.

[53] The best source on this whole vexed topic is Scholes, *The Puritans and Music*. Puritan aversion to the organ in churches (but not in the home and secular settings) was mainly symbolic: to them the organ represented the whole of Roman Catholic ceremony and theology. In this they may have been right: the Puritans removed organs from Oxford college chapels in order to put an end to high church services, and Anthony Wood records that when the organs were restored after the Restoration, high church services also reappeared (Davies, *Worship and Theology . . . 1603–1690*, p. 253).

[54] Davies, *Worship of the English Puritans*, p. 209.

[55] *A Christian Directory* [Rooy, p. 93].

[56] Richard Cox, *Original Letters* [Knappen, *Tudor Puritanism*, p. 127].

[57] John Milton, *The Reason of Church-Government* [*CPW*, 1:766].

[58] John Cotton, quoted in Miller, *Seventeenth Century*, p. 437.

[59] The best source on Puritan music is Scholes, *The Puritans and Music*.

[60] Morison, *Intellectual Life*, p. 156.

[61] John Jewel, *Zurich Letters* [Davies, *Worship and Theology . . . 1534–1603*, pp. 385–86].

[62] Collinson, p. 380.

[63] Millar Maclure, *The Paul's Cross Sermons, 1534–1642* (Toronto: University of Toronto Press, 1958), p. 165.

[64] Good starting points on the Puritan imagination include the following: Sacvan Bercovitch, *The American Puritan Imagination* (Cambridge: Cambridge University Press, 1974); Barbara K. Lewalski, *Protestant Poetics and the Seventeenth-Century Religious Lyric* (Princeton: Princeton University Press, 1979); E. Beatrice Batson, *John Bunyan: Allegory and Imagination* (London: Croom Helm, 1984).

[65] Bercovitch, "Introduction" to *The American Puritan Imagination*, comments, "In keeping with their intellectual outlook the colonists' writings were highly figurative, abounding in metaphor, parallel, allusion, type and trope, and controlled by a variety of sophisticated rhetorical devices" (pp. 4–5).

[66] Thomas Watson, *The Beatitudes*, p. 143.

[67] Ralph Venning, *The Plague of Plagues*, p. 165.

[68] Samuel Bolton, *The True Bounds of Christian Freedom*, p. 84.

[69] *The Allegory of Love* (Oxford: Oxford University Press, 1936), p. 334.

[70] Quoted in New, p. 70.

[71] *The Whole Doctrine of the Sacraments* [Holifield, p. 37].

[72] See Hill, *Society and Puritanism*, pp. 62–74; and Knott, p. 37.

[73] *The Laws of Ecclesiastical Polity* [Davies, *Worship of the English Puritans*, p. 186].

[74] *The Saints' Everlasting Rest*, p. 128.

[75] John Geree, *The Character of an Old English Puritan* [Collinson, p. 361].

[76] *Worship and Theology . . . 1603–1690*, p. 191.

[77] *Eikonoklastes* [*CPW*, 3.505]. William Hinde wrote, "If any man will rest in his book prayers and never strive to speak unto God out of his own heart, such a man in my opinion comes far short of the power and practice, comfort and fruit of true prayer" (*Life of John Bruen* [R. C. Richardson, p. 47]).

[78] For an analysis of Puritan meditation books, see U. Milo Kaufmann, *The Pilgrim's Progress and Traditions in Puritan Meditation;* and Charles E. Hambrick-Stowe, *The Practice of Piety: Puritan Devotional Disciplines in Seventeenth-Century New England.*

[79] One minister's diary records the number of such family services that he attended over a four-year span. The totals were 57, 48, 64, and 47 (Davies, *Worship of the English Puritans*, p. 283).

[80] Oliver Heywood, *Diary* [Davies, *Worship of the English Puritans*, p. 282].

[81] *Demonstration of Family Duties* [R. C. Richardson, p. 90].

[82] *Society and Puritanism*, pp. 443–81.

[83] *Family*, p. 141.

[84] *Works* [Wakefield, p. 55].

[85] Important studies on the Puritan Sabbath include the following: W. B. Whitaker, *Sunday in Tudor and Stuart Times* (London: Houghton, 1933); James T. Dennison, *The Market Day of the Soul;* Winton U. Solberg, *Redeem the Time: The Puritan Sabbath in Early America;* Christopher Hill, *Society and Puritanism*, ch. 5; R. J. Bauckham, "Sabbath and Sunday in the Protestant Tradition," pp. 311–44 in *From Sabbath to Lord's Day: A Biblical, Historical, and Theological Investigation*, ed. D. A. Carson (Grand Rapids: Zondervan, 1982).

[86] Nicholas Bownde, *The Doctrine of the Sabbath* [Bauckham, "Sabbath and Sunday," p. 324].

[87] Gervase Babington, *A Very Fruitful Exposition of the Commandments* [Dennison, p. 36].

[88] *CLII Lectures Upon Psalm LI* [Hill, *Society and Puritanism*, p. 175].

[89] *The Puritan Doctrine of the Sabbath* [Dennison, p. 48]. Bownde criticized people who "think that the whole observation of the Sabbath is in the use of the public exercises, so that as soon as they be out of the church doors they are ready to talk of all worldly affairs."

[90] *The Marrow of Theology*, p. 299.

[91] *The Catechizing of Families* [Hill, *Society and Puritanism*, p. 166]. Hill cites examples of manufacturers and businessmen who tried to force their employees to work seven days a week (p. 152).

[92] *The Doctrine of the Sabbath Vindicated* [Hill, *Society and Puritanism*, p. 177]. William Gouge had no supper on Saturday evenings so as to prevent his servants from having to stay up late, and on Sundays no servant stayed home to prepare a meal (Hill, p. 181).

[93] *Society and Puritanism*, p. 152.

[94] *The Spectator*, No. 112 [Hill, *Society and Puritanism*, p. 217].

[95] Milton, quoted in Hill, *Society and Puritanism*, p. 199; Wither, *Hymns and Songs of the Church* [Hill, *Society and Puritanism*, p. 212].

[96] *The Doctrine of the Sabbath* [Hill, *Society and Puritanism*, p. 171].

[97] *The Practice of Piety* [Hill, *Society and Puritanism*, p. 182].

[98] *A Godly Exhortation* . . . [Knappen, *Tudor Puritanism*, p. 448].

[99] A. B., *The Sabbath Truly Sanctified* [Dennison, p. 133].

[100] *The Marrow of Theology*, pp. 298–300. Ames's division of the doctrine into the two parts of rest and sanctification of that rest was standard among Puritan writers.

[101] *Works* [Hill, *Society and Puritanism*, p. 151].

[102] Ibid., p. 174.

[103] *The Divine Appointment of the Lord's Day* [Dennison, p. 176].

[104] Dennison, p. 176; Hill, *Society and Puritanism*, p. 197.

[105] *The Saint's Qualification* [Hill, *Society and Puritanism*, p. 176].

[106] *Hymns and Songs of the Church* [Hill, *Society and Puritanism*, p. 212].

[107] *The Church History of Britain* [Dennison, p. 43].

[108] *The Christian's Two Chief Lessons* [McGee, p. 247].

[109] *The Marrow of Theology* [Emerson, *Puritanism in America*, p. 26].

[110] Quoted in Miller, *Seventeenth Century*, p. 435.

[111] *History of the Plymouth Plantation* [Schneider, p. 22].

[112] *The Bruised Reed* [George, p. 414].

[113] *New England's Tears* . . . [McGee, p. 155].

[114] *The Beatitudes*, p. 231. The idea of spiritual fellowship elicited some of the Puritans' most sensuous language. Robert Coachman called it "the most pleasant dew and sweet ointment, the one ravishing the eye, the other delighting the smell" (*The Cry of a Stone* [McGee, p. 206]). Robert Bolton wrote that "if once this divine flame of brotherly love be kindled by the Holy Ghost in the hearts of true-hearted Christians . . . it is never put out . . . but burns in their breast . . . with mutual warmth of dearest sweetness here upon earth" (*Instructions for a Right Comforting Afflicted Consciences* [McGee, pp. 205–6]).

[115] *A Consolatory Letter to an Afflicted Conscience* [McGee, p. 205].

[116] *Correction, Instruction: or, a Treatise of Afflictions* [McGee, p. 205].

[117] *Rebukes for Sin by God's Burning Anger* [McGee, p. 186].

[118] *The Saints' Cordials* [McGee, p. 195]. Elsewhere Sibbes wrote that it is dangerous to neglect "the benefit of their holy conference, their godly instructions, their divine consolations, brotherly admonitions and charitable reprehensions" (*A Consolatory Letter* . . . [McGee, p. 195]).

[119] *A Body of Divinity* [McGee, p. 202]. In his book on the Beatitudes, Watson wrote, "If you would be pure, walk with them that are pure. . . . Association begets assimilation" (p. 195).

[120] Knappen, *Two Elizabethan Puritan Diaries*, p. 120.

[121] *The Cry of a Stone* [McGee, p. 198].

[122] Quoted by Miller, *Seventeenth Century*, p. 435.

CHAPTER 8

[1] Letter of 1528 [Plass, 3:1178].

[2] Tyndale, *Works* [Hughes, p. 14]. The preface to the Geneva Bible stated that the Scriptures were intended "both for the learned and unlearned of what nation and tongue soever they were" [Trinterud, p. 218].

[3] Quoted in Warfield, pp. 188–89. Edward Reynolds, one of the writers of the Westminster Confession, expressed the wish that "every family might have a Bible in it" (*An Explication of the Fourteenth Chapter of the Prophet Hosea . . .* [Rogers, p. 401]).

[4] Quoted in F. F. Bruce, *History of the Bible in English,* 3d ed. (New York: Oxford University Press, 1978), p. 96.

[5] Perry, p. 238.

[6] *Christ the Fountain of Life* [Carden, p. 14].

[7] *The Saints' Everlasting Rest* [New, p. 27].

[8] William Riley Parker, *Milton: A Biography* (Oxford: Oxford University Press, 1968), 1:4.

[9] *Winthrop Papers* [McGee, p. 244].

[10] *Military Duties Recommended to an Artillary Company* [Carden, pp. 12–13].

[11] Henry Newcome, *Autobiography* [R. C. Richardson, p. 104].

[12] *The English Works* [Knott, p. 169].

[13] *The Marrow of Theology*, p. 188.

[14] William Hinde, *Life of John Bruen* [R. C. Richardson, p. 102].

[15] *A Companion for Communicants* [Carden, pp. 8–9].

[16] *Works* [Warfield, p. 303].

[17] *The Works of Ephesus Explained* [John Wilson, p. 209]. Luther and Calvin had first established this critique of custom and reason. Luther had said, "All customs, no matter how good they are, must give way to the Word of God" (Address to the Diet at Augsburg, 1530 [Plass, 3:1181]). Calvin had affirmed that "we desire to follow Scripture alone as a rule of faith and religion, without mixing with it any other thing which might be devised by the opinion of men apart from the Word of God" (1536 *Confession of Faith* [Jarman, p. 110]).

[18] *Works*, 13:40–41.

[19] *The Unlawfulness and Danger of Limited Episcopacy* [Rogers, p. 349].

[20] *Body of Divinity* [Packer, p. 19]. Thomas Gataker wrote, "But there is God's own mark set upon every sentence in this book . . . by the Spirit of God himself" (*A Wife in Deed* [Rogers, p. 371]).

[21] *Tears of Repentance* [Carden, p. 4].

[22] *Works*, 16:297, 309. Increase Mather believed that the Bible "ought to be received on that sole account of the authority of the speaker. . . . Because of the authority of the speaker, men have infinite reason to hear and fear, and to believe and obey" (*The Latter Sign Discoursed . . .* [Carden, p. 3]).

[23] *An Explication of the Fourteenth Chapter of the Prophet Hosea* [Rogers, p. 409]. Luther had been particularly adamant on the reliability of Scripture; he wrote to King Henry VIII, "God's Word is above all; God cannot err and deceive" (Plass, 3:1368). On another occasion Luther expressed his certainty that "this Holy Scripture . . . will not deceive me" (lecture on Gen. 37:9 [Plass, 2:839]).

[24] *Works* [Warfield, p. 273].

[25] Luther, *Works* [John Warwick Montgomery, "Lessons from Luther on the Inerrancy of Holy Writ," in *God's Inerrant Word* (Minneapolis: Bethany Fellowship, 1974), p. 67]; Calvin, *Commentary on Hebrews* [Kenneth S. Kantzer, "Calvin and the Holy Scriptures," in *Inspiration and*

Interpretation, ed. John F. Walvoord (Grand Rapids: Eerdmans, 1957), p. 142]. On the same page Kantzer quotes eight additional passages where Calvin used the word "infallible" or "inerrant" to describe the Bible.

[26] *A Free Disputation Against Pretended Liberty of Conscience* [Warfield, p. 247].

[27] *The Marrow of Theology*, pp. 185–86.

[28] Baxter, *Works* [Warfield, p. 273]; Owen, *Works*, 14:273.

[29] *Remains* [Warfield, pp. 244–45].

[30] *Works* [Warfield, p. 273].

[31] William Tyndale, *Prologue to the Book of Genesis* [Knott, p. 20]; Samuel Rutherford, *A Free Disputation Against Pretended Liberty of Conscience* [Warfield, p. 256]; Increase Mather, *David Serving His Generation* [Carden, p. 7].

[32] Cartwright, *The Second Reply* [Emerson, *Puritanism in America*, p. 20]; Gough, Prologue to the *Enchiridion* of Erasmus [Trinterud, p. 38]. Thomas Gataker called Scripture "the only sure touchstone of all saving truth" (*Shadows Without Substance* [Rogers, p. 433]).

[33] William Whittingham, *Reformation of the Church* [Jarman, p. 110]; John Eliot, *The Christian Commonwealth* [Carden, p. 5]. Arthur Hildersham wrote that "there is no good work any man can do but he may have clear direction for it in the Word of God" (*CLII Lectures Upon Psalm LI* [Kaufmann, p. 47]).

[34] *The Divine Right of Church-Government* [Rogers, p. 331].

[35] *The Marrow of Theology*, p. 187. John Owen wrote that Scripture is God's "safe rule and infallible guide for the due performance of all the duties, towards himself and one another, which he requires of us in the whole course of our obedience. . . . We go to them [the Scriptures] . . . to learn our own duty, to be instructed in the whole course of our obedience" (*An Exposition of . . . Hebrews* [Kaufmann, p. 46]).

[36] *The Works of John Whitgift* [Jarman, p. 21].

[37] *A Brief and Plain Declaration* [Trinterud, p. 243]. Walter Travers spoke of establishing "a just and lawful manner of government according to the word of God" (*A Full and Plain Declaration* [Jarman, p. 66]).

[38] *The Marrow of Theology*, p. 187.

[39] *Christian Directions* [Kaufmann, pp. 45–46].

[40] *Divine Meditations and Holy Contemplations* [Kaufmann, p. 46].

[41] *The Works of John Whitgift* [Davies, *Worship and Theology . . . 1534–1603*, pp. 51–52].

[42] *Works* [Knappen, *Tudor Puritanism*, p. 355].

[43] H. Ainsworth and F. Johnson, *An Apology or Defense of Such True Christians as Are Commonly . . . Called Brownists* [Knappen, p. 356]. The extension of biblical authority to all areas of life is reminiscent of the practice of such Reformers as Calvin and Luther, who not only cited the Bible in political matters but also, for example, used it as a scientific authority to condemn the Copernican system (see Rogers, p. 96).

[44] *A Treatise of Miscellany Questions* [Rogers, p. 346]. Thomas Gataker showed a similar contentment to believe conclusions "deduced from Scripture" and then applied to a current situation (*Shadows Without Substance* [Rogers, p. 334]).

[45] Preface to Willard's *Brief Discourse Concerning That Ceremony of Laying the Hand on the Bible in Swearing* [Lowrie, p. 33].

[46] Frederic Farrar, *History of Interpretation* (1886; reprint, Grand Rapids: Baker, 1961), p. 199.

[47] Ibid., p. 200.

[48] The examples are cited from H. H. Rowley, "The Interpretation of the Song of Songs," in *The Servant of the Lord and Other Essays on the Old Testament* (London: Lutterworth, 1952), pp. 196–97.

[49] *Obedience of a Christian Man* [Knappen, p. 357].

[50] *Shadows Without Substance* [Rogers, p. 301].

[51] *Scripture-Light, the Most Sure Light* [Warfield, p. 252]. John Ball noted similarly that "there is but one proper and natural sense, though sometimes things are so expressed as that the things themselves do signify other matters" (*A Short Treatise* . . . [Warfield, p. 189]).

[52] *Clavis Cantici* [Lewlaski, p. 122]. John White made a similar distinction when he wrote that "such allegorical senses of Scripture, we must not easily admit, unless the Scripture itself warrant them" (*A Way to the Tree of Life* [Warfield, p. 253]).

[53] *Tentations* [Warfield, p. 253].

[54] *A Chain of Principles* [Warfield, p. 234].

[55] *Works*, 14:276.

[56] *Of Reformation* [*CPW*, 1:566].

[57] *A Way to the Tree of Life* [Warfield, p. 231].

[58] *Works* [Warfield, pp. 231–32].

[59] Farrar, *History of Interpretation*, p. 296.

[60] *A Short Treatise* . . . [Warfield, p. 189].

[61] John Lightfoot, *Works* [Warfield, p. 304].

[62] *Works* [Packer, p. 21]. John Owen wrote, "This is the genuine and proper way of the interpretation of Scripture, when from the words themselves, considered with relation unto the persons speaking them, and all their circumstances, we declare what is their determinate mind and sense" (*The Works* [Kaufmann, p. 39]).

[63] *The Art of Prophesying* [Breward, p. 338].

[64] Quoted in Rogers, p. 424.

[65] *An Answer to Two Questions* [Carden, p. 5]. Other Puritans spoke of the Scriptures' "consonancy and harmony within themselves" and "the marvellous consent of all parts and passages (though written by divers and several penmen)" (Edward Reynolds, *An Explication of the Fourteenth Chapter of the Prophet Hosea* [Rogers, p. 409]; George Gillespie, *A Treatise of Miscellany Questions* [Warfield, p. 176]).

[66] The statement in Romans 12:6 that if a person's gift is prophecy he should prophecy "in proportion to our faith" was construed by Calvin to mean that a person should not break the *content* of the faith in prophecy. The phrase continues to be used today, but I have discovered that hardly anyone who uses it has a good explanation of what the phrase itself means.

[67] *An Exposition of the Epistle to the Hebrews* [Kaufmann, p. 109]. *The Scots Confession* declared, "We dare not receive or admit any interpretation which is contrary to any principal point of our faith, or to any other plain text of Scripture, or to the rule of love" [Rogers, p. 404].

[68] *The Art of Prophesying* [Breward, p. 338]. Richard Bernard rejected any interpretation that does not "agree with the principles of religion, the points of catechism set down in the creed, the Lord's Prayer, the Ten Commandments, and the doctrine of sacraments" (*The Faithful Shepherd* [Packer, p. 23]).

[69] *God's Eye on His Israel* [Rogers, p. 407]. Elsewhere Gataker wrote, "The whole doctrine of faith is to be received, that is contained in holy Writ; and that collation of Scripture with Scripture may afford much light unto places more obscure" (*Shadows Without Substance* [Rogers, p. 407]).

[70] *The Papers Which Passed at New-Castle*. . . [Rogers, p. 412].

[71] John Lightfoot, *Works* [Warfield, p. 304].

[72] *Works* [Packer, p. 23]. John Ball wrote, "Always it is to be observed that obscure places are not to be expounded contrary to the rule of faith set down in plainer places of the Scripture" (*A Short Treatise* . . . [Warfield, p. 187]).

[73] "Sole Fide: The Reformed Doctrine of Justification," in *Soli Deo Gloria: Essays in Reformed Theology*, ed. R. C. Sproul (Philadelphia: Presbyterian and Reformed, 1976), p. 11.

[74] *Prologue to Jonah* [Clebsch, p. 164]. Samuel Rutherford divided biblical content into "Law and Gospel" (*The Trial and Triumph of Faith* . . . [Rogers, p. 357]).

[75] *The Art of Prophesying* [Breward, pp. 341–42].

[76] *A Treatise of Miscellany Questions* [Warfield, p. 176].

[77] Edward Reynolds, for example, spoke of "the mercy and grace of God in the promises" and "the threatenings of God set forth in his Word, and executed in his judgments upon wicked men" (Sermon on Hosea [Rogers, p. 374]). The *Westminster Confession* (XIV, sec. ii) used the terms "commands," "threatenings, and promises" contained in the Bible [Kaufmann, p. 203].

[78] *The Literary Impact of the Authorized Version* (Philadelphia: Fortress, 1963), pp. 29–34.

[79] *The Marrow of Theology*, pp. 187–88.

[80] *The Soul's Conflict* [Lewalski, p. 167].

[81] *An Introduction to the Holy Scriptures* [Kaufmann, p. 70].

[82] *David's Instructor: A Sermon* [Rogers, p. 300].

[83] Wither, *Preparation to the Psalter* [Lewalski, p. 80]; Milton, *Reason of Church-Government* [CPW, 1:816].

[84] George Gillespie, *A Treatise of Miscellany Questions* [Warfield, p. 175].

[85] *The Art of Prophesying* [Kaufmann, p. 81].

[86] *A Commentary Upon the Whole Book of Judges* [Kaufmann, p. 82].

[87] *A Short Treatise . . .* [Warfield, p. 186].

[88] *Rhetorica Sacra* [Lewalski, p. 83].

[89] Wither, *A Preparation to the Psalter* [Baroway, p. 466]; Sibbes, *The Soul's Conflict* [Lewalski, p. 166].

[90] Lewalski, pp. 78, 83.

[91] *The Marrow of Theology*, p. 187.

[92] Ambrose, *Prima, Media, and Ultima* [Kaufmann, p. 203]; Gouge, *Christian Directions* [Kaufmann, p. 205].

[93] *The New Covenant* [Coolidge, p. 145].

[94] *The Works* [Knott, p. 32].

[95] *A Few Sighs From Hell* [Knott, p. 137].

[96] Preface to *The First Tome or Volume of the Paraphrases of Erasmus Upon the New Testament* [Knott, p. 26]. This echoes the view of Luther that "Scripture certainly does not contain words that are merely to be read, . . . but it is full of words that are to be lived, . . . not to speculate and philosophize about but to turn into life and action" (dedicatory remarks to an interpretation of Ps. 118 [Plass, 1:84]).

[97] *A Treatise of the New Covenant* [Rogers, p. 385].

[98] *Another Sermon* [John Wilson, p. 144].

[99] Mather, *Substance of Sermons* [Carden, p. 40]; Lukin, *An Introduction to the Holy Scriptures* [Kaufmann, p. 238].

[100] *An Explication of the Hundred and Tenth Psalm* [Rogers, p. 356].

[101] Gillespie, *A Treatise of Miscellany Questions* [Warfield, p. 175]; Udall, Preface to *The First Tome . . .* [Knott, p. 26].

[102] *The Divine Authority of the Scriptures Asserted* [Knott, p. 36].

[103] John Foxe, *Acts and Monuments* [Knott, p. 13].

CHAPTER 9

[1] "Modern Education and the Classics," in *Essays Ancient and Modern* (New York: Harcourt, Brace, 1932, 1936), p. 169.

[2] Miller/Johnson, 2:700.

[3] Ibid., 1:14.

[4] Ibid., 2:701.

[5] *Magnalia Christi Americana*, bk. 4, pt. 1.

[6] Crawford, pp. 12–13. The same source furnishes data about the establishing of schools in New England.

[7] Ellwood P. Cubberly, *A Brief History of Education* (Boston: Houghton Mifflin, 1922), pp. 195–96.

[8] Knappen, *Tudor Puritanism*, p. 469. Foster Watson's history of the English grammar schools concludes that "the English Grammar Schools gained much of their vitality and inspiration from the national life, in its most intense manifestation in Puritanism" (pp. 538–39).

[9] *Book of Discipline* [Porter, *Tudor England*, p. 198].

[10] Quoted in Miller, *Seventeenth Century*, p. 69.

[11] Ashley, p. 142.

[12] J. W. Ashley Smith, *The Birth of Modern Education*, p. 12. Maurice Ashley calls the Commonwealth years "a period of lively activity in education," with the London of the 1650s "a centre of original philosophic and scientific thought" (p. 142).

[13] James, pp. 314–26. Regarding the decline of education after the Restoration, Schlatter writes, "Plainly, the Church of England, in conjunction with the government, was willing to sacrifice much of the progress which had been made by the Puritans, in order to stamp out dissent entirely" (p. 46).

[14] Greaves, *Puritan Revolution and Educational Thought*, p. 15. Elsewhere Greaves notes that "with the exception of the Presbyterians, Puritans evidenced more interest in educational questions than issues of ecclesiastical polity" (*Society and Religion*, p. 329).

[15] Quoted in Miller, *Seventeenth Century*, p. 74. Greaves, *Puritan Revolution and Educational Thought*, documents in detail how the English Puritans defended knowledge, learning, and reason against the anti-intellectual attacks of the sectaries in mid-seventeenth-century England.

[16] *The New Covenant* [Axtell, p. 12].

[17] *The Autobiography of Richard Baxter* [Axtell, p. 12].

[18] *Christ the Fountain of Life* [Miller/Johnson, 1:22].

[19] Quoted in Miller, *Seventeenth Century*, pp. 67 and 171. Cotton Mather made similar claims: "Every grace enters into the soul through the understanding" (*Cares About the Nurseries* [Edmund Morgan, *Puritan Family*, p. 89]). Mather also theorized that in order to believe the Catholic doctrine of transubstantiation a person must "altogether lose all the use of common sense and natural reason, in those very things which God himself has made them judges in" (Quoted in Miller, *Seventeenth Century*, p. 71).

[20] *The Cup of Blessing* [Miller/Johnson, 1:39].

[21] Cotton, *A Practical Commentary* . . . [Miller/Johnson, 1:24]; Hubbard, *The Happiness of a People* [Miller/Johnson, p. 1:24].

[22] *Reasonable Religion* [Middlekauff, p. 297].

[23] Morison, *Founding of Harvard College*, p. 337.

[24] *The Judgment of Non-Conformists, of the Interest of Reason in Matters of Religion* [Miller, *Seventeenth Century*, p. 72]. Baxter also theorized that "the most religious are the most truly and nobly rational."

[25] *Scripture-Light* . . . [Warfield, p. 234].

[26] Quoted in Miller, *Seventeenth Century*, p. 69.

[27] *New England's First Fruits* [Miller/Johnson, 2:701].

[28] *Sermons and Discourses on Several Occasions* [Miller/Johnson, 1:18].

[29] Hooker, *The Soul's Preparation for Christ* [Miller/Johnson, 1:12]; Perkins, *The Foundation of Christian Religion Gathered into Six Principles* [Axtell, p. 12]. Richard Rogers recorded in his *Diary* that he experienced "much heaviness" because of his "wants in knowledge" (Knappen, *Two Elizabethan Puritan Diaries*, p. 59).

³⁰ *What the Pious Parent Wishes* [Edmund Morgan, *Puritan Family*, p. 87].

³¹ *To My Father* [*The Complete Poetical Works of John Milton*, ed. Douglas Bush (Boston: Houghton Mifflin, 1965), p. 100].

³² Porter, *Tudor England*, p. 185.

³³ Ibid., p. 198. The "Order of Schools" drawn up under the auspices of Knox asserted the necessity of schools "wherein youth may be trained in the knowledge and fear of God" (Frederick Eby, *Early Protestant Educators* [1931; reprint New York: AMS Press, 1971], p. 275). All of this is very reminiscent of a similar emphasis in Luther, who praised the council of Nürnberg for maintaining a school that contributed to the students' "eternal salvation as well as to their temporal well-being and honor" (*A Sermon on Keeping Children in School* [Luther, *Works*, 46:214]).

³⁴ *New England's First Fruits* [Miller/Johnson, 2:702].

³⁵ Ibid., p. 715.

³⁶ *Massachusetts Laws of 1648* [Edmund Morgan, *Puritan Family*, p. 88].

³⁷ *Cares About the Nurseries* [Edmund Morgan, *Puritan Family*, p. 90].

³⁸ *A Good Wife God's Gift* [Emerson, *English Puritanism*, p. 215]. Luther and Calvin had said similar things about the limitations of purely humanistic learning. Luther said, "For we certainly want to provide not only for our children's bellies, but for their souls as well. At least this is what truly Christian parents would say about it" (*To the Councilmen of Germany, That They Establish and Maintain Christian Schools* [Luther, *Works*, 45:349]). On the same subject, Calvin wrote that "a knowledge of all the sciences is mere smoke, where the heavenly science of Christ is wanting" (Commentary on 1 Cor. 1:20).

³⁹ *To the Christian Nobility* . . . [Luther, *Works*, 44:205–7].

⁴⁰ Statutes of Emmanuel College [Porter, *Tudor England*, p. 182].

⁴¹ *New England's First Fruits* [Miller/Johnson, 2:702].

⁴² *Of Education* [CPW, 2:397].

⁴³ *Vindiciae Literarum* [Greaves, *Puritan Revolution and Educational Thought*, p. 122]. Henry Thurman, while an Oxford student, had as an ideal "the study of humane learning, in subordination to divinity" (*A Defence of Humane Learning in the Ministry* [Greaves, p. 37]).

⁴⁴ *Victoria County History of Lancashire* [Derek Wilson, p. 136].

⁴⁵ *CPW*, 2:366–67.

⁴⁶ *To the Councilmen* . . . [Luther, *Works*, 45:369–70]. Calvin was similarly committed to the liberal arts. In his academy at Geneva, of the twenty-seven weekly lectures, three were in theology, eight in Hebrew and the Old Testament, three in ethics, five in Greek orators and poets, three in physics and mathematics, and five in dialectic and rhetoric. Texts included works by Virgil, Cicero, Ovid, Livy, Homer, Aristotle, Plato, and Plutarch (Eby, p. 253; W. Stanford Reid, "Calvin and the Founding of the Academy of Geneva," *Westminster Theological Journal*, 18 [1955], pp. 13, 16).

⁴⁷ *A Godly Form of Household Government* [Knappen, *Tudor Puritanism*, p. 468].

⁴⁸ Morison, *Intellectual Life*, p. 89. The phrase "good literature" comes from Cicero's phrase *bonae literae*.

⁴⁹ *Magnalia Christi Americana* [Morison, *Harvard College in the Seventeenth Century*, 1:324]. Mather once voiced the dream he had to "fill the country with a liberal education" (*The Serviceable Man* [Miller, *Nature's Nation*, p. 48]).

⁵⁰ J. W. Ashley Smith, p. 71. Morison, *Intellectual Life*, similarly concludes that "Puritanism in New England preserved far more of the humanist tradition than did non-puritanism in the other English colonies" (p. 17).

⁵¹ *The Divine Right of Church-Government* [Rogers, p. 284]. In Germany, Philip Melanchthon expressed the same theory of education: "For some teach absolutely nothing out of the Sacred Scriptures; some teach the children absolutely nothing but the Sacred Scriptures; both of which are not to be tolerated" (quoted in *A History of Religious Educations*, ed. Elmer L. Towns [Grand Rapids: Baker, 1975], p. 152).

[52] Miller/Johnson, 1:20.

[53] *The Faithful Shepherd* [Haller, *Rise of Puritanism*, p. 138]. Mark Curtis documents that "the Puritan interest in the reform of the Church gave them strong convictions about the usefulness of university education" (p. 190).

[54] Quoted in Miller, *Seventeenth Century*, p. 85. William Shurtleff said in a sermon that "the knowledge not only of the learned languages but of the whole circle of arts and sciences may be of use to a Gospel minister" (*The Labour That Attends the Gospel Ministry* [Morison, *Harvard College in the Seventeenth Century*, 1:166]).

[55] T. G. Wright, pp. 244–53.

[56] Quoted in Miller, *Seventeenth Century*, p. 311. Cotton Mather praised John Cotton for the same qualities, calling him "a most universal scholar, and a living system of the liberal arts and a walking library" (*Magnalia Christi Americana* [Mitchell, p. 102]).

[57] *Studies in Medieval and Renaissance Literature* (Cambridge: Cambridge University Press, 1966), p. 122. An art historian similarly concludes, "Where they had so much in common it is not always possible to draw a distinction between the reflection of Renaissance and of Reformation ideas. . . . At first . . . the two worked in harmony and many of the most Renaissance-conscious men of the mid-century were the most extreme Protestants" (Eric Mercer, *English Art, 1553–1625* [Oxford: Oxford University Press, 1962], pp. 6–7).

[58] See C. H. Conley, *The First English Translators of the Classics* (New Haven: Yale University Press, 1927). Conley speaks of "the inherent harmony between Protestantism and classicism" (p. 76). On the other hand, it is important to note also Conley's conclusion that "the translation movement . . . begun by Puritans was brought to an end by Puritans" (p. 116), suggesting that as the Renaissance and Reformation developed, tensions between them became much more pronounced.

[59] Joan Simon, *Education and Society in Tudor England* (Cambridge: Cambridge University Press, 1967), p. 402, concludes that "humanistic insistence on the need to disseminate education had received a fresh impetus at the Reformation." For documentation of the extent to which the curriculum of Puritan education consisted of classical texts, see the following sources: Mark H. Curtis, *Oxford and Cambridge in Transition, 1558–1642*; H. McLachlan, *English Education Under the Test Acts, Being the History of the Non-Conformist Academies, 1662–1820* (Manchester: Manchester University Press, 1931); J. W. Ashley Smith, *The Birth of Modern Education*; Irene Parker, *Dissenting Academies in England* (Cambridge: Cambridge University Press, 1914).

[60] Quoted in Miller, *Seventeenth Century*, p. 160.

[61] The quoted phrases come, *seriatim*, from John Milton, *An Apology Against a Pamphlet* [*CPW*, 1:923]; 1642 Charter of Harvard College [Kenneth Murdock, *Increase Mather: The Foremost American Puritan* (Cambridge: Harvard University Press, 1926), p. 45]; 1650 Charter of Harvard College [Morison, *Harvard College in the Seventeenth Century*, 1:6]; *New England's First Fruits* [Miller/Johnson, 2:701]; Parliamentary Propagation Act of 1641 [James, p. 322].

[62] *The Christian's Portion* [George, p. 347].

[63] Miller/Johnson, 2:706.

[64] *A Sermon Touching the Use of Humane Learning* [Miller, *Seventeenth Century*, p. 82]. In another place Reynolds wrote that we know God's judgments in two ways, "the one natural, by sense; the other spiritual, by faith" (*A Treatise of the Passions and Faculties of the Soul of Man* [Rogers, p. 248]).

[65] Miller/Johnson, 2:719.

[66] The strongest case for Puritan influence on modern science is Robert K. Merton's book *Science, Technology, and Society in Seventeenth Century England*. See also Christopher Hill, *Intellectual Origins of the English Revolution* (Oxford: Oxford University Press, 1965); and John Dillenberger, *Protestant Thought and Natural Science* (Garden City, N.Y.: Doubleday, 1960). The topic has generated an enormous quantity of scholarly debate; for some key essays in the debate and full bibliographic suggestions, see Charles Webster, ed., *The Intellectual Revolution of the Seventeenth Century* (London: Routledge and Kegan Paul, 1974). Webster steers clear of the causal argument in observing that "English science rose into prominence along with puritanism" (p. 15).

[67] *The Unreasonableness of Infidelity* [Greaves, *Puritan Revolution and Educational Thought*, p. 12].

⁶⁸ *The Logician's School-Master* [Miller, *Seventeenth Century*, p. 162].

⁶⁹ *A Brief Exposition . . . Upon the Whole Book of Ecclesiastes* [Miller, *Seventeenth Century*, p. 212].

⁷⁰ Morison, *Intellectual Life*, p. 89.

⁷¹ *Discourse Concerning the Danger of Apostasy* [Miller/Johnson, 1:21]. Mather was probably alluding to Luther, who had written, "I am convinced that without knowledge of literature pure theology cannot at all endure, just as heretofore, when letters have declined and lain prostrate, theology, too, has wretchedly fallen and lain prostrate; nay, I see that there has never been a great revelation of the Word of God unless he has first prepared the way by the rise and prosperity of languages and letters. . . . Certainly it is my desire that there shall be as many poets and rhetoricians as possible, because I see that by these studies, as by no other means, people are wonderfully fitted for the grasping of sacred truth and for handling it skillfully and happily" (Letter to Eobanus Hessus [Robert Ulic, *A History of Religious Education* (New York: New York University Press, 1968), pp. 110–11]).

⁷² *Institutes of the Christian Religion.* 2.2.15. Elsewhere Calvin wrote, "The sons of Cain, though deprived of the Spirit of regeneration, were yet endued with gifts of no despicable kind; just as the experience of all ages teaches us how widely the rays of divine light have shone on unbelieving nations, for the benefit of the present life; and we see . . . that the excellent gifts of the Spirit are diffused through the whole human race" (Commentary on Gen. 4:20).

⁷³ Not all Puritans agreed with the majority viewpoint that I outline. William Dell was the most vocal disparager of pagan learning. He wrote, for example, that students should "learn the Greek and Latin tongues especially from Christians, and so without the lies, fables, follies, vanities, whoredoms, lust, pride, revenge, etc., of the heathens, especially seeing neither their words nor their phrases are meet for Christians to take in their mouths; and most necessary it is that Christians should forget the names of their gods and muses, which were but devils and damned creatures, and all their mythology and fabulous inventions and let them all go to Satan from whence they came" (Foster Watson, p. 535).

⁷⁴ *Woe to Drunkards* [Miller/Johnson, 1:22]. The same emphasis was present in Luther, who wrote, "The fine liberal arts, invented and brought to light by learned and outstanding people — even though those people were heathen — are serviceable and useful to people for this life. Moreover, they are creations and noble, precious gifts. . . . [God] has used them and still uses them according to his good pleasure, for the praise, honor, and glory of his holy name" (Comment inscribed in a book of classical poetry [Plass, 1:450]).

⁷⁵ *A Presidential Address* [Miller/Johnson, 2:721].

⁷⁶ *A Commencement Sermon* [Miller/Johnson, 2:706].

⁷⁷ *The Christian's Portion* [George, p. 347].

⁷⁸ *A Congregational Church Is a Catholic Visible Church* [Miller, *Seventeenth Century*, p. 180].

⁷⁹ Greaves, *Puritan Revolution and Educational Thought*, p. 39.

⁸⁰ *CPW*, 2:377.

⁸¹ *Book of Discipline* [Porter, *Tudor England* , p. 199].

⁸² Cairns, p. 331.

⁸³ *A Christian Directory* [Tichi, p. 58]. Luther had written in a similar vein, "I shall say nothing here about the pure pleasure a man gets from having studied, even though he never holds an office of any kind, how at home by himself he can read all kinds of things, talk and associate with educated people" (*A Sermon on Keeping Children in School* [*Luther Works*, 46:243]).

⁸⁴ *Treatise on the Necessity of Humane Learning for the Gospel Preacher* [Ashley Smith, p. 28]. Calvin also valued the arts for their own sake: "Although the invention of the harp and of similar instruments of music may minister to our pleasure rather than to our necessity, still it is not to be thought altogether superfluous; much less does it deserve . . . to be condemned" (Commentary on Gen. 4:20).

⁸⁵ *The Mourner's Cordial Against Excessive Sorrow* [Lowrie, p. 225].

⁸⁶ *Heavenly Merchandise* [Lowrie, p. 205].

CHAPTER 10

[1] Miller, *Seventeenth Century*, p. 421.

[2] *Works* [Breen, p. 8].

[3] E. Digby Baltzell, *Puritan Boston and Quaker Philadelphia*.

[4] *The High Esteem Which God Hath of the Death of His Saints* [Miller, *Nature's Nation*, p. 38].

[5] *A Model of Christian Charity* [McGiffert, p. 32].

[6] *A Reply to an Answer* [Walzer, p. 182].

[7] *The Throne Established by Righteousness* [Miller/Johnson, 1:275].

[8] *Connecticut Records* [Edmund Morgan, *Puritan Family*, p. 145].

[9] Morgan, p. 145.

[10] Emerson, *Puritanism in America*, p. 134.

[11] Ibid.

[12] *The Parable of the Wicked Mammon* [Campbell, p. 111].

[13] *The Saints' Cordials* [McGee, p. 202].

[14] Unidentified source, quoted in Miller, *Seventeenth Century*, p. 416.

[15] Miller/Johnson, 1:197–98.

[16] *A Sermon Preached at Paul's Cross* [Hyma, p. 182].

[17] *A Treatise of the Vocations* . . . [White, p. 245].

[18] *A Holy Commonwealth* [Schneider, p. 15].

[19] *God's Promise* [Carroll, p. 133].

[20] *The Character of a Good Ruler* [Miller/Johnson, 1:252].

[21] Quoted in Miller, *Seventeenth Century*, p. 423.

[22] *A Survey* [Carroll, pp. 132–33].

[23] Timothy H. Breen and Stephen Foster, "The Puritans' Greatest Achievement: A Study of Social Cohesion in Seventeenth-Century Massachusetts," in Vaughan and Bremer, pp. 110–27.

[24] *A Treatise of the Vocations* . . . [Edmund Morgan, *Political Ideas*, p. 56].

[25] Richard Bernard, *The Ready Way to Good Works* [George, p. 156].

[26] Hill, *Society and Puritanism*, p. 136.

[27] *Works* [George, p. 172].

[28] *A Sermon Made in the Shrouds in Paul's* [Hyma, p. 181].

[29] *Spittle Sermon* [Hill, *Puritanism and Revolution*, p. 234].

[30] *Philanthropy in England, 1480–1660* (London: Allen and Unwin, 1959).

[31] Ibid., pp. 17, 20, 151.

[32] *Diary* [Knappen, *Two Elizabethan Puritan Diaries*, p. 107].

[33] *Acts and Monuments* [Emerson, *English Puritanism*, p. 50].

[34] Hill, *Society and Puritanism*, p. 277. Knappen, *Tudor Puritanism*, concludes that the typical Puritan minister "opened his purse to needy prisoners, assisted struggling students through the university, and sold his crops to the poor below the market rate" (p. 344).

[35] Hyma, p. 86.

[36] *London's Charity Enlarged* [Jordan, p. 213].

[37] *New-England Pleaded With* [Miller, *Nature's Nation*, p. 30].

[38] *The Day of Trouble Is Near* [Miller, *Nature's Nation*, p. 31].

[39] McGiffert, pp. 114–16.

[40] Keayne's last will is reprinted in McGiffert, pp. 117–21.

[41] *Chapters from A Christian Directory*, ed. Tawney, pp. 102–12.

[42] *Meditations and Disquisitions Upon the First Psalm* [McGee, p. 192].

[43] *Breast-Plate of Faith and Love* [McGee, p. 192].

[44] *A Spiritual Antidote Against Sinful Contagion* [McGee, p. 192].

[45] Quoted in White, pp. 190–91. Here is another sample of Perkins's denunciations: "In the calling of the merchant and tradesman, there is false weights, and false measures. . . ; setting a gloss on wares by powdering, starching, blowing, dark shops . . . and all manner of bad dealing. . . . In the landlord, there is racking of rents, taking immoderate fines, enclosing of grounds that have lain common time out of mind: and the cause is want of sobriety and temperance in diet and apparel. In the husbandman and cornmonger, there is exceeding injustice in hoarding up grain till the time of further advantage: and in taking whatsoever they can get for their own, though it be to the shedding of the blood of the poor" (White, p. 192).

[46] *The Last Work of a Believer* [Rooy, p. 108].

[47] *The Life of Faith* [Rooy, p. 109].

[48] *Conscience, With the Power and Cases Thereof* [George, pp. 155–56]. Cotton Mather spoke an identical language of moral concern: "Neighbors! you stand related unto one another. And you should . . . excel in the duties of good neighborhood. . . . The orphans and widows, and so all the children of affliction in the neighborhood, must be visited and relieved with all agreeable kindness" (*Bonifacius* [Miller, *American Puritans*, pp. 216–17]).

[49] *Parentator* [Edmund Morgan, *Puritan Family*, p. 4].

[50] *A Serious Exhortation to the Present and Succeeding Generation in New England* [Edmund Morgan, *Puritan Family*, p. 102].

[51] *The Marrow of Theology*, p. 236.

[52] *Of the Good Education of Children* [Emerson, *English Puritanism*, p. 153].

[53] *Tudor Puritanism*, p. 348.

[54] *Works* [Hill, *Puritanism and Revolution*, pp. 227–28].

[55] Ibid., p. 231.

[56] *Puritanism and Revolution*, p. 222.

[57] *Commentary Upon . . . Malachi* [Hill, *Society and Puritanism*, p. 277].

[58] *God's Doings, and Man's Duty* [Hill, *Puritanism and Revolution*, p. 234].

[59] Thomas Fuller, *Worthies* [Hill, *Society and Puritanism*, p. 138]. Fuller also records that John White of Dorchester encouraged everyone to work, "piety breeding industry, and industry procuring plenty unto it"; significantly, "a beggar was not then to be seen in the town" (Hill, p. 138).

[60] *David Serving His Generation* [Carden, p. 5].

[61] The characterization of Puritanism as espousing the individualism of the common person and the contrast to Renaissance humanistic individualism comes from Eric Mercer, *English Art, 1553–1625* (Oxford: Oxford University Press, 1962), p. 6. Haller says about the Puritans that "a lively expectation of becoming 'somebody' does not conduce a willingness to remain nobody. Men who have assurance that they are to inherit heaven have a way of presently taking possession of the earth" (*Rise of Puritanism*, p. 162).

[62] William Tyndale, *The Obedience of a Christian Man* [Campbell, p. 117].

[63] Hugh Latimer, *A Most Faithful Sermon Preached Before the King's Most Excellent Majesty* [White, p. 123].

[64] William Perkins, *Works* [Hill, *Puritanism and Revolution*, p. 237].

[65] Samuel Willard, *The Character of a Good Ruler* [Miller/Johnson, 1:254].

[66] William Dell, *The Way of True Peace and Unity* [Woodhouse, p. 312].

[67] Stone, *Crisis*, p. 745.

[68] Perry, p. 192. The best collection of primary documents on the democratic spirit of the Puritans in *Puritanism and Liberty*, ed. A. S. P. Woodhouse.

[69] *Letter to Clarendon* [Baltzell, p. 80].

[70] Hanserd Knollys, *A Glimpse of Sion's Glory* [Woodhouse, p. 234].

[71] *Christ Above All Exalted* [McGee, p. 191].

[72] *The Way of True Peace and Unity* [Woodhouse, pp. 308–9]. Thomas Adams similarly claimed that "it is not the birth, but the new birth, that makes men truly noble" (*The Holy Choice* [Walzer, p. 235]).

[73] *The Soul's Vocation* [Miller, *Errand into the Wilderness*, p. 46].

[74] *Animadversions* [Haller, *Liberty and Reformation*, p. 55].

[75] Quoted in Miller, *Seventeenth Century*, p. 408.

[76] Election sermon of 1669 [Miller, *Seventeenth Century*, p. 421].

[77] *The Tenure of Kings and Magistrates* [*CPW*, 3:206].

[78] Miller/Johnson, 1:273.

[79] Foster, p. 156.

[80] Margaret James writes that "Puritanism helped to bring about the birth of the spirit of modern democracy" (p. 25). A. S. P. Woodhouse believes that the Puritans contributed "the habits of thought and feeling on which democracy must necessarily rely, and in whose absence it would inevitably break down" ("Religion and Some Foundations of English Democracy," *Philosophical Review*, 61, no. 4 [Oct. 1952]: 510).

CHAPTER 11

[1] Quoted in Crawford, p. 495.

[2] Philip Stubbes, *Anatomy of Abuses* [Crawford, pp. 499–500].

[3] Quoted in Scholes, p. 235. Knappen, *Tudor Puritanism*, pp. 434–35, draws attention to the same evidence and attributes the whitewashing to Elizabeth's injunction.

[4] Crouch, pp. 136–37; Scholes, p. 222.

[5] A beginning bibliography would include the following items: Crouch, *Puritanism and Art: An Inquiry into a Popular Fallacy* (1910); Edward Dowden, *Puritan and Anglican: Studies in Literature* (London: Kegan Paul, 1910); Scholes, *The Puritans and Music* (1934); Roland Frye, *Perspective on Man: Literature and the Christian Tradition* (Philadelphia: Westminster, 1961), pp. 171–79; Sasek, *The Literary Temper of the English Puritans* (1961); Sacvan Bercovitch, *The American Puritan Imagination* (Cambridge: Cambridge University Press, 1974); Daly, *God's Altar: The World and the Flesh in Puritan Poetry* (1978); John Wilson, "Calvin and the Arts," *Third Way*, 2, no. 2 (1978): 3–5; Lewalski, *Protestant Poetics and the Seventeenth-Century Religious Lyric* (1979); Emory Elliott, ed., *Puritan Influences in American Literature* (Urbana: University of Illinois Press, 1979); Alan Sinfield, *Literature in Protestant England, 1560–1660* (London: Croom Helm, 1983); E. Beatrice Batson, *John Bunyan: Allegory and Imagination* (London: Croom Helm, 1984).

[6] Hans-Peter Wagner, *Puritan Attitudes Towards Recreation in Early Seventeenth-Century New England* (Frankfurt: Verlag Peter Lang, 1982).

[7] Solberg, pp. 46–52, is an example of such misinterpretation.

[8] *Christian Warfare* [Foster, p. 106]. William Perkins wrote, "Rest from labor with the refreshing of the body and mind is necessary, because man's nature is like a bow, which being always bent and used is soon broken in pieces" (*The Whole Treatise* [Wagner, pp. 53–54]).

[9] *The Poor Man's Help* [Wagner, p. 46]. According to Thomas Cartwright the sixth commandment is broken when a person "useth not the honest recreation, wherewith his health may be maintained: for we must not think that there are no more ways to kill a man's self but with a knife" (Pearson, p. 403).

[10] Scholes, pp. 110–11.

[11] Miller/Johnson, 2:171.

[12] Quoted in Wagner, p. 22.

[13] Francis White, quoted in Wagner, p. 45.

[14] William Burkitt, *The Poor Man's Help* [Wagner, p. 50].

[15] William Perkins, *A Treatise of the Vocations or Callings of Men* [Breward, p. 471].

[16] McNeill, p. 40.

[17] Cotton Mather, *A Christian at His Calling* [Foster, p. 107].

[18] Richard Baxter, *A Christian Directory* [Weber, p. 262].

[19] *A Christian Directory* [Wagner, pp. 48–49].

[20] The rules were these: (1) recreations must be "of the best report," (2) they "must be profitable to ourselves and others, and they must tend to the glory of God," (3) their purpose "must be to refresh our bodies and minds," and (4) their use "must be moderate and sparing" of time and "affections" (*Cases of Conscience* [Sasek, p. 113]).

[21] *A Christian Directory* [Sasek, p. 114].

[22] *A Christian Directory* [Weber, p. 261]. Baxter also wrote, "To redeem the time is to see that we cast none of it away in vain; but use every minute of it as a most precious thing, and spend it wholly in the way of duty" (*A Christian Directory* [Kitch, p. 170]).

[23] Walzer, p. 210.

[24] *Tetrachordon* [*CPW*, 2:597].

[25] I have taken all of the examples in this paragraph from Alice Morse Earle, *The Sabbath in Puritan New England* (New York: Scribner, 1893), pp. 246–47.

[26] Quoted in Fleming, p. 21.

[27] *Grace Abounding to the Chief of Sinners*, pp. 12–13.

[28] Schnucker, pp. 356–64, has a section on the topic.

[29] Louis B. Wright, *Colonial America*, p. 169.

[30] Quoted in Seaver, p. 38.

[31] These examples are taken from Davies, *Worship and Theology . . . 1603–1690*, p. 165.

[32] Peter Lewis, p. 61.

[33] *Letters and Journals* [Haller, *Liberty and Reformation*, p. 111]. Baillie's final verdict is a small classic: "The humour of this people is very various, and inclinable to singularities, to differ from all the world, and one from another, and shortly from themselves."

[34] Richard Sibbes, *Beams of Divine Light* [George, p. 131].

[35] *Autobiography*, p. 102.

[36] Frances M. Caulkins, *History of Norwich, Connecticut* [Edmund Morgan, *Puritan Family*, p. 50].

[37] *Life and Letters of John Winthrop* [Edmund Morgan, *Puritan Family*, p. 50].

[38] *Diary* [Edmund Morgan, *Puritan Family*, pp. 97–98].

[39] Ibid.

[40] *Diary* [Wagner, pp. 102–3].

[41] *Diary* [Greven, *Protestant Temperament*, p. 67].

[42] *Works* [George, p. 282].

[43] Ibid., p. 279.

[44] *Of Domestical Duties* [Haller, "Puritan Art of Love," p. 251].

[45] *The Well-Ordered Family* [Edmund Morgan, *Puritan Family*, p. 44].

[46] *A Christian Directory* [Schlatter, p. 11].

[47] *The History of New England* [Edmund Morgan, *Puritan Family*, p. 44].

[48] *The Copy of a Letter Written . . . to His Sister* [Edmund Morgan, *Puritan Family*, p. 44].

[49] White, p. 161.

[50] Quoted in Greven, *Protestant Temperament*, p. 52.

[51] During the sixteenth and seventeenth centuries, literacy among women increased, their share in opinion-shaping was enhanced, their role as wives and mothers was exalted, their chances for education increased somewhat, and their legal status improved. Although the laws allowed husbands to beat their wives, Puritan preachers denounced it from the pulpit. The first professional women painters, publishers of music, and poets of significance date from the Puritan Protectorate. Puritans were not necessarily the main cause of such gains, but they played their role in this cultural movement of their time. For a brief comment, see Christopher Hill, *The Intellectual Origins of the English Revolution* (Oxford: Oxford University Press, 1965), pp. 274–75; more detailed studies include Ulrich, *Good Wives;* and Roberta Hamilton, *The Liberation of Women: A Study of Patriarchy and Capitalism,* ch. 7.

[52] *Tudor Puritanism,* p. 352.

[53] Louis B. Wright, *Colonial America,* pp. 166–68.

[54] *An Admonition to the Parliament* [*Puritan Manifestoes,* p. 21].

[55] *Reformation of the Church* [Jarman, p. 110].

[56] R. C. Richardson, pp. 80–81.

[57] Collinson, p. 380.

[58] Quoted in Miller, *Seventeenth Century,* p. 470.

[59] Ibid.

[60] The source is Bruno Ryves, quoted in Scholes, p. 233. See also John Phillips, *The Reformation of Images: Destruction of Art in England, 1535–1660* (Berkeley: University of California Press, 1973).

[61] Scholes, p. 233.

[62] Thomas Becon, *The Catechism of Thomas Becon* [Elliott, pp. 63–64].

[63] Benjamin Wadsworth, *A Course of Sermons on Early Piety* [Edmund Morgan, *Puritan Family,* p. 93].

[64] John Robinson, *Of Children and Their Education* [Greven, *Child-Rearing Concepts,* pp. 13–14].

[65] *Diary of Samuel Sewall* [Stone, *Family,* p. 212].

[66] Diaries of Cotton Mather [Stone, *Family,* p. 212].

[67] *Diary of Cotton Mather* [Greven, *Protestant Temperament,* p. 67].

[68] Quoted in Greven, *Protestant Temperament,* p. 70.

[69] Ibid.

CHAPTER 12

[1] *Life and Letters of John Winthrop* [Edmund Morgan, *Puritan Family,* p. 51]. Winthrop's terminology here is reminiscent of Richard Baxter's classic *The Saints' Everlasting Rest,* which took as its theme Hebrews 4:9 ("There remaineth therefore a rest to the people of God"). That text, wrote Baxter, presupposes for every person "an end towards which he moveth for rest. . . . This can be only God, the chief good. He that taketh anything else for his happiness is out of the way [from] the first step. The principal damning sin is to make anything besides God our end or rest" (p. 32).

[2] *Winthrop Papers* [McGee, p. 45].

[3] Miller/Johnson, 2:715.

[4] *A Complete Body of Divinity* [Daly, p. 63].

[5] Richard Steele, *The Tradesman's Calling* [Kitch, p. 116].

[6] *The Fountain Opened* [Lowrie, p. 227]. Richard Rogers wrote in his diary, "I see again that faith and godliness are the upholders of our joy, and make an hard estate easy and a prosperous fruitful" (Knappen, *Two Elizabethan Puritan Diaries*, p. 100).

[7] *A Collection of Original Papers Relative to the History of the Colony of Massachusetts Bay* [Hyma, p. 231].

[8] *Works*, New, p. 43. Richard Rogers wrote, "The Lord knoweth that . . . patience and continual delighting in the Lord of my salvation are the riches which I have desired to be furnished with" (*Diary* [Knappen, *Two Elizabethan Puritan Diaries*, p. 88]).

[9] *The First Sermon* . . . [John F. Wilson, p. 40].

[10] *The Beatitudes*, p. 232.

[11] Quoted in James Fulton Maclear, " 'The Heart of New England Rent': The Mystical Element in Early Puritan History," in *The New England Puritans*, ed. Sydney V. James (New York: Harper and Row, 1968), p. 52.

[12] *The Calling of the Ministry* [Brown, p. 80].

[13] *A Holy Commonwealth* [Schneider, p. 15].

[14] *The Plague of Plagues*, p. 284. In the same conclusion Venning called holiness "the beauty of earth and Heaven, without which we cannot live well on earth, nor shall ever live in Heaven" (p. 282).

[15] *The Art of Prophesying* [Breward, p. 349].

[16] Quoted in Schücking, p. 51.

[17] *Diary* [Knappen, *Two Elizabethan Puritan Diaries*, p. 118].

[18] *Bowels Opened* [George, p. 113].

[19] *Works* [Porter, *Reformation and Reaction*, p. 139].

[20] *Christian Calling* [Miller/Johnson, 1:319].

[21] *The Principles of the Christian Religion* [Schlatter, p. 189].

[22] *English Literature in the Sixteenth Century Excluding Drama* (Oxford: Oxford University Press, 1954), p. 190.

[23] Schlatter, p. 11. Perry writes in a similar vein, "The puritan's other-worldliness was not a withdrawal from the world, but a living *in* the world in accordance with other-worldly standards" (p. 305).

[24] Richard Greenham, *Works* [Hill, *Society and Puritanism*, p. 443].

[25] Swinnock, *The Christian Man's Calling* [Schlatter, p. 189]; Steele, *The Tradesman's Calling* [Schlatter, p. 195]. Richard Rogers recorded his resolve to make "godliness in every part" of his life "mine occupation and trade" (*Diary* [Knappen, *Two Elizabethan Puritan Diaries*, p. 64]).

[26] *Works* [Breen, p. 12].

[27] Quoted in Davies, *Worship of the English Puritans*, pp. 9–10.

[28] *The Gospel-Covenant* [McGiffert, p. 35]. Schneider writes regarding the Puritans, "Religion was not a department or phase of social life; it was the end and aim of all life" (p. 23).

[29] Quoted in Watkins, p. 64.

[30] *The Saints' Everlasting Rest* [Kaufmann, p. 216].

[31] *The Memoirs of Walter Pringle of Greenknow; or, Some Few of the Free Mercies of God to Him* [Watkins, p. 63].

[32] *A Sermon Wherein Is Showed That It Is the Duty and . . . Care of Believers . . . to Live in the Constant Exercise of Grace* [Elliott, p. 179].

[33] *Diary* [McGee, pp. 15–16]. The Puritan Thomas Case claimed that the difficulties of life are the occasion "to mind what new duty God expects, what new grace he is to exert and exercise" (*Correction, Instruction: or, a Treatise of Afflictions* [McGee, p. 35]).

34 Cited in Watkins, p. 65.

35 *The Soul's Conflict* . . . [Lewalski, pp. 160–61].

36 *The Practical Christian* [Kaufmann, p. 213].

37 *Prima, Media, and Ultima* [Kaufmann, p. 206].

38 *A Man in Christ* [Daly, p. 74].

39 *Wonderful Works* [Middlekauff, p. 283].

40 *Works* [Miller, *Errand into the Wilderness*, p. 77].

41 *The Saints' Everlasting Rest*, p. 173.

42 *A Christian Directory* [Kitch, p. 114].

43 *The Reformed Pastor*, p. 102.

44 Quoted in Lowrie, p. 174.

45 *Beams of Divine Light* [George, p. 412].

46 Quoted in Emerson, *English Puritanism*, p. 148.

47 *Works* [Perry, p. 220].

48 *Grace Abounding to the Chief of Sinners*, pp. 16–17.

49 *Wonder-Working Providence* [James F. Maclear, "New England and the Fifth Monarchy . . . ," in Vaughan and Bremer, p. 72].

50 *A New Pathway Unto Prayer* [Bailey, *Thomas Becon*, p. 23].

51 *Of Plymouth Plantation* [Emerson, *Puritanism in America*, p. 42]. Cotton Mather was equally optimistic about prospects in New England: "The God of heaven had carried a nation into a wilderness upon the designs of a glorious reformation" (*Magnalia Christi Americana* [Schneider, p. 31]).

52 Willard, *The Fountain Opened* [Lowrie, p. 234]; Milton, *Areopagitica* [*CPW*, 2:558].

53 *Of Education* [*CPW*, 2:379].

54 Richard Sibbes, *Works* [Rooy, p. 63].

55 *Balm for Bleeding England and Ireland* [McGee, p. 44].

56 *The Works of John Robinson* [Perry, p. 355].

57 *Letters of Samuel Rutherford* [Hill, *God's Englishman*, p. 226].

58 *Letters* [Hill, *God's Englishman*, pp. 226–27].

59 *Works* [Hill, *God's Englishman*, p. 231].

60 *The Christian's Two Chief Lessons* [Miller, *Errand Into the Wilderness*, p. 87].

61 *The Saint's Daily Exercise* [Miller, *Errand*, p. 88]. Richard Sibbes said that "it is not so much the having of grace as grace in exercise that preserves the soul" (*Works* [Miller, *Errand*, p. 88]).

62 *Heaven Ravished* [John Wilson, p. 192].

63 Quoted in Bremer, p. 24.

64 *CPW*, 2:515.

65 Quoted in Joseph C. McLelland, *The Reformation and Its Significance Today* (Philadelphia: Westminster, 1962), p. 74.

66 *The Saints' Everlasting Rest*, pp. 34–35.

67 *A Serious Exhortation to the Present and Succeeding Generation in New England* [Edmund Morgan, *Puritan Family*, p. 102].

68 *Works*, 14:311.

69 *Works* [Hill, *God's Englishman*, p. 238].

70 *The Marrow of Theology*, p. 193.

[71] *Essays to Do Good* [Perry, p. 257].

[72] *The Minister* [Middlekauff, p. 191].

[73] Baltzell, p. 44.

[74] *The Parable of the Ten Virgins* [Strier, p. 145]. Strier notes that "the stress on experience is central to historical Protestantism" (p. 145).

[75] Sibbes, *A Learned Commentary* . . . [Strier, p. 145]; Tyndale, *Works* [Campbell, p. 204].

[76] *The Beatitudes*, pp. 172, 174.

[77] John Field, *The Second Part of a Register* [Seaver, p. 51].

[78] Quoted in Miller, *Seventeenth Century*, p. 42.

[79] William Perkins, *Works* [George, p. 138].

[80] *The Hurt of Hearing Mass* [Murray, p. 17].

[81] *Works* [Hill, *Puritanism and Revolution*, p. 237].

[82] *Reliquiae* [Mitchell, p. 272].

[83] Dickens, p. 138.

[84] Sibbes, *Yea and Amen* [George, p. 383]; Owen, *Works*, 14:314, 311.

[85] *The Responsibility of Mind in a Civilization of Machines* (Amherst: University of Massachusetts Press, 1979), p. 73.

[86] *Certain Sermons* [Rogers, p. 245].

[87] *Magnalia Christi Americana* [Emerson, *Puritanism in America*, p. 25].

[88] Samuel Willard, *The Truly Blessed Man* [Lowrie, p. 39].

[89] Quoted in Brown, p. 181.

[90] *The Calling of the Ministry* [Brown, p. 79].

[91] Trinterud, p. 214.

[92] Richard Sibbes, *Beams of Divine Light* [George, p. 131]. William Adams said that the believer "hath much business to do in and about the world, which he is vigorously to attend, and . . . upon which he is to bestow affection" (quoted in Emerson, *Puritanism in America*, pp. 141–42).

[93] Richard Sibbes, *The Saint's Cordials* [George, p. 125].

[94] Richard Sibbes, *Light From Heaven* [Kaufmann, p. 134].

[95] Jeremiah Burroughs, *Two Treatises* . . . [Hyma, p. 243].

[96] *Works* [George, p. 229].

[97] *The Saints' Everlasting Rest*, p. 35. In *A Christian Directory* Baxter wrote, "Though God need none of our good works, yet that which is good materially pleaseth Him, as it tendeth toward His glory, and our own and others' benefit, which He delighteth in." [Merton, p. 61].

[98] Increase Mather, *David Serving His Generation* [Carden, p. 5].

[99] Introduction to *Puritanism in America* [no pagination].

[100] *Memoirs of the Life of Colonel Hutchinson*, p. 4.

[101] *A Golden Chain* . . . [Breward, p. 177].

[102] *The Beatitudes*, p. 251.

[103] Ibid., p. 235.

[104] Anne Bradstreet, *Works* [Daly, p. 82].

[105] Ralph Venning, *The Plague of Plagues*, p. 264.

[106] Cotton Mather, *Magnalia Christi Americana* [Foster, p. 121].

[107] John Owen, *Works*, 16:82.

[108] Answer to the opening question of the *Westminster Shorter Catechism*.

[109] Thomas Watson, *The Beatitudes*, p. 251.

[110] Thomas Cartwright, quoted in Pearson, p. 403.

[111] Lucy Hutchinson, Preface to *Memoirs of the Life of Colonel Hutchinson*, p. 5.

[112] Thomas Adams, *Works* [Ball, p. 3].

[113] *A Treatise of the Vocations or Callings of Men* [Breward, p. 464].

[114] *The Saints' Everlasting Rest*, p. 45.

[115] *Works* [Ball, p. 58].

[116] *Works* [Perry, p. 277].

Bibliography

The following bibliography is limited to the works cited most frequently in the footnotes, where they appear in abbreviated form. Some additional, less frequently cited sources are included in the further readings at the end of chapters and in footnotes containing complete publication information.

Ames, William. *Conscience with the Power and Cases Thereof.* 1639; reprint Norwood, N.J.: Walter J. Johnson, 1975.

————. *The Marrow of Theology,* ed. John D. Eusden. Boston: Pilgrim, 1968.

Ashley, Maurice. *Oliver Cromwell and the Puritan Revolution.* London: English Universities Press, 1958.

Avis, Paul D. L. *The Church in the Theology of the Reformers.* Atlanta: John Knox, 1981.

Axtell, James. *The School Upon a Hill: Education and Society in Colonial New England.* New York: W. W. Norton, 1976.

Babbage, Stuart B. *Puritanism and Richard Bancroft.* London: S.P.C.K., 1962.

Bailey, Derrick Sherwin. *Sexual Relation in Christian Thought.* New York: Harper and Brothers, 1959.

————. *Thomas Becon and the Reformation of the Church in England.* Edinburgh: Oliver and Boyd, 1952.

Ball, Bryan W. *The English Connection: The Puritan Roots of Seventh-day Adventist Belief.* Cambridge: James Clarke, 1981.

Baltzell, E. Digby. *Puritan Boston and Quaker Philadelphia.* New York: The Free Press, 1979.

Baroway, Israel. "The Bible as Poetry in the English Renaissance: An Introduction." *Journal of English and Germanic Philology* 32 (1933): 447–80.

Baxter, Richard. *Chapters from A Christian Directory,* ed. Jeannette Tawney. London: G. Bell and Sons, 1925.

————. *The Autobiography of Richard Baxter.* London: J. M. Dent, 1931.

————. *The Reformed Pastor,* ed. William Brown. Edinburgh: Banner of Truth Trust, 1974.

————. *The Saints' Everlasting Rest.* Westwood, N.J.: Fleming H. Revell, 1962.

Bolton, Samuel. *The True Bounds of Christian Freedom*. Edinburgh: Banner of Truth Trust, 1964.

Breen, T. H. *The Character of the Good Ruler: A Study of Puritan Political Ideas in New England, 1630–1730*. New Haven: Yale University Press, 1970.

Bremer, Francis J. *The Puritan Experiment: New England Society from Bradford to Edwards*. New York: St. Martin's, 1976.

Breward, Ian, ed. *The Work of William Perkins*. Appleford: Sutton Courtenay, 1970.

Brown, John. *Puritan Preaching in England*. New York: Scribner, 1900.

Bunyan, John. *Grace Abounding to the Chief of Sinners and The Pilgrim's Progress*, ed. Roger Sharrock. London: Oxford University Press, 1966.

Cairns, Earle E. "The Puritan Philosophy of Education." *Bibliotheca Sacra* 104 (1947): 326–36.

Campbell, W. E. *Erasmus, Tyndale, and More*. London: Eyre and Spottiswoode, 1949.

Carden, Allen. "The Word of God in Puritan New England: Seventeenth-Century Perspectives on the Nature and Authority of the Bible." *Andrews University Seminary Studies* 18 (Spring 1980): 1–16.

Carroll, Peter N. *Puritanism and the Wilderness: The Intellectual Significance of the New England Frontier, 1629–1700*. New York: Columbia University Press, 1969.

Clebsch, William A. *England's Earliest Protestants, 1520–1535*. New Haven: Yale University Press, 1964.

Cole, William G. *Sex in Christianity and Psychoanalysis*. New York: Oxford University Press, 1966.

Collinson, Patrick. *The Elizabethan Puritan Movement*. Berkeley: University of California Press, 1967.

Coolidge, John S. *The Pauline Renaissance in England: Puritanism and the Bible*. Oxford: Oxford University Press, 1970.

Crawford, Mary Caroline. *Social Life in Old New England*. New York: Grosset and Dunlap, 1914.

Crouch, Joseph. *Puritanism and Art: An Inquiry into a Popular Fallacy*. London: Cassell, 1910.

Curtis, Mark H. *Oxford and Cambridge in Transition, 1558–1642*. Oxford: Oxford University Press, 1959.

Daly, Robert. *God's Altar: The World and the Flesh in Puritan Poetry*. Berkeley: University of California Press, 1978.

Davies, Horton. *The Worship of the English Puritans*. Westminster: Dacre, 1948.

————. *Worship and Theology in England: From Andrewes to Baxter and Fox, 1603–1690*. Princeton: Princeton University Press, 1975.

————. *Worship and Theology in England: From Cranmer to Hooker, 1534–1603*. Princeton: Princeton University Press, 1970.

Demos, John. *A Little Commonwealth: Family Life in Plymouth Colony*. New York: Oxford University Press, 1970.

Dennison, James T. *The Puritan Doctrine of the Sabbath in England, 1532–1700.* Pittsburgh: Pittsburgh Theological Seminary thesis, 1973.

Dickens, A. G. *The English Reformation.* New York: Schocken Books, 1964.

Elliott, Emory. *Power and the Pulpit in Puritan New England.* Princeton: Princeton University Press, 1975.

Emerson, Everett, ed. *English Puritanism from John Hooper to John Milton.* Durham, North Carolina: Duke University Press, 1968.

————. *Puritanism in America, 1620–1750.* Boston: Twayne, 1977.

Eusden, John Dykstra. *Puritans, Lawyers, and Politics in Early Seventeenth Century England.* New Haven: Yale University Press, 1958.

Fleming, Sanford. *Children and Puritanism.* New Haven: Yale University Press, 1933.

Forrester, W. R. *Christian Vocation.* New York: Scribner, 1953.

Foster, Stephen. *Their Solitary Way: The Puritan Social Ethic in the First Century of Settlement in New England.* New Haven: Yale University Press, 1971.

Frye, Roland M. "The Teachings of Classical Puritanism on Conjugal Love." *Studies in the Renaissance,* 2 (1955): 148–59.

George, Charles H., and Katherine George. *The Protestant Mind of the English Reformation, 1570–1640.* Princeton: Princeton University Press, 1961.

Gooch, G. P. *English Democratic Ideas in the Seventeenth Century.* Cambridge: Cambridge University Press, 1927.

Greaves, Richard L. *Society and Religion in Elizabethan England.* Minneapolis: University of Minnesota Press, 1981.

————. *The Puritan Revolution and Educational Thought: Background for Reform.* New Brunswick: Rutgers University Press, 1969.

Green, Robert W., ed. *Protestantism and Capitalism: The Weber Thesis and Its Critics.* Boston: D. C. Heath, 1959.

Greven, Philip, ed. *Child-Rearing Concepts, 1628–1861.* Itasca, Ill.: F. E. Peacock, 1973.

————. *The Protestant Temperament: Patterns of Child-Rearing, Religious Experience, and the Self in Early America.* New York: Knopf, 1977.

Halkett, John. *Milton and the Idea of Matrimony.* New Haven: Yale University Press, 1970.

Haller, William. *Liberty and Reformation in the Puritan Revolution.* New York: Columbia University Press, 1955, 1963.

————. *The Rise of Puritanism.* New York: Columbia University Press, 1938.

Haller, William, and Malleville Haller. "The Puritan Art of Love." *Huntington Library Quarterly* 5 (1941–42): 235–72.

Hambrick-Stowe, Charles E. *The Practice of Piety: Puritan Devotional Disciplines in Seventeenth-Century New England.* Chapel Hill: University of North Carolina Press, 1982.

Hamilton, Roberta. *The Liberation of Women: A Study of Patriarchy and Capitalism.* Winchester, Mass.: Allen Unwin, 1978.

Harkness, Georgia. *John Calvin: The Man and His Ethics.* Nashville: Abingdon, 1958.

Hawyard, F. H. *The Unknown Cromwell*. London: Allen and Unwin, 1934.

Hill, Christopher. *Change and Continuity in Seventeenth-Century England*. Cambridge: Harvard University Press, 1975.

————. *God's Englishman: Oliver Cromwell and the English Revolution*. New York: Harper and Row, 1970.

————. *Puritanism and Revolution: Studies in Interpretation of the English Revolution of the Seventeenth Century*. London: Secker and Warburg, 1958.

————. *Society and Puritanism in Pre-Revolutionary England*. New York: Schocken Books, 1964.

Holifield, E. Brooks. *The Covenant Sealed: The Development of Puritan Sacramental Theology in Old and New England, 1570–1720*. New Haven: Yale University Press, 1974.

Hudson, Winthrop S. "The Ministry in the Puritan Age," in *The Ministry in Historical Perspectives*, ed. H. Richard Niebuhr and Daniel D. Williams. New York: Harper and Brothers, 1956, pp. 180–206.

Hughes, Philip E. *Theology of the English Reformers*. Grand Rapids: Eerdmans, 1965.

Hunt, Morton M. *The Natural History of Love*. New York: Knopf, 1959.

Hutchinson, Lucy. *Memoirs of the Life of Colonel Hutchinson*, ed. James Sutherland. London: Oxford University Press, 1973.

Hyma, Albert. *Christianity, Captitalism and Communism: A Historical Analysis*. Ann Arbor: George Wahr, 1937.

Irwin, Joyce L., ed. *Womanhood in Radical Protestantism, 1525–1675*. New York: Edwin Mellen, 1979.

James, Margaret. *Social Problems and Policy During the Puritan Revolution, 1640–1660*. 1930; reprint New York: Barnes and Noble, 1966.

Jarman, Robert D. *The Regulative Principle of Scripture: The Origin of a Cardinal Doctrine in the Early Elizabethan Puritan Movement*. Unpublished thesis, Trinity Evangelical Divinity School, 1977.

Johnson, James Turner. *A Society Ordained by God: English Puritan Marriage Doctrine in the First Half of the Seventeenth Century*. Nashville: Abingdon, 1970.

Jordan, W. K. *The Development of Religious Toleration in England*, 2 vols. Cambridge: Harvard University Press, 1932, 1936.

Kaufmann, U. Milo. *The Pilgrim's Progress and Traditions in Puritan Meditation*. New Haven: Yale University Press, 1966.

Keeble, N. H. *Richard Baxter: Puritan Man of Letters*. Oxford: Oxford University Press, 1982.

Kitch, M. J., ed. *Capitalism and the Reformation*. London: Longmans, Green, 1967.

Knappen, M. M. *Tudor Puritanism: A Chapter in the History of Idealism*. Chicago: University of Chicago Press, 1939.

————, ed. *Two Elizabethan Puritan Diaries*. 1933; reprint Gloucester, Mass.: Peter Smith, 1966.

Knott, John R., Jr. *The Sword of the Spirit: Puritan Responses to the Bible*. Chicago: University of Chicago Press, 1980.

Lerner, Laurence. *Love and Marriage: Literature and Its Social Context.* New York: St. Martin's, 1979.

Lewalski, Barbara K. *Protestant Poetics and the Seventeenth-Century Religious Lyric.* Princeton: Princeton University Press, 1979.

Lewis, Peter. *The Genius of Puritanism.* Haywards Heath, Sussex: Carey, 1977.

Lowrie, Ernest Benson. *The Shape of the Puritan Mind: The Thought of Samuel Willard.* New Haven: Yale University Press, 1974.

Luther, Martin. *Luther's Works,* ed. Jaroslav Pelikan and Helmut T. Lehmann, 55 vols. St. Louis: Concordia; and Philadelphia: Fortress, 1955–1976.

Mather, Cotton. *Magnalia Christi Americana,* 2 vols. New York: Russell and Russell, 1967.

McGee, J. Sears. *The Godly Man in Stuart England: Anglicans, Puritans, and the Two Tables, 1620–1670.* New Haven: Yale University Press, 1976.

McGiffert, Michael, ed. *Puritanism and the American Experience.* Reading, Mass.: Addison-Wesley, 1969.

McNeill, John Thomas. *Modern Christian Movements.* Philadelphia: Westminster, 1954.

Merton, Robert K. *Science, Technology, and Society in Seventeenth Century England.* New York: Howard Fertig, 1970.

Micklem, Nathaniel, ed. *Christian Worship: Studies in Its History and Meaning.* Oxford: Oxford University Press, 1971.

Middlekauff, Robert. *The Mathers: Three Generations of Puritan Intellectuals.* New York: Oxford University Press, 1971.

Miller, Perry. *Errand into the Wilderness.* Cambridge: Harvard University Press, 1956.

————. *Nature's Nation.* Cambridge: Harvard University Press, 1967.

————. *The New England Mind: From Colony to Province.* Cambridge: Harvard University Press, 1953.

————. *The New England Mind: The Seventeenth Century.* Cambridge: Harvard University Press, 1939, 1954.

Miller, Perry, and Thomas H. Johnson, eds. *The Puritans,* rev. ed., 2 vols. New York: Harper Torchbooks, 1963.

Milton, John. *Complete Prose Works,* 8 vols. New Haven: Yale University Press, 1953–. Abbreviated *CPW.*

Mitchell, W. Fraser. *English Pulpit Oratory from Andrewes to Tillotson.* London: S.P.C.K., 1932.

Morgan, Edmund S., ed. *Puritan Political Ideas, 1558–1794.* Indianapolis: Bobbs-Merrill, 1965.

————. *The Puritan Family: Religion and Domestic Relations in Seventeenth-Century New England.* 1944; reprint New York: Harper and Row, 1966.

————. "The Puritans and Sex," in *Pivotal Interpretations of American History,* ed. Carl N. Degler. New York: Harper and Row, 1966. 1:4–16.

Morgan, Irvonwy. *The Godly Preachers of the Elizabethan Church.* London: Epworth, 1965.

Morison, Samuel Eliot. *Harvard College in the Seventeenth Century*, 2 vols. Cambridge: Harvard University Press, 1936.

―――――. *The Founding of Harvard College*. Cambridge: Harvard University Press, 1935.

―――――. *The Intellectual Life of Colonial New England*. New York: Washington Square Press, 1956.

Murray, Iain, ed. *The Reformation of the Church: A Collection of Reformed and Puritan Documents on Church Issues*. London: Banner of Truth Trust, 1965.

New, John F. H. *Anglican and Puritan: The Basis of Their Opposition, 1558–1640*. Stanford: Stanford University Press, 1964.

Old, Hughes Oliphant. *Worship that is Reformed According to Scripture*. Guides to the Reformed Tradition. Atlanta: John Knox, 1984.

Owen, John. *The Works of John Owen*, 16 vols., ed. William H. Goold. London: Banner of Truth Trust, 1966.

Packer, J. I. "The Puritans as Interpreters of Scripture." In *A Goodly Heritage*. London: Puritan Studies Conference, 1958, pp. 18–26.

Pearson, A. F. Scott. *Thomas Cartwright and Elizabethan Puritanism, 1535–1603*. Cambridge: Cambridge University Press, 1925.

Perry, Ralph Barton. *Puritanism and Democracy*. New York: Vanguard, 1944.

Plass, Ewald M., ed. *What Luther Says: An Anthology*, 3 vols. St. Louis: Concordia, 1959.

Porter, H. C. *Puritanism in Tudor England*. Columbia, S.C.: University of South Carolina Press, 1971.

―――――. *Reformation and Reaction in Tudor Cambridge*. 1958; reprint Camden, Conn.: Archon Books, 1972.

Powell, Chilton Latham. *English Domestic Relations, 1487–1653*. 1917; reprint New York: Russell and Russell, 1972.

Puritan Manifestoes: A Study of the Origin of the Puritan Revolt, ed. W. H. Frere and C. E. Douglas. London: S.P.C.K., 1954.

Reinitz, Richard, ed. *Tensions in American Puritanism*. New York: John Wiley and Sons, 1970.

Richardson, Herbert W. *Nun, Witch, Playmate: The Americanization of Sex*. New York: Harper and Row, 1971.

Richardson, R. C. *Puritanism in North-West England: A Regional Study of Chester to 1642*. Manchester: Manchester University Press, 1972.

Robertson, A. M. *Aspects of the Rise of Economic Individualism*. New York: Kelley and Millman, 1959.

Rogers, Jack Bartlett. *Scripture in the Westminster Confession*. Grand Rapids: Eerdmans, 1967.

Rooy, Sidney H. *The Theology of Missions in the Puritan Tradition*. Grand Rapids: Eerdmans, 1965.

Sasek, Lawrence A. *The Literary Temper of the English Puritans*. 1961; reprint New York: Greenwood, 1969.

Schlatter, Richard B. *The Social Ideas of Religious Leaders, 1660–1688*. 1940; reprint New York: Octagon Books, 1971.

Schneider, Herbert Wallace. *The Puritan Mind*. New York: Henry Holt, 1930.

Schnucker, Robert Victor. *Views of Selected Puritans, 1560–1630, on Marriage and Human Sexuality*. Iowa City: University of Iowa Dissertation, 1969.

Scholes, Percy A. *The Puritans and Music in England and New England*. London: Oxford University Press, 1934.

Schücking, Levin L. *The Puritan Family: A Social Study from the Literary Sources*. New York: Schocken Books, 1970.

Seaver, Paul S. *The Puritan Lectureships: The Politics of Religious Dissent, 1560–1662*. Stanford: Stanford University Press, 1970.

Smith, J. W. Ashley. *The Birth of Modern Education: The Contribution of the Dissenting Academies, 1660–1800*. London: Independent Press, 1954.

Smith, H. Shelton et al., eds. *American Christianity: An Historical Interpretation with Representative Documents*, vol. 1. New York: Scribner, 1960.

Smith, Wilson, ed. *Theories of Education in Early America, 1655–1819*. Indianapolis: Bobbs-Merrill, 1973.

Solberg, Winton U. *Redeem the Time: The Puritan Sabbath in Early America*. Cambridge: Harvard University Press, 1977.

Stannard, David E. *The Puritan Way of Death: A Study in Religion, Culture, and Social Change*. New York: Oxford University Press, 1977.

Stenton, Doris Mary. *The English Woman in History*. London: Allen and Unwin, 1957.

Stone, Lawrence. *The Crisis of the Aristocracy, 1558–1641*. Oxford: Oxford University Press, 1965.

————. *The Family, Sex and Marriage in England, 1500–1688*. New York: Harper and Row, 1977.

Strier, Richard. *Love Known: Theology and Experience in George Herbert's Poetry*. Chicago: University of Chicago Press, 1983.

Tawney, R. H. *Religion and the Rise of Capitalism*. New York: Harcourt, Brace, 1926.

Tichi, Cecilia. *New World, New Earth: Environmental Reform in American Literature from the Puritans Through Whitman*. New Haven: Yale University Press, 1979.

Trinterud, Leonard J., ed. *Elizabeth Puritanism*. New York: Oxford University Press, 1971.

Ulrich, Laurel Thatcher. *Good Wives: Image and Reality in the Lives of Women in Northern New England, 1650–1750*. New York: Knopf, 1982.

————. "Vertuous Women Found: New England Ministerial Literature, 1668–1735," in *Puritan New England*, ed. Alden T. Vaughan and Francis J. Bremer. New York: St. Martin's, 1977, pp. 215–31.

Vaughan, Alden T., and Francis J. Bremer, eds. *Puritan New England: Essays on Religion, Society, and Culture*. New York: St. Martin's, 1977.

Venning, Ralph. *The Plague of Plagues*. London: Banner of Truth Trust, 1965.

Wagner, Hans-Peter. *Puritan Attitudes Towards Recreation in Early Seventeenth-Century New England*. Frankfurt: Verlag Peter Lang, 1982.

Wakefield, Gordon S. *Puritan Devotion: Its Place in the Development of Christian Piety*. London: Epworth, 1957.

Walzer, Michael. *The Revolution of the Saints: A Study in the Origins of Radical Politics*. Cambridge: Harvard University Press, 1965.

Warfield, Benjamin B. *The Westminster Assembly and Its Work*. New York: Oxford University Press, 1931.

Watkins, Owen C. *The Puritan Experience: Studies in Spiritual Autobiography*. New York: Schocken Books, 1972.

Watson, Foster. *The English Grammar Schools to 1660: Their Curriculum and Practice*. Cambridge: Cambridge University Press, 1980.

Watson, Thomas. *The Beatitudes*. (Edinburgh: Banner of Truth Trust, 1977).

Weber, Max. *The Protestant Ethic and the Spirit of Capitalism*, trans. Talcott Parsons. New York: Scribner, 1930.

White, Helen C. *Social Criticism in Popular Religious Literature of the Sixteenth Century*. New York: Macmillan, 1944.

Wilson, Derek. *The People and the Book: The Revolutionary Impact of the English Bible, 1380–1611*. London: Barrie and Jenkins, 1976.

Wilson, John F. *Pulpit in Parliament: Puritanism During the English Civil Wars, 1640–1648*. Princeton: Princeton University Press, 1969.

Woodhouse, A. S. P., ed. *Puritanism and Liberty*. Chicago: Chicago University Press, 1951.

Wright, Louis B. *Life in Colonial America*. New York: Capricorn Books, 1965.

——————. *Middle-Class Culture in Elizabethan England*. Chapel Hill: University of North Carolina Press, 1935.

Wright, Thomas G. *Literary Culture in Early New England, 1620–1730*. 1920; reprint New York: Russell and Russell, 1966.

Index of Persons

The index includes persons referred to or quoted in the text, persons quoted in the notes, and all items listed in Further Reading at the end of chapters. It does not include authors who are merely named in the notes.

276

Webster, Charles, 258
Weston, William, 124, 198, 203
Whately, William, 44–45, 46, 50, 51, 55, 94
Whichcote, Benjamin, 97
White, Francis, 190
White, Helen C., 185
White, James F., 122
White, John, 146, 253, 260
Whitefield, George, xi
Whitgift, John, 4, 9
Whittingham, William, 197
Wigglesworth, Michael, 200–201
Wilcox, Thomas, 92
Willard, Samuel, 5–6, 14, 16, 17, 20, 53, 58, 60, 62, 76, 77, 78, 79, 81, 82, 83, 84, 85, 170, 171, 174, 176, 182, 206, 210, 212, 216, 225, 229, 236, 239

William and Mary, 10
Williams, Roger, 199
Wilson, Derek, 13, 154, 243
Wing, John, 51
Winthrop, John, 10, 18, 19, 49, 50, 59, 77, 139, 174, 175, 179, 184, 190, 194, 196, 206, 207, 209, 234
Wither, George, 130, 132, 150, 151
Wood, Anthony J., 3
Woodhouse, A. S. P., 185, 261
Woodrow, Robert, 35
Wordsworth, William, 104

Index of Topics

Arts, the, 3–4, 168, 189, 261

Bible: 137–54, 219; as literature, 149–52; authority of, xii, 13, 15, 112–15, 140-43; in education, 162–63; interpretation of, 143–52; translation of, 137–40
Body, human, 4, 44–45, 195, 210

Calling; vocation, 15–16, 26–29, 174
Children, 78-85, 194-95, 200
Church, xv, 11-34
Clothing, 3, 47
Common, sanctity of the, 25, 209–210
Common grace, 168–69
Common person, 182–84
Covenant, 15, 79, 87, 185
Creation, doctrine of, 15, 210, 217

Democracy, 182–84, 248, 261

Economics, 14, 56–71
Education, 7, 13–14, 79–80, 156–71
Emotion, 4, 5–6, 50–51, 216

Failings of the Puritans, 187–202
Family, xiii–xiv, 73–88

Humanism, 165–67, 257

Iconoclasm, 117–18, 199
Intolerance, 5, 198–99

Liberal arts education, 164–70, 256–58

Male chauvinism, 195–96
Marriage, 39–55, 73–88
Moderation, 33–35, 64–66
Money, 3, 30–33, 56–71
Music, 3–4, 122-24, 189, 224

Persecution of Puritans, x–xi, 13, 118, 226
Person, view of, xiv, 16
Physical world, 4, 15, 205, 210
Preacher, Puritan ideal of, 92–94
Preaching, 90–108, 124–26, 193
Priesthood of all believers, 52, 119, 146, 182, 183, 248
Puritans: failings, 187–202; history, 7–10; holistic philosophy and lifestyle, xi–xii, 24–26, 31, 48–49, 164–70, 208–210, 216–18; key doctrines, 14–16; leading traits, 11–14, 16–21; modern misconceptions about, ix–x, 1–7, 23, 32–33, 39–40, 57, 174, 179, 187–89; persecution of, x–xi, 13, 118, 226; strengths, ix–xvi, 205–222

Reason, 4, 159–60
Recreation, 3, 189–91
Renaissance, 165–67, 257

Sabbath, 129–32, 191–92, 249
Sacramental view of life, 15, 125–26, 209–210
Sacraments, 122
Sacred-secular dichotomy, 24–26, 44, 208, 228
Science, 168, 257–58
Scripture. See Bible.
Self, view of, 6, 220
Sex, 2, 39–55, 192–93, 232
Social action, 173–85

Tolerance, 5
Tradition, negative attitude toward, 17, 113
Truth, 126, 167–70

Vocation, 15–16, 26–29, 174

Women, status of, 51–53, 76–78, 195–96, 263
Work, 3, 23–36, 190–91, 214–15
Worship, 18–19, 110–34